D0442233

America: The Middle Period

Essays in Honor of Bernard Mayo

America
The Middle Period
Essays in Honor of
Bernard Mayo

Edited by John B. Boles
Towson State College

University Press of Virginia

Charlottesville

THE UNIVERSITY PRESS OF VIRGINIA
Copyright © 1973 by the Rector and Visitors
of the University of Virginia

First published 1973

ISBN: 0–8139–0478–1
Library of Congress Catalog Card Number: 73–81766
Printed in the United States of America

Dedicated to
BERNARD MAYO
a trusted friend, devoted scholar, and extraordinary teacher,
and to his wife,
PEG,
in appreciation of their having enriched
the University of Virginia
and our individual lives

740504

Contents

Preface

FOR three decades at the University of Virginia, Bernard Mayo charmed undergraduates with his witty lectures and gracious manners; for thirty years he frightened, challenged, and inspired scores of graduate students. The Mayo seminar became known as both the most demanding and rewarding experience of one's graduate education. In his famous (and infamous) seminars on the middle period of American history, Professor Mayo applied his extraordinary critical faculties to his students' papers, but he did so with kind intent. To his small groups of awed students he displayed an incredible command of the factual events of history, an amazing ability to ask the right questions, and a phenomenal eye and ear for style. One principle Mayo drove home again and again with unerring effectiveness: never be satisfied with less than your absolute best. And Mayo was never satisfied with an unambitious best! No survivor of his seminar will ever be content without trying to measure up to his mentor's expectations.

Mayo's range covered virtually every aspect of the Middle Period (which he defined as the years from 1763 to 1865): he produced and inspired work in political, intellectual, social, diplomatic, and religious history. His students have followed him in their interest in biography and the *beaux-arts*. This collection of articles only partly reflects the breadth of his interests and the depth of our appreciation. The Corcoran Department of History at Virginia has long had a galaxy of great scholars, but for every one of his students, graduate training was "the Mayo treatment," and each has maintained an ever-increasing recognition of the intellectual debt owed him. We each know that nothing we can say or write can repay what he has given us. Instead, we each offer this collection as "a peppercorn for Mr. Mayo."

Each of Bernard Mayo's students has helped in the compilation and publication of this *festschrift*. Those unable to contribute an essay have supported the project in other ways. I would like to thank Pendleton Gaines especially for his warm encouragement. Mrs. Peggy Mayo has been a cheerful confidant, a pleasure to work with as well as to know. Professors W. W. Abbot and Merrill D. Peterson of the University of Virginia have been trusted advisers. Peg Beverly, Cindy Eckes, Stacie Sernocky, and Kathie Young, secretaries in the history department of Towson State College, have aided me immeasurably. As always, my wife Nancy has been an irreplaceable helpmate. Of course, the University of Virginia has made this whole affair possible—by employing Bernard Mayo and by enrolling the contributors as students. A grant from the Corcoran Foundation of the University of Virginia contributed to the publication, as did generous grants from the Towson State College Research Committee and the Towson Foundation, Incorporated. To all of the above I convey my appreciation.

JOHN B. BOLES

Baltimore, Maryland
March 1, 1973

Bernard Mayo: An Appreciation

Pendleton Gaines

THE first time I saw Bernie Mayo was in a second-story seminar room in the Alderman Library of the University of
Virginia. An unusually warm February sun, bolstered by a boom-
ing library furnace, had made most of the fifteen or so students
drowsy. It was the first meeting of Bernie's Age of Jefferson that
semester. (I was later to find out that whatever Middle Period
course you took from Bernie, it always became the Age of Jefferson.) It was 1946. Most of the students, like myself, were former
G.I.'s. I had not been in an academic classroom for four years. A
polite, rather earnest, little man started rattling off the names of
books about Jefferson, Jay, Monroe, Randolph, and other historical characters, some major and some minor, and throwing out
an occasional comment on each volume. Most of it was Greek to
me, and I began to wonder if I was in the right room. I did have a
diploma and had majored in history, but I was just vaguely aware
of about one book in ten that he mentioned. I hadn't even heard of
many of the characters. Maybe this was a political science or
philosophy class.

Then, out of the blue and apropos of absolutely nothing, an old
country boy made his one contribution to the discussion of the day.
I might add that it was his only contribution for many days. Still
influenced by World War II headlines, he allowed that Jefferson
had treated Burr pretty shabbily. He seriously asked Mayo if there
wasn't a parallel here with Hitler's treatment of the Jews!

A pall descended upon the room. Bernie's face gradually turned
red, and a slight tremor appeared in both voice and hand. He
calmly launched into a twenty-minute disquisition on Republicanism versus Federalism, emphasizing the roles of Jefferson and
Marshall. He cited at least a dozen books and articles, all of which
apparently showed that Jefferson's personal animus toward Burr
was indeed small, if it existed at all. In fact, I got the impression
they were old college roommates. The entire class was overwhelmed by the enormity of this man Mayo's knowledge. Much
later I found out that this sophomoric remark had so upset Bernie
that he couldn't even eat much that night.

I absorbed two lessons that afternoon, never to be forgotten. Don't make positive statements about history to a man of Mayo's erudition, or as far as that goes, to any other person knowledgeable in a given field, without knowing at least something about the subject. That's not a bad policy; I have tried to follow it ever since. Bernie really drove it home to me that day. My other observation was less important but more intriguing. Here was a Maine native who had attended his state university, a maverick Down-Easter who had spent most of his adult life in and around Washington, a Yankee liberal who admired virtually all the Rooseveltian reforms—yet here he was defending the apostle of the least possible government against Hamilton, the great government centralizer. Though in Charlottesville a scant five years, Bernie was beginning to show his Jeffersonianism. The Rotunda, the colonnades, the serpentine walls, the Georgian buildings, Monticello, the Blue Ridge, and even the rolling hills of Albemarle were beginning to have their effect. This gradual process continued slowly until today the conversion to Jeffersonianism is complete. Jefferson's head may be Dumas Malone's, but his heart is Bernard Mayo's.

I have known Bernie for more than twenty-five years. While in graduate school, after getting over my original fear of the man, I eagerly visited him several times a week, or at least as often as he would see me. I took every graduate course he offered. Then, after I received my degree in 1950, I was lucky enough to return to Charlottesville once or twice each year, always visiting Mayo. For the last ten or twelve years, since I have become slightly disabled, I have just seen him once, in 1969, though we have kept up a rather desultory correspondence. Two patterns emerge through the haze of my many recollections of Bernie, one important and the other less important but equally fascinating. First, Mayo was a superb teacher in the best sense of the word. Second, he gradually fell under the influence of Jefferson so that today he is a genuine Jeffersonphile. Other memories of this many-faceted man abound. But these are the two that loom largest for me.

Bernie's greatness as a teacher is simple to explain. His enthusiasm for his subject was so infectious his students readily caught it. He knew so much about everything historical that we were all eager to rush to the Alderman stacks to find out more about the subject than he knew, or better yet, find some minuscule matter on which he was wrong. I never succeeded in either, but it wasn't from lack of trying. Bernie loved to mention some obscure fact from an even more obscure historical journal and then chide his class for not knowing what he was talking about. I guess I heard him say a thousand times, "Really, Mr. Smith (or Brown or Jones or Gaines), if we don't know these elementary facts, how can we expect to understand the period!" And Bernie was telling us such earth-shaking facts as that the boxwoods at Ash Lawn were planted after the house itself was built, that Henry Clay really did drink Old Crow whiskey, or some equally significant bit of historical unimportance!

Bernie was a good lecturer but not a great one. He was effective with large groups but by no means sensational. His commencement address when I was at Wofford College was spirited and effective, but somewhat pedestrian. His undergraduate classroom lectures at the University usually weren't too fascinating for the nonhistory majors. In his lectures he seemed to miss the give and take of students. It was in small groups, seminars and the like, that he excelled. He wasn't just excellent there, he was utterly magnificent.

Two things helped make Bernie a great teacher: knowledge of and enthusiasm for his subject and total bibliographical recall. He just happened to know as much history as anybody I ever met. It was not just the political, social, economic, and intellectual facts, or even the deeper forces, movements, causes, and results of a period. It was all the little incidental stuff: Peggy Eaton's peccadillos or the Little Magician's latest trick. Mayo assumed (often too generously) that his graduate students knew the basic facts of the period and would embellish as only he could. Sometimes it was downright infuriating the way Bernie knew all the little extraneous, insignificant details of a given time.

The response he evoked from his students at times was one of despondency. I have never felt as stupid and ignorant, before or since, as I did in his seminars. More than once I thought seriously about taking up some less strenuous discipline. Yet, although Mayo might make us all angry, he never really humiliated a student before the entire class. It was a pretty narrow line he walked. We all might feel like ignoramuses, but it was always unanimous. Much later I realized how effective Bernie had been. By making all sorts of statements, some true and some outlandish, he had us all dying to find out more about the subject. Like Socrates in those Athenian groves, Mayo on those lovely grounds asked the great questions. We never found all the answers. But, after all, the search is what education is all about. Every time I reach for a book today to learn some new fact or check on an old one, I may not always realize it, but there is a little bit of Bernie urging me on. That is a debt I shall never be able to repay. And I am not alone in this indebtedness.

Bernie really taught English as much as he did history. What a literary stylist he was! His Bibles were Wooley and Scott, along with Fowler. Term papers, theses, and dissertations had to be rewritten ad infinitum. He wrote so beautifully himself that he insisted each of his students' final products be as well done as possible. One of the first stories I heard at Virginia was that Allan Nevins had in some book review hailed Bernie's book on Clay as a model of literary style for other historical writers to emulate. Mayo in fact wrote too well. He was in such demand to edit volumes and write introductions, pamphlets, book reviews, articles in professional journals, and all the rest, that it curtailed his own output of original work. He published more than his share, but many of us always suspected he could have produced more of his own if he hadn't been doing all sorts of other literary tasks. Doing them beautifully, of course: eye-catching introductions, alliterative phrases, transitional sentences, balanced paragraphs, meaningful conclusions, and exact footnoting.

Bernie was such a literary perfectionist that all smart graduate students realized they would probably have to revise their theses or dissertations forever unless they did something about it. Thus the trick was to leave the University at the end of the academic year (for example, by having a job if possible) and then simply to flood Bernie with so much material that he couldn't disapprove it. I knew one student who finally turned in, and had approved, all six chapters of his thesis in April. His master's degree was then actually awarded that June. This tactic worked sometimes with theses, but it was much more difficult as far as dissertations were concerned. I tried this technique. Both my thesis and dissertation were written under Bernie's supervision. I was teaching at a small Alabama college when I completed my thesis and took my master's orals. Bernie was away most of that year teaching at Harvard, Columbia, or some eastern school. He was so popular that he was always in great demand at other universities. I managed to send in so many chapters by mail in such a short period of time that he simply did not have the heart to reject my thesis. I tried to make him feel that he would be taking bread out of four poor Gaineses' mouths if he did. It worked.

I also employed the other gimmick that sometimes worked with Bernie. As a thesis subject I chose to write on a somewhat obscure Virginia governor of the early 1840s, James McDowell. His chief distinction had been to fall off a barge into the water, almost drowning, while dedicating the completion of a major portion of the James River and Kanawha Canal near Buchanan. In other words, I tried to write about somebody or something Bernie did not either know or care too much about. I never had nerve enough to write on Jefferson's family, friends, foreign policy, or anything else remotely connected with Jefferson. My ploy worked pretty well on the thesis level, but the dissertation was another story.

To put it mildly, Bernie was death on dissertations. They had to be both historically and stylistically near-perfect. You could spend a lifetime writing for him—as one of the contributors to this volume almost did. In a moment of weakness, Bernie approved the Virginia Constitutional Convention of 1850–51 as my dissertation subject. For a short time I thought I had him. How wrong I was! He not only read and corrected each chapter many times, but had two others do the same: Thomas Perkins Abernethy, who had forgotten more Virginia history than anybody else had ever known; and the University's own political scientist, George Spicer, who probably knew more about the history of Virginia's government, including its constitutional development, than anyone alive. So I was trapped, both as to content and style. Mayo had won again, as he always did.

The other thing that helped make Mayo a great teacher was his unbelievable knowledge of historiography. I have been associated with many colleges and universities, and may indeed have known historians who knew as many facts as Bernie, but I have never known anyone who approached his bibliographic knowledge of a given period. He must have slept with every obscure journal or book even remotely concerned with America of the eighteenth and nineteenth centuries. Much of the time he also knew the background of the articles or books. For example, he not only knew that Dexter Perkins wrote the best book on the Monroe Doctrine, but he knew the whys and wherefores of Perkins's writing the book. Bernie's encyclopedic knowledge of historiography was awesome. To some of us it seemed that he had *invented* the Middle Period.

In his seminar Bernie got at least one of us wound up each day on some subject the student thought he really knew something about: internal improvements, the Barbary pirates, or even the Grecian influence on the architecture of Monticello. Mayo would quietly lead the student on and on. Then gently but firmly Bernie would let him have the shaft, mentioning at least three books and five articles on the subject with which no one in the class, including the speaker, was even vaguely familiar. The balloon was deflated. We would at that time hear the usual refrain about the complete impossibility of us knowing anything important about a certain subject when we did not even know the elementary, basic facts. I can still hear Bernie playing that tune over and over again. All of us received this needle at one time or another.

Mayo was the embodiment of the old adage about an educated man being one who might not have certain information but who knew exactly where to find it. Bernie was such a believer in historiography that he announced early in his seminar on The Age of Jackson that the only question on the final exam would be to write a bibliography of the period covered, with a brief critical commentary on each work cited. (Even that seminar seemed to revolve more around Monticello than it did The Hermitage.) I immediately concluded that the only way out of this dilemma was to read every book review or article bearing on the period in five or six major historical journals. Reading all the works themselves was out of the question. At exam time I must have set a record for the number of blue books filled in one three-hour period. Bernie's only reference to me about that exam was a caustic comment made several months later that though I had mentioned a lot of works, my criticisms were often shallow and superficial. You could never really win with Bernie! In stressing the importance of historiography, he was far ahead of his time. During the past decades many courses in historical research and bibliography have crept into hundreds of college and university catalogs. Today they are routine requirements for graduate students.

One of Bernie's most able students was Joe Harrison, a contributor to this collection. Joe wrote me recently, giving a succinct definition of Bernie's greatness as a teacher: "Urbanity and wit, enormous learning, a real interest in the quality of his students' minds, and a connoisseur's feeling for the past—these and a constant demand for perfection, accompanied by the flattering convention that we were all competing in the historical big leagues —seem to me the essence of his quality as a teacher."

Mayo's gifts as a brilliant teacher and superb supervisor of historical writing are undeniable. But how many of us know the subtle change that has come over this man who has lived for more than thirty years in the shadow of the squire of Monticello? Any civilized person living in Athens today has to become a lover of the Periclean Age. A similar person residing in Florence must become a lover of the Renaissance. Likewise, any such person living at the University of Virginia under the very shadow of Monticello must become a lover of Jefferson. This is particularly true of a historian specializing in the Revolutionary and Middle Periods. The surrender of the Yankee liberal, the Washington New Dealer, was the most natural thing in the world. Mind you, Bernie is no blind, uncritical devotee of the sage of Monticello. But there is no doubt that thirty years in Charlottesville have turned this man into an unabashed aficionado of Jefferson.

Shortly after moving to Charlottesville, Mayo started editing books as well as writing pamphlets and articles about Jefferson. That was to be expected; Jefferson material was plentiful in Alderman Library and indeed throughout Albemarle. In 1946 he told us in class that Jefferson was not wholly unlike Franklin Roosevelt: he might even use doubtful means to achieve desirable ends. He cited the location of the University of Virginia as an example, hinting that there may have been a little skulduggery when Jefferson, as chairman of the commission appointed by the assembly to find a suitable site for the proposed university, won out over those from the Valley who wanted the university located there. Bernie said that some engineers may have stretched a point or two about the centrality of Jefferson's site, but that obviously it was the only place to build the university!

There was much of Virginia's history that Bernie did not like, although like all good historians in those days, he attempted to be critically aloof and nonmoralistic in both his writings and teachings. But it was obvious that many things displeased him: the Tidewater oligarchy, stress on family ties, uneven justice, unequal representation, restricted suffrage, lack of public funds for education or even for good roads, and all the rest. Of course the existing Byrd machine was anathema to Bernie, as it was to all good liberals. Although anything is provable if you look hard enough in the writings of Jefferson, Shakespeare, or the Bible, Bernie was certain that Jefferson would be a liberal were he still living. He reminded us again and again that Jefferson's essentially agrarian society had long since turned into a highly complex industrial one.

The first time Bernie visited my home in Lexington, he was the very model of a somewhat disinterested history teacher. Yes, the Shenandoah Valley was exquisite, the Washington and Lee University campus lovely, and the Virginia Military Institute properly austere. My father, who for thirty years had held the same position Lee did after the War, regaled Mayo with many Lee stories. He even told Bernie the moving account of Lee's stroke and his death in the bay window of our dining room, in sight of his beloved Blue Ridge. Mayo was properly polite and attentive, but his little condescending smile showed that it was obvious to him that we were all living in the past, pleasant, yes, but still the past. Yet another year in Jefferson's shadow began to make a difference in Bernie.

He returned to visit in Lexington the following year, 1949. This time he wanted to know all about the Lee residence on the Washington and Lee campus. I showed him our garage, which had been the stable for Lee's horse, Traveler. He even tolerated a monument recently placed there by the United Daughters of the Confederacy marking Traveler's old stable! Mayo spent hours in Lee Chapel where the great Confederate and many of his relatives are entombed. Bernie wanted to know exactly the Washington-Custis-Lee kinship. He visited the Jackson house on the campus and Stonewall's grave in the town cemetery. He and my father swapped Virginia stories by the dozens, many dealing with the Carters, Randolphs, Harrisons, and even the Byrds. This was no polite interest; his increasing knowledge of Jefferson was making him more sympathetic toward all things Virginian. The liberal from Washington was gradually succumbing.

It is interesting that the first of Bernie's many published works on Jefferson was issued in 1942, two years after he moved to Charlottesville. There is no doubt that Thomas Jefferson was getting to Bernard Mayo. In the early 1960s he was Thomas Jefferson Professor at the University, and in 1965, I think it was, he moved into Pavilion IV on the Lawn for a seven-year stay. Surely a residence on the Lawn is the apogee of a successful teaching career at Mr. Jefferson's academical village.

The main thrust of these comments has been to emphasize Mayo's unique qualities as a teacher in the complete sense of the word and to show the gradual but increasing influence Jefferson had on him. I cherish many other memories of Bernie as a friend.

In a huge symbolic expansion, the famous remark of Wellington that the battle of Waterloo was won on the playing fields of Eton may be taken as a reasonable interpretation of history. Within the theater of human affairs our eyes focus upon the stage where the spotlight of historical notoriety fleetingly illumines the men and women who strut and fret their little hour. But behind the scenes, unseen yet everywhere dominant, are the teachers of our youth, the Bernard Mayos. Whether the social order be the religious pattern of the Middle Ages, the totalitarianism of Russia, or the democracy of our Western world, this at least is certain: any given civilization is and will always be what teachers like Bernard Mayo choose to make it.

America: The Middle Period

Essays in Honor of Bernard Mayo

1 Charles Thomson and the Creation of "A New Order of the Ages"

J. Edwin Hendricks

THE reverse side of the seal of the United States bears the motto *Novus Ordo Seclorum*, or "A New Order of the Ages." This inscription may tell more about the nature of the American Revolution than all the histories of it. It tells too of its author, Charles Thomson, secretary to the Continental Congress, who altered a passage from Virgil to produce a statement of purpose for the revolutionary generation that laid the groundwork for the formation of the United States. The men who fathered the American Revolution were conscious of the earthshaking impact of what they were doing. In official proclamations, in the Declaration of Independence, and even on the Great Seal they made plain to the world their intention to create "A New Order of the Ages."

Charles Thomson's role in establishing this new order was an important one, though largely unknown today. Passing references to his activities as a Philadelphia revolutionary or as "perpetual" secretary to the Continental Congress appear in some history books; but his activities in Philadelphia are eclipsed by the more famed actions of Sam Adams in Boston, and his work as secretary is relegated to that of a reporter of events. Thomson even contributed to his own obscurity by destroying his private papers late in life because they contained evidence discrediting some who had become leaders in the new nation.[1]

A good example of the neglect of Thomson's role in revolutionary events is the traditional story of the adoption of the Great Seal of the United States. This is the seal that is still affixed to official documents of the United States and that is most frequently visible on the back of the one dollar bill. Most students of this period know that Franklin, Jefferson, the French artist Du Simitière, and others submitted various designs to Congress and that from them a seal was constructed and adopted. What is not known

---

[1] See Edmund C. Burnett, s.v. "Thomson, Charles," *Dictionary of American Biography;* Lewis R. Harley, *Life of Charles Thomson* (Philadelphia, 1900); and John J. Zimmerman, "Charles Thomson, 'The Sam Adams of Philadelphia,'" *Mississippi Valley Historical Review,* 45 (1958): 464–80.

is that Congress, unable to agree on any of the proposals submitted, turned all the reports and designs over to Thomson. He then took parts from the earlier proposals and incorporated them into the present design. From *E Pluribus Unum* on the front to the all-seeing eye atop a pyramid on the back, the seal arrangements were his. And he contributed the two inscriptions on the back, *Annuit Coeptis* and *Novus Ordo Seclorum*, from his own extensive knowledge of the Latin classics by changing two lines from Virgil to fit the idealism of the revolutionary age.[2]

Novus Ordo Seclorum was particularly apt as a motto for the Revolution and for the life of Charles Thomson. Daniel Boorstin states that the Revolution was a "series of events by which we separated ourselves from the British Empire and acquired a national identity."[3] It took both these accomplishments to achieve "A New Order of the Ages," and Thomson had a vital part in both these achievements.

It is as hard to say when Charles Thomson began his part in the separation of the colonies from the mother country as it is to pinpoint the start of that process. Perhaps it was in 1739 when he with his father and two brothers left their home near Londonderry in Northern Ireland and traveled across the ocean to the New World. The father died as the ship approached the Delaware Capes, but he doubtlessly had instilled in his young sons the dream of escape from the rigors of life in an Ulster which was dominated by absentee landlords and harsh English political control.[4] Certainly there were foreshadowings of the revolutionary Thomson in the 1750s when he supported the struggle of the Delaware Indians to preserve their property from the proprietors of the Pennsylvania colony. He gained experience as a propagandist in writing *An Enquiry into the Causes of Alienation of the Delaware and the Shawanese Indians from the British Interest, and into the Measures Taken for Recovering Their Friendship*, in

[2] Virgil, *Eclogues*, 4. 5; Department of State, *Seal of the United States* (Washington, D.C., 1957), pp. 7–10. Committee reports and sketches, including Thomson's original sketch on which *Novus Ordo Seclorum* first appeared are in the Papers of the Continental Congress, item 23, roll 31, National Archives, Washington, D.C., and are published in part in Thomas Jefferson, *The Papers of Thomas Jefferson*, ed. Julian P. Boyd et al. (Princeton, N.J., 1950–), I, 494–97.

[3] Boorstin, *The Genius of American Politics* (Chicago, 1953), p. 70.

[4] Accounts of Thomson's arrival in America are found in John F. Watson, *Annals of Philadelphia and Pennsylvania in the Olden Time* (2 vols., Philadelphia, 1850), I, 567–68; "American Biography," *American Quarterly Review*, 1 (1827): 28–30; and Harley, pp. 15–20.

which he described the unethical means the Penns had used to defraud Chief Teedyuscung and his tribesmen of their lands. Benjamin Franklin had the book published in London in 1759 as part of an attempt to remove the proprietors and turn Pennsylvania into a royal colony.[5]

Thomson's principal revolutionary activities came with the passage of the Stamp Act. His opposition to that act and to the Townshend duties that followed gained him a reputation as "the life of the cause of liberty" in Pennsylvania and led John Adams to refer to him as the "Sam Adams of Philadelphia." [6]

Thomson's work as a Philadelphia revolutionary well illustrates the early stages of a revolt against an established government.[7] He propagandized through newspapers, pamphlets, and letters. He formed and participated in small groups that worked behind the scenes to further the cause of rebellion. He called mass meetings and carefully planned their agenda so that the end results were those which he desired. Along with his fellow revolutionaries in Boston and New York, he developed and refined the tools of economic boycott and the committees of correspondence which grew into committees of safety to keep reluctant revolutionaries in line.[8] Thomson's efforts to secure support from the "mechanics and artisans" of Philadelphia, notably among the carpenters, are especially interesting in the light of recent emphasis on the role of the lower classes in rebellions. He saw to it that carefully staged "peaceful" public demonstrations came to the verge of violence and backed away after successfully showing the intensity of the

---

[5] Lawrence C. Wroth, *An American Bookshelf, 1755* (Philadelphia, 1934), pp. 17–18, discusses the publication of Thomson's *Enquiry*. For Franklin's role, see Carl Van Doren, *Benjamin Franklin* (New York, 1938), pp. 285ff.

[6] John Adams, *The Adams Papers; Diary and Autobiography of John Adams*, ed. L. H. Butterfield et al. (5 vols., Cambridge, Mass., 1961), II, 115.

[7] Thomson is featured prominently in Arthur M. Schlesinger, Sr., *The Colonial Merchants and the American Revolution* (New York, 1918), pp. 42–59, 114, 251; and Merrill Jensen, *The Founding of a Nation* (New York, 1968), pp. 357–58, 473–74, 525–26. A more complete version is in Zimmerman.

[8] Thomson outlines his activities in undated accounts to Dr. David Ramsay and William Henry Drayton, both of South Carolina, Thomson Papers, Library of Congress, Washington, D.C. Both accounts are printed in *New-York Historical Society Collections*, 11 (1878): 215–29, 274–86. A corrected version of the Ramsay letter is in Paul H. Smith, "Charles Thomson on Unity in the American Revolution," *Quarterly Journal of the Library of Congress*, 28 (1971): 158–72.

sentiments of the participants. That is to say, he served as the director of the Philadelphia "mob" in the early stages of revolution.[9]

The rebels secured the repeal of the Stamp Act and the Townshend duties, except the one on tea, and attempted to establish a "new order" for themselves within the British Empire. At the same time they established a new political order within the colonies and fixed themselves firmly as leaders of this new group of political activists. Then in rapid order came the Tea Act, the Boston Tea Party, the Intolerable Acts, and the assembling of the First Continental Congress. When the British reacted to the Boston Tea Party by enacting the Intolerable Acts, Thomson again was active in rallying support for the threatened Massachusetts radicals.

When Pennsylvania officialdom, headed by Speaker of the Assembly Joseph Galloway, opposed the calling of the Continental Congress, Thomson and his fellow Philadelphia radicals used their committees of correspondence to call an extralegal provincial assembly, which forced the regularly elected assembly to choose delegates for the Congress. Galloway and the moderates sought to have the last word by excluding the radical Thomson from the Pennsylvania delegation. But in August 1774, as the delegates from the other colonies arrived in Philadelphia, Thomson and other Pennsylvania radicals met them. After many "conversations" and an agreement "made out of doors," the delegates chose Thomson as secretary to the First Continental Congress. Galloway and the moderates expressed displeasure at this choice of "one of the most violent sons of Liberty . . . in America" but found themselves powerless to prevent the action.[10]

Thomson's first and perhaps greatest contribution to the Continental Congress was to bring to that body a reputation for honesty and openness which few revolutionary governments have posessed. While serving the Delaware chief Teedyuscung and his Indians, Thomson had earned the name "the man who talks the truth" by his insistence on revealing the entire truth of disputed matters. Within a short time this reputation was extended to his position as secretary to Congress and the official proclamations and information emanating from that office. So reliable were Thomson's reports, even during the dark days of the war, that it became a

[9] James H. Hutson, "An Investigation of the Inarticulates: Philadelphia's White Oaks," *William and Mary Quarterly*, 3d ser., 28 (1971): 19–25.

[10] Thomson to Drayton, n.d., Thomson Papers, Lib. Cong.; Adams, *Diary*, II, 115; Joseph Galloway to William Franklin, Sept. 5, 1774, *New Jersey Archives*, 1st ser. (Newark, 1880–86), X, 477.

common method of attesting the truth to assert that "it's as true as if Charles Thomson's name was to it." [11]

The influence of Thomson and the more violent element in the Congress was seen too when the delegates rejected Galloway's proposal to accept a position within the British Empire which would have provided the colonies with an intercolonial assembly subordinate to Parliament. Then the Congress used the revolutionary device of economic boycott and adopted an "Association" which urged all the colonies not to trade with Britain until she had recognized colonial rights and demands. Thomson, though not a voting member of Congress, doubtlessly had a part in shaping the Association; it was quite similar to the means of protest that he had urged on Philadelphia in response to the Stamp Act and Townshend duties. He plunged immediately into an effort to bring Pennsylvania into compliance with the suggestions from the Congress. The "life of the cause of liberty" was at work on both colonial and intercolonial levels seeking to secure a new order in which colonial rights would be respected.[12]

In May 1775 the Second Continental Congress convened and asked Thomson to continue his services as secretary. Thomson, to this point a violent radical or at least willing to use violent means to secure his desires, began to shift toward a slightly more moderate position; or perhaps the pendulum swing of revolution began to leave one of its initial movers behind. With the coming of Lexington and Concord and the publication of Tom Paine's *Common Sense*, the movement toward independence began to grow. Thomson favored the drive for independence that resulted in the adoption of the Declaration on July 4, 1776, but he opposed the excesses of that movement within Pennsylvania as the radicals destroyed the old provincial government and adopted the radically democratic Pennsylvania constitution of 1776. The road to a new order had its pitfalls.[13]

---

[11] Joseph H. Jones, *The Life of Ashbell Green* (New York, 1849), p. 48; Watson, pp. 568–70; John Adams to William Lee, July 20, 1780, John Adams, *The Works of John Adams*, ed. Charles Francis Adams (10 vols., Boston, 1850–56), VII, 231.

[12] Edmund C. Burnett, *The Continental Congress* (New York, 1941), is the best account of the actions of the Continental Congress.

[13] Theodore Thayer, *Pennsylvania Politics and the Growth of Democracy* (Harrisburg, 1953), pp. 172–75; Thomson to Drayton, n.d., Thomson Papers, Lib. Cong. See also David Hawke, *In the Midst of a Revolution* (Philadelphia, 1961), pp. 183–86, 191–96; and Gordon Wood, *The Creation of the American Republic, 1776–1787* (Chapel Hill, N.C., 1969), pp. 226–37.

Thomson's activities now shifted entirely to the congressional scene. Leaving Pennsylvania and Philadelphia politics behind, he devoted himself to his job as the extralegal Congress sought to give itself a somewhat legal status by adopting the Articles of Confederation. The primary task of the new order of government was to win the struggle for separation from the mother country. Throughout the long and difficult war, Thomson served as secretary to the Congress. In addition to recording and publishing the journals of Congress, he accumulated other secretarial and semiexecutive duties. His office served as a depository of official documents and public papers and handled the correspondence between the Congress and the various states. Thomson gathered reference volumes and records of the state laws and constitutions for the use of the delegates to Congress. He was designated keeper of the Great Seal of the United States and was responsible for affixing it to public documents. He arranged public functions for the Congress, ordered its supplies, and temporarily performed the functions of the president, the secretary for foreign affairs, and other offices when they were vacated by resignation or death. Above all, Thomson served as the sole connecting link within the Congress from its beginning in 1774 until its end in 1789. The delegations from the states frequently changed membership; when new members sought advice on proper procedures and precedents, Thomson was there to provide the information. When members sought to verify their memories of past actions, Thomson gave a quick reference to the proper journal or secret minute book. When the independence of the United States was declared, and as it was secured through a long and frequently arduous war, Thomson presided over his office as secretary and contributed greatly to the accomplishment of that first step toward a new order—the separation of the colonies from the British Empire.[14]

At the same time, the colonists were moving toward the second part of Boorstin's thesis—the acquisition of a national identity, the complex attitude on the part of a group of people that sets them apart from all similar groups, the sense of uniqueness that ties them

[14] Thomson's role as perpetual secretary to the Continental Congress has never been adequately chronicled. Burnett, in *Continental Congress*, pays the secretary many tributes, but his emphasis is elsewhere. Careful study of the *Journals of the Continental Congress*, ed. Worthington C. Ford et al. (34 vols., Washington, D.C., 1904–47); Burnett's edition of the *Letters of the Members of the Continental Congress* (8 vols., Washington, D.C., 1921–36); and the Papers of the Continental Congress indicates that Thomson's role was far greater than has been traditionally accepted.

together. Such a national bond had been developing in the British settlements in North America since the early days of colonialism. The process was a long one, and for many was not completed until long after the American Revolution and the actual establishment of a separate nation.

Thomson's experience in acquiring his own sense of national identity illustrates many of the component parts of that nationalism which developed in most Americans by the end of the eighteenth century. Thomson may or may not have begun his part in achieving separation from the British Empire when he and his family came to the New World, but certainly the choice of a new homeland began the process of his identification with America. This process continued for the rest of his long life. In almost all areas of cultural development Thomson's growth was of an American inclination, and finally an American individual emerged who was devoted to the nation that was being formed in hopes of establishing "A New Order of the Ages."

Thomson's educational, religious, scientific, and agricultural activities showed remarkable parallels to the patterns of development of the new nation. His attitude toward education was manifested early. When the ten-year-old boy arrived in Delaware in 1739, he and his brothers found that the ship's captain had made away with the money their dead father had deposited in the ship's safe. Forced to find lodging and support for themselves, the brothers agreed that Charles should be placed in the home of a New Castle blacksmith. Charles watched one member of the family make a nail, went to the forge, and made a nail so well constructed that the family determined to have him apprenticed to them to be trained as a smith. But somewhere the youngster had acquired a burning desire for an education. He knew that if he became a smith this desire would never be fulfilled; so he packed his belongings on his back and left. As he walked along, a lady of the neighborhood offered him a ride. Thomson convinced her of his sincere desire to be a scholar; she took him home and with the aid of his older brother placed him in a school.[15]

After some preliminary training Thomson entered the academy of Dr. Francis Alison at New London, Pennsylvania. Dr. Alison was a classical scholar educated at the University of Glasgow, but he insisted that his students study English grammar, English lit-

[15] Watson, I, 568. Deborah Logan, Philadelphia contemporary of Thomson's and a frequent visitor during Thomson's retirement years, gives a similar account; see Miscellaneous Manuscripts, Historical Society of Pennsylvania, Philadelphia.

erature, mathematics, science, and other subjects. One day Thomson's tendency to solve problems on his own, coupled with a wanderlust, caused him to leave school and walk forty-five miles to Philadelphia to purchase a bound volume of the *Spectator* for the use of himself and his fellow students. Dr. Alison was so impressed with his pupil's action that he did not administer the usual punishment for runaways.[16]

After completing his studies at Dr. Alison's, Thomson operated a subscription school in a converted cooper's shop for a short time and in 1750 moved to Philadelphia. Here he took a position as tutor of Latin and Greek in Benjamin Franklin's Academy of Philadelphia, the forerunner of the University of Pennsylvania. Thomson taught at the school for five years and then took a position as Latin master and head of the Friend's Public School of Philadelphia. Here Thomson could shape his own curriculum; he included many subjects of a practical rather than scholarly nature. After running the school for about three years Thomson left teaching and went into business.[17]

Thomson, who had no children, saw to the education of his servants and slaves even to the point of sending them away to school on occasion. Sometime in the 1760s he set forth a rather significant "Plan of an American University." [18] He proposed:

As all habits especially the active ought to be early acquired, along with their studies at home youth should be taught to look much abroad; not to plunge into the gaities and fopperies of the idle but to view towns, fields, forts, harbours, and magazines, and to converse with men of all characters, professions, and trades and to inform themselves of their lives manners and connections. To this they should learn address and agility of body and even to wield the weapons and handle the tools of the several callings they are inspecting. Why should letters disqualify a man to take up a foile, mount in the great saddle or rein in the hunting horses. The ingenious mechanics the workers in stores and metals and improvers in trade, navigation and agriculture ought to be searched out and conversed with, no less than the professors of speculative science. Thus blending the active and contemplative life

[16] Thomas Clinton Pears, "Francis Alison, Colonial Educator," *Delaware Notes*, 17th ser. (1944), pp. 9–22; George Morgan, "The Colonial Origin of Newark Academy," ibid., 8th ser. (1943), pp. 7–30; Benjamin Rush, *Autobiography of Benjamin Rush*, ed. George W. Corner (Princeton, N.J., 1948), pp. 289–94.

[17] Harley, p. 33; Thomas H. Montgomery, *A History of the University of Pennsylvania to A.D. 1770* (Philadelphia, 1900), pp. 142, 148, 162–66; Thomas Woody, *Early Quaker Education in Pennsylvania* (New York, 1920), pp. 45, 180–81, 202–20.

[18] Thomson Memo Book, Thomson Papers, Hist. Soc. Pa.

would enliven and polish both and produce models of men as Xenophon or Sr. Walter Raleigh. . . .

For want of such a plan of Education many a man miscalled great is less useful to Society than the meanest peasant and many a gentleman of family of less consequence to it than the little boy in his kitchen.

Not such the worthies that adorned Queen Elizabeth's court, nor the race of private Gentlemen who were the supports of British liberty from her age down to the Revolution. Cards, dress and ruffling did not then engross their time; expensive diversions and amusements did not drain their Estates. They thought themselves obliged to be good for something. They thought, they studied, they exercised, they entered on life with a resolution to excell and thereby acquired great knowledge of affairs as well as letters.

Youth wholesomely educated, under a sober manly discipline would supersede the cobweb penalties of laws; and vices acquired by mean habits and an effeminate Education that now occupy our tribunals would then disappear.

Thomson's "American University" was to be an organized community in which youths progressed through stages of development by means of public examinations and promotions to the next step toward maturity.

In his proposals, in his life, and in the new order of which he was a part, Thomson held firmly to the maxim that he had placed at the beginning of his "Plan of an American University": "Learning should be connected with Life and qualify its possessor for Action, else it is just so much lumber, serving at best as an idle Amusement." These words seem strange coming from a Latin and Greek master, but they reflected an emerging American attitude which affected Thomson, a pragmatism which insisted on education being useful. This was not to deny the need for a sound educational background in the classics but simply to add another element to the usual eighteenth-century educational program.

Thomson's religious heritage, too, was similar to the developing religious patterns of America. He was born to Scotch-Irish Presbyterian parents and received much of his formal religious training under Dr. Alison, an "Old Side" Presbyterian. Thomson was enough of a product of the Enlightenment to allow reason to sway him from the faith of his ancestors. On one occasion he horrified the minister-teacher by proclaiming rebelliously that he did not know his catechism and had no intention of learning it, but would develop his own beliefs from a study of the Scriptures.[19] While still a young man he undertook a study of Eastern religions and made careful note of all the similarities between Buddhism and the deism

[19] Rush, p. 294.

of the Enlightenment.[20] Thomson had already proved himself to be a rationalist in other areas. As he said in his *Enquiry*, "It becomes Men of Wisdom and Prudence to leave nothing to Chance where Reason can decide." [21] On another occasion he stated, "I rest satisfyed that whatever is, either is, or will be ordered by the best." [22]

Yet he retained a devout, if not orthodox, faith. He apparently served some time as an elder in a Presbyterian church in Philadelphia and in his retirement years occasionally attended the Lower Merion Baptist Church near his home and gave it the property on which the church still stands. In 1779 he had an argument with the president of Congress, Henry Laurens. Thomson stated that the differences between the two began when Laurens, a true rationalist, failed to convince Thomson "that Moses, the man of God and deliverer of Israel, was an imposter and that he deceived the Israelites at Mount Sinai by his having had the knowledge of the use of gun powder." Apparently this was too much rationalism for Thomson to accept.[23] Thomson spent his retirement translating the Septuagint and the New Testament from the Greek and publishing the entire Bible in his own version of an Americanized English. He also complied a Harmony of the four Gospels using the words of his own translation.[24]

So Thomson became ultimately an unorthodox but devout Christian. This juxtaposition of Christianity and rationalism was typical of American religious attitudes of the day. Even such a noted rationalist as Thomas Jefferson cannot be called a true deist. He was instead a theist, a rationalist who had not quite relinquished the idea of a personal God. This attitude was shared by Thomson and probably by most enlightened Americans of his time.

Thomson's scientific interests were active and varied. Much of his interest was practical, a search for solutions to problems that he faced. On one occasion he read a paper to a group of friends on the best time and method of planting strawberries. At other times he investigated the possibilities of silk culture in America, of pre-

[20] Thomson Memo Book, Thomson Papers, Hist. Soc. Pa.

[21] P. 112.

[22] Thomson to Susannah Wright, July 20, 1758, Miscellaneous Collection, American Philosophical Society Library, Philadelphia.

[23] *Journals of Continental Congress*, XIV, 1008 ff.; *Letters of Continental Congress*, IV, 392–408; and Thomson Papers, Lib. Cong.

[24] Thomson, *The Holy Bible Containing the Old and New Covenant, Commonly Called the Old and New Testament* (4 vols., Philadelphia, 1808); Thomson, *A Synopsis of the Four Evangelists* (Philadelphia, 1815). See John F. Lyons, "Thomson's Bible," *Journal of the Presbyterian Historical Society*, 15 (1938–39): 211–20.

serving cloth and paper by applying cedar oil, and of cures for such ailments as toothaches and burns. He even developed a method of absorbing and disguising the unpleasant taste of the rum that he distilled to make it "scarcely distinguishable" from West Indian rum. His emphasis on "useful" science resulted in the transformation of a small self-improvement group of young men into the "American Society for promoting and propagating useful knowledge, held in Philadelphia." This group merged with the older Philosophical Society to form the American Philosophical Society, held at Philadelphia, for Promoting Useful Knowledge. This group not only united some of the greatest inquiring minds of the continent but also brought together many of the leaders of the American Revolution.[25]

Thomson joined Jefferson and others in a curiosity about the continent in which they lived, and he contributed a long appendix to Jefferson's *Notes on the State of Virginia*. Thomson supported Jefferson's attempt to persuade Europeans that the American continent was not a debilitating one and that indeed American animals and men grew as large, if not larger, than those of Europe. Thomson particularly tried to prove that American Indian males were not lacking in "ardor for their females" and that their "organs of generation" were not smaller than those of European males—both charges that the European scientist Buffon had levied.[26] Resuming his scientific activities after the Revolution, Thomson maintained an active correspondence with Jefferson, ranging over such scientific subjects as improved lighting devices, the efficiency of steam power, the nature of balloon flights, and the relative virtues and dangers of mesmerism.[27] For Thomson, and for most Americans at this time, science had to be "useful" and to serve the needs of the America in which it was developing. They were not unaware of the science of Europe; they rather sought to use it for their own needs and to insure that American accomplishments were judged in such a light as to cast credit on their native land.

For Thomson science and agriculture were intermingled, and

[25] The Thomson memo book, Thomson Papers, Hist. Soc. Pa., contains many of Thomson's papers and notes on various topics. See also J. Edwin Hendricks, "Charles Thomson's Philadelphia Rum," *Pennsylvania Magazine of History and Biography*, 89 (1965): 115; Brooke Hindle, "The Rise of the American Philosophical Society, 1766 to 1787" (Ph.D. diss., University of Pennsylvania, 1949).

[26] Thomas Jefferson, *Notes on the State of Virginia*, 1787 edition annotated by William Peden (Chapel Hill, N.C., 1955), pp. xviii–xix.

[27] Much of the Thomson-Jefferson correspondence is in the Thomson Papers, Lib. Cong. Early portions are printed in Jefferson, *Papers*, VI–XI.

both were useful to the emerging nation. Whether seeking new
and better ways to grow strawberries, trying to introduce mulberry
trees and silk worms, grape culture and wine making, or shipping
seeds and plants for an Englishman's garden, he emphasized both
individual and national development. Thomson helped found the
Philadelphia Agricultural Society and read a paper to one of its
early meetings. The paper was well received, and Thomson published it as a book in 1787. Interestingly, not even the avid American Thomson could let the volume stand on its own but indicated
that it was based on Arthur Young's 1771 *Farmer's Tour through
England*.[28] Although Thomson did include some material from
Young's books, *Notes on Farming* is primarily of interest because
of its efforts to introduce such American agricultural improvements
as feeding pumpkins to cattle for fodder and using the leaves from
American trees for both feed and compost. He later applied many
of his ideas in improving his farmlands during his retirement.

Thomson even had a specific and important role in the physical
growth of the American nation. In 1787, while the Constitutional
Convention was meeting in Philadelphia, Thomson presided over
the Confederation Congress meeting in New York and forced the
Congress to stay in session until it adopted the Northwest Ordinance. That ordinance provided for the first time in the annals of
political history a process whereby a nation could peacefully add
territory to its boundaries. The territories thus created could become states on an equal basis with the earlier states, a process
which provided for the orderly growth and development of the new
nation. He also had a role in the prohibition of slavery in the Northwest Territories; this set the trend for the ultimate abolition of
slavery in the rest of the United States.[29]

Thomson was an early example of "the American success story."
He personified inquisitiveness, intelligence, social mobility, political responsibility, and material and cultural success. After acquiring a good classical education at Dr. Alison's, Thomson went
to Philadelphia as a teacher. He soon made political and social connections with Benjamin Franklin, the leading Quakers of the colony (among them Isaac Norris and John Dickinson), and left

[28] *Notes on Farming* (New York, 1787); Brooke Hindle, *The Pursuit of
Science in Revolutionary America* (Chapel Hill, N.C., 1956), pp. 3–59.

[29] Frederick D. Stone, "The Ordinance of 1787," *Pennsylvania Magazine
of History and Biography*, 13 (1889): 335; and Frederick S. Rolater,
"Charles Thomson, Secretary of the Continental Congress, 1774–1789"
(M.A. thesis, University of Southern California, 1965), pp. 139–47, 162–
64, and 200 ff.

teaching to enter business. Earlier he had married Ruth Mather, the daughter of a man of moderate means, thereby apparently acquiring some operating capital. The Stamp Act gave him the opportunity to enter active political life, and he quickly achieved a position of leadership. His importing business faltered because of boycotts and other troubles with the British, and he sold out to become a distiller and operator of a cordial store. His participation in the American Philosophical Society expanded his acquaintances among the city's leadership. After the death of his first wife, he married Hannah Harrison, niece of John Dickinson and heiress to Harriton, the seven-hundred-acre plantation where Bryn Mawr now stands. Here he retired at the close of fifteen years as secretary of the Continental Congress; he renewed his interest in agriculture, improved and increased his holdings, and devoted himself to his biblical translations, making much the same contribution to an American culture as Noah Webster did with his dictionary.

Thomson's success story even had a happy ending since he lived to see the new order come into being. In many ways he had contributed to it, and in many ways he was a part of it. He agitated, organized, recorded, investigated, and worked for the nation he loved until he died in 1824 at the age of ninety-five. Thomson's career was a remarkable record for an orphan immigrant boy whose sole possessions when he arrived in this land were the ability to make a good nail and a desire to become a scholar. It had all been possible because of the "New Order of the Ages" that he not only helped form but also entitled.

2   Thomas Jefferson and the Fine Arts of Northern Italy: "A Peep into Elysium"

George Green Shackelford

I N 1787 Thomas Jefferson traveled in Italy to learn about rice; this essay omits details of the agricultural quest and seeks instead to reconstitute the cultural opportunities that he savored there. As he wrote to Charles Bellini, who taught Italian at the College of William and Mary and advised the young Jefferson on purchasing copies of European paintings, he lacked words to express how much he enjoyed the "architecture, sculpture, painting [and] music" of the Europeans.[1] Yet the marquis de Chastellux had observed as early as 1782 that Jefferson called his home "Monticello, . . . a name which bespeaks its owner's attachment to the language of Italy and above all to the Fine Arts, of which Italy was the cradle and is still the resort." [2]

Credited with introducing his countrymen to the principles of architectural neoclassicism, Jefferson has been hailed as the American Palladio.[3] But it was not until the 1940s that his biographers named any building which he had inspected in Italy.[4] Nor did they earlier note any persons as sources of his inspiration regarding the fine arts: his professional architectural colleague, Charles-Louis Clérisseau; the professional artists, John Trumbull and Maria Cosway; Louis XVI's curator of paintings, the comte d'Angeville; and the talented connoisseur, Madame de Tott, all contributed to preparing Jefferson's taste for what he was to see of the fine arts in northern Italy.

[1] Jefferson to Bellini, Sept. 30, 1785, *The Papers of Thomas Jefferson*, ed. Julian P. Boyd et al. (Princeton, N.J., 1950—), VIII, 569.

[2] François-Jean, marquis de Chastellux, *Travels in North America in the Years 1780, 1781 and 1782*, trans. and ed. Howard C. Rice, Jr. (2 vols., Chapel Hill, N.C., 1963), II, 390.

[3] Fiske Kimball, *Thomas Jefferson, Architect*, 2d ed. Frederick D. Nichols (New York, 1968), pp. 81–83, et passim.

[4] In chronological order these were: Bernard Mayo, *Jefferson Himself: The Personal Narrative of a Many-Sided American* (Boston, 1942); Marie Kimball, *Thomas Jefferson* (3 vols., Philadelphia and New York, 1943–50); and Dumas Malone, *Jefferson and His Time* (Boston, 1948—).

Especially was this true of Mrs. Maria Hadfield Cosway, an Anglo-Italian beauty. One can only speculate upon the nature of their friendship, but there is no doubt that they shared interests in children, education, music, nature, and especially painting. He practiced his Italian on her, and he sometimes was able to persuade her to leave her ultrasophistocated and foppish friends such as the duc de Biron and examine leisurely the paintings located in the royal palaces in and around Paris. Doubtless she spoke to him on such occasions of the paintings in the private and public collections at Florence, where she had grown up and to whose academy she had been elected as a youthful painter, or of those at Turin, where she had passed about a year before coming to London in the early 1770s.[5]

In his *Notes on Virginia*, Jefferson wrote as if the commonwealth's General Assembly had established as a component of a plan for the broader diffusion of knowledge "a public library and gallery, by laying out a certain sum annually in books, paintings and statues."[6] At best, this was exaggeration. He himself may have contemplated such a state art gallery, but the legislative bill for a central research library died a-borning, and even it had made no provision for gallery, paintings, or sculpture.[7] As a youth, however, Jefferson had compiled lists of painters and their works;[8] and as a mature man he displayed at Monticello his own collection of paintings.

Within the concept that the fine arts possess an essential unity, Jefferson's interest in paintings is as important as his more familiar concern with architecture. There has been general approbation of Jefferson's interest in and influence upon the latter: no one appears to have condemned him either for having bastardized neoclassicism or for having imprisoned Americans in architectural patterns two milleniums out-of-date and a hemisphere removed from their place of origin. Neoclassicism was the mode in all of the fine arts in Jefferson's day, and he preferred it also to the exclusion of its im-

[5] Helen D. Bullock, *My Head and My Heart: A Little History of Thomas Jefferson and Maria Cosway* (New York, 1945). The universities at Milan, Padua, and Pavia in this period conferred doctorates on women. See Edith Wharton, *The Valley of Decision* (2 vols., New York, 1902), II, 92–93, 189.

[6] Thomas Jefferson, *Notes on Virginia*, ed. William Peden (Chapel Hill, N.C., 1954), p. 149.

[7] Thomas Jefferson, "A Bill for the More General Diffusion of Knowledge" and "A Bill for Establishing a Public Library," *Papers*, II, 526–35, 544–45.

[8] Marie Kimball, *Jefferson*, I, 154, 322, quoting pocket notebook in Library of Congress accompanying notes dated 1769.

mediate predecessors—the medieval, the baroque, and the Georgian. Like his contemporaries, he believed that his age was
harmoniously attuned both to the Renaissance and to the classic
era. Remarkably, many of those who accept Jefferson's taste in
architecture condemn his taste in painting and sculpture, although
according to the standards of his time the latter two were insepa-
rable from the first of the fine arts. They castigate him for his
occasional excessive praise for neoclassical paintings that were the
rage everywhere in the Western world and for his alleged reference to "the old red faded things of Rubens." [9]

At least once, Jefferson backed down when an artistic friend,
Madame de Tott, showed him the error of his extravagant praise.[10]
Furthermore, he thought enough of Rubens to display at Monticello a copy of his *Diogenes and His Lantern*. He also possessed
three copies of works by Raphael. Within the standards of his day
in the young United States of America, Jefferson was a considerable art collector, even though few of his paintings were originals other than portraits. Then, as now, the greatest works of the
old masters were institutionalized; only copies were available to the
general public. When he could obtain an original by a good contemporary, such as Grueze, the Peales, Houdon, Benjamin West,
or Trumbull, he did so.[11]

Jefferson himself complained that his appreciation of the fine
arts was more book-learned than acquired by firsthand observation.[12] His biographers often state his indebtedness to architectural
and gardening books, but none have alluded to the guidebooks that
he used in European cities, not merely to get about from one place
to another but as sources of information about noted buildings and
art collections. The Virginia bibliophile retained these guidebooks
in his library for later use, such as helping to plan the city of
Washington.[13] By reference to these and to contemporary and near-
contemporary travelers' accounts, we can detail some of the monuments and paintings that Jefferson saw in northern Italy and
hazard brief speculation upon their influence on his mature taste in

[9] See, for example, Merrill D. Peterson, *Thomas Jefferson and the New
Nation: A Biography* (New York, 1970), pp. 351–52.

[10] Jefferson to Madame de Tott, Feb. 28 and April 5, 1787, Madame de
Tott to Jefferson, March 4, 1787, *Papers*, XI, 187–88, 198–99, 270–73.

[11] Marie Kimball, *Jefferson*, III, 114, 323–24; Marie Kimball, *The
Furnishings of Monticello* (Charlottesville, Va., 1940), pp. 7–13.

[12] Jefferson to Bellini, Sept. 30, 1785, *Papers*, VIII, 568–69.

[13] Jefferson to Pierre Charles L'Enfant, April 10, 1791, *The Writings of
Thomas Jefferson*, ed. Andrew A. Lipscomb and Albert E. Bergh (20
vols., Washington, D.C., 1903–4), VII, 162.

the fine arts. Because he relied so heavily on his three principal Italian guidebooks, *Guide pour le voyage d'Italie en poste,*[14] *Nouva guida di Milano,*[15] and *Beautés de Gênes,*[16] he did not himself make notes on much more than agricultural, financial, and utilitarian matters during his hurried Italian tour. At its conclusion, he had so strained his constitution that he suffered a spell of sickness which, after his official correspondence was done, long left him unable to write detailed, retrospective letters to his familiars about what he had seen during what he told Maria Cosway had been only "a Peep . . . into Elysium." [17]

Alas! Jefferson never went to Rome for a month's visit [18] in order to improve his concept of what was chaste and correct. Nor did Jefferson the architect ever go to Venice or Vicenza to see a building designed by Palladio. All that Thomas Jefferson knew from his own experience about Italy, he gained in the spring of 1787 when he traveled through the Piedmontese provinces of the king of Sardinia, the Austrian duchy of Milan, and the Republic of Genoa. As minister resident at Paris and former treaty commissioner, he had sought without result authority from Congress to go thither officially to survey opportunities for American commerce. Although Secretary for Foreign Affairs John Jay could grant him leave only to travel for his health, the minister comported himself as though his status as a commercial agent had been approved.[19] He imposed upon himself a strict timetable and limited itinerary

[14] [Anonymous], *Guide pour le voyage d'Italie en poste, nouvelle édition, avec les changements dans les postes, et augmentées de routes des états de terre ferme de S. M. le Roy de Sardaigne* . . . (Genoa: Gravier, 1793; xerox copy at Virginia Polytechnic Institute and State University, Blacksburg). No copy of the 1786 Turin edition bought by Jefferson in Turin can be found. See E. Millicent Sowerby, *The Catalogue of the Library of Thomas Jefferson* (4 vols., Washington, D.C., 1952–59), IV, 128–33.

[15] [Carlo Bianconi], *Nuova guida di Milano, per amanti delle belle arte e delle sacre e profane antichita milanesi* . . . (Milan, 1787; microfilm at V.P.I. & S.U.). This is the same edition bought by Jefferson in that city and included in his sale to the Library of Congress.

[16] [Giacomo Brusco], *Description des beautés de Gênes et de ses environs, ornée de differentes vues, de tailles douce: et de la carte topographique de la ville* (Genoa, 1781; copy at University of Virginia Library, Charlottesville). This is the same edition bought by Jefferson in that city and included in his sale to the Library of Congress.

[17] Jefferson to Maria Cosway, July 1, 1787, *Papers,* XI, 519.

[18] Jefferson to Thomas Mann Randolph, Sr., Aug. 11, 1787, ibid., XII, 2–22.

[19] Jefferson to Jay, Oct. 23, 1786, Jay to Jefferson, July 27, 1787, ibid., X, 484–85, XI, 627–28.

from which he did not depart in order to gratify his architectural and artistic interests.[20]

In planning his journey from Nice to Turin to Milan to Genoa and back to Nice, Jefferson was prepared for the discomfort, noise, dirt, and disorder along the way. He employed a regular valet named Petitjean for the whole trip, and he hired additional local valets and messenger boys to show him the lay of the land in strange cities.[21] Jefferson, ever a humane man, steeled himself in advance against being "persecuted" by the sound of the "cruel whip of the postillion." [22] There were, however, compensations for such disagreeable sensations, even though he customarily made light of his sightseeing visits to palaces, art galleries, and museums. In a splendid letter to Lafayette, he welcomed the chance "to see what I have never seen before and shall never see again. In the great cities, I go to see what travellers think alone worthy of being seen; but I make a job of it, and generally gulp it all down in a day." [23]

When Jefferson later suggested a seven-month continental itinerary for Thomas Mann Randolph, Jr., he recommended spending most of the time in and about the great cities: after prolonged study in the vicinity of Paris, a month each at Rome and Naples; two weeks at Florence; a week each at Geneva, Genoa, Milan, and Turin; four days each at Bordeaux and Marseilles; three days each at Leghorn and Dijon; two days each at Lyons, Nantes, and Nîmes; and one day each at Nice and Pisa.[24] He himself was never to go east of Milan or south of Genoa, at both of which he spent less time than he wished.

When Jefferson crossed the Var River from France into the kingdom of Sardinia on April 10, 1787, he had been absent from Paris for six weeks.[25] It is likely that he did not secure his visas

[20] Jefferson to Maria Cosway, July 1, 1787, ibid., XI, 519. Jefferson did not charge these expenses to the government.

[21] Jefferson to William Short, March 15 and April 12, 1787, ibid., XI, 214–15, 287. See also Jefferson, entry for May 1, 1787, Account Book, p. 457, xerox copy at UVa Lib. James A. Bear, Jr., curator of Monticello, kindly made available to the author his transcript of the Account Book. There are minor variations between the author's and Bear's reading of entries, particularly in place names, which here are modernized. The spelling of major French and Italian cities is anglicized here; minor place names are given the national spelling of today.

[22] Jefferson to Madame de Tott, April 3, 1787, *Papers*, XI, 271.

[23] Jefferson to Lafayette, April 11, 1787, ibid., XI, 283.

[24] Jefferson to Thomas Mann Randolph, Sr., Aug. 11, 1787, ibid., XI, 20–22.

[25] Entries for Feb. 28 and April 10, 1787, Jefferson Account Book, pp. 454, 456.

until he determined at Marseilles that he would go to Italy. He had arranged with the Parisian banker Ferdinand Grand for a letter of credit and a list of bankers on whom he might draw along his way.[26] He had not sought letters of introduction from the Sardinian ambassador to the Court of Versailles, the conte di Scarnafis, an unrelenting advocate of absolutism who had been haughty in transmitting his government's refusal to enter into a commercial treaty.[27] However, Jefferson had secured a few letters of scholarly introduction from the philosophical Abbés Arnoux and Chalut,[28] from his one-time Albemarle neighbor Philip Mazzei, who was then at Paris seeing through the press his *Recherches sur les États-Unis*,[29] and from a Milanese gentleman named Gaudenzio Clerici, whom Jefferson may have met in America and who claimed friendship with David Ramsay, the South Carolina botanist and historian. More dilettante than *philosophe*, Clerici was a country cousin of a prominent noble family of Milan. In vain, he urged the American minister leisurely to enjoy "the serenity and mildness of the Italian climate [which made that country] the Garden of Europe." Jefferson may not have been aware of the younger man's interesting and important associations, since he did not attempt to see Clerici when passing through the latter's countryside along the Ticino between Novara and Milan. In later years, however, he guided to Clerici's door a number of young Americans on their grand tour.[30]

---

[26] Jefferson to Grand and Grand to Jefferson, Feb. 28, 1787, *Papers*, XI, 184–85.

[27] De Scarnafis to the American Commissioners, Feb. 2, 1785, ibid., VII, 632–33. Jefferson used the French version of the minister's name, which in its Italian version was Filippo Ottone Ponte, conte di Scarnafiggi. He had been a student of Giambatista Beccaria at the University of Turin. See Antonio Pace, *Benjamin Franklin and Italy*, American Philosophical Society *Memoirs*, vol. 47 (Philadelphia, 1958), 95 passim. See also Philip Mazzei, *Memoirs of the Life and Peregrinations of the Florentine, Philip Mazzei, 1730–1816*, trans. Howard Mararro (New York, 1942), p. 326.

[28] Jefferson to the Abbés Arnoux and Chalut, April 12, 1787, *Papers*, XI, 287–88. The abbés provided entrée to André Sasserno at Nice, who in turn gave Jefferson letters for the Abbé Deleuze at Turin and conte Francesco dal Verme at Milan. Mazzei considered Arnoux and Chalut "very ignorant" (*Memoirs*, p. 293). Deleuze may be a misreading of conte Giuseppi Angelo Saluzzo of the Turin Academy of Sciences. Pace, p. 63.

[29] Jefferson to Mazzei, April 4, 1787, *Papers*, XI, 266–67. Mazzei's opus is *Recherches historiques et politiques sur les États-Unis . . . par un citoyen de Virginie* (4 vols., Paris, 1787).

[30] Gaudenzio Clerici to Jefferson, March 5, 1787, Jefferson to Clerici, Aug. 15, 1787, and Aug. 31, 1788, Clerici to Jefferson, Jan. 20, 1789, *Papers*, XI, 199–200, XII, 38–39, XIII, 553–54, XIV, 475.

When Jefferson discovered that he could not learn about Italian
rice at Marseilles,[31] he determined to travel in Italy for the briefest
period necessary to accomplish that purpose. Ever a discriminating
bibliophile, Jefferson bought maps and guidebooks of Turin,
Milan, and Genoa "while in those cities," [32] both for immediate use
and for subsequent rumination. The American diplomat proceeded
to the Piedmontese port of Nice, whence he arranged to cross the
Maritime Alps through the Tende Pass and then to descend the
plain of the Po as far as the rice fields situated in the great triangle
between Vercelli, Milan, and Pavia.[33]

While refreshing himself at Nice, Jefferson visited the royal
botanical garden and called upon most of the persons to whom he
carried letters of introduction.[34] The American diplomat declared
that Nice was handsome, possessed good accommodations, and
enjoyed a "superb" climate. The rather straight-laced Virginian
lamented that its society was "gay and dissipated," but he may
have told himself that such was the natural consequence of absolutism in the kingdom of Sardinia.

Learning that the snows were "not yet enough melted to allow
carriages to pass," Jefferson engaged at Nice mules and muleteers
to convey him, his valet, and his portmanteau through the Tende
Pass. The road through the pass was then considered an engineering marvel, by whose sixty-nine *lacets*, or hairpin curves, one
ascended to the 4,230-foot-high Col de Braus.[35] In good weather,
Jefferson assured Maria Cosway, "you may go in your chariot in
full trot from Nice to Turin, as if there were no mountain," [36]

[31] Jefferson to Short, April 7, 1787, ibid., XI, 280–81.

[32] Jefferson to L'Enfant, April 10, 1791, *Writings*, VII, 162. Jefferson
also recommended that tourists buy Joseph Addison's *Remarks on Several
Parts of Italy* (London, 1745 and later eds.), but he did not buy until 1788
the copy of Addison's book which he sold to the Library of Congress
(Sowerby, IV, 128–33).

[33] Entry for April 10, 1787, Jefferson Account Book, p. 456. See also Jefferson to Mazzei, April 4, 1787, to Short, April 7, 1787, *Papers*, XI, 266–
67, 280.

[34] Entries for April 6–10, 1787, "Notes of a Tour into the Southern Parts
of France . . . and Northern Italy, in the year, 1787," ibid., XI, 429–30,
463n; entry for April 13, 1787, Jefferson Account Book, p. 456. He visited
the commandant, the director of the Royal Tobacco Factory, a banker, and
two merchants.

[35] Jefferson to Short, April 12, 1787, *Papers*, XI, 287; entries for April
[14]–15, 1787, Jefferson Account Book, p. 456; *Italie en poste*, pp. 48–49;
Karl Baedeker, *Italy: Handbook for Travellers . . . , First Part: Northern
Italy* (9th remodeled ed., Leipzig and London, 1892), p. 80.

[36] Jefferson to Maria Cosway, July 1, 1787, *Papers*, XI, 520.

utilizing the well-organized system of engaging successive teams of horses to draw one's chaise from one way-station, or post, to the next about ten miles distant. He noted, and perhaps ate as a local delicacy, the speckled trout of the River Roya in its stretches just below the great Gorge of Saorgo. "Further on," Jefferson wrote, "we come to the Chateau of Saorgo, where a scene is presented, the most singular and picturesque I ever saw. The castle and village seem hanging to a cloud in front. On the right is a mountain cloven through to let pass a gurgling stream; on the left a river over which is thrown a magnificent bridge. The whole form a basin, the sides of which are shagged with rocks, olive trees, vines, herds, etc." [37] He went so far as to declare to Mrs. Cosway, "I insist on your painting it." [38] The chateau was a fortresslike castle "in the Oriental style"; the French in 1792 destroyed it and its adjacent fortified barracks. In its wild, romantic setting it must have resembled a Shangri-la, set on an irregular triangular platform whose nearly equal sides were about seventy yards in length.[39] It is tempting to give to Maria Cosway's painting of roseate cliffs viewed from a rocky mountain torrent the title *The Gorge of Saorgo*.[40]

Once he reached the plain of the Po, the flat countryside permitted Jefferson to travel swiftly in a two-horse carriage with a postillion and a cock horse. During the four changes of post horses between Cuneo and Turin, he jotted down impressions of the rich agricultural lands through which he passed.[41] He lunched at Racconigi, the site of the palazzo of the Carignano branch of the house of Savoy, whose park and gardens have been attributed to Louis XIV's landscape architect, André Le Nôtre. The façade of the edifice is about a hundred yards from the village and separated from the latter only by a grille, but Jefferson does not record entering either the grounds or the palazzo, famous for its great soaring

[37] Entry for April 14, 1787, "Notes of a Tour," ibid., XI, 432. His description of Saorgo to Mrs. Cosway was based on this. His spelling of "Saorgio" has been modernized.

[38] Jefferson to Maria Cosway, July 1, 1787, ibid., XI, 520. Earlier he had begged in his famous "My Head and My Heart" letter that she paint Niagara Falls, the junction of the Potomac and the Shenandoah, the Natural Bridge of Virginia, and Monticello; Jefferson to Maria Cosway, Oct. 12, 1786, ibid., X, 445.

[39] Baedeker, p. 80, and the author's observations.

[40] Cosway Collection, College of Santa Maria della Grazie, Lodi, Italy.

[41] Entry for April 15, 1787, "Notes of a Tour," *Papers*, XI, 433; entry for April 16, 1787, Jefferson Account Book, p. 456; *Italie en poste*, pp. 48–49.

roccoco hall. Not far from Racconigi he crossed the Po where it was about fifty yards wide on a wooden roadway built on "swinging batteaux" that were moored to the river bank by cables supported at their midsection by canoes. Another traveler remarked that the canoes used on the Po near Turin were dugouts, just like the canoes of the North American Indians; it is curious that Jefferson, a collector of Indian artifacts and recorder of their languages and customs, did not make a similar observation.[42]

Jefferson arrived at Turin in the late afternoon of April 16 and took lodgings at the Hôtel d'Angleterre for what proved to be a four-night stay. He must have followed local custom by joining at common table about a dozen persons for a table-d'hôte dinner. Unfortunately, the American epicure commented only on the wines of the region, a "red wine of Nebiule," similar to the present-day Fraisci, which he found so "pleasing" that he exclaimed: "It is about as sweet as the silky Madiera, as astringent on the palate as Bordeaux, and as brisk as Champagne." He also noted favorably the "thick and strong" red wine of Monferrato, similar to today's Dolcetti.[43]

Once Jefferson determined that he could not obtain at Turin the desired information about rice, he felt free to devote several days to cultivating his appreciation of the history and fine arts of Piedmont, of which Maria Cosway surely had told him something. On the first and second nights of his visit, he attended comedies at what may have been the semiprivate theater of the ducca di Carignano. He devoted the daylight hours of April 17 and 18 so completely to sightseeing that he left little time for seeing those to whom he bore business letters.[44] Former Treaty Commissioner Jef-

[42] Entries for April 15–16, 1787, "Notes of a Tour," *Papers*, XI, 433–34; and for the same dates, Jefferson Account Book, p. 456. See also *Italie en Poste*, pp. 48–49; "An American" [Timothy Dwight], *A Journal of a Tour in Italy in the Year 1821* (New York, 1824), p. 466; Baedeker, p. 55; and Richardson Wright, *The Story of Gardening* (New York, 1934), pp. 270–96.

[43] Entries for April 16–19, Jefferson Account Book, p. 456. Quotation from entries for April 17–18, "Notes of a Tour," *Papers*, XI, 435. See also Charles Pinot-Duclos, *Voyage en Italie, ou considerations sur l'Italie* (Paris, 1791 ed.), p. 324. Pinot-Duclos made his trip in 1767 when he was historiographer of France and secrétaire perpetuelle of the Académie Française. Professor Raimondo Luraghi kindly furnished the author with comments on wines in the course of conducting him to eighteenth-century places of interest at Turin.

[44] Entries for April 17–19, Jefferson Account Book, p. 456; Maria Cosway to Jefferson, July 9, 1787, *Papers*, XI, 568–69 and 464n. He visited two bankers and two or three merchants, whom he questioned concerning the potential market for American tobacco, whale oil, and fish products.

ferson was painfully aware that the king of Sardinia had rebuffed America's invitation to negotiate a treaty of amity and commerce, saying that he would not initiate such a move until U.S.-Sardinian trade through Nice expanded enough to make it mutually advantageous.[45] At Turin, Jefferson bought £13.10 worth of "maps," which may have been one or more of the guidebooks *Italie en poste*, Carlo Bianci's *Nuova guida di Milano*, and Giacomo Brusco's *Beautés de Gênes*.[46]

In seeing the sights of Turin, it was conventional to devote a morning to the Palazzo Reale, the Duomo, the adjacent royal chapel of the Santissima Sindone, and the church of San Lorenzo.[47] Characteristically, Jefferson did not record his sensations upon viewing these. One must reluctantly conclude that he might have agreed with his fellow classicist, the Irish Jesuit priest John Chetwode Eustace, that Guarino Guarini and Filippo Juvara, the principal architects of Turin's palazzi and churches, were too baroque in preferring

the twisted, tortured curves and angles of Borromini, to the unbroken lines and simple forms of antiquity. Novelty, not purity, and *prettyness* instead of majesty, seem to have been their sole object. Hence, this city does not . . . present one chaste model, one single grand specimen in the ancient style, to challenge the admiration of travellers. Every edifice . . . , whether church or theatre, hospital or palace, is encumbered with whimsical ornaments, is all glare and glitter, gaiety and confusion. In vain does the eye seek for repose, the mind long for simplicity. Gilding and flourishing blaze on all sides, and we turn away from the gaudy show, dazzled and disgusted.[48]

It would have been remarkable if Jefferson had expressed approbation of Guarini's churches of Santissima Sindone and San Lorenzo. A man of his own times, he doubtless agreed with his bitter critic and fellow American, Timothy Dwight, that these early eighteenth-century churches "had nothing remarkable, except the nondescript barbarisms of their cupolas." [49]

---

[45] De Scarnafis to the American Commissioners, Feb. 2, 1785, *Papers*, VII, 632–33. See also Jefferson to C. W. F. Dumas, Dec. 9, 1787, to John Adams, July 1, 1787, ibid., XII, 407, XI, 516; and Dumas Malone, *Jefferson and the Rights of Man* (Boston, 1951), pp. 40–49.

[46] Entry for April 17, 1787, Jefferson Account Book, p. 456; Sowerby, IV, 128–33.

[47] Pinot-Duclos, p. 325.

[48] Eustace, *A Classical Tour through Italy* (8th ed., 3 vols., London, 1841), III, 166–69. Based on travels in 1802, the book is marred by Francophobia, but it accurately reflects the classicists' distaste for both the Gothic and the baroque.

[49] Dwight, p. 466. See also Seigfried Geidion, *Space, Time and Architecture: The Growth of a New Tradition* (Cambridge, Mass., 1941), pp. 55–

It was conventional to visit the University of Turin and the nearby academy and archives in the afternoon. Because Jefferson had a letter of introduction to the Abbé Deleuze, a professor of the academy, he surely visited those precincts.[50] Before the 1790s, the university occupied a position more similar to those of the Renaissance and to the one that Jefferson was to found in Virginia than to its contemporary institutions. Students were "considered as part of the court, and admitted to all its balls and amusements." The university was housed in a "most extensive building" of two stories built about an arcaded court; it boasted a library of "more than fifty thousand volumes," a museum for its "numerous collections of statues, vases, and other antiquities; . . . a hall of anatomy, admirably furnished, and an observatory." Furthermore, the university was "endowed for twenty-four professors, all of whom gave daily lectures." Associated with, but not a part of, the university was the academy, which enjoyed "a considerable degree of reputation,"[51] and which Jefferson must enviously have contemplated. How ironic that the despot-ridden Piedmont should possess the gallery and research library for which the virtuous Commonwealth of Virginia refused all support!

Apparently the news that an American savant was in the city spread enough to make Jefferson an object of momentary curiosity. Gaudenzio Clerici later wrote him that "The . . . Marquis de Cacciapiatti and his Brother the Chevalier told me . . . of either having seen or having heard that Monsr. de Jefferson was, at the time of their coming thro' Turin, quietly philosofizing in the Capital."[52]

Jefferson took horses to visit the basilica church of Superga and the royal palazzi of Moncalieri and of Stupinigi. The sight of the mountain of Superga from the banks of the Po is far more compelling than that of Monticello from the Rivanna, but the view from both of those eminences reveals rolling plains to the east and high mountains to the north and west. Since it was, after all, Jefferson who popularized the name Piedmont as an American geo-

---

61; and Richard Pommer, *Eighteenth-Century Architecture in Piedmont: The Open Structures of Juvarra, Alfieri & Vittone* (New York, 1967), pp. 7–11. For Dwight's unflattering view of Jefferson, see Timothy Dwight, *The Character of Thomas Jefferson as Revealed in His Writings* (Boston, 1839).

[50] Pinot-Duclos, p. 325; "Notes of a Tour," *Papers*, XI, 464n.

[51] Eustace, III, 167–69. The academy also served as a preparatory school for civil and military service. Wharton, I, 91–92.

[52] Clerici to Jefferson, July 14, 1787, *Papers*, XI, 585–86.

graphic term, he might have exclaimed over the similarities of terrain. But he made no note of it. The basilica, built to commemorate Piedmontese success in breaking the French seige of 1706 and to serve as a royal mausoleum, was a monument to be looked at. Accordingly, the scale of its classical portico, curved interior, forest of pillars, and carved reredoses is very great. After this excursion, Jefferson recorded only his irritation over the custom of local coachmen. Although it took an hour for their six-horse carriages to ascend the mountain, "on the descent" they raced "to prove the brilliance of themselves and of their steeds."

It was not the season for the court to be in residence at Moncalieri when Jefferson visited its Palazzo Reale located on the southern slope of the mountain of Superga. The reddish, rectangular complex with its round corner towers had been rebuilt often, but one could still discern that it once had been a fortress. From observing there lesser members of the house of Savoy and retired courtiers, the sturdy American republican may have thought that the palazzo gave tangible illustration of the diminishing relevance of monarchical institutions.[53]

At Stupinigi the Palazzina di Caccia or hunting lodge had been begun in 1729. Its first and great architect was Filippo Juvara, of whose work little was left after thirty years of additions and rebuilding. His initial concept was that only the king, a few courtiers, and several servants would sleep at the lodge; all others would be permitted to come from Turin, five or six miles to the northeast, only when invited. The edifice was to be one room thick, giving maximum visual effect for least expense. Its great room, the salone centrale, was a stage for sumptuous entertainment located at the junction of four spraddled wings, two of which were devoted to royal apartments and two to banqueting halls. When Jefferson visited the Stupinigi, the palazzina had become a palazzo, swollen to accommodate the prolific royal family and their entourage. The salone centrale had been raised from its original two stories to three, and it presented on its ceiling a fresco of Diana departing at dawn for the chase and on its roof a huge statue of a stag. Sacheverell Sitwell has endorsed the statement that this room is "one of the most successful of baroque interiors," but Richard

---

[53] Entry for April 18, Jefferson Account Book, p. 456; "Notes of a Tour," *Papers*, XI, 435; Short to Jefferson, Oct. 18, 1788, ibid., XIV, 27; Eustace, III, 167–69; Baedeker, p. 38. Quotation is from Pinot-Duclos, pp. 328–29. When Pinot-Duclos went to Superga, one of the carriages overturned and was dragged, but without human injury. The palazzo is now a military academy.

Pommer in his authoritative work on Piedmontese architecture makes it clear that, however fine Stupinigi had been to begin with, this room and the building of which it is a part had become a contradictory mess by the time Jefferson saw it.[54]

Before leaving Turin, Jefferson must have viewed from the exterior and may have inspected some of the nine "hospitals" of the city, which provided many social services in addition to medical and nursing care—"provisions and employment to the poor, education to the orphans, a dowry to unmarried girls, and an asylum to the sick and decayed." [55] One would like to think that one so keenly desirous as Jefferson of support for such services in Virginia visited these hospitals, but his ecclesiastical suspicions may have prevailed. There was no uncertainty, however, of his interest in Turin's straight streets and broad avenues inherited from Roman days, but he did not say that they reminded him of Philadelphia, as did Timothy Dwight. His protégé William Short later declared that Turin was "the handsomest city . . . in Europe on account of its regularity" both of streets and of buildings, even though the surface of the latter appeared more "unfinished" than that of English and American townhouses.[56]

Jefferson's postchaise brought him to the famous Albergo de Tre Re in Vercelli, the rice-market town, on April 19. There he made clandestine arrangement to see how rough rice was husked and to smuggle some seed rice out of the country. That he secreted a small packet on his own person was very daring because Sardinian law prescribed death as the penalty for exporting seed rice. Understandably the American diplomat did not linger. After clearing customs and crossing the River Agogna the next day, he hastened through Novara to Milan, where he lodged at the Albergo Reale.[57]

In Milan, the conte Francesco dal Verme befriended Jefferson and directed him "to those objects which precisely merited most attention" in the Lombard capital during his visit of three nights and two days. An acquaintance of Benjamin Franklin and John Adams and a man who actually had visited the United States in

---

[54] Entry for April 18, 1787, Jefferson Account Book, p. 456; Hugh Thomas, "Stupinigi," *Great Houses of Europe*, ed. Sacheverell Sitwell (London, 1970), pp. 198–205; Pommer, pp. 61–78.

[55] Eustace, III, 106.

[56] Dwight, pp. 465–66; Short to Jefferson, Oct. 18, 1788, *Papers*, XIV, 27.

[57] "Notes of a Tour," *Papers*, XI, 22–24; entries for April 19–20, 1787, Jefferson Account Book, pp. 436–37.

1783–84, dal Verme was good company as well as good cicerone, and Jefferson subsequently sent him from Paris a gift of books which included his own *Notes on Virginia*. He also directed to him several young Americans on their grand tour.[58] It is likely that Jefferson and his new-found Milanese friends, enlightened aristocrats, discussed the controversial reforms of the Hapsburg emperor Joseph II in the duchy of Milan. The conte dal Verme was a man to Jefferson's liking. Not only did the nobleman tell him about a pendulum odometer suitable for carriages, but he displayed a fanciful interest in the scientific and pseudoscientific interests of the age. Making a gracious reference to the marquis de Chastellux's account of his visit to Jefferson at Monticello, dal Verme exclaimed that he would like to "be transported in a Baloon" to America.[59]

Besides dal Verme, Jefferson met also at Milan the conte Luigi di Castiglioni. Unfortunately, the American's visit was so brief that he could not have accepted, as did William Short about eighteen months later, Castiglioni's invitation to inspect his own and his relatives' villas about a dozen miles from the city on the way to the Italian lakes. From Short's account, his patron would have enjoyed such an excursion not only for the beauties of the landscape but also because Castiglioni and his in-laws proved to be "zealous botanist[s] . . . , as much attached to American plants & trees as . . . to Americans, themselves." [60]

In Milan, Jefferson singled out three houses as especially noteworthy: the Casa Candiani, the Casa Roma, and the Casa Belgiojoso. The first two of these palazzi he identified as recent works by the architect Appiani, and he stated his preference for the first-named. However, it was the Palazzo Belgiojoso that he described. The architect Martin had built this edifice in the mid-eighteenth century on the Via Moroni, a block north of the Piazza della Scala. Its small cabinet especially pleased Jefferson, because its ceiling was composed of small hexagons, in the center of each of which were painted alternately cameo medallions and classic busts. Its salon was worthy of special remark, also, because its walls and

[58] Entries for April 23–24, 1787, "Notes of a Tour," *Papers*, XI, 437, 464; Jefferson to dal Verme, Aug. 15, 1788, ibid., XIII, 42–43; and entries for April 20–23, 1787, Jefferson Account Book, p. 456. It is not known whether Jefferson acted upon his memorandum to visit a certain Abbé de Regibus, or whether he meant instead the brothers Reycends, who were book dealers. Pace, p. 12.

[59] Dal Verme to Jefferson, Feb. 12, 1788, *Papers*, XII, 587–88; Jefferson, "Notes of a Tour," ibid., XI, 437.

[60] Short to Jefferson, Oct. 28, 1788, ibid., XIV, 41–43.

floor were sheathed in scagliola work, or marble dust of various colors so reconstituted as to be "scarcely distinguishable from the finest marbles." [61]

It is remarkable that Jefferson did not mention the splendid Palazzo Clerici nearby, built in the first half of the eighteenth century. Among its furnishings other than fine tapestries is a large fresco by Giovanni Battista Tiepolo depicting how the chariot of the sun, driven by Mercury, illumines the world.[62] Stendhal observed that the Milanesi believed that the "true patent of nobility" was to build a fine palazzo. Jefferson might have concurred with Stendhal's admiration of the rather academic style of Guiseppe Piermarini's 1778 rebuilding of the La Scala Theatre, and even with Stendhal's acidulous observation that new "social requirements" outmoded interior arrangements appropriate to palazzi built in the sixteenth century by Palladio and his school, and that "the main features of the Italian residence which seems . . . worth preserving are the bedrooms, which are lofty [and] salubrious." [63]

Almost surely Jefferson visited what is now the Brera Gallery, then known as the Palazzo di Scienze, Lettere, e Arti, which housed a college recently secularized and expanded by Emperor Joseph II. A decade before, while a Jesuit institution of "great extent and magnificence," it had a student body of twelve hundred. Built by Francesco Maria Richini in the sixteenth century, it was a typical north Italian collegiate complex located in the central city around a courtyard and enclosed by two stories of arcaded loggias. The great picture gallery for which the Brera has been famous since 1809 was not, of course, there for Jefferson to see, but there were smaller and less notable collections of paintings and sculpture in its halls to give him "much amusement." [64]

[61] "Notes of a Tour," ibid., XI, 437. World War II bomb damage of the area was very heavy but much has been restored. The Casa Belgiojoso should not be confused with the present Gallery of Modern Art, formerly the Villa Reale and before that the Villa Belgioioso which was built by Leopold Pollak in 1790 for conte Lodovico Barbiano de Belgioioso. The latter sold it to the Cisalpine Republic to give to Napoleon who resided there, as did Eugène Beauharnais afterwards. Baedeker, pp. 95, 96, 110; Ente Provinciale per il Turismo di Milano, *Tutta Milano* (Milan, 1969), p. 38.

[62] Ente Provinciale Turismo, *Milano* [Milan, 1969?], p. [9]; *Tutta Milano*, p. 39.

[63] Marie Henri Beyle [Stendhal], *Rome, Naples and Florence*, trans. Richard N. Coe (New York, 1960), pp. 36–38, 337.

[64] Jefferson to George Wythe, Sept. 16, 1787, *Papers*, XII, 127. See also Baedeker, p. 97; Touring Club Italienne, *L'Italie en une volume*, ed. Cesar Chiodi, Les Guides Bleus series, 1952 ed., p. 45.

The Biblioteca Ambrosiana was in 1787 much the same as it is today. Since Jefferson owned a good copy of Leonardo da Vinci's painting of *St. John* [65] and was fascinated by mechanical contrivances, he may have gone to the Biblioteca to view its celebrated collection of da Vinci manuscripts and drawings. By the same reasoning, Jefferson may have gone to the refectory of the late Dominican convent attached to the suburban church of Sante Maria della Gazie to see Leonardo's *Last Supper*, even though that fresco was flaking and fading. Despite Jefferson's anticlerical predilections, he could not ignore the Duomo of Milan. Without knowing whether he examined its interior with care, we may assume that he climbed to its roof, just as he advised younger Americans to climb to the top of church steeples in order to perceive the scope of cities. The author of the Virginia Statute for Religious Freedom left no doubt, however, of his opinion of the Duomo in particular and of Italian churches in general: "The Cathedral of Milan [is] a worthy object of philosophical contemplation, to be placed among the rarest instances of the misuse of money. On viewing the churches of Italy it is evident without calculation that the same expense would have sufficed to throw the Appenines into the Adriatic and thereby render it terra firma from Leghorn to Constantinople." Jefferson, to be sure, was far from complaining, as did Father Eustace fifteen years later, that the enlightened despot Joseph II had curtailed construction of the Duomo.[66]

When the Ospedale Maggiore of Milan loomed up before him, Jefferson presumably relied upon his guidebook, for he recorded no data even though its secular nature should have guaranteed that he would give free rein to his long-standing interest in prisons and hospitals. Since the fifteenth century, the Ospedale's series of rectangular courts had housed the medical, nursing, and other social services of the duchy. Its buildings were of a transitional style combining Gothic and Renaissance architectural features. Sometimes referred to as Milan's Ca' Grande, there were three hundred rooms in the lazaretto or wards, and another portion of the immense edifice housed twelve hundred working convalescents. Although its rooms were airy and clean, the huge structure was surrounded by a stream whose convenience for sewage purposes must have induced fevers that periodically reduced the number of inmates.

[65] Marie Kimball, *Jefferson*, I, 114.

[66] "Hints to Americans Travelling in Europe," *Papers*, XIII, 272; see also ibid., XIII, 268; Eustace, III, 125, 128–29.

Jefferson, the classicist, probably visited the Basilica di San Lorenzo Maggiore, where the city's major Roman remains were located – sixteen marble Corinthian columns that in the third century A.D. had led to the baths of Roman Mediolanum.[67]

Jefferson resisted the temptation to travel more widely in Italy before returning to France via Genoa. As he wrote to Maria Cosway, "I took a peep only into Elysium. I entered it at one door, and came out at another. . . . I calculated the hours it would have taken to carry me on to Rome. But they were exactly so many more than I could spare. Was not this provoking? In thirty hours from Milan I could have been at [Venice]." [68] He left Milan after breakfast on April 23. On his way south, he resumed his agricultural notes. He broke his journey to visit the former Carthusian monastery, the Certosa di Pavia, about five miles north of Pavia, but he remarked neither on its superb Lombard Romanesque architecture nor on its disestablishment several years earlier by Joseph II. The property of the former abbey had produced an income £1,200 a year, which the emperor diverted to support an expansion of the hospitals and educational institutions of Milan and Pavia.

At Pavia, the traveler lodged at the Albergo Croce Bianco, famous as an hostelry for more than a century. He visited the botanical gardens, but if he went elsewhere in the university of which they are a part, he did not say so. Because of his interest in educational institutions, he may quickly have taken a turn about its "noble library, grand halls for lectures, anatomical galleries, . . . and several well-endowed colleges." Since the fourteenth century, this university had produced great men, such as the scientist Volta and the early master of the University of Paris, Pietro di Pavia.[69]

From Pavia, Jefferson traveled south without significant delay to the Republic of Genoa. Discharging his old equipage and employing a new one, the weary traveler drove into the splendor-loving city, whose mythological foundation Janus sited so as to face toward both Italy and France. Dissatisfied with his initial lodgings, he moved to the French-style Hôtel du Cerf, where he engaged a room overlooking the Mediterranean. During three days in Genoa he spent almost £80 in sightseeing and transportation.

Thomas Jefferson left record of having visited only one of the

---

[67] Eustace, III, 130–31.

[68] Jefferson to Maria Cosway, July 1, 1787, *Papers*, XI, 519–20.

[69] Entries for April 23–24, 1787, Jefferson Account Book, p. 456; Eustace, III, 107–9; Baedeker, pp. 141–44; and *Italie en Poste*, p. 33 and plate 19.

city's famous palazzi and two others in its suburbs. The first of these "lofty palaces" was the Palazzo Marcello Durazzo, then owned by the marchese Jean Luc Durazzo, to whom he brought a letter of introduction from the marchese Jean Baptiste di Spinola, a kinsman of the minister of the Republic of Genoa resident at the Court of Versailles, Christoforo Vicenzo di Spinola.[70] Located on the up-hill side of the Via Balbi, this palazzo was thought to have been built in the late sixteenth century by the architect Galeazzo Alessi, reputedly a student of Michelangelo and a contemporary of Palladio; but it probably was more the work of Bartolomeo Bianci. It had been much improved by the later addition of an eighteenth-century façade, vestibule, and double stairway that was the work of Andrea Taglifici. Although Jefferson urged all Americans who came to Italy to go thither, he noted only a bench with straight legs and caned seat which particularly pleased him. There was good reason for his taciturnity: his guidebook, Brusco's *Beautés de Gênes*, devoted five pages to the palazzo's paintings and contained a fine illustration of the street façade.[71] According to Brusco, the frescos of the Palazzo Marcello Durazzo were executed in the Bolognese style of Jacques Bena, Simone da Pesaro, and Domenique Piola. Of about eighty paintings, listed by artists and title, more than one-half were by such famous men as Caravaggio, both Agostino and Annibale Carracci, Guido Renni, Rubens, Titian, Vandyke, and Veronese. Remarkably for that day, Brusco's guidebook differentiated between originals and those which were copies or "of the school of" so-and-so. Among the family portraits were several by Hyacinthe Rigaud, who had painted Louis XIV.[72]

Inasmuch as Jefferson was acquainted with marchese di Spinola, he may have visited his palazzo and possibly others of the Spinola family. Spinola once had made courteous inquiries about a possible

[70] *Papers*, XI, 464; Pace, pp. 96, 97, 114–15, 119, identifies Minister Resident Spinola as Christoforo Vincenzo Spinola. Julian P. Boyd et al. in Jefferson's *Papers* identifies him as Jean Baptiste de Spinola. It may be that the latter was in fact the person to whom Jefferson was intended to present the letter of introduction.

[71] Entries for April 24–28, 1787, Jefferson Account Book, p. 456; "Notes of a Tour," *Papers*, XI, 440–41, 464; Jefferson to Short, Feb. 28, 1789, ibid., XIV, 598. See also Brusco, p. 11; quotation from Eustace, III, 82–97, 102. He presented letters of introduction from Le Clerc to the bankers Bertrand, Ricard & Bramerel and from Guide to the merchant Aimé Regny.

[72] Brusco, pp. 51–56; John Canaday, *The Lives of the Painters* (4 vols., New York, 1969), IV, passim. See also Editors of *Réalités*, *Great Houses of Italy* (New York, 1968), pp. 128–31.

treaty of amity and commerce between the two republics, and such acts were cherished by the treaty commissioners. The Genovese diplomat's palace near the Palazzo Garibaldi of that day was called the Palazzo *alla catena*. By no means so splendid as the Palazzo Marcello Durazzo, it nonetheless boasted three Guido Renis and a Correggio among about a dozen important paintings.

As a man who not only provided his own house with many windows but amplified them by skylights, Jefferson may have nodded agreement when he read in his guidebook and at the same time observed for himself that the cathedral church of San Lorenzo was "of the rather heavy gothic variety" with "badly lighted aisles." [73] As a resolute anticlerical, he was indifferent as to whether the churches of Genoa were, in the words of the Irish Jesuit Father Eustace, guilty of too much "ornament and glare," but he probably agreed they possessed too little of "the first of architectural graces, simplicity." [74]

The Palazzo Doria Pamphili glistens whitely on the western verge of Genoa for everyone to see. In Jefferson's day it was called the Palazzo Doria Principe.[75] Whether or not Jefferson met at Paris Monsignor Guiseppi Doria Pamphili who had served as Papal Nuncio at Versailles in the early 1760s, his failure to mention this "earliest" and "most familiar" of the "great" palazzi of the city fits into his usual pattern. This celebrated structure had been begun early in the sixteenth century for Admiral Andrea Doria, and it had been embellished with statuary and gardens designed by Fra Montorsoli that reached from the mountains to the shingle. Jefferson, as a "modern," English-style gardener, presumably found its Renaissance gardens of parterres and geometric forms too old-fashioned. Brusco's *Beautés de Gênes* gave this palazzo and its pleasure grounds not only lengthy description but a full-page illustration which emphasized its obsolete forecourt and crenellated, bastionlike walls along the sea.[76]

The American minister took pleasure in consulting with the marble-cutters of Genoa about mantlepieces for future delivery to Virginia. From the craftsmen he selected Antonio Capellano, whose establishment was situated on the waterfront near the Ponte della Legne. When William Short was planning to pass through Genoa two years later, Jefferson asked him to obtain prices for carving several different "chimney pieces" for which he

---

[73] Brusco, p. 110, 11.   [74] Eustace, III, 82–97, 102.   [75] Pace, p. 50.
[76] Brusco, plate 1 et seq. See also *Great Houses of Italy*, pp. 124–27.

supplied sketches for the architraves, freizes, and cornices. "You can tell Capellano," said Jefferson, "that you make the enquiry for the person to whom he furnished notes of the price of marble in April 1787, and from that circumstance I shall give him a prefer-ence to other workmen, at an equal price." [77]

In visiting the suburbs of Genoa, the Virginia horticulturist was happy to view the extent and excellence of the conte Durazzo's gardens at Nervi to the east and of the principe Lomellino at Sestri to the west. He advised American travelers in later years to visit the former because it possessed a vegetable garden surpassed only by "Woburn [Abbey's] farm in England." The flower gardens of the principe Lomellino, he exclaimed, were the "finest I ever saw out of England." [78]

Since there was no continuous road from Genoa to Nice, Jef-ferson embarked in a felucca on April 28, 1787, even though he was never a good sailor under the best of circumstances. Hardly out of the harbor, the little ship was beset by a fierce southwesterly wind which is called locally the *libeccio,* of which he should have had ample warning from reading Brusco's guidebook. The Gulf of Genoa was put into so nasty a chop that not only did he become "mortally sick," but the captain thought that conditions were severe enough to put into the little fishing port of Noli, about forty miles west of Genoa. Ironically, there was a good road from Genoa as far as Noli.

Instead of continuing a comfortable voyage on a placid sea as he had envisioned, he decided to go on by land, "clambering [up] the cliffs of the Appenine[s], sometimes on foot, sometimes on a mule according as the path was more or less difficult." Two days of alternating between the rich, narrow pockets of coastal plain and the desolate mountains behind them would not have been enough for a less-determined traveler to reach Nice on May 1, 1787, and to cross the Var River into France the next day. [79] Genoa believed she enjoyed military security by not building roads for her western neighbors to use as invasion routes. But Jefferson the physiocrat railed against having to traverse these corniches, or mountain pathways usually bearing only pedestrian traffic. In-stead of these, he observed, there should be a fine road "along the

---

[77] Jefferson to Short, Feb. 28, 1789, *Papers,* XIV, 598.

[78] "Hints for Americans Travelling in Europe," *Papers,* XIII, 270.

[79] Jefferson to Martha Jefferson, May 4, 1787, ibid., XI, 348; Brusco, p. 7; Pinot-Duclos, pp. 11–18. Twenty years before, Pinot-Duclos's boat had suffered somewhat the same fate.

margin of the sea," which would create "one continued village" and on which "travellers would enter Italy without crossing the Alps." [80]

It is a paradox that Jefferson, the lover of art and architecture, wrote so little about the fine arts that he enjoyed while in northern Italy. Consultation of his guidebooks and pocket account book, more than of his correspondence or notes about his tour, have made possible this reconstruction of a list of the "worthy" great buildings and collections of paintings that, as he wrote Lafayette, he was in the habit of visiting. [81] Hazardous as is such a speculative synthesis, it is even more hazardous to attempt to attribute to these "worthy" sights any specific influence on Jefferson. In reality, much of what he saw there was little different from what he already had seen and discussed with his intimates at Paris, or even from what he had learned from books and discussion with Bellini and others at Williamsburg. Except for the marble mantlepieces that he wanted to order for Monticello, the influence of what he saw in northern Italy was subliminal.

If there be evidence of the influence of northern Italy's fine arts upon Thomas Jefferson, it is to be found in three places: in the houses he built for himself at Monticello and Poplar Forest; in the capital city that he helped build for the nation; and in the university that he built for his fellow citizens' enlightenment.

It would be excessive to claim for the palazzi of Genoa, with their use of hillside basements for service functions, any influence on the way that Jefferson made coherent the housekeeping rooms of the basement of Monticello. There are plenty of prototypes for the piazzas with which he terminated the wings of the Monticello he rebuilt, [82] without claiming for the Palazzo Marcello Durazzo any kinship. But it is undeniable that Monticello did become more of an Italian palazzo than it had been. French influences are usually claimed for the remodeling of the house, but he did designate the north and south porches as piazzas. It may be that he popularized in America the term *piazza* just as he did the geographical term *Piedmont*. Despite Jefferson's annotated derivation from Palladio of so many of the details of Monticello, that residence is nonetheless an amalgam of all that he had read and all that he had seen.

[80] "Notes of a Tour," *Papers*, XI, 441–43. Spanish possession of an enclave between Genoa and Nice, 1598–1713, left a residue of calculated insularity.

[81] Jefferson to Lafayette, April 11, 1787, ibid., XI, 283.

[82] Fiske Kimball, *Jefferson, Architect*, p. 161, plates 6, 31, 147.

Jefferson placed his collection of paintings and sculpture in Monticello. Unusual as these were in America then, they were not so much Italianate as international in kind, variety, and manner of display. Although the collection of antiquities enjoyed international vogue, it was, on the other hand, peculiarly Italian because of the archeological excavations at Herculaneum, Pompeii, and Rome. The north Italian princes of both church and state clamored for and displayed such ancient treasures in their collections, some of which Jefferson must have seen, since their owners' conspicuous display was very competitive.[83] Jefferson's own cultural competitiveness with Buffon over anthropological matters led him to write his *Notes on Virginia*, as is so well known. He displayed at Monticello, not some fine Roman bronze or marble statue, but fossilized bones of a mammoth and American Indian artifacts,[84] thus yielding to the European collectors nothing in nationalistic pride or antiquity.

Surely it is not too speculative to attribute to the universities at Turin, Milan, and Pavia some influence on Jefferson's plans for the University of Virginia. His plans for the latter originally called for a large square cortile surrounded by arches on piers and punctuated by pavilions, suggesting a subtle kinship to Pavia's smaller, but similar, courts. The derivation of the Rotunda from the Pantheon at Rome and from Palladio is well known, but many forget that its great room originally was ringed by one-story columns in pairs,[85] instead of the gigantic, two-story ones now there. Because the use of columns in pairs was a practice which does not seem to have been as popular in France or England as in northern Italy, the latter's influence would appear to have been greater.

At Monticello, Jefferson planted a few of the Lombardy poplars that he cherished as the tree of liberty. Later he caused double rows of the poplars to be set between the White House and the Capitol at Washington.[86] From the piano nobile of Monticello, he could look out through arcaded piazzas and columned porticoes upon scenes which, if they were not Elysian, were at least an arcadian Piedmont.

---

[83] Wharton, I, 289–94, II, 3, 13.

[84] Marie Kimball, *Furnishings of Monticello*, p. 10.

[85] William A. Lambeth and Warren H. Manning, *Thomas Jefferson as an Architect and a Designer of Landscapes* (Boston and New York, 1913), plate XVI.

[86] Malone, *Jefferson and His Time*, IV, 47–48.

3 How the "Common Man" Voted in Jefferson's Virginia

Norman K. Risjord

S ELDOM has the average person shaped the course of human events. Mute, colorless, and timid, he rarely attracts enough attention to make any imprint on the documents from which history is written. A chance conversation recorded by a diarist, a barren entry in a list of taxables, an anonymous act of heroism are his only monuments left to posterity. The "common man" can never be rescued from anonymity, but he can be analyzed, at least in numerical terms, and traced through the course of time.

In recent years political historians have looked more closely at the role of the average citizen in the early American political system. On the one hand, they have sought to define democracy by asking such questions as How many persons could vote? and of those, How many wanted to vote? [1] And, on the other hand, they have examined the governing elite to determine how representative it actually was. Several studies utilizing roll call analysis have discovered factions in both state legislatures and the national Congress that appear to reflect basic differences in American society,[2] while other research has indicated that the ruling elite was significantly democratized by the entry of persons of lower social and economic status in the period from the Revolution to the presidency of Thomas Jefferson.[3] Useful as such work has certainly been, it

[1] J. R. Pole, "Historians and the Problem of Early American Democracy," *American Historical Review*, 67 (1962): 626–46, summarizes critically the early literature on the subject. More recent statements are: Jackson T. Main, "Government by the People: The American Revolution and the Democratization of the Legislatures," *William and Mary Quarterly*, 3d ser., 21 (1964): 165–90; and J. R. Pole, *Political Representation in England and the Origins of the American Republic* (New York, 1966).

[2] Jackson T. Main, *Political Parties before the Constitution* (Chapel Hill, N.C., 1972); Mary P. Ryan, "Party Formation in the United States Congress, 1789 to 1796," *William and Mary Quarterly*, 3d ser., 28 (1971): 523–42; Norman K. Risjord and Gordon Den Boer, "The Evolution of Political Parties in Virginia, 1782–1800" (forthcoming in the *Journal of American History*).

[3] Jackson T. Main, *The Upper House in Revolutionary America, 1763–1788* (Madison, Wis., 1967); Sidney Aronson, *Status and Kinship in the*

still does not penetrate below the "upper crust" of society. Still un-resolved is the problem of the role of the average citizen. To what extent did he feel that the system reflected his interests, and how much did he participate in its functions? Conversely, how concerned were political leaders about the views and attitudes of the "common man"? The answers to these questions will go a long way toward defining the nature of early American democracy.

The revolutionary state governments were all founded, at least in theory, on the "just consent of the governed." In several states the legislatures actively sought to involve the governed in the political process. They permitted spectators to attend legislative sessions and undertook to publish journals of their proceedings. In 1782 the Virginia assembly adopted a standing order that permitted any member to demand a roll call vote on any question. The results would be entered upon the journal and published at public expense on the reasoning that "the relation between the constituent and representative, renders it necessary that the former should be well informed of the conduct of the latter, in discharge of the important trust to him committed, to the end that the people may have it in their power to encourage the meritorious servants, and discountenance the undeserving." [4]

There is some evidence to indicate that Virginia voters took advantage of the opportunity thus presented. In 1785, for instance, a western farmer wrote his assemblyman a long diatribe against paper money, concluding with the request that he "have the yeas and Nays taken on the money Question." [5] Quite clearly, this constituent intended to hold his public servants accountable at election time. On another occasion—this time in the late 1790s—a victorious Republican candidate for the House of Delegates from the Tidewater county of James City boasted that his defeated opponent had "met the reward for his inconsistency." [6] The loser had voted Antifederalist/Republican in the 1788–92 sessions but in the mid-1790s sided more often with the Federalists. His opponent

Higher Civil Service: Standards of Selection in the Administrations of John Adams, Thomas Jefferson, and Andrew Jackson (Cambridge, Mass., 1964); James K. Martin, "Political Elites and the Outbreak of the American Revolution: A Quantitative Profile in Continuity, Turnover, and Change, 1774–1777" (Ph.D. diss., University of Wisconsin, 1969).

[4] *Journal of the House of Delegates of Virginia, 1782* (Richmond, 1828), p. 23.

[5] George Skillern to Archibald Stuart, Botetourt, Nov. 4, 1785, Archibald Stuart Papers, Virginia Historical Society, Richmond.

[6] Littleton W. Tazewell to Henry Tazewell, Feb. 16, 1798, Tazewell Family Papers, Virginia State Library, Richmond.

obviously kept track of his erratic voting behavior and assumed that the voters did too.

Such examples, of course, could be multiplied without proving much about the nature of the representative system. Far more useful are electoral poll lists, a few of which survive in Virginia for the 1780s and 1790s. A chance discovery of several election polls in the Virginia State Library inspired a systematic search, and the result was the acquisition of fifteen polls from nine counties, with at least one sample from every geographical subsection of the state.[7] They also included every type of election held at that time—for the House of Delegates, the state senate, the ratifying convention of 1788, for presidential electors in 1789, and the federal House of Representatives.[8] The poll lists give the name of each voter (common names like Smith and Jones were often followed by some further identification, such as a plantation name) and the candidate for whom he voted. By locating each voter in the county tax lists [9] one can construct a profile of the Virginia electorate, and with this one can try to answer some of the central questions concerning the state's representative system. Were party differences (i.e., Federalist-Antifederalist or Federalist-Republican) reflected in differences among the voters? If so, what were the most important factors in voting behavior? Wealth? Residence? Family ties? [10] Did the voters have a meaningful choice? Did the candidates differ in wealth, or was it a choice between two gentlemen expounding different principles? Or was it merely a popularity contest in which neither candidates nor voters evidenced any differences? Did the

[7] The Archives Division, Va. State Lib., has a box labeled "Election Poll Lists," but it contains only a few polls, and two are badly damaged. A better source was the county deed books, in which election results were recorded amidst the land transactions of the day—evidently the most readily available paper for the county clerk.

[8] Most of the polls date from 1788–89. The fact that these were preserved may suggest how hard-fought those contests were and how important they were considered.

[9] Virginia had two basic taxes, a land tax and a personalty tax. The land tax was assessed on acreage by valuation, which was a better indicator of wealth than mere acreage. The personalty tax was a levy on white adult males, slaves (with different rates for those over and under sixteen), horses, carriages, and (until 1788) cattle. I used only the slave figures, which complement the land valuation figure as an indication of how much of the acreage was actually farmed.

[10] Because the counties were subdivided into tax districts, the tax lists gave some clue as to residence. Family relationships were investigated in only two counties (Accomac and Amherst); in neither did it appear to be a significant factor.

election attract a significant turnout among eligible voters? And, finally, was the turnout representative of the social structure of the county? Or did only the wealthy and the educated appear at the polls?

The most important election in Virginia during the postrevolutionary period was the first federal election of 1789. It focused on issues, rather than personalities, and both Federalists and Antifederalists campaigned vigorously on the assumption that control of the new federal government would determine whether the Constitution was a viable structure or an empty parchment. Washington felt that for the Federalists "to be shipwrecked in sight of the port would be the severest of all possible aggravations to our Misery." James Madison, running for a seat in the House of Representatives, confessed that he "electioneered" more intensely than he ever had in his life.[11] The congressional election and the contest over presidential electors were both fought in multiple-county districts. Thus party identification was likely to be a more important determinant of voting behavior than residential proximity or personal acquaintance.

Madison's opponent in this congressional election was James Monroe, and fortunately one poll survives from this epic contest. It was held in Amherst County, February 2–4, 1789.[12] As a prominent figure in both the Philadelphia convention and the Virginia ratifying convention, Madison was one of the leading Federalists in the state. Only the most uninformed of voters could have been unaware of his political principles. Monroe, though an ally of Madison's through the legislative battles of the mid-1780s, had voted against the Constitution in the ratifying convention because he felt it went too far toward governmental centralization without enough safeguards for the rights of citizens. His Antifederalist friends persuaded him to run for Congress in the hope of securing amendments to the Constitution.[13] Neither candidate was a resident of Amherst. Madison lived in Orange County seventy-five miles away, and Monroe lived in Fredericksburg, over a hundred miles from Amherst Count House.

Amherst is located in the central Piedmont, cupped between the James River and the Blue Ridge. Socially and politically it was

[11] Washington to Madison, Sept. 23, 1788, Washington Papers, Library of Congress, Washington, D.C.; Madison to Edmund Randolph, Nov. 23, 1788, Madison Papers, Lib. Cong.

[12] Amherst County Deed Book F, 1787–1790, pp. 296–98, Va. State Lib.

[13] Monroe to Jefferson, Fredericksburg, Feb. 15, 1789, *Papers of Thomas Jefferson*, ed. Julian P. Boyd et al. (Princeton, N.J., 1950–), XIV, 557–59.

dominated by the Cabell family, whose scions held one or both of the county's seats in the House of Delegates, and the district senate seat as well, throughout the 1780s. William Cabell, Sr., proprietor of nearly 18,000 acres in the county, was a personal friend of Patrick Henry,[14] and his sons usually voted with Henry in the assembly. Friendship and family influence evidently coincided with economic interest, however, for the Amherst delegates voted consistently with a debtor-oriented bloc of Piedmont and Southside delegates on the various economic issues (taxation, British debts, paper money) that agitated the Virginia assembly in the mid-1780s.[15] In the Virginia ratifying convention the Amherst delegates, both Cabells, voted against the Constitution, as did the delegates from the neighboring counties in the upper James River valley. Public sentiment in Amherst was clearly Antifederal. Though Madison won the district congressional seat, Monroe carried Amherst by 236 votes to 145. Approximately 84 percent of Madison's voters and 79 percent of Monroe's were found in the county tax lists for 1789, and the breakdown of the electorate by wealth in Table 1 is instructive.[16]

As might be expected, the wealthy were more inclined to appear at the polls than the poor. Planters owning £400 or more in real estate had a turnout of 61 percent (57 percent among those owning twenty-five or more slaves), while only 19 percent of those in the £0–24 category voted (15 percent among those owning no slaves). Even so, the turnout among the poor was not bad for an eighteenth-century election, where the voter had to travel many miles to the

[14] Robert D. Meade, *Patrick Henry, Practical Revolutionary* (Philadelphia and New York, 1969), pp. 282, 373.

[15] For the means used to determine voting behavior and party affiliation of members of the Virginia assembly throughout this essay, see Risjord and Den Boer.

[16] Usually about 70% to 90% of the voters in the elections investigated here could be identified. Polls were taken and taxes were collected orally; hence names were often phonetically spelled, with radical variations from one list to another. Where the identification was uncertain, the voter was omitted. Some of the unidentified voters were probably planters' sons who were allowed to vote even though they paid no real estate taxes; others may have been tenants who were allowed to vote even though they did not meet the qualification of land ownership (50 acres of unimproved or 25 acres of improved land). A number of voters, for instance, paid taxes on slaves and horses but could not be located in the land books.

The categories of wealth in the tables are arbitrary, but they were determined only after several counties were sampled. Since the only purpose here is to determine factors in voting behavior, much definition of these categories beyond "poor," "middling," and "wealthy" was not deemed necessary.

Table 1. Amherst County election, 1789: House of Representatives

a. Distribution of voters by land valuation (expressed in pounds Virginia currency)

Wealth	Madison voters	% of Madison's total	Monroe voters	% of Monroe's total	All county tax-payers	% of county total
£0–24	8	7	22	12	157	19
£25–74	24	22	70	36.5	280	35
£75–149	19	17	37	19	128	15
£150–399	39	35	45	23	185	23
£400–799	14	13	12	6	44	5
£800–1,499	4	4	3	1.5	10	1.5
£1,500—	2	2	4	2	10	1.5
Total	110	100	193	100	814	100

b. Distribution of voters by slave ownership

Slaves	Madison voters	% of Madison's total	Monroe voters	% of Monroe's total	All county tax-payers	% of county total
0	28	27	63	31.5	617	50
1–4	22	21	59	30	293	24.5
5–12	24	22	56	29	202	18
13–24	18	18	14	7	63	5
25–49	9	9	3	1.5	23	2
50–99	3	3	2	1	7	.5
Total	104	100	195	100	1,205	100

county court house and cast his ballot orally in the presence of the candidates (or, in this case, their stand-ins). Moreover, it should be noted that the poorest voters dominated this election. Those with fewer than five slaves (or less than £150) cast more ballots for Monroe than Madison received altogether. That, of course, is the most striking feature of the election. In terms of landed wealth, Monroe's voters closely approximated the social structure of the county, while Madison's voters were wealthier than the county norm in almost every category. In general terms, a poor man was twice as likely to vote for Monroe, while a wealthy man was twice as likely to vote for Madison.

Monroe's score among the wealthy was inflated by the Antifederal bias among the Cabell family. Of his seven wealthy supporters (£800 or more) four were Cabells. The Higginbothams were similarly united behind Monroe, while members of the Rose family consistently supported Madison. A year earlier Hugh Rose had been an unsuccessful pro-Constitution candidate for the ratifying convention. The number of voters involved in these family blocks was very small, however, certainly not enough to influence the outcome. Other families, related by blood or marriage, divided between the two candidates; so family ties cannot be considered an important factor in voting behavior.

Residence was even less important. The county was divided into two tax collection districts—the Amherst parish and the Lexington parish. The first was evidently the eastern half of the county, bordering on the James River, and the second was the western half (the village of Lexington was just across the mountains in Rockbridge County). There was thus some topographical, and perhaps economic, variation between the two districts. The eastern part was gently rolling, rather fertile land, with easy access to river transportation and the Richmond market. The western district was, by comparison, remote, rocky, and hilly, though it has some very good land in the valleys of the Tye and Piney rivers. Many of the very wealthy, including the Cabells and Roses, resided in the eastern district, but otherwise there was little difference in the social composition of the two halves of the county. Nor was there any difference in voting behavior. The two candidates received the same proportion of votes in each district as they did in the county as a whole.[17]

In summary, wealth—whether determined by extent and fertility of landholdings or by capital investment in production (slaveholding)—was the most important single determinant of voting behavior, and the wealthy showed a decided preference for the Federalist candidate, while the poor inclined toward Antifederalism.

A similar pattern emerged in Greensville County, which lies astride the fall line on the North Carolina border. It was a fairly prosperous county (only a third of its taxpayers possessed no slaves, as opposed to half in Amherst) in the heart of the tobacco country. Its delegates to the ratifying convention voted in favor of the Constitution, but from 1788 on the county's delegates in the assembly voted consistently Antifederalist and Republican. Two polls survive from the first elections of 1789. The first, taken on January 17, involved a contest for the state senate between Edward

[17] I am indebted to Donna J. Byrne, who compiled most of the statistics on wealth, residence, and genealogy among voters in this election as an undergraduate term paper project.

Carrington, a Richmond lawyer (though he represented Powhatan in the House of Delegates), and John Pride, an Amelia County planter. Carrington was a brother-in-law of John Marshall and a Federalist leader in the assembly; Pride voted against the Constitution in the ratifying convention. In the poll of January 17 Pride carried Greensville 53 to 37 and got enough support elsewhere to win the senate seat. Carrington then became a candidate for the district congressional seat in a second poll on February 2. His opponents in that contest were Thomas Rivers (of unknown party) and Theodorick Bland of Prince George, who was one of the most prominent Antifederalists in the state (second only to Patrick Henry and George Mason). In Greensville, Bland defeated Carrington 38 to 8 (with 14 votes for Rivers), and he won the district congressional seat.[18]

Because of the light turnout in both elections [19] and because both involved clear-cut party contests, the two polls were combined for purposes of voter analysis (Table 2).[20] Because the sample is small, the distribution is not even, and minor deviations distort the percentages. Of the four wealthy Antifederalists (£1500 plus), for instance, two had served the county in the House of Delegates in the mid-1780s where they had voted with Patrick Henry's debtor faction. Thus political and personal considerations may have been more important in their behavior than wealth. Except for that variation and the failure of the very poor to vote at all, the Antifederalist vote closely approximates the county norm, while the Federalist vote was largely confined to planters of substance. Two-thirds of the Federalist total came from planters of £150 or more, and 72 percent of the Antifederalist vote came from planters of less than £150 real property.[21]

[18] Greensville County Deed Book I, 1781–92, pp. 239–41, Va. State Lib.

[19] There were 374 white males who owned at least 25 acres. There is no way of determining how many were adults and how many had "improved" their land, but it seems likely that nearly all could have voted if they wanted to.

[20] A total of 121 persons voted in one or both elections. Only two voted Federalist in the senate election and Antifederalist in the congressional one; both were omitted from the analysis. No one split his ticket in the opposite direction. Those who voted for Thomas Rivers were included only if they also voted for a candidate of known party in the senate election. Ninety-three percent of the voters were found in one or both of the tax books.

[21] I am indebted to Erik Olson, who compiled the statistics on Greensville voters as an undergraduate term paper project. Olson also traced a number of voters in Catherine Lindsay Knorr, *Marriage Bonds and*

Table 2. Greensville County elections, 1789: state senate and federal House of Representatives

a. Distribution of voters by land valuation (expressed in pounds Virginia currency)

Wealth	Federalist voters	% of Federalist total	Antifed voters	% of Antifed total	All county taxpayers	% of county total
£0–24	0	0	3	4.5	31	9
£25–74	3	10	24	38	121	31
£75–149	7	22.5	19	30	114	29.5
£150–399	14	45	8	13	79	20
£400–799	7	22.5	1	1.5	21	6
£800–1,499	0	0	4	6.5	11	3
£1,500—	0	0	4	6.5	5	1.5
Total	31	100	63	100	382	100

b. Distribution of voters by slave ownership

Slaves	Federalist voters	% of Federalist total	Antifed voters	% of Antifed total	All county taxpayers	% of county total
0	3	8	12	19	155	33
1–4	9	23	23	36	172	37
5–12	17	47	20	31	111	24
13–24	7	20	7	10	23	5
25–49	1	2	1	2	7	1
50–99	0	0	1	2	1	
Total	37	100	64	100	469	100

Cumberland County in the southern Piedmont was also in this congressional district, but there it was not possible to pinpoint any differences among the voters in the contest between Carrington and Bland.[22] Cumberland was in the heart of Virginia Antifederalism, and Bland won by 150 to 31. The sparse vote makes analysis difficult (only 25 of Carrington's voters could be identified, for

Ministers' Returns of Greensville County, Virginia, 1781–1825 (Pine Bluff, Ark., 1955), but with no positive results. He found that most of the Federalists were related by blood or marriage, possibly because they were so few and so socially homogeneous. On the other hand, some of the largest families in the county—Avent, Harris, Johnson, and Rives—split their votes between the two parties.

[22] Cumberland County Deed Book, no. 6 (1779–90), Feb. 2, 1789, Va. State Lib.

example). Both candidates had sizable plantations in the county, though neither resided there permanently. Each candidate obtained about two-thirds of his total vote from the tax district in which he owned land.

One poll involving the presidential contest survives from the first federal elections. This was taken in Isle of Wight County on January 7, 1789.[23] Virginia selected presidential electors by popular balloting in districts, and in most districts the contest was hard-fought. During the autumn Edward Carrington reported to Madison from Richmond that "the voice of this State runs pretty unanimously for Genl. Washington as Presid[en]t and Mr. H[enry] is putting in agitation the name of [George] Clinton for vice Presid[en]t which takes well with the Anti's."[24] The Anti-federalists distrusted John Adams for his political writings and suspected that he had been corrupted by his long service in England.[25]

Party views were thus well disseminated, at least among the political leaders, and in the Isle of Wight contest the candidates for presidential elector were fairly easy to distinguish. The Federalist candidate was Samuel Kello, wealthy planter and mill-owner,[26] who represented neighboring Southampton County in the ratifying convention. His opponent was General Joseph Jones of Dinwiddie, commander of the Southside militia and the leading Antifederalist in the southeastern counties. Isle of Wight was overwhelmingly pro-Constitution, and Kello won the election, 209–72. As in the congressional contests, the voters tended to divide along lines of wealth. Those who held no slaves, for instance, constituted half of Jones's total but only a fourth of Kello's. Wealthy slave-owners (those who possessed thirteen or more) made up 10 percent of Kello's total vote and only 1 percent of Jones's.

Why did Virginians' voting behavior follow lines of economic status? The best explanation seems to be that the legislative factions of the 1780s formed in response to economic issues—taxation, British debts, paper money, judicial reform. A creditor-oriented

[23] Isle of Wight poll for Presidential Elector, Jan. 7, 1789, Executive Papers, Box 58, Va. State Lib.

[24] Carrington to Madison, Richmond, Nov. 9, 1788, Madison Papers.

[25] Theodorick Bland to St. George Tucker, Feb. 8, 1789, Tucker-Coleman Papers, College of William and Mary, Williamsburg, Va. In the electoral college all ten of Virginia's votes went to Washington, but in the vice-presidential balloting Adams received only five votes. Clinton got three; John Hancock and John Jay, one each.

[26] Kello possessed 700 acres and 13 slaves in Southampton and advertised his mill in the Richmond *Virginia Gazette*, April 5, 1787.

group of delegates was led by Madison after he returned from Congress in 1785, while a prodebtor faction looked for leadership to Patrick Henry, or to one of his lieutenants while Henry was governor from 1784 to 1786. Because the Constitution affected all these economic issues in one way or another, the factional division continued through the debate on ratification. Indeed, the contest over the Constitution and the first federal elections intensified loyalties and hardened party lines.[27] Thus the voters evidently perceived the economic issues at stake, and most of them voted what they felt to be their interest.

Such voting was easier, however, in the contests for federal offices where the issues were relatively clear and the candidates easy to identify. In contests for the state House of Delegates the correlation between partisan voting and wealth is not so clear. This is illustrated by two polls from Accomac County, one taken in 1787, the other in 1790. Unlike all other poll lists discussed here, these were found in the papers of one of the candidates, John Cropper.[28] In Virginia's system of oral voting there was always the possibility that the wealthy and influential might be able to intimidate the small freeholders. How would the freeholders have reacted if they knew that one of the candidates was going to retain the poll list for future reference? Whatever Cropper's purpose, there is no evidence of intimidation, for the poorest voters generally favored his opponent.

There were four candidates in the 1787 election, and the two with the most votes went to the House of Delegates. The results were:

Edmund Custis	(1,238 acres valued at £595, 27 slaves)	385
John Cropper	(640 acres valued at £1,021, 16 slaves)	355
Jabez Pitt	(500 acres valued at £224, 10 slaves)	345
Levin Joynes	(501 acres valued at £73, 14 slaves)	242

Cropper had served in the assembly since 1784, and his voting record was generally creditor-nationalist (he remained a Federalist in the 1790s). Custis, the other winner, had no previous political service, but the next year he represented the county in the ratifying convention and voted against the Constitution. Pitt was elected to the House of Delegates in 1788, where he voted consistently Antifederalist (i.e., in favor of radical amendments and a second

[27] For a more detailed description of this process, see Risjord and Den Boer.

[28] John Cropper Papers, Va. Hist. Soc.

federal convention). Joynes subsequently represented the Eastern Shore counties in the state senate from 1788 to 1792 and voted Federalist. The four thus divided evenly in their subsequent political affiliations, though there was virtually no difference among them in wealth. Since Cropper was the only one with prior political service, the question is, To what extent did the voters seem to be aware of differences among the candidates' positions?

The fact that the two winners were of opposite political faiths suggests that the voters made no distinction. Moreover, no one seems to have thought of weighting his ballot by voting only once. Nearly everyone voted for two candidates, and 106 men voted for both Cropper and Custis, accounting for 30 percent of Cropper's vote and 27 percent of Custis's. Table 3, then, counts only those voters who seem to have demonstrated a preference—by voting for Cropper and not for Custis, or vice versa. The economic pattern

Table 3. Accomac County election, 1787: House of Delegates

a. Distribution of voters by land valuation (expressed in pounds Virginia currency)

Wealth	Cropper voters	% of Cropper's total	Custis voters	% of Custis's total	All county tax-payers	% of county total
£0–24	41	19	63	30	330	30
£25–74	89	42	88	41.5	430	40
£75–149	30	15	23	10	128	12.5
£150–399	33	16	27	13	115	11.5
£400–799	11	5.5	7	3.5	35	3.5
£800–1,499	5	2.5	2	1	17	2
£1,500—	0		2	1	4	.5

b. Distribution of voters by slave ownership

Slaves	Cropper voters	% of Cropper's total	Custis voters	% of Custis's total	All county tax-payers	% of county total
0	46	21	92	37	664	44
1–4	79	36	94	38	506	33
5–12	72	33	49	20	275	18
13–24	21	10	8	4	59	4
25–49	2	1	2	1	9	1
50–99	0		0		0	
Total	220	100	245	100	1,513	100

is similar to that noted in the federal elections. Though Custis had some friends and relatives among the wealthy, his voters reflect the social structure of the county, while Cropper's are generally wealthier. The significant difference is in the voting behavior of the poor. Since there was no outward social or economic difference between the candidates, the freeholders must have been reacting to ideology, rhetoric, or personalities. Did they oppose Cropper because of his record of opposing debtor relief and favoring high taxes in the assembly? Or did Custis make some sort of pitch to the poor before the election? Either way, the evidence suggests that there was a good deal more voter awareness than historians have ever suspected.

The number of people who voted for both candidates, however, suggests that voter identification was not so sharp in state contests as in federal ones. This is further illustrated by a second Accomac poll for the House of Delegates, held in 1790.[29] There were only three candidates in this election. Cropper received 454 votes, Thomas Custis (who did not vote enough in the House of Delegates to be categorized, but was probably a Federalist[30]) received 368, and Edmund Custis, 327. The turnout—about 600 voters among 1,137 taxpaying landowners[31]—is impressive, but nearly a third failed to vote along party lines. A total of 183 freeholders voted for both Cropper and Edmund Custis, which was 40 percent of Cropper's total and 56 percent of Custis's. However, among those who voted for Cropper and not for Custis (or vice versa), the distribution by wealth was even more pronounced than in the earlier election. Indeed, of all the polls examined, this is the only one in which the percentage of the poorest freeholders (i.e., those with less than £75 real estate) in the Antifederalist column exceeded their percentage of the entire county (Table 4).

If Virginia's voters were able to distinguish candidates by party and to identify party with economic interest, as the evidence ex-

[29] Ibid. I am indebted to Mrs. Judy Gitchel, who compiled the statistics on this election as an undergraduate term paper project. She also found that each candidate did slightly better in his own tax district, but the difference was not enough to affect the outcome.

[30] The Custises were related by marriage to President Washington (though the Eastern Shore branch only remotely so), and most of them were Federalists. Edmund was evidently the maverick of the family. Moreover, nearly all of the delegates from Accomac in the early 1790s were Federalists.

[31] The statistic of 1,137, taken from the 1790 land book, includes women and free Negroes. The total number of voters is only approximate because some votes were given to persons other than the three candidates.

Table 4. Accomac County election, 1790: House of Delegates

a. Distribution of voters by land valuation (expressed in pounds Virginia currency)

Wealth	Cropper voters	% of Cropper's total	Custis voters	% of Custis's total	All county tax-payers *	% of county total
£0–24	46	27	23	33	330	30
£25–74	67	39	30	43	430	40
£75–149	25	14	11	16	128	12.5
£150–399	22	12	3	4	115	11.5
£400–799	8	6	2	3	35	3.5
£800–1,499	3	2	1	1	17	2
£1,500—	0		0		4	.5
Total	1,717	100	70	100	1,059	100

b. Distribution of voters by slave ownership

Slaves	Cropper voters	% of Cropper's total	Custis voters	% of Custis's total	All county tax-payers	% of county total
0	57	21.5	39	38	664	44
1–4	114	52.5	52	51	506	33
5–12	43	24.5	11	11	275	18
13–24	2	1	0		59	4
25–49	1	.5	0		9	1
50–99	0		0		0	
Total	217	100	102	100	1,513	100

* To save labor the figures for all county taxpayers are the same as those calculated for 1787 (see Table 3). Samples of this and other counties indicate that there is no important change in the social structure in a period of only three years.

amined so far suggests, what happened when there was no party contest? Two extant poll lists involved elections of this sort, both from Buckingham County in 1788. The first, held on March 10, involved the election of delegates to the ratifying convention; the second, undated but probably held in April, was a poll for the House of Delegates. Buckingham, located in the Piedmont on the south side of the James, was heavily Antifederal. The Cabells were almost as strong there as in neighboring Amherst, and on the other side of it was Prince Edward, Patrick Henry's homeland. In the contest there were three candidates for the county's two seats in the ratifying convention.[32] Charles Patteson, who led the balloting with 288 votes, owned 1,571 acres valued at £719 and 11 slaves. He had served in the House of Delegates in 1784 and 1787 but cast few votes. David Bell, the other winner with 243 votes, owned 426 acres valued at £112 and no slaves. He had the least wealth among the candidates, but there were a number of wealthy Bells in the county, and he probably stood to inherit property. In 1793, for instance, he advertised for sale 1,000 acres in Buckingham, which were part of a still larger tract.[33] The third candidate was Joseph Cabell, 223 votes, who owned 899 acres valued at £1,231 and 24 slaves. The most prominent of the candidates, Cabell served in the senate in the early 1780s and in the house in 1787–88, but he did not cast enough roll call votes to permit party identification. There was thus little to distinguish the three candidates in terms of wealth or past political behavior. In the convention Patteson and Bell voted against the Constitution.

An analysis of the voters (all but sixteen of whom were found in the tax books) indicates that they made no distinction either (Table 5). Despite the lack of perceptible differences among the candidates, the turnout was comparable to other elections examined —about 50 percent of the eligible voters.[34] The voters were a fair cross section of the county population. Though free Negroes were excluded from the vote in Virginia, one mulatto, owner of 388 acres, was on this poll list. As elsewhere, the wealthy were slightly more disposed to appear at the poll than the poor; yet neither wealthy nor poor showed any particular preference for one candidate. It was strictly a popularity contest.

The same was true of the assembly election.[35] Again, three candidates vied for the two seats in the House of Delegates. Joseph Cabell, who led with 278 votes, is described above. Thomas Anderson, the other winner, with 242 votes, owned 1,600 acres valued at £2,453 and 26 slaves. His voting record in the house was thin, but he voted twice with the Antifederalists in favor of a second convention and drastic amendments to the Constitution. The third

[32] "Poll lists" box, Va. State Lib. There were evidently about 350 voters, though I have only 205 names. Pages two, four, and six (out of seven in all) are missing.

[33] Advertisement in Richmond *Virginia Gazette*, May 15, 1793.

[34] Of the 729 taxpayers listed in the land books, 702 were white males owning at least 25 acres.

[35] "Poll lists" box, Va. State Lib. In this election there were 337 voters. A fourth candidate, John Cabell, received only three votes and was omitted from the calculations.

Table 5. Buckingham County election, 1788: convention to ratify the federal Constitution

a. Distribution of voters by land valuation (expressed in pounds Virginia currency)

Wealth	Patteson voters	% of Patteson's total	Bell voters	% of Bell's total	Cabell voters	% of Cabell's total	All county taxpayers	% of county total
£0–24	26	24.5	16	21	24	28	160	22
£25–74	37	35.5	30	39	25	30	311	42.5
£75–149	21	20	18	24	12	14	117	14.5
£150–399	14	13	10	13	16	19	92	13
£400–799	6	5	0	0	5	6	20	3
£800–1,499	2	2	0	0	1	1	12	2
£1,500—	0	0	2	3	2	2	17	3
Total	106	100	76	100	85	100	729	100

b. Distribution of voters by slave ownership

Slaves	Patteson voters	% of Patteson's total	Bell voters	% of Bell's total	Cabell voters	% of Cabell's total	All county taxpayers	% of county total
0	49	40	35	37	42	40	421	50
1–4	50	40	41	43	34	32	286	33
5–12	21	17	17	18	25	23.5	125	14
13–24	3	3	1	1	4	3.5	25	2.5
25–49	0	0	1	1	1	1	4	.5
50–99	0	0	0	0	0	0	0	
Total	123	100	95	100	106	100	861	100

candidate, with 140 votes, was Hickerson Barksdale, owner of 857 acres valued at £238 and 12 slaves. He served the county in the House of Delegates from 1785 to 1787, voting with the Henryites on the few times he was present.[36] Thus the candidates were indistinguishable in economic and political terms. Voter distribution was again random (Table 6).

Where the candidates could not be distinguished by party or political issue, the voters themselves failed to divide in any meaningful manner. Indeed, so indifferent were they to the outcome that they took the loser in the first Buckingham contest (Joseph Cabell) and raised him to first place in the second, almost as if they were eager to avoid hurt feelings. Conversely, in every election during the 1780s where there was a genuine party contest, a significant number of voters followed their own interests. The poorest classes tended to vote for candidates identified with debtor interests and Antifederalism, the "middling sort" divided evenly, and the wealthy showed a preference for creditor-oriented Federalism. The next question, then, is this: to what extent did this orientation by wealth carry over into the party battles between Federalists and Republicans in the 1790s?

Unfortunately only a few poll lists survive for the 1790s. As party lines hardened after 1793 most counties leaned heavily toward one side or the other. As a result, local party contests were rare (even in the congressional elections), and county clerks may have seen no need to keep the poll lists after the winner was certified. The first example is a Botetourt County poll for the House of Delegates and the state senate in April 1792.[37] This is also the only poll list found for a county west of the Blue Ridge. Botetourt is in the upper James River valley, south of Lexington, and like most western counties it favored the Constitution. There were three candidates for the two house seats—George Hancock and Martin McFerran, Federalists, and William Norvel, an unknown who never held office. Hancock was a gentleman farmer whose parents were wealthy slaveowners in South Carolina. Though trained in the law, he apparently did not need to practice his profession.[38]

---

[36] In 1785 he voted twice against the amendment that would have given Congress authority to regulate commerce, he voted with the debtor side two out of three times on economic issues.

[37] "Poll lists" box, Va. State Lib.

[38] Robert D. Stoner, *A Seedbed of the Republic: A Study of the Pioneers in the Upper Valley of Virginia* (Roanoke, 1962), pp. 294–96. The tax books of 1790 (the 1792 ones are illegible) credit him with 56 acres and 10 slaves. The acreage is clearly incorrect; in 1786 he was taxed for 806 acres.

Table 6. Buckingham County election, 1788: House of Delegates

a. Distribution of voters by land valuation (expressed in pounds Virginia currency)

Wealth	Cabell voters	% of Cabell's total	Anderson voters	% of Anderson's total	Barksdale voters	% of B'ksdale's total	County taxpayers	% of county total
£0–24	32	16.5	36	20	16	16	160	22
£25–74	75	39	65	36	33	32.5	311	42.5
£75–149	30	15.5	31	17	28	27.5	117	14.5
£150–399	43	22	33	18	17	17	92	13
£400–799	7	4	8	5	5	5	20	3
£800–1,499	2	1	3	1.5	0	0	12	2
£1,500—	4	2	4	2.5	2	2	17	3
Total	193	100	180	100	101	100	729	100

b. Distribution of voters by slave ownership

Slaves	Cabell voters	% of Cabell's total	Anderson voters	% of Anderson's total	B'ksdale voters	% of B'ksdale's total	All county taxpayers	% of county total
0	77	33	73	34	29	27	421	50
1–4	89	38	87	40	49	46	286	33
5–12	53	23	46	21	23	21	125	14
13–24	8	4	6	3	5	4	25	2.5
25–49	4	2	4	2	2	2	4	.5
50–99	0		0		0		0	
Total	231	100	216	100	108	100	861	100

McFerran was a farmer who owned 319 acres valued at £526 and no slaves, while Norvel possessed 376 acres valued at £126 and 7 slaves.

Each of the 322 voters exercised both of his ballots, and the results were: Hancock, 302; McFerran, 191; and Norvel, 151. Since Hancock had the support of 94 percent of the voters, the main competition was between McFerran and Norvel. A comparison of their supporters revealed no important differences.[39] Those with less than £75 real estate made up 57 percent of McFerran's total, 58 percent of Norvel's, and 69 percent of the county as a whole. McFerran did slightly better among the wealthy (those with more than four slaves made up 8 percent of his total and 4 percent of Norvel's), but on the whole there is no significant difference between the two. In short, parties and issues do not seem to have been involved; it was a contest of personalities, status, and reputation.

This suspicion is confirmed by the simultaneous contest for the district senate seat between John Preston and Daniel Trigg, both from Montgomery County to the southwest. Preston, whose father was a hero of the Indian wars and one of the largest landowners in the southwest, had supported the Constitution.[40] Trigg's politics are not known, but his uncles, Abram and John, were prominent Antifederalists in Bedford and Montgomery.[41] Preston won by the lopsided margin of 260 to 57. This result might reflect the generally Federalist complexion of Botetourt, except that 51 of those who voted for Trigg also voted for Hancock and McFerran in the house contest. One can only conclude that in this relatively poor, undeveloped region, where 69 percent of the taxpayers had less than £75 and 82 percent of the male population were not slaveholders, the electorate chose the candidates with the highest standing and reputation in the community, without regard to their political affiliation.

Westmoreland County, in contrast, was both the wealthiest and the most socially divided of all the counties examined. It was located in the Northern Neck, between the Potomac and the Rappa-

[39] A disappointing sample, only 57%, could be found in the tax lists for 1790. This may reflect the mobility of the Valley population.

[40] He served in the senate from 1792 to 1800. He voted Federalist in 1795 and Republican in 1798, the only years in which the senate held roll calls on party-determining issues.

[41] Abram and John Trigg both voted against the Constitution in the ratifying convention, and both became Republican congressmen, John from 1797 to 1804 and Abram from 1797 to 1809.

hannock rivers, a long-settled region dominated by the princely domains of Carters, Lees, Fitzhughs, and Washingtons. Almost 60 percent of the taxpayers were slaveowners, whereas in every other county except Accomac less than half owned slaves. The wealthy (those possessing land worth £400 or more) made up 11 percent of the landowners, in contrast to 8 percent in Amherst, for instance. Westmoreland also had a larger "poor white" class than any other county examined – a third of the landowners possessed land worth less than £25 (the same class in Amherst numbered only 19 percent of the total). The Northern Neck was heavily Federalist in 1788–89, but it gradually turned Republican in the course of the 1790s, except for Westmoreland. That county was the home of "Light-Horse Harry" Lee, cavalry general in the Revolution and personal friend of President Washington. His influence no doubt helped to keep the county in the Federalist column, as did the numerous Washingtons who also resided there.[42]

On March 12, 1793, the county held an election for the federal House of Representatives. The candidates were Walter Jones and John Heath, both from neighboring Northumberland County.[43] Jones possessed a degree in medicine from Edinburgh and had held the rank of physician general in the Revolutionary army, but it is doubtful that he was still actively practicing. The tax books list him as possessing a plantation of 636 acres and 21 slaves. Jones had served in the ratifying convention and voted in favor of the Constitution. By 1797 when he was finally elected to Congress he was a Republican, but it is not clear what the voters considered him in 1793. At least privately he was critical of Hamilton's financial policies, but then so was Henry Lee.[44] In any case, Jones carried Federalist Westmoreland by 137–95, though he lost the election. His opponent, John Heath, was a lawyer who had served as a commonwealth's attorney in the 1780s. His plantation, Springfield, listed 27 slaves. His stand on the Constitution is unknown, but in two terms in Congress (1793–97) he voted Republican.

[42] The 1792 land book lists five Washingtons, all nephews of the president. George himself is credited with 0 slaves and 2 horses in the 1793 personalty book. Though most of his holdings were in Fairfax and Fauquier, he probably still possessed the Ferry Farm in Westmoreland, which he and his mother had received jointly on his father's death. In any case, he is placed in the wealthiest categories in the accompanying tables.

[43] Westmoreland County Records, vol. 7, 1790–98, pp. 115–17, Va. State Lib. A third candidate, Francis L. Lee, party unknown, received only two votes.

[44] Jones to [Henry Lee], June 20, 1792, Charles Lee Papers, Va. State Lib.; Henry Lee to Madison, Jan. 8, 23, 1792, Madison Papers.

Though there was no apparent economic difference between the candidates, Jones revealed an interesting feature of the campaign in a letter to a friend: "I am at present cap in hand to the Electors of five Counties, and have little doubt I shall succeed—however (mirabile dictu) I have a very active opponent in Johnny Heath; though his addresses are principally in his own language, *to the yeomanry,* I am not too Secure." Jones himself refused to make any appeals to "the Vulgar Heart." [45] A breakdown of the Westmoreland vote indicates that Heath's campaign had little effect on the poor, but he did succeed in alienating the rich (Table 7).[46] Among Jones's supporters were four Washingtons, including the president himself. Perhaps the differences between the candidates were so fine that only the knowledgeable elite was aware of them. It is also possible that the president's preference influenced a number of voters, which would obscure any economic differential that might have existed. There is no way of determining the extent of the president's influence, however, since he voted next to last.

Whatever issues may have separated the congressional candidates, it is clear that there was no substantial difference among the contenders in the poll for the House of Delegates, held on April 30, 1793.[47] The results were: Richard Lee, 256; Willoughby Newton, 191; and Daniel McCarty, 160. "Squire Richard" Lee of Lee Hall, an uncle of Light-Horse Harry, possessed an estate of 4,098 acres and 39 slaves.[48] He had served in the House of Delegates from 1776 to 1792 voting frequently but almost completely at random. Unlike other Northern Neck delegates, he had failed to follow Madison's lead in the mid-1780s, and his record on the Constitution in the 1788–89 sessions is mixed but generally Antifederalist. After he won this election in 1793, his record in the House was consistently Federalist through the next two sessions. Newton, the other winner, had no previous political service, but his votes in the House in 1793 and again in 1796 were also Fed-

[45] Jones to St. George Tucker, Jan. 5, 1793, Tucker-Coleman Papers. In Heath's only previous service in the assembly (1782), he voted for debtor relief and tax postponement.

[46] The only land book surviving for Westmoreland in this period is 1792, and that is clearly incomplete. Thus the land valuation statistics are not very meaningful, and no estimate of turnout was attempted. I am indebted to Gwen Williams, who compiled the statistics on this election as an undergraduate term paper project.

[47] Westmoreland County Records, vol. 7, pp. 118–21.

[48] He is missing from the incomplete 1792 land book, and he died in 1795. The acreage figure given is that in the hands of his executors in 1797. The acreage figure for Willoughby Newton, below, is also for 1797.

Table 7. Westmoreland County election, 1793: House of Representatives

a. Distribution of voters by land valuation (expressed in pounds Virginia currency)

Wealth	Jones voters	% of Jones's total	Heath voters	% of Heath's total	All county tax- payers	% of county total
£0–24	7	20	5	24	54	33
£25–74	9	25	8	35	39	24
£75–149	8	22	7	33	24	15
£150–399	3	8	1	4	18	11
£400–799	3	8	1	4	13	8
£800–1,499	1	3	0		1	1
£1,500—	1	3	0		2	2
Town lots only	4	11	0		12	7
Total	36	100	22	100	163	100

b. Distribution of voters by slave ownership

Slaves	Jones voters	% of Jones's total	Heath voters	% of Heath's total	All county tax- payers	% of county total
0	22	21	13	16	260	41
1–4	39	37	32	40	223	35
5–12	24	23	32	40	111	17
13–24	12	11	3	4	29	4.5
25–49	8	7	0		12	2
50–99	1	1	0		3	.5
Total	106	100	80	100	636	100

eralist. His plantation numbered 832 acres and 12 slaves. McCarty, a son-in-law of George Mason, lived in Fairfax County, but he also owned a plantation of 4,557 acres and 70 slaves in Westmoreland. He won election to the House in 1794–95, and he too was consistently Federalist.

There was thus little difference economically or politically among the three candidates, and the voters accordingly behaved as friends and neighbors.[49] Newton's own tax district gave him 81 percent of his total vote, while the other tax district gave Lee 72

[49] Since nearly every voter exercised both of his votes and there were only three candidates, there was no way of determining degrees of partisanship as was attempted in the Accomac polls. Hence all the votes cast for each candidate were used in the following calculations.

percent of his total and McCarty 63 percent of his. The figures for Lee and McCarty are lower because they lived in the same district and hence divided the loyalties of the voters. Because residence was such an important factor, supporters of each candidate differed little economically (Table 8).[50]

The most interesting feature of this election was the apparent bloc voting. In all the other polls examined the names seem to have been listed in the order of the voter's appearance, and no particular pattern could be found. But this poll contains blocs of six to ten men who voted for the same two candidates (the pair-

Table 8. Westmoreland County election, 1793: House of Delegates

Distribution of voters by slave ownership

Slaves	Lee voters	% of Lee's total	Mc-Carty voters	% of Mc-Carty's total	New-ton voters	% of New-ton's total	All county tax-payers	% of county total
0	59	30	31	22	44	32	260	41
1–4	73	37	48	34.5	54	39	223	35
5–12	47	24	44	32	28	20	111	17
13–24	11	5.5	9	6.5	8	6	29	4.5
25–49	3	2.5	5	3.5	4	3	12	2
50–99	2	1	2	1.5	0		3	.5
Total	195	100	139	100	138	100	636	100

ing of candidates varies, of course, with each bloc), and the members of each bloc lived in the same tax district. Moreover, the tendency toward bloc voting increased toward the end of the poll. It requires only a little imagination to see the clusters of freeholders waiting outside the court house for the strategic moment to rush in with their verbal choices. How important was the "bandwagon" effect? Possibly, when nothing else distinguishes the candidates, every maneuver is important. One final incident adds to the suspicion that the election was more hotly contested than the lack of issues seems to have warranted. The three candidates voted, as usual, near the end of the day. Lee and Newton, following gentlemanly custom, voted for their opponents. McCarty voted for himself.

[50] Since the land book for 1792 is so incomplete, only slaveholding was determined in this poll. Of each candidate's total, the following number of voters could be found in the personalty book: Lee, 76%; McCarty, 87%; Newton, 72%.

Four years later, April 24, 1797, a poll for congressional and assembly seats involved many of the same candidates, but this time there were evident party differences.[51] Walter Jones was again a candidate for the House of Representatives, and his opponent was James Ball of Lancaster County. Jones won the election this time, and his record in Congress over the next two years was consistently Republican.[52] Ball, who was probably a distant cousin of Washington's, was elected to the House of Delegates in 1799 and voted Federalist on every party issue.[53] Jones's victory, by a margin of 127 to 70, reflected the rising Jeffersonian sentiment in Westmoreland, but the electorate did not divide along lines of wealth (Table 9).

We do not know, of course, the extent to which voters were aware of party differences between the two candidates. The stance of prominent persons may have afforded them some clue. Daniel McCarty, ungracious loser four years earlier, voted for Jones (and McCarty's subsequent senatorial record was Republican); indeed, he was the wealthiest of Jones's supporters. On the other hand, the former president journeyed down from Mount Vernon to vote a straight Federalist ticket.[54] He voted this time in the middle of the poll; the next half dozen voters acted quite independently.

The accompanying assembly contest indicates that at least a third of the voters were unconcerned with parties. For the district senate seat McCarty was unopposed, and everyone—including Washington—voted for him. There were four candidates for the two house seats: Henry Lee, John P. Hungerford, and two others, Muse and Turner, who were not identified by first name. Nor can the latter two be identified by party. Lee was the most prominent Federalist in the county, having recently completed a term as governor. Hungerford had no prior political service, but his record in the House of Delegates over the next three years was Republican.[55]

[51] Westmoreland County Records, vol. 7, pp. 428–32.

[52] Manning J. Dauer, *The Adams Federalists* (Baltimore, 1953), pp. 309, 314.

[53] There were eight party-determining votes in the 1799 session, ranging from commentaries on Adams's foreign policy to reaffirmation of the resolutions of 1798.

[54] Washington is not listed in the Westmoreland land book for 1797 (which is incomplete), and in the personal property book he was taxed for only two horses and no slaves. He voted for Henry Lee in the House of Delegates contest.

[55] Hungerford voted Republican on nine of eleven party issues in the 1797–99 sessions.

Table 9. Westmoreland County election, 1797: House of Representatives

a. Distribution of voters by land valuation (expressed in pounds Virginia currency)

Wealth	Ball voters	% of Ball's total	Jones voters	% of Jones's total	All county tax-payers	% of county total
£0–24	7	16	18	25	117	32
£25–74	16	36	21	29.5	106	29
£75–149	7	16	16	22	58	16
£150–399	7	16	11	15	55	14.5
£400–799	4	9	5	7	24	6
£800–1,499	0		0		2	.5
£1,500—	3	7	1	1.5	7	2
Total	44	100	72	100	369	100

b. Distribution of voters by slave ownership

Slaves	Ball voters	% of Ball's total	Jones voters	% of Jones's total	All county tax-payers *	% of county total
0	19	36	22	23	260	41
1–4	17	32	44	45	223	35
5–12	12	22	23	24	111	17
13–24	2	4	5	5	29	4.5
25–49	2	4	2	2	12	2
50–99	1	2	1	1	3	.5
Total	53	100	97	100	636	100

* To save labor, the 1793 figures from Table 8 are repeated here. There were 2,379 slaves in the county in 1793 and 2,305 in 1798; changes in slaveholding patterns in the interim would be negligible.

Hungerford led the race with 155 votes, and Lee received 134 (there were 208 voters in all). Though the county had shifted since 1793 from Federalist to Republican, the old war hero Henry Lee still had a strong personal following. A little over a third of the freeholders voted for both Lee and Hungerford. Parties, however, were a factor, and the extent of partisan voting can be measured by comparing the congressional and assembly contests. Among the James Ball voters (presumably Federalists) who also voted in the House of Delegates contest, 39 supported Lee, 12 favored Hungerford, and 16 voted for both. Of the Jones voters (presumably Republicans) who participated in the assembly election, 34 stood up for Hungerford, 19 for Lee, and 44 for both. Thus, only about half of the electorate voted a straight party ticket.

Among those who did demonstrate a party preference (i.e., by voting for only Lee or Hungerford, not both) there was a clear relationship between party and wealth (Table 10).[56] Both candidates lived in the same tax district, and there was no residential pattern to the voting. There was a considerable difference between them in wealth, however. Henry Lee's palatial Stratford Hall commanded a domain of 1,367 acres and 30 slaves, while Hungerford possessed a modest plantation of 200 acres and 12 slaves. Lee may

Table 10. Westmoreland County election, 1797: House of Delegates

a. Distribution of voters by land valuation (expressed in pounds Virginia currency)

Wealth	Lee voters	% of Lee's total	Hunger-ford voters	% of Hunger-ford's total	Voting for both	% of total voting for both
£0–24	0		9	37	6	18
£25–74	8	33.5	8	33.5	10	30.5
£75–149	6	25	4	17	6	18
£150–399	3	13	2	8.5	9	27.5
£400–799	5	20	1	4	1	3
£800–1,499	0		0		0	
£1,500—	2	8.5	0		1	3
Total	24	100	24	100	33	100

b. Distribution of voters by slave ownership

Slaves	Lee voters	% of Lee's total	Hunger-ford voters	% of Hunger-ford's total	Voting for both	% of total voting for both
0	4	11.5	19	37	19	28
1–4	12	34	22	43	28	41
5–12	11	31	8	16	19	28
13–24	3	10	1	2	2	3
25–49	4	11.5	1	2	0	
50–99	1	3	0		0	
Total	35	100	51	100	68	100

[56] Of the 208 who voted in the assembly contest, only two voted for neither Lee nor Hungerford. A total of 81 (39%) could be found in the incomplete land book and 154 (74%) in the personalty book.

thus have symbolized an elitist Federalism, while Hungerford represented a more common Republicanism, but which factor—the candidate or the party—was more important cannot be determined.

Firm conclusions about voters' conceptions of the Federalist and Republican parties will have to await the discovery of more poll lists for the 1790s. But it seems likely that the assembly contest in Westmoreland will prove to be less typical than the congressional one. In the 1780s economic issues were paramount in Virginia politics; that voters acted by wealth and interest is not surprising. But by the mid-1790s a host of noneconomic factors was influencing voter behavior—the French Revolution and the symbols it evoked, foreign relations and national pride, Washington's retirement and the accession of Adams as head of the Federalist party, to name only a few. Only factors of this sort, it would seem, can explain the results of an Essex County congressional poll in 1793.

Essex is in the middle Tidewater on the south bank of the Rappahannock. It was Antifederalist in 1788 and consistently Republican thereafter. There were three candidates for the congressional seat, none a resident of the county. Francis Corbin was a planter/lawyer educated in England, who possessed an estate of 750 acres and 22 slaves in Middlesex and a similar farm in Caroline. He had served in the House of Delegates since 1784, an ally and correspondent of Madison's, though he remained a Federalist in the 1790s. John Roane, who possessed 1,000 acres and 19 slaves in King William, came from a prominent Antifederalist family. In the House of Delegates he had consistently supported a second convention and substantive amendments to the Constitution. The third candidate was Anthony New, who trailed in Essex but won the district. New owned 482 acres and 11 slaves in Caroline, and he too was an Antifederalist in the House of Delegates in 1788–90. In Congress (1793–1805) he was a Republican. The results of the election in Essex were: Roane, 173; New, 126; and Corbin, 94.[57] The lopsided margin showed the Antifederalist/Republican complexion of the county, but there are no important differences among the supporters of each candidate. If anything, Corbin did slightly better among the poor voters than the Republicans did. Clearly, noneconomic factors were at work, notably the rhetoric that accompanied the birth of a national party system.

Let us, then, return to the question posed at the beginning of

[57] Essex County poll, March 1797, Essex County Deed Book, no. 33, Va. State Lib.

this essay. How well did the Virginia political system function? It worked remarkably well, despite domination by the gentry. Very rarely was there an electoral contest in which there was any apparent difference in social or economic status between the candidates. Not only were the candidates invariably wealthy, they were often the wealthiest men in the county. Yet the turnout (usually from 40 to 60 percent) suggests that the gentry were able to interest the average citizen in the process. It may be, as Charles Sydnor has suggested, that the practice of oral voting actually enhanced the voter's conception of his importance by calling public attention to his choice.[58] Probably more important was the public occasion. Court days, when most elections were held, were important events in an isolated, rural society. The practice of treating the voters to whisky, rum, or wine enlivened the festivities and enhanced the turnout.

The wealthy were more likely to appear at the polls than the poor, but, in general, the electorate was a fair cross section of the county taxpayers. Indeed, the poorest voters were a majority of the electorate on every occasion. Nor is there much evidence that the wealthy objected to this situation. The law that permitted planters to vote in every county in which they held the requisite amount of land has often been cited as evidence of planter domination, but there is no evidence that the opportunity was much used.[59] There were seldom more than two or three nonresident voters on any poll list. Indeed, the number of nonresidents was often exceeded by those who voted twice. And these were almost always small freeholders, probably because more prominent men would be recognized.[60] Nearly all the double-voting appears toward the end of the lists—probably at the end of a long day for the harried county clerk. On no occasion was it enough to alter the outcome—perhaps it was undertaken on a dare or a bet, or maybe it was just a convivial voter testing the system.

It was, finally, an intelligent electorate, able to associate candidates with voting records and issues. The gentry dominated the system, but despite their economic homogeneity they generally managed to represent different points of view. When such differences existed, the electorate divided along economic lines, until

[58] Charles Sydnor, *Gentlemen Freeholders: Political Practices in Washington's Virginia* (Chapel Hill, N.C., 1952), p. 34.

[59] Sydnor calls nonresidents "a significant force" (p. 40).

[60] The amount of double voting is hard to measure because of the tendency to repeat names in a family. However, when a name appears twice on a poll list and only once on a tax list, one's suspicions are aroused.

the 1790s when national politics and partisan rhetoric complicated the issues. When no important difference separated the candidates, other factors—hero worship, residence, family ties—influenced voter behavior. Yet personalities and social stature remained important, even after the formation of national political parties. Even in the late 1790s about a third of the electorate seemed unconcerned with party differences, at least to the extent of supporting two candidates with opposite views.

Virginia was not yet a democracy, but it had a solid foundation for it. The "common man" was an integral part of the system. With the help of a little Jeffersonian rhetoric he would begin to recognize his power.

4   Alexander Hamilton
as Public Administrator: A Reappraisal

John S. Pancake

ALEXANDER HAMILTON has long been admired as one of the most brilliant of the Founding Fathers, but for many years his reputation was overshadowed by the Jeffersonian tradition. In the late nineteenth and early twentieth centuries, however, a Hamiltonian renaissance created a new and heroic image of the first secretary of the Treasury. Legendary figures of the American past who had been conceived in the smoke of battle or the forests of frontier were giving way to the new ideal of the industrial giant and the business magnate.

Hamilton emerged as the great organizer of the new American nation. Writers of the Progressive era created a new cult of business efficiency, and Hamilton became their hero. Theodore Roosevelt admired him extravagantly. Henry Cabot Lodge and Arthur Vandenberg represented successive generations of statesmen who studied Hamilton's example, and questions of national policy were often prefaced by the phrase "If Hamilton were alive today. . . ." In 1948 Leonard White, in his administrative history of *The Federalists*, concluded: "Alexander Hamilton was the greatest administrative genius of his generation, and one of the great administrators of all time." [1]

For almost a century, then, Americans have looked to Hamilton as the model of genius in public administration. It would appear appropriate, therefore, to examine the man around whom the legend has been created. In making such an appraisal there is no intention to deprecate Hamilton's genius as an innovative statesman. Almost alone among the Founding Fathers he had early recognized that a strong central government must be a great energizing force in the critical years of the new nation, and he pursued this goal with relentless purpose. As secretary of the Treasury he was determined to use governmental power to achieve stability and prosperity. The questions here raised concern Hamilton's conduct as a public administrator, that is, as a subordinate

---

[1] White, *The Federalists: A Study in Administrative History, 1789–1801* (New York, 1948), pp. 125–26.

to the president and as presiding officer of the most important department of the executive branch.

Hamilton had no traditional family or regional roots, and almost all of his public life was spent in the service of the government of the United States: as an officer on the staff of the commander in chief and in a regiment of the Continental Line, as a member of the Confederation Congress, and as a delegate to the Constitutional Convention. He played a decisive role in the New York ratifying convention of 1788; and his brilliant *Federalist* essays, written in conjunction with James Madison and John Jay, provided an invaluable handbook for those who campaigned for the new government.

Hamilton's qualifications for the Treasury were well known to Washington, not only on the basis of their former association but from the many recommendations of acquaintances. James Madison, whom Washington consulted often in the first months of the new administration, thought that Hamilton was *"perhaps best qualified* for that *species of business."* [2]

The task that Hamilton undertook was formidable. He was determined to establish the public credit of the new government and to do it on terms that would satisfy government creditors. His proposals for funding the national debt at par, assuming the debts of the states, and creating a national banking system were breathtaking in their scope. The sureness with which Hamilton moved to his objectives, the public confidence that he created, and the ultimate success that he achieved attest to the superior quality of his statesmanship.

At the same time that he was dealing with these larger problems of public credit, Hamilton was also engaged in the very critical business of building the administrative structure of the new government. The problem of converting a constitutional blueprint into a working model is one that has often wrecked new governments created out of revolution. It is perhaps for this achievement as much as for any other that we call the men of the Revolution the "Founding Fathers."

Hamilton's Treasury Department was the largest in the government, both in numbers and in the range of its activity. By 1792 the central Treasury office employed over ninety persons with about thirteen hundred employees in the field. The department thus constituted the largest nonmilitary administrative organiza-

[2] Madison to Thomas Jefferson, May 27, 1789, *The Papers of Thomas Jefferson*, ed. Julian P. Boyd et al. (Princeton, N.J., 1950–), XV, 153.

tion that had ever existed in American history. It goes without saying that Hamilton attempted to fill these positions with men of honesty and integrity as well as ability. Nonetheless, it would have been surprising if the host of subordinate appointments did not contain some incompetents and even a few rogues.[3]

But the appointment of William Duer to the position of assistant secretary constituted a serious mistake and one that Hamilton should have avoided. Duer was an eighteenth-century wheeler-dealer. He had performed honorable service as a soldier in the Continental army, had served in the Congress on the Board of War, and was serving on the Treasury Board of the Confederation government in 1789. He had also made a more than modest fortune from government contracts and other business ventures. He had married "Lady Kitty," the daughter of General William Alexander, self-styled Lord Stirling. The Reverend Manasseh Cutler reported that "Colonel Duer . . . lives in the style of a nobleman. I presume he had not less than fifteen different sorts of wine at dinner . . . besides most excellent bottled cider, porter and several other kinds of strong beer." [4]

Duer had been a business partner of another notable speculator, Daniel Parker, in the firms of William Duer and Co., Duer and Parker, Parker and Duer, and Daniel Parker and Co. He had also acquired a considerable amount of state and continental paper as well as soldiers' certificates. He was secretary of the Treasury Board in 1787 when that body and Congress approved the sale of lands in the Northwest Territory to Cutler and his Ohio Company Associates. These, in turn, made a confidential agreement for the resale of part of the land to the Scioto Company, of which Duer and Daniel Parker were the prime movers. In other words, Duer as secretary of the Treasury Board helped obtain approval for a massive land speculation deal for Duer the partner of the Scioto Company. John C. Miller, in his biography, says: "That Hamilton knew of Duer's shady dealings is certain." [5]

Early in 1790 the Scioto Company's grandiose colonization scheme ran into trouble because it could not meet its payments to

[3] White, pp. 122–23.

[4] William Parker Cutler and Julia Perkins Cutler, *The Life, Journals and Correspondence of Rev. Manasseh Cutler* (2 vols., Cincinnati, 1888), I, 241.

[5] Joseph Stancliffe Davis, "William Duer," *Essays in the Early History of American Corporations* (2 vols., Cambridge, Mass., 1917), I, 121, 131–40; Miller, *Alexander Hamilton: Portrait in Paradox* (New York, 1959), p. 245.

the government for its land. Hamilton's Report on Public Credit of January 1790, prepared with Duer's assistance, recommended that the price of public lands be reduced to twenty cents an acre, payable in government certificates. Such a proposal not only had the obvious advantage of reducing the price of public lands but of enhancing the value of government securities. Duer had a good deal of both.[6]

At the time that the accounts of the old Treasury Board were transferred to the new Department of the Treasury, Duer was charged with over $200,000 worth of Treasury indents (interest payments). Neither the new secretary nor his subordinates made any effort either to collect the funds or to call on Duer for an accounting. It was not until almost three years later that Duer's business failures finally induced Comptroller Oliver Wolcott to bring suit for recovery—recovery that was never made. During his tenure as assistant secretary, Duer also, according to a well-founded account, took Treasury warrants "to deposit as collateral security for some of his private engagements."[7]

It seems probable that Hamilton did not know of this last transaction, but he could scarcely have been unaware of the irregularities in Duer's Treasury Board accounts or of his speculative activities in western lands. "Lady Kitty" and Elizabeth Hamilton were cousins, and the Hamiltons were also well acquainted with Daniel Parker, Postmaster Samuel Osgood (former president of the Treasury Board), Secretary of War Henry Knox, and his redoubtable wife, all of whom were associates of Duer in one or another of his speculative schemes.[8]

Yet it was not until Duer became notoriously active in the speculation of government securities that he finally resigned, whether at the prompting of the secretary of the Treasury or not is uncertain. Duer was obviously using his knowledge of Hamilton's plans for funding and assumption to trade in state and continental paper. This was illegal, for by law a government officer was forbidden to "purchase by himself, or another in trust for him, any public lands or other public property" or to have any dealings in "the purchase or sale of any public securities of any State, or the

---

[6] Alexander Hamilton, *The Papers of Alexander Hamilton*, ed. Harold C. Syrett, Jacob E. Cooke, et al. (New York, 1962–), VI, 56, 91.

[7] Ibid., XI, 131–32; Seth Johnson to Andrew Craigie, Dec. 24, 1793, quoted in Davis, I, 192.

[8] Rufus King, "Memorandum," Dec. 21, 1788, *Life and Correspondence of Rufus King*, ed. Charles R. King (6 vols., New York, 1894–1900), I, 623–24.

United States." William Constable, a noted speculator himself, remarked in October 1789 that Duer was "working with Jno. Hopkins at buying up soldiers' pay. . . . He may not only incur censure but be turned out." But Duer did not resign until six months later. Even then, Hamilton's attitude was hardly that of a superior toward an unfaithful subordinate. "While I truly regret, my dear friend, that the necessity of your situation compels you to relinquish a station in which public and personal considerations combine to induce me to wish your continuance, I cannot but be sensible to the force of motives by which you are determined. And I interest myself in your happiness too sincerely not to acquiesce in whatever may redound to your happiness." [9]

The irony was obviously unintentional, for Hamilton soon afterward became one of the principal promoters of the Society for Useful Manufactures. This venture seems to have been launched at least partly to demonstrate the validity of Hamilton's assumptions in his Report on Manufactures. The S.U.M. was incorporated in New Jersey in 1791 under terms that were remarkable for their generosity (although subsequent corporation history has demonstrated that in New Jersey all things are possible). What is noteworthy is that the directors elected the ubiquitous Colonel Duer "governor" of the Society. He was still the man with the Midas touch, and enthusiastic plans were made for the production of everything from pasteboard and pottery to blankets and beer. [10]

The fortunes of the S.U.M. bloomed quickly and then faded. Its directors' meeting in the spring of 1792 was somewhat embarrassing because "Governor" Duer's financial schemes had collapsed and he was lodged in the New York City jail. Yet Hamilton and his fellow directors did not despair. Hamilton called upon William Seton, cashier of the Bank of New York, for loans that may have amounted to as much as $80,000. Seton's cooperation was predictable in view of the fact that Hamilton had been instrumental in founding the Bank of New York and that it was the depository of government funds. Hamilton had opposed the establishment of a branch of the Bank of the United States in New York, and when he was overruled he informed Seton, "Ultimately, it will be incumbent upon me to place the public funds in the

[9] *U.S. Statutes at Large*, I, 67; Constable to Robert Morris, Oct. 28, 1789, quoted in Broadus Mitchell, *Alexander Hamilton* (2 vols., New York, 1957–62), II, 164; see also ibid., II, 155ff., and Miller, 244–46; Hamilton to Duer, April 4–7 (?), 1790, Hamilton, *Papers*, VI, 346.

[10] Davis, "The 'S.U.M.': The First New Jersey Corporation," *Essays*, I, 349–409.

keeping of the branch; but *it may be depended upon* that I shall *precipitate nothing*, but shall so conduct the transfer as not to embarrass or distress your institution." [11]

Using negative evidence, historians have unanimously cleared Hamilton of the charge of using his position for his own profit— of what lawyers would call "malfeasance." But what of the scarcely less serious charge of what today would be termed "conflict of interest"? Was such a concept unknown to the Founding Fathers? Shortly after his appointment as secretary of the Treasury, Hamilton received a letter from General "Light-Horse Harry" Lee, asking for "an opinion concerning the domestic debt. Will it speedily rise, will the interest accruing command specie or any thing nearly as valuable, what will become of the indents already issued?" Hamilton replied, "You remember the saying with regard to Caesar's Wife. I think the spirit of it applicable to every man concerned in the administration of the finances of a Country. With respect to the Conduct of such men—*Suspicion* is ever eagle-eyed. And the most innocent things are apt to be misinterpreted." [12]

What, then, of Caesar's wife's cousin? What of the responsibility of a public administrator for the actions of a subordinate? In *The Federalist* Hamilton is explicit in pointing out that public administrators have "the responsibility . . . for the fitness and competence of the persons on whom they bestow their choice, and the interest they will have in the respectable and prosperous administration of affairs, will inspire a sufficient disposition, to dismiss from a share in it, all such, who, by their conduct, shall have proved themselves unworthy of the confidence reposed in them." [13]

If it did not occur to Hamilton that his promotion of the Society for Useful Manufactures and his continued association with Duer conflicted with his position as secretary of the Treasury, it was publicly brought to his attention. The Report on Manufactures of December 5, 1791, was inevitably linked with the charter of the S.U.M., which the legislature of New Jersey had approved two weeks earlier. "A Farmer" in the *National Gazette* addressed "Five letters to the Yeomanry of the United States: Containing some

[11] Philip Livingston to Hamilton, March 24, 1792, Hamilton to Seton, May 25, 1792, Seton to Hamilton, June 11, 1792, Hamilton, *Papers*, XI, 174–75 and n, 424–25, 505–6; Davis, I, 477; Hamilton to Seton, Nov. 25, 1791, Hamilton, *Papers*, IX, 539.

[12] Lee to Hamilton, Nov. 16, 1789, Hamilton to Lee, Dec. 1, 1789, Hamilton, *Papers*, V, 517, VI, 1.

[13] *The Federalist*, ed. Jacob E. Cooke (Middleton, Conn., 1961), p. 449 (no. 66).

Observations on the Dangerous Scheme of Governor Duer and Mr. Secretary Hamilton . . . ." Said the "Farmer,"

It may be thought improper at this early period to offer any observations on the justice or wisdom of the report of the Secretary of the Treasury on manufactures. It is true, we might have waited for the deliberations of Congress on the subject; but Congress having adopted a new method of legislating, by referring the most important business of the country to the different Secretaries, and adopting their reports, experience justifies a belief, that the principles of this report will also be adopted, and will come forward under the sanction of the legislature in the form of a law. The Secretary of the Treasury, and his friends in New York, have already prepared the way, by procuring one of the most arbitrary and unjust laws to be enacted by the commonwealth of New-Jersey, that ever disgraced the government of a free people; a law granting to a few wealthy men . . . unconstitutional privileges highly injurious to the citizens of that state.

And "Brutus" told the "Freemen of Pennsylvania" that the great issue before the country was not Federalists versus Antifederalists; "it is the Treasury of the United States against the people." [14]

The final episode in Hamilton's relationship with Duer came in the panic of 1792. The wildcat speculation that precipitated the panic was caused in part by an attempt by Duer and a group of associates to corner government securities. They were caught short when another group attempted a corner of specie, and banks had to call their loans to thwart it. In an effort to stave off the crash Hamilton used Treasury funds to purchase government securities, although not with the intention of saving Duer. In any event, the move came too late and Duer was ruined. The Treasury now stepped in and filed suit for the old shortage in his Treasury accounts. Hamilton never joined in the general condemnation of Duer and several years later said of his former associate, "He is a man who, with a great deal of good zeal, has in critical times rendered valuable service to the country." [15]

Hamilton seems to have been flawed in two respects, both of which have damaged the reputations of many public administrators: conflict of interest and what the twentieth century calls "cronyism." In both cases he, like his successors, found the public quick to condemn and reluctant to forgive.

The cabinet dissension between Hamilton and Jefferson is familiar to all students of the history of the early Republic. Their differences were rooted in conflicting ideologies that in turn were

[14] Philadelphia *National Gazette*, Aug. 27 and Sept. 1, 1792.

[15] Davis, I, 284–307; Hamilton to ——, n.d., *The Works of Alexander Hamilton*, ed. Henry Cabot Lodge (10 vols., New York, 1904), X, 50.

reflected in conflicting notions of policy, foreign and domestic. Out of this conflict the first major parties were born, and the two-party system became the American way of politics.

The dissension first surfaced in the form of complaints by Jefferson that Hamilton was meddling in State Department matters that were essentially none of his business. It was difficult to determine departmental lines in the first Washington administration. There were only three departments—Attorney General Edmund Randolph was not, strictly speaking, a member of the cabinet, but he was usually present at conferences of department heads. With such a small official family Washington thought he could utilize the combined resources of his aides on all important matters of state. Nor did he seem concerned about departmental boundaries when, for example, he solicited Jefferson's opinion on the constitutionality of the Bank of the United States. And Hamilton justifiably pointed out that income to the Treasury might be vitally affected by trade restrictions that were imposed as the result of foreign policy decisions.

The complaints about interdepartmental interference more probably represented a surface expression of deeper differences. It is difficult to tell to what extent these were personal; the mask of eighteenth-century courtesy often conceals them from the historian's view. Jefferson, in later life, characterized Hamilton as being "of acute understanding, disinterested, honest, and honorable in all private transactions." And Hamilton, on at least one great occasion, demonstrated his respect for Jefferson. On the other hand Jefferson often expressed his conviction that Hamilton was a monarchist, and the latter called Jefferson an "intriguing incendiary." Such expressions can be, for the most part, put down to partisan polemics.[16]

The immediate cause for their antagonism was in the area of foreign policy. Early in his administration Washington made it clear that he intended to pursue a course of neutrality as strictly as circumstances permitted. With this basic objective both Jefferson and Hamilton agreed. The great difference lay in the means by which the objective could be attained. Jefferson was fully aware that the United States was a second-rate power. He was also aware that the United States was indebted to France for her assistance in the winning of independence and that she symbolized the strug-

[16] "Anas," Feb. 4, 1818, Thomas Jefferson, *The Writings of Thomas Jefferson*, ed. Paul Leicester Ford (10 vols., New York, 1892–99), I, 166; "Catullus," Sept. 29, 1792, Hamilton, *Papers*, XII, 504.

gle for liberty against tyranny. Both factors weighed heavily with public opinion, and Jefferson never discounted this important political factor. There was also the commercial Treaty of 1778 with France, the only trade agreement of any importance that the new nation had been able to ratify. So far as trade with Britain was concerned, Jefferson hoped, perhaps unrealistically, that if strong measures against Great Britain resulted in losses to American commerce, France would take up the slack. In any event, "in the case of the two nations with which we have the most intimate connections, France & Britain, my system was to give satisfactory distinctions to the former, of little cost to us, in return for the solid advantages yielded to us by them; & to have met the English with some restrictions which might induce them to abate their severities against our commerce." So wrote Jefferson to the president in the fall of 1792. "I have always supposed," he continued, "this coincided with your sentiments." [17]

When Jefferson and his friend Madison talked of discriminating duties, embargoes, and other retaliatory measures against Great Britain, Hamilton was appalled. The idea of a commercial "cold war" was, in his view, an invitation to disaster. The two most salient considerations in Hamilton's mind were British sea power and the critical importance of British trade to the American economy. His own financial plans, particularly the heavy debt incurred by funding and assumption, were based on commercial prosperity. In short, Hamilton favored a policy which would at all costs avoid giving offense to England. In his determination to see this policy implemented he vigorously opposed Jefferson in cabinet discussions—to the point, in fact, that Washington was finally forced to ask them for opinions in writing in order to keep them from each other's throat. But Hamilton did more than voice his opposition. In his zeal to impose his will on the president he went beyond not only interdepartmental boundaries but the limits of propriety.

The first occasion was the Nootka Sound crisis. Spain and England clashed in the Pacific Northwest, and it appeared that the two nations might go to war. Several factors threatened to embroil the United States in the quarrel. The British in Canada posed a threat both by their continued occupation of forts on the American side of the international boundary and because it appeared that in the event of war they might wish to pass troops through American territory in order to attack Spain in Florida and the Trans-Mis-

[17] Jefferson to Washington, Sept. 9, 1792, Jefferson, *Writings*, VII, 139–40.

sissippi. The United States' relations with Spain were also somewhat delicate. The Florida boundary was still unsettled, and the
United States was concerned over the fact that Spain controlled
the mouth of the Mississippi. Various plots and rumored con-
spiracies in the years since 1783 had made the Old Southwest a
veritable powder keg in Spanish-American diplomacy.[18]

The Nootka Sound episode was the occasion for the first enun-
ciation of American neutrality, and the first demonstration of the
divergent views of Jefferson and Hamilton. Far from sitting idly
by, Washington was determined to take whatever advantage might
be made of the situation. He made it clear that the United States
intended to remain neutral, but he determined to promote a settlement of the Mississippi question by offering Spain assurances that,
beyond the navigation of the river and the boundary settlement,
the United States posed no threat to Spanish interests in North
America. He was also prepared to give Spain positive assurances
of limited support against Great Britain. In the summer of 1790
he dispatched his former aide, Colonel David Humphreys, on a
secret mission to Spain by way of Paris. Humphreys carried a letter
to Lafayette, presumably to keep the French informed, and one to
Diego Gardoqui in Spain that contained the president's overture:
"That all persons who may be employed in the intercourse between
the Dominions of his most Catholic Majesty and the United States
may serve to promote a mutual good understanding, and to advance
reciprocally the substantial interests of the two nations (which, I
am convinced, are not only entirely compatible with, but may be
highly promotive to each other) is the constant and ardent wish of,
Sir Your etc." [19]

In the meantime Hamilton was pursuing his own line of diplomacy with the British. His channel of communication was Major
George Beckwith, a British agent dispatched by Lord Dorchester,
the governor general of Canada, to New York to gather intelligence. Beckwith had been on similar missions before, and Hamilton was personally acquainted with him. Whitehall had as yet
sent no accredited representative to the United States; so Beckwith
served as a sort of minister without portfolio. Washington knew
of Beckwith's presence in New York and, in fact, encouraged

[18] William K. Manning, "The Nootka Sound Controversy," American
Historical Association, *Annual Report, 1904* (Washington, D.C., 1905),
pp. 279–478.
[19] Washington to Diego Gardoqui, Aug. 10, 1790, *The Writings of
George Washington*, ed. John C. Fitzpatrick (39 vols., Washington, D.C.,
1931–44), XXXI, 82.

Hamilton to cultivate him. Washington obviously expected Hamilton to report to him in detail, and Hamilton did so—but with some startling omissions and alterations. A comparison of Hamilton's reports to Washington and those of Beckwith to Dorchester reveal that Hamilton deliberately attempted to discredit the American minister in London, Gouverneur Morris, in the eyes of both Washington and the British. He also gave Beckwith the impression that Secretary of State Jefferson did not speak for prevailing administration policy.[20]

But by far the most serious indiscretion was his attempt to scuttle Humphreys's secret mission to Spain. While Washington and Jefferson were hoping for a mutual security understanding with Spain, Hamilton was proposing to Beckwith that the United States might be willing to secure its objectives as an ally of Great Britain. According to Beckwith, Hamilton told him, "The navigation of the river Mississippi we must have, and that shortly, and I do not think the bare navigation will be sufficient. . . . We consider ourselves perfectly at liberty to act with respect to Spain in any way most conducive to our interests, even to the going to war with that power, if we shall think it adviseable to join You." [21]

As it happened, Humphreys's mission never had much chance for success. Spain and Britain adjusted their differences, and the threat of war passed. Washington seems to have suspected a deliberate attempt to discredit Morris, although he did not guess the source. Washington's message to Congress in December 1790 suggested "such encouragements of our own Navigation as will render our commerce . . . less dependent on foreign bottoms." Madison followed the president's lead by introducing retaliatory legislation aimed at England, but Congress refused to pass it.[22] The British, however, were impressed to the extent of sending an accredited envoy to the United States a few months later.

The new representative was George Hammond, and Hamilton cultivated him as assiduously as he had Beckwith. With the outbreak of the war in Europe in 1792 American neutrality became increasingly precarious. The gyrations of Citizen Genêt did serious damage to Jefferson's attempts to "give satisfactory distinctions" to France. The president's apparent unwillingness to clarify his

[20] Julian P. Boyd, *Number 7: Alexander Hamilton's Secret Attempt to Control American Foreign Policy* (Princeton, N.J., 1964), pp. 66–72, 27, 151, 153–54.

[21] Beckwith to Lord Dorchester, Sept. 29–30 (?), 1790, Hamilton, *Papers*, VII, 73–74.

[22] Second Annual Address, 1793, Washington, *Writings*, XXXI, 167.

position on the divergent views of Jefferson and Hamilton led to the former's resignation at the end of 1793. Hamilton was then left with a clear field, and he continued to promote his policies despite increased British restrictions on American trade and her continued occupation of the Northwest posts. Britain refused to recognize the American principle that "free ships make free goods" or even that American goods were neutral if bound to a French port. England's interpretation of neutral rights with regard to rules of blockade and contraband grew increasingly narrow. But Hammond reported to Grenville that "in the justice of these principles Mr. Hamilton perfectly coincided and assured me that he would be responsible for the concurrence of all the members of this administration in the admission of their propriety to the fullest extent." [23]

Even Hamilton was unprepared for the severity with which Britain implemented its edicts. Two Orders in Council of 1793 were followed by devastating raids on American shipping not only in European waters but in the West Indies. To Hamilton such highhandedness seemed "inexplicably mysterious," betraying "strong tokens of deep-rooted hatred." [24] Congress was in a savage mood when it passed a thirty-day embargo in April 1794 and authorized an increase in the army. The pillaging of American shipping, the continued occupation of the Northwest forts, and the suspicion that Dorchester was inciting Indian raids on the frontier brought England and the United States to the brink of war. Washington decided to send a special mission to England to seek a settlement.

He chose Chief Justice John Jay for the task, and it was Hamilton who drafted most of his instructions, completely bypassing Secretary of State Edmund Randolph. Hamilton's advice to Jay accorded with a summation of his views which he had drawn up a few weeks before. Conciliation of Britain was even more important than before. " 'Tis as great an error for a nation to overrate us as to underrate itself. Presumption is as great a fault as timidity. 'Tis our error to overrate ourselves and underrate Great Britain; we forget how little we can annoy, how much we may be annoyed." [25]

But Hamilton was prepared to go even further in the pursuance of his policy. Jay had been instructed, over Hamilton's objection,

[23] Hammond to Lord Grenville, April 2–May 17 (?), 1793, Hamilton, *Papers*, XIV, 273.

[24] Quoted in Miller, 392.

[25] Hamilton to Washington, April 14, 1794, Hamilton, *Works*, V, 110. See the entire letter, pp. 97–115, for Hamilton's arguments in favor of conciliating Great Britain.

to sound out the representatives of Sweden and Denmark on the possibility of common diplomatic action against British maritime policy. The two Baltic powers did, in fact, form a "league of armed neutrality" and issued an invitation to the United States to join them. After some cabinet discussion it was decided to instruct Jay, who was already in London, not to commit himself to the proposal. Whatever slight leverage the situation might have given the United States was nullified by Hamilton's prompt revelation of the cabinet decision to Hammond, who in turn relayed it to London. The reply of the British foreign secretary, Lord Grenville, to Hammond's news indicated that it was "very acceptable. . . . From the weight and influence of Mr. Hamilton, and from the opportunities which he undoubtedly has of knowing the views and plans of his Government; there is great reason to suppose that his opinion on this subject must be well founded. . . . You should still attend to this subject, and . . . renew it from time to time in conversation with those whom you may have reason to think well disposed." [26]

It may be noted in passing that Jay did obtain the two principal objectives of his mission: peace with England and evacuation of American territory. But the commercial concessions that he made appalled Washington and precipitated a political explosion which rocked the nation. Hamilton had avoided offending England, but he had deeply affronted public opinion in the United States.

It is doubtful if Hamilton's indiscretions—which would surely have been labeled as breaches of the national security in the twentieth century—affected the outcome of Jay's mission. Nor is there any question of Hamilton's patriotism. In fact, it was the zeal engendered by his passionate conviction of the rightness of his policy that led him to attempt to undermine the policies of the administration. But in so doing, Hamilton violated basic principles of public administration. Less than two years before he had written:

Difference of opinion between men engaged in any common pursuit, is a natural appendage of human nature. When only exerted *in the discharge of a duty*, with delicacy and temper, among liberal and sensible men, it can create no animosity; but when it produces officious interferences, dictated by no call of duty—when it volunteers a display of itself in a quarter, where there is no responsibility, to the destruction and embarrassment of one who is charged with an immediate and

[26] Lord Grenville to Hammond, Oct. 2, 1794, *Instructions to the British Ministers to the United States, 1791–1812*, ed. Bernard Mayo, American Historical Association, *Annual Report, 1936* (Washington, D.C., 1941), p. 67.

direct responsibility—it must necessarily beget ill-humor and discord between parties.

Applied to members of the executive administration of any government, it must necessarily tend to occasion, more or less, distracted councils, to foster factions in the community, and practically to weaken the government.

Moreover the heads of the several executive departments are justly to be viewed as auxiliaries to the executive chief. *Opposition to any measure of his, by either of those heads of departments, except in the shape of frank, firm, and independent advice to himself, is evidently contrary to the relations which subsist between the parties. And it cannot well be controverted that a measure becomes his, so as to involve the duty of acquiescence on the part of the members of his administration.*[27]

Only slightly less reprehensible was Hamilton's failure to communicate to the president fully and frankly his conversations with Beckwith and Hammond. Surely his former aide knew the value Washington placed on every scrap of intelligence about his opponents. To repeat, Hamilton was certainly not guilty of actually subverting American policy, but his conduct seems to fall far short of that expected of administrators, whom Hamilton himself described as "men who, for ability and integrity, deserve his [the president's] confidence." [28]

Although these episodes in Hamilton's career point to specific flaws in his role as public administrator, they should also be viewed in the context of his whole administrative career. Did Hamilton as public administrator lose sight of his responsibility as a public servant? Hamilton was, from an early age, driven by ambition. At the age of fourteen he had written, "I contemn the grov'ling and condition of a Clerk or the like, to which my Fortune &c. condemns me and would willingly risk my life tho' not my Character to exalt my Station." [29] (One of the remarkable facets of Hamilton's make-up was that he never allowed his driving urge for power and place to impugn his integrity.) It is obvious, both from the context of the letter and of Hamilton's later career, that what he sought was not wealth but fame and honor. Did he also have an inordinate desire for power?

The power on which Hamilton discoursed at length and with enormous insight was governmental power. When he first appeared in the Confederation Congress in 1782 he brought with him a

---

[27] "Metellus," Oct. 24, 1792, Hamilton, *Papers*, XII, 615. Italics added.

[28] "Public Conduct . . . of John Adams . . . ," Oct. 1800, Hamilton, *Works*, VII, 338.

[29] Hamilton to Edward Stevens, Nov. 11, 1769, Hamilton, *Papers*, I, 4.

resolution from the legislature of New York which urged the calling of a new constitutional convention. With the possible exception of James Madison, Hamilton was the most consistent and vehement advocate of increasing the power of the national government during the decade of the 1780s. Unlike Madison and most other nationalists, Hamilton only thinly concealed his lack of respect for the state governments, and within the privacy of the Constitutional Convention his contempt for them was undisguised. He advocated a national congress which would have "unlimited power of passing *all laws* without exception." He believed that "the evils operating in the States . . . must soon cure the people of their fondness for democracies," and so "we must . . . annihilate the state distinctions and state operations." This need to be free of the states was especially important because the government that Hamilton envisioned must not only possess authority but energy. "Energy in Government is essential to that security against external and internal danger, and to that prompt and salutary execution of the laws, which enter into the very definition of good government," he told the convention.[30] And again, "A government ought to contain it itself every power requisite to the full accomplishment of the objects committed to its care, and to the complete execution of the trusts for which it is responsible; free from every other control, but a regard to the public good and to the sense of the people." [31]

What was the locus of national power in the American system? Said Hamilton, in *The Federalist*, "The administration of government, in its largest sense, comprehends all the operations of the body politic, whether legislative, executive or judiciary, but in its most usual and perhaps its most precise signification, it is limited to executive details, and falls peculiarly within the province of the executive department." It was here that the power of government could be generated. "Energy in the executive is a leading character in the definition of good government." [32]

It was as the president's aide—as mayor of the executive palace —that Hamilton saw the opportunity to fulfill his ambition. Deliberately he refused to become a candidate for the Senate and discouraged those who suggested his appointment to the Supreme Court. As secretary of the Treasury he could be at the controls of the engine of government. He could be Rousseau's Legislator, that

[30] Hamilton's speech to the Constitutional Convention, June 18, 1787, *The Records of the Federal Convention*, ed. Max Farrand (4 vols., New Haven, Conn., 1966), I, 300 (Yates), 291 (Madison), 297 (Yates).

[31] *The Federalist*, ed. Cooke, p. 233 (no. 37), p. 195 (no. 31).

[32] Ibid., p. 486 (no. 72), p. 471 (no. 70).

"superior intelligence, acquainted with all the passions of men, but liable to none of them." [33] For Hamilton had never been convinced of the efficacy of republican government. He accepted it only because he knew that it was the only kind of government that was acceptable to the American people.

He did not deny the power of the people to determine their own fundamental law or to choose their own rulers. What he feared was that they would be unable to determine what was best for them, what constituted the long range "public interest," "general happiness," or "common good." The individual and regional interests of the people were part of the overall public good, but the public good was more than the sum of individual interests. Only the wise and the able had the vision to see beyond the constant shifts of popular opinion. "The people are turbulent and changing; they seldom judge or determine right," he told the convention. It was for this reason that Hamilton proposed a president and Senate elected for life.[34] Only if removed from the direct influence of the whims of shifting public opinion could the "disinterested, discreet and temperate rulers" make long-term public policy. His notes for his speech to the convention contain a striking sentence: "There ought to be a principle in government capable of resisting popular will." [35]

If public opinion was not the guide to administrative action, what was? In the conduct of his office as secretary of the Treasury, Hamilton often did not consult Washington, sometimes acted on his own in the absence of an executive decision, and occasionally even circumvented the president. It is here suggested that Hamilton had come to identify the "public good" with the state, that as a public administrator his primary goal was the enhancement of the position and prestige of the government of the United States.

Hamilton saw no conflict of interest between his position as secretary of the Treasury and his promotion of the Society of Useful Manufactures simply because, in his mind, there was none. His concern for the success of the enterprise was not on account of the profits that might accrue to him but because it would further his dream for an industrialized American economy. Fighting for

[33] Jean Jacques Rousseau, *The Social Contract*, trans. and ed. Charles Frankel (New York, 1947), 35.

[34] *Records of the Federal Convention*, I, 299–300; see also Cecelia Kenyon, "Alexander Hamilton: Rousseau of the Right," *Political Science Quarterly*, 73, no. 2 (June 1958): 161–78.

[35] Hamilton to the Supervisors of the City of Albany, Feb. 18, 1789, Hamilton, *Papers*, V, 256; *Records of the Federal Convention*, I, 309.

the success of his financial system, he was not particularly concerned about its effect on people—he brushed aside Madison's arguments on the injustices resulting from the speculation in government paper. He was concerned that the government of the United States attain national and international respectability as a responsible creditor and the proud possessor of a national banking system. His fear of alienating Great Britain had less to do with its effects on seamen or farmers, or even merchants, than the effect on the income to the Treasury and the consequent damage to his financial program. Thus Hamilton as a public administrator lost touch with the people. His power, authority, and energy were the power and authority and energy of the government of the United States.

Perhaps these concepts and these goals do produce something that can be called "the public good" which serves the interests of the people. But when executors of public policy remove themselves from the popular will, they appear to be asking a greater reliance on their infallibility and integrity than is consistent with republicanism. It is pertinent to ask whether Alexander Hamilton—and his spiritual descendants of the twentieth century—would really identify themselves as servants of the people. It is pertinent to ask whether they seek to enhance the power and prestige of the state in order to enhance their own power and prestige.

It may be appropriate to add an epilogue to Hamilton's public career. Whether or not he ever considered becoming president, he never ran for political office after 1787. He frequently appealed to the public for support of his measures, but he never asked them to vote for him. Whether he realized it or not, Hamilton had no personal political base. In New York he depended on the influence of others, notably his father-in-law, General Philip Schuyler. In national politics, by his own admission, President Washington "was an *Aegis very essential to me*" [36]; after Washington's death and the rupture with John Adams, Hamilton found himself peculiarly alone. Neither the "new" Federalists who attempted to reconstruct the party nor the die-hards of the Essex Junto looked to him for leadership. He himself expressed his disgust at Jefferson's appeals for popular support. His own attempt to found a new party drew no response, and he ruefully concluded that he should "withdraw from the scene. Every day proves to me more and more, that this American world was not made for me." [37]

There is some indication that Hamilton sensed that his concept

[36] Hamilton to Tobias Lear, Jan. 2, 1800, Hamilton, *Works*, X, 357.
[37] Hamilton to Gouverneur Morris, Feb. 27, 1802, ibid., X, 425–26.

of the relationship of the people to government was flawed, and that this was somehow linked with the waning of his own destiny. In the spring of 1804, less than three months before his fatal appointment with Aaron Burr, he wrote to an unknown friend:

> Arraign not the dispensations of Providence, they must be founded on wisdom and goodness; and when they do not suit us, it must be because there is some fault in ourselves which deserves chastisement; or because there is a kind of intent, to correct in us some vice or failing, of which, perhaps, we may not be conscious; or because the general plan requires that we should suffer partial ill.
> In this situation it is our duty to cultivate resignation, and even humility, bearing in mind, in the language of the poet, "that it was pride that lost the blest abodes." [38]

Alexander Hamilton may have been dead before Burr's bullet ever reached its mark.

---

[38] Hamilton to ——, April 2, 1804, ibid., X, 456.

5   George Cranfield Berkeley
and the *Chesapeake-Leopard* Affair of 1807

Edwin M. Gaines

O N June 1, 1807, Vice Admiral George Cranfield Berkeley issued an order which enraged a nation. In command of the North Atlantic Station for His Majesty's Navy, Berkeley instructed his ships to stop the United States frigate *Chesapeake* if they met her at sea and to search her for deserters.[1] The admiral's order precipitated the shocking attack on June 22 by H.M.S. *Leopard* upon the U.S.S. *Chesapeake*.

The *Leopard* hailed the American frigate, signaling that she carried dispatches and wished to send a man aboard.[2] Since this procedure was not unusual, Commodore James Barron, skipper of the *Chesapeake*, agreed to the request. But when he was shown Berkeley's order, he, of course, refused to allow the search for deserters. Barron was well aware of United States naval policy with regard to the search of national ships by foreign powers. In 1798 Captain Isaac Phillips had allowed his sloop, the U.S.S. *Baltimore*, to be stopped and searched by John Loring of H.M.S. *Carnatic*. Fifty men were removed from the *Baltimore*. Phillips was promptly courtmartialed, and the American government issued orders forbidding search or impressment aboard its national ships. The English government was duly informed.[3]

Upon receiving word that Barron refused to comply with the admiral's request, the *Leopard* attacked. The *Chesapeake* was totally unprepared for the broadsides, and carnage ensued. One of her officers, while bemoaning that the guns were not ready to fire,

[1] Vice Admiral George Cranfield Berkeley to the respective captains and commanders of His Majesty's ships and vessels on the North American Station, June 1, 1807, Admiralty Papers, 1/497, Public Record Office, London.

[2] Entry of June 22, 1807, Logbook of the *Chesapeake*, May 9, 1807–Feb. 21, 1809, Library of Congress, Washington, D.C.; entry of June 22, 1807, Logbook of the *Leopard*, Jan. 28, 1807–Aug. 16, 1807, Adm 51/1702.

[3] Bradford Perkins, *The First Rapprochement, England and the United States, 1795–1805* (Philadelphia, 1955), p. 99; *Instructions to the British Ministers to the United States, 1791–1812*, ed. Bernard Mayo, American Historical Association, *Annual Report, 1936* (Washington, D.C., 1941), p. 172.

also lamented that "those we thought to be our best friends were
. . . murdering us in cool blood." [4] The *Chesapeake*'s sole act of
defense was to fire one shot after Lieutenant William Allen had
raced to the galley and returned with a live coal in his hands.[5]
Three men aboard the *Chesapeake* were killed and eighteen
wounded.

Three lieutenants from the *Leopard* and a number of petty
officers from various English vessels who could readily recognize
any English deserters then boarded the stricken ship. After a
careful search, they took only four men from the *Chesapeake*.
Three of these were Americans who had previously served in the
Royal Navy, but not aboard any of the ships listed in Berkeley's
order. One was a British deserter, but he had enlisted under an
assumed name, and his true identity was therefore unknown to
Barron.[6]

The United States, having tried since 1793 to solve by diplomatic means the vexatious problem of impressment, reacted
vehemently against this wanton British attack within sight of the
Virginia coast.[7] Shocked by such treatment of a neutral's national
ship, the new nation was far more united against Great Britain at
this moment than it was when war finally came in 1812. President
Thomas Jefferson wrote to a friend, "Never since the battle of
Lexington have I seen the country in such a state of exasperation
as at present and even that did not produce such unanimity." [8]
Seventy years later historian Henry Adams observed, "This famous
event . . . more than any other single cause tended to exasperate
national jealousies and to make England and America permanently
hostile." [9] Even as late as 1916 the Wilsonian campaign cry, "He

---

[4] *The Proceedings of the General Court Martial Convened for the Trial
of Commodore James Barron, Captain Charles Gordon, Mr. William Hook,
and Captain John Hall, of the United States Ship Chesapeake, in the Month
of January, 1808* (Washington, D.C., 1822), p. 147.

[5] Ibid., p. 60.

[6] For a more complete account of the *Chesapeake-Leopard* encounter and
its effect upon the United States, see Edwin M. Gaines, "The *Chesapeake*
Affair: Virginians Mobilize to Defend National Honor," *Virginia Magazine
of History and Biography*, 64 (April 1956): 131–42.

[7] For an excellent discussion of U.S. and British diplomacy during the
early years, see H. C. Allen, *Great Britain and the United States, A History
of Anglo-American Relations, 1783–1952* (New York, 1955), pp. 300–325.

[8] Jefferson to du Pont de Nemours, July 14, 1807, Jefferson Papers,
Lib. Cong.

[9] Adams, *History of the United States of America during the Second
Administration of Thomas Jefferson* (9 vols., New York, 1890), II, 27–30.

kept us out of war," was accompanied by the anti-British slogan, "Remember the *Chesapeake*," in the keynote address at the Democratic National Convention.[10]

The man chosen by the British Admiralty in 1806 for the potentially explosive North Atlantic command did not bring a large supply of tact and patience to his task. However, his lineage was good and his friends were well-placed. His grandfather, the third earl of Berkeley, had served for ten years (1717–27) as First Lord of the Admiralty; his father, a general, had seen action against the forces of Bonnie Prince Charlie in 1745.[11] George Cranfield himself, a second son of the fourth earl, began his naval career early, leaving Berkeley Castle in Gloucestershire when only thirteen, in 1766, to serve under his illustrious cousin, Admiral Augustus Keppel. In the following two years young Berkeley received his first taste of the new world while surveying the Gulf of St. Lawrence.[12]

As a lieutenant, Berkeley was commended for his action against the French navy at Ushant in 1778. He returned to Newfoundland waters during the American Revolution, where he played havoc with American privateers, capturing nine in all. His greatest recognition by the navy came as a result of the battle of the "Glorious first of June" (1794).[13] Although he received one of the relatively few gold medals for bravery against the French fleet, his strategy in handling his man-of-war came under serious fire.[14] A head wound which he suffered in this action sidelined him for several years. Nevertheless the intemperate sea veteran was able to continue as a active and controversial figure, for he—as often was the custom of the day—combined his military career with a political one.

His first venture into politics, in 1774, proved to be a fiasco, a typical result of his stubborn and outspoken manner. As a lieutenant he stood for Parliament against the Admiralty's wishes, and in a bitter campaign was severely defeated. Subsequently he was reprimanded and temporarily placed on the inactive list. His suc-

[10] Walter Millis, *Road to War: America, 1914–1917* (Boston, 1935), p. 318.

[11] Also a Knight of the Garter, James, third earl of Berkeley (1680–1736), married Lady Louisa Lennox, daughter of the first duke of Richmond (*Gentleman's Magazine*, 25 [London, 1756], p. 42).

[12] John Knox Laughton, s.v. "Berkeley, George Cranfield," *Dictionary of National Biography*.

[13] Ibid.

[14] A. Aspinall, *Politics and the Press c. 1780–1800* (London, 1949), p. 85.

cessful political debut came in 1781 with his election to Parliament from Gloucester. He continued to represent his home county, where his brother served as lord lieutenant, until 1812.[15]

As early as 1784 Berkeley, along with his friend Henry Phipps, became a supporter of the Young Pitt.[16] His marriage in that same year to Emily Charlotte, daughter of Lord George Lennox, gained for him a number of powerful and loyal in-laws. With the support of his relatives and political allies, he was promoted to rear admiral in 1799. During the Addington ministry (1801–4), George Cranfield Berkeley as a vociferous member of the Opposition reached such a crescendo of harangue that the government-subsidized *Royal Standard* launched a violent attack upon him personally and upon his service record. The admiral sued but only collected damages for libel concerning his personal bravery. The newspaper accusations and the subsequent trial were representative of the near-sensational controversies evoked by this man.[17]

Upon Pitt's return to power, Berkeley, once again rewarded for his political services and backed by powerful family connections, was promoted to vice admiral. When a major post, command of the North Atlantic Station, fell open in early 1806 upon the sudden death of Admiral Andrew Mitchell, Berkeley was awarded the plum.[18]

At this time both the prime minister, Lord Grenville, and the First Lord of the Admiralty, Thomas Grenville, were close friends of the irascible admiral. Even after the fall of the "all Talents" ministry in March 1807, Berkeley enjoyed unusual support in the Portland government. His old friend and political ally Phipps was First Lord of the Admiralty. Two loyal brothers-in-law, the Duke of Richmond as Ireland's lord lieutenant and Henry Bathurst as president of the Board of Trade, were also in the ministry.[19] No

[15] Laughton.

[16] Berkeley's political career is outlined in *Gentlemen's Magazine and Historical Chronicle*, 88 (London, 1818): 370–71.

[17] Aspinall, p. 85.

[18] Mitchell died Feb. 25, 1806, in the Atlantic post, and Berkeley was notified of his appointment to succeed him on May 3 (Captain Beresford to Admiralty, March 6, 1806, and Admiralty to Berkeley, May 3, 1806, Adm 2/931).

[19] Charles Lennox, fourth duke of Richmond, and son of George Henry Lennox, was a brother of Berkeley's wife, whose sister married Henry Bathurst. See sketch of George Henry Lennox in *Gentleman's Magazine*, 75 (London, 1805): 294. Berkeley's half-sister, Mary Elizabeth Nugent, married George Nugent-Temple Grenville, first marquis of Buckingham (George Fisher Russell Barker, s.v. "Grenville, George Nugent-Temple,"

one's word carried more weight with Foreign Minister George Canning than did that of Bathurst. Together they formulated the Orders in Council. Without the support of these and other powerful friends and relatives, Berkeley would doubtlessly not have been named to command the seething North Atlantic. Yet even some of them, especially Lord Grenville and Henry Phipps, had misgivings that Berkeley was the man best suited for the post.[20]

On July 22, 1806, Admiral Berkeley sailed into his summer headquarters of Halifax, Nova Scotia. His command stretched from the Gulf of St. Lawrence southward past Florida into the Caribbean. Included in his roster of warships were three ships of the line, one fifty-gun cruiser, four frigates, and twelve smaller vessels. Naval yards at the winter command post in Bermuda had recently built fifteen schooners, swelling his manpower to around four thousand seamen.[21] In deploying his forces against the French, Admiral Berkeley indicated that the Norfolk area was the critical sphere. He reported to the Admiralty soon after his arrival,

The Chesapeake seems to be not only the general rendezvous of the French Ships, but in fact is the only one with sufficient depth of water for them to enter to refit, therefore it ought to be made the Rendezvous of the principal strength of the English Squadron, which in war time ought to consist of three line of Battle Ships, two of which with two Frigates and a Brig should be constantly cruising off the Capes or in Hampton Roads. . . . This force would be able to protect trade from the Capes of Virginia to New York to Nantucket.[22]

Ultimately this policy, adhered to by Berkeley, proved far more drastic to the United States than to the inconvenienced French.

The Halifax commander had a lion's share of routine headaches. There was constant confusion over the boundary between the United States and Canada in the Bay of Fundy. Fishing rights, alleged smuggling, and citizenship privileges were a few of the harassing issues that resulted almost daily from this geographical controversy. Even more vexing was the unkind outcome of months

---

DNB; Buckingham to Bathurst, Nov. 25, 1807, *The Memoirs of the Court and Cabinets of George III*, from the original documents by the Duke of Buckingham and Chandos, K.O. [4 vols., London, 1855], IV, 212).

[20] Lord Grenville to Thomas Grenville, Oct. 23, 1807, Grenville Papers, British Museum, no. 41852; Phipps to Bathurst, Oct. 7, 1807, *Report on the Manuscripts of J. B. Fortescue, Esq. Preserved at Dropmore*, ed. Walter Fitzpatrick (10 vols., London, 1892–98), IV, 187.

[21] Berkeley to William Marsden, July 23, 1806, March 27, 1807, Adm 1/496, 497; Report to Admiralty of List of Bermuda Built Schooners, Adm 1/497, f243.

[22] Berkeley to Marsden, April 30, 1807, Adm 1/497.

of British vigilance to prevent the French warships, enjoying diplomatic immunity in the Chesapeake Bay area, from escaping. Somehow they more often than not made their dash for freedom successfully.[23]

American reaction to the bellicose conduct of H.M.S. *Leander* in April 1806 gave Berkeley additional difficulties. The *Leander*, accompanied by two other British warships, was engaged in searching merchant vessels for men and contraband just outside New York harbor. One schooner, seeking cover of the port, was pursued by the *Leander*, which proceeded to fire a warning volley "accidentally" into the ship rather than over her head. The action, which took place in the harbor itself, resulted in the death of an American sailor, John Pierce. Irate New Yorkers rioted, and angry protests were raised in every section of the country. President Thomas Jefferson felt obliged to issue a proclamation forbidding the *Leander* and two sister ships from entering American waters.[24] Later when one of the three banned warships, the *Cambrian*, entered Hampton Roads, the population rose up in arms. The American government lodged a biting protest, and the hapless pilot who had steered the vessel in was tried and jailed.[25] Thus Berkeley found three of his sloops denied port facilities on the mainland. Adding salt to the admiral's wounds was the ignominious necessity of returning Captain Whitby of the ill-starred *Leander* to England for court-martial (to be acquitted). Though this ship's actions elevated American anger to a dangerous pitch, subsequent protests and retaliations by the United States only served to infuriate the uncompromising and uncomprehending commander of the North Atlantic Station. He termed the presidential order barring his ships an outright "aggression."[26]

Unquestionably the foremost problem confronting the admiral was that of manpower. As the newly constructed Bermuda schooners set sail, some means had to be found of manning them from North Atlantic reserves. Berkeley protested against the need

[23] Berkeley to Marsden, Aug. 14 and Jan. 30, 1807, Adm 1/497; Captain Douglas aboard H.M.S. *Bellona* to Berkeley, Dec. 27, 1807, and Berkeley to Admiralty, Jan. 2, 1808, Adm 1/498.

[24] *Instructions to the British Ministers*, p. 223, contains a concise account of the incident.

[25] David Erskine to Foreign Secretary Viscount Howick, Jan. 6, 1807, Foreign Office Papers, 5/52, PRO. Erskine asked Secretary of State James Madison to bar only the commanding officers of the three ships, but Madison replied that this would be no inconvenience for the English since all they had to do was change captains.

[26] Berkeley to Marsden, May 31, 1807, Adm 1/497.

of furnishing almost one hundred sailors on a single occasion for four additions to the Royal Navy. Expanding the works further impoverished his supply of seagoing personnel. His complaints to the Admiralty were constant.[27]

Potentially the most dangerous, and certainly the most irritating, source of depletion for his North Atlantic command was the ever-present threat of mutiny and desertion. During the twelve months preceding the *Leopard's* attack there were at least three mutinous actions in the North Atlantic squadron outside of the Norfolk area in which a sizable number of men made their way to the mainland.[28] In addition, each spring the fancies of young Halifax seamen turned to thoughts other than those of warships, and Berkeley reported it was all the militia could do to keep them from escaping to the provinces. The most galling loss from desertions occurred near the entrance to the Chesapeake Bay. Often after jumping ship, deserters, according to the indignant admiral, "openly paraded the streets of Norfolk, bearing the American flag . . . and bidding defiance to their Officers when spoken to." [29]

To meet these shortages of manpower created by expanding needs and increasing desertions, Berkeley employed the policy of impressment. The demand for additional seamen was occasionally satisfied easily when merchant vessels conveying immigrants to America were encountered. The Irish particularly were subject to this human highjacking—sometimes by the shipload.[30] But when Americans, or those calling themselves such, fell victim to the practice, trouble inevitably followed.

The fundamental dispute arose, of course, from a conflict in nationality laws. The United States Constitution provided for the formation of a uniform system of naturalization. Although laws to this effect were in operation by 1790, in most instances the administration was left to the discretion of local officials, and a multiplicity of systems arose. Often citizenship could be acquired by simply taking an oath and paying the necessary fee.[31] At var-

[27] Berkeley to Marsden, April 10, 1807, Adm 1/497.

[28] Erskine to James Madison, Jan. 4 and Jan. 6, 1807, FO 5/52.

[29] Berkeley to Marsden, June 30 and March 23, 1807, Adm 1/497.

[30] Berkeley to Marsden, April 14, 1807, Adm 1/497. Such had been the case of the *George Washington* in Jan. 1807 and the *La Patriote* and *Cybelle* somewhat later that year.

[31] An able examination of the existing laws and conflicts in citizenship is contained in Ralph Robinson, "Retaliation for the Treatment of Prisoners in the War of 1812," *American Historical Review,* 49 (Oct. 1943): 65–70.

iance with these practices was English common law, which recognized that everyone born a British subject remained one until his death, regardless of personal preferences. Adding to this basic disagreement, which remained until the Anglo-American Treaty of 1870, were the not infrequent abuses in securing American citizenship papers, or "protection." One recalls the story of the lady selling certificates of protection who had constructed a cradle large enough to accommodate a man; in court she could declare that indeed she had known the man from his cradle.[32] But humor was not evident when the report of a single American enslaved in the British navy reach the public. One such forcible seizure was considered by the overwhelming majority of Americans as a grievous and intolerable national insult.[33]

Admiral Berkeley's conduct of impressment entailed two features that were certain to increase United States resentment. If doubt existed about a sailor's citizenship, the admiral's rule of thumb was to press the unfortunate individual into service and await the outcome. Even though release might be secured eventually, the delay of months or years was almost unendurable, sometimes fatal, to the luckless individual. The other characteristic Berkeley imprint was reflected in his steadfast contention that anyone who "had shared the bounty" in His Majesty's Navy was a Englishman forever—regardless of birth, citizenship papers, or prior service.[34]

It is important to note that this latter belief was the established policy of his subordinates until the case of Richard Dickens in early 1807. Dickens was an American sailor aboard Captain John E. Douglas's flagship *Bellona* off Norfolk. He was forcibly detained from returning to his own country. When the American government learned of Douglas's refusal to release him unless ordered to by Berkeley, who also declined, Secretary of State James Madison lodged a "vehement" protest with David Erskine, British minister to the United States. The result was that on April 27, Berkeley received an order from the Admiralty stating that the sailor in question was to be returned. He was further requested "to acquaint Captain Douglas that he was incorrect in

[32] Bernard Mayo, *Henry Clay: Spokesman of the New West* (Boston, 1937), p. 462n.

[33] A realistic and sensible picture of the sensitivity on the part of Americans in general is painted by Allen, p. 281.

[34] This position was never officially sanctioned by the English government at any time (ibid., p. 336).

refusing . . . to discharge an American Citizen named Dickens from the *Bellona*, on plea that he had entered voluntarily on board another British Ship and had afterwards accepted the Bounty." [35] This order was the first instance of the Admiralty's acknowledgment that United States citizens, despite having shared in the bounty, were not subject to the restrictions of British sailors.

This principle bears heavily on the first of two groups of desertions, involving ten men, that occurred in the Chesapeake area during the five months before the departure of the U.S.S. *Chesapeake* in June 1807. In late February, near Hampton Roads, five crew members of H.M.S. *Melampus* seized the gig while the ship's officers were engaged in merriment and made their way ashore under a belated hail of musketry.[36] Three of the malcontents— William Ware, Daniel Martin, and John Strachan—were Americans. Subsequent British testimony revealed that the first two had joined voluntarily and the last-named, after being impressed, joined with the others in participating in the bounty.[37]

At once the venerable British consul at Norfolk, John Hamilton —who despite his loyalty to England during the Revolution was beloved by the local populace—sought the return of these three from American authorities. The commanding officer of the area, colorful Captain Stephen Decatur, referred Hamilton to the recruiting officer of the *Chesapeake*, then fitting out at the Roads. This young officer, Lieutenant Arthur Sinclair, stated that only a civil magistrate could force his cooperation. The persistent Ham-

---

[35] Berkeley to Marsden, Feb. 2, 1807, and Marsden to Berkeley, March 10, 1807, FO 5/55.

[36] Commodore James Barron to the Hon. Robert Smith, April 7, 1807, quoted in John C. Emerson, *The Chesapeake Affair of 1807* (Portsmouth, Va., 1954), p. 7.

[37] Though it has never been established whether the three were born in America, all, from at least childhood, grew up in American houses as American citizens. Ware, who claimed Pipe Creek, Maryland, as his birthplace, was half Indian. Martin was a mulatto, and Strachan, white (ibid.; Erskine to George Canning, Sept. 1, 1807, FO 5/52; statement of Captain Crafts, in Norfolk *Gazette and Public Ledger*, Sept. 2, 1807, who had the three men as crewmen on his brig *Neptune* in 1805). Even Madison admitted there was a question of whether the involved men were pressed or enlisted voluntarily, and that one had probably not been born in America. Yet he insisted, correctly, that all were American citizens and no British deserters would be enlisted in American armed forces as stated by longtime standing orders of both the secretary of war and the secretary of the navy (Madison to Erskine, Aug. 21, 1807, and Erskine to Canning, Sept. 1 and Oct. 5, 1807, FO 5/52).

ilton then applied to his friend, Thomas Parker, the mayor of Norfolk.[38] In turn Mayor Parker sought advice from the distinguished Virginia jurist and legislator, Littleton Waller Tazewell. In a lengthy decision Tazewell ruled that there was no provision for delivering up escaped nationals, although the state did have a statute enabling magistrates to apprehend deserters from merchant vessels. Hamilton thought the answer satisfactory and was further reassured by the return of two merchant seamen, for whom he had applied during these negotiations, to their mother ship the *Herald*. The consul informed Berkeley of the reasonableness of the American position. He noted that it was Tazewell who had introduced legislation into the Virginia assembly of 1805 making it possible for masters of British freighters to recapture escaped crewmen. The United States had not yet enacted any national law regarding seamen of foreign vessels.[39]

The matter might temporarily have rested there. However, the thorough-going British consul also forwarded a report to Erskine, saying he believed all five men from the *Melampus* were aboard the *Chesapeake*, then fitting out at Norfolk. Secretary Madison at first gave Erskine the stock reply that no treaty article covering the return of deserters existed between the two countries.[40] Then the secretary of state questioned Commodore James Barron, just arrived in Norfolk before taking command of the *Chesapeake* and proceeding to his new post as commander of American forces in the Mediterranean. Barron replied that he was aware of the navy's rule against enlisting foreign citizens aboard United States warships. He added that Martin, Strachan, and Ware were among the *Chesapeake*'s complement, that they had served aboard the *Melampus*, but that they were Americans. Madison apprised Erskine of these facts, and the matter was dropped.[41]

During these diplomatic exchanges, another five men escaped from the British navy to Sewell's Point, at Hampton Roads. Henry Saunders, Jenkin Ratford, Richard Herbert, George North, and William Hill overcame a petty officer accompanying them on a work detail and fled the sloop *Halifax*. Their former commander reported that the last-named three had joined the crew of the *Chesapeake*.[42] Ironically, only one of the five had done so, a British

[38] Hamilton to Berkeley, March 21, 1807, Adm 1/497.

[39] Parker to Hamilton, March 10, 1807, Hamilton to Berkeley, March 21, 1807, Adm 1/497.

[40] Erskine to Canning, July 17, 1807, FO 5/52.

[41] Barron to Robert Smith, April 7, 1807, quoted in Emerson, p. 7.

[42] Captain Townsend to Berkeley, March 7, 1807, Adm 1/497.

subject, Ratford, who enlisted under the alias of John Wilson, unknown to Commodore Barron.[43]

As reports of the desertions reached Berkeley at his Bermuda winter headquarters, the admiral waxed much warmer than the mild weather. Indignantly he informed the Admiralty of these two group desertions. In periodic outbursts he constantly deplored with incredulity the "insolence" of American authorities, the "lofty" language of the secretary of state, and the other "indignities" at United States ports that reflected on the British flag and honor. Soon his temper appeared to overcome his better judgment. On March 23, the American station commander angrily reported: "I am sorry to say that according to the best intelligence I can procure above 10,000 English Seamen . . . are at present employed in the Service of the Americans." The reasons offered by Berkeley for desertion seem more accurate than the figures produced. He observed, "The higher wages given both in their Men of War and trading ships cannot be withstood by the Men, and the open and avowed protection given to them certainly requires some explanation from the American Government, as the answer given to all demands from us is that the Treaties with Great Britain contain no Article which can authorize the demand from us, or Compliance from them." [44]

The vituperative admiral vehemently recommended a more vigorous policy toward the United States against such losses of manpower. At the same time Erskine was repeatedly urging upon his government a clause in the proposed treaty between the two nations which dealt with "Seamen who desert from His Majesty's Ships of War." He observed that it was of great importance, not necessarily because of the number who deserted, but in order to remove the ever-present temptation to desert.[45] Certainly it seems that the constant threat of desertion rather than the number of men lost from His Majesty's Navy was the more worrisome item.

In addition practically every report or letter from a junior officer who visited an American seaport contained some reference to the galling experience of encountering a sailor formerly in the English navy. Significantly, when such men were repossessed or reimpressed by the British, they were charged not only with "Desertion and Mutiny" but also with "Contempt." Typical was one chagrined English captain's report of a visit to Norfolk, where he

---

[43] As quoted in Emerson, p. 113.
[44] Berkeley to Marsden, March 23, 1807, Adm 1/497.
[45] Erskine to Howick, April 22, 1807, FO 5/52.

met a former crewman parading under the American flag. The latter greeted Captain James Townsend with a "contemptuous gesture" and the assertion that he was now "in the Land of Liberty." [46] Emotion-provoking scenes could hardly be endured with complacency by the rulers of the sea, and they certainly increased the British navy's reluctance to compromise.

Such accounts soon had a telling effect on Berkeley. Early in 1807 intelligence reports, particularly those relating to the forthcoming departure of the United States frigate *Chesapeake*, had begun to rile him considerably. First dispatches from his junior officers of Norfolk assured him that three of the men who had escaped from the *Halifax* and some of the deserters from the *Melampus* had enlisted aboard the American vessel. On March 24, Captain Townsend reported from the *Halifax* that "there are from information 35 Englishmen aboard the *Chesapeake*." As reports continued to come in, the number of British deserters alleged to be aboard the *Chesapeake* mounted. By April 28 Berkeley confidently advised the Admiralty that the *Chesapeake*'s crew was "composed chiefly of Deserters from our Ships." [47]

These inaccurate protests and allegations, along with such sweeping estimates that over "10,000 English Seamen" were in the Americans' service, came at a critical time, for the unhappy admiral's correspondence was invariably taken to Foreign Minister Canning upon arrival.[48] It was just at this serious juncture that William Pinkney and James Madison were laboring dilligently to negotiate a treaty between the two countries which would redress American maritime grievances. George Canning, with the North Atlantic background as painted by Admiral Berkeley, could hardly have been sympathetic to American protests. This in part explains his vacillations during the drawn-out negotiations, which ended in failure.[49]

On May 4, after firing home one of his typically descriptive protests to the Admiralty and Canning, the ruffled Berkeley left his winter headquarters at Bermuda.[50] He sailed northward for

[46] Court-martial of John Wilson, alias Jenkin Ratford, Aug. 28, 1807, Adm 1/497.

[47] Berkeley to Marsden, March 23, 1807, Capt. Townsend to Berkeley, March 7, 1807, and March 24, 1807, Berkeley to Marsden, April 28, 1807, Adm 1/497.

[48] Berkeley to Marsden, March 23, 1807, Adm 1/497.

[49] All the communiqués that dealt with the number of deserters, as reported by Berkeley, had notations by Admiralty officials to place the reports before Canning at once.

[50] Entry of May 4, 1807, Logbook of the *Leopard*, Adm 51/1702.

Halifax aboard the *Leopard*, commanded by his confidant and old friend, Captain S. P. Humphreys, whom Berkeley had hand-picked to skipper this vessel, his flagship. On their ten-day voyage to Halifax the two officers must have spent hours discussing their irritations with the Americans. Within a fortnight of the arrival of the fifty-gun cruiser at the summer command post, news of another, even more grievous "hostile act" reached their ears.[51]

The incident had occurred on May 2 when H.M.S. *Driver*, commanded by Captain Love, anchored in the Charleston, S.C., harbor for supplies. This was one of the three English warships forbidden to enter United States waters by the president's proclamation of the preceding year after the *Leander* affair. The sloop's appearance created an uproar in the sensitive and proud seaboard city. Charlestonians had long chafed at the ineffectual measures taken by the president to arrest British maritime abuses. Now, at the sight of one of the banned participants, they rioted. The United States port officer there, Michael Kaltersen, felt compelled to notify the British ship that it had twenty-four hours' grace in which to depart; otherwise the harbor batteries would be brought into action. The *Driver* protested but shortly sailed from Charleston Bay.[52]

For George Berkeley this proved to be the last straw. "Such an aggression," as he called it, was not to be endured without retaliation. When news of the Charleston incident reached him on May 31, the admiral immediately dashed off an indignant letter to the Admiralty. He included no indication of the action he planned to take. There was only the hint that previously he had used threats of force in a letter shown by Erskine to Madison which had "produced a sort of conciliatory message from the Secretary." [53]

The next day Berkeley issued his historic order requiring his ships at sea, upon meeting the United States frigate *Chesapeake*, to search her for deserters from seven ships (named in the margin) "according to the custom and usage of civilized nations, on terms of amity with each other." Thus the North Atlantic commander was claiming a right never assumed by the Admiralty— the right to search the national ships of neutrals. The credulity of Admiral Berkeley asserted itself once more. His search order spoke of the "many seamen" who had deserted from the listed ships of his command and "entered on board the U.S.S. *Chesapeake*." Confident that the haul would be great, he did not list H.M.S.

---

[51] Berkeley to Marsden, May 31, 1807, Adm 1/497.
[52] Charleston *Peoples Friend and Daily Advertizer*, May 12, 1807.
[53] Berkeley to Marsden, May 31, 1807, Adm 1/497.

Melampus in his order. He know from Erskine of his shaky claim to the three American citizens.[54]

Within ten days the *Leopard* was making her way from Halifax to the Virginia bay. As she sailed southward she performed the menacing procedure, practically discontinued after Trafalgar, of exercising her "great guns."[55] She also delayed long enough en route to impress from the first American ship encountered, thus filling out her complement.[56] The commanding officer was still Berkeley's friend and favorite, Captain Humphreys, who had spent the past forty-five days with his admiral. Humphreys had been present when the order of June 1 was drawn up, and he certainly knew the letter and intent of that document. Ironically, the ship arrived off Hampton Roads only hours before the *Chesapeake*'s departure.[57]

This background of events, threatening a calamitous setback to Anglo-American relations, was influenced by many diverse factors. The Napoleonic Wars and the ensuing necessity for strong maritime measures by the English navy perhaps constituted the most obvious roadblock to amicable relations between the two countries. American public opinion had been fanned to a potentially inflammatory degree by the number, severity, and proximity of England's wartime practices along the United States seaboard. The stage was set for a national explosion.

Admiral Berkeley triggered just such a tragedy when he penned his order of June 1, 1807. His influential alliance of friends and relatives had placed him on the seething North Atlantic seaboard. The all-powerful Admiralty had refused to allow the government to act in any manner that was not consistent with Berkeley's interpretation and illustration of events in the Atlantic. The admiral's own personality—particularly his impetuosity, credulity, and bumptiousness—compelled him to act in a manner offensive to all Americans. In ordering what he considered retaliatory action, he attempted to uphold a position previously and later considered untenable by the English government. The result was the tragic *Chesapeake-Leopard* affair.

---

[54] Berkeley to the respective captains and commanders of His Majesty's ships and vessels on the North American Station, June 1, 1807, Adm 1/497.

[55] Entries of June 11 and 15, 1807, Logbook of the *Leopard*, Adm 51/1702.

[56] Entry of June 14, 1807, ibid.   [57] Entry of June 21, 1807, ibid.

6 William Lowndes and the Tariff:
Common-Sense Nationalism

Carl J. Vipperman

WHEN the first session of the Fourteenth Congress met in December 1815, its members faced the difficult task of providing solutions to profound national problems. Three years of war and the few months of peace since had shown that the most critical problems concerned bad currency, bad roads, and infant American industries. These industries had been nourished by embargo and war only to be exposed to the cutthroat competition of British merchants now dumping their goods on the American market. A national bank and a system of internal improvements were looked upon as remedies to correct the problems of currency, communications, and transportation; and Congress was expected to recommend protective tariffs to preserve the industries that the war had fostered.[1]

Representative William Lowndes, member of the slaveholding, rice-planting aristocracy of South Carolina and prominent War Hawk congressman since 1811, received the first important appointment of his career this session when he was named chairman of the powerful Committee of Ways and Means. By virtue of this appointment Lowndes became primarily responsible for the nation's revenue program, which since 1789 had depended principally on import duties. Named to Ways and Means with Lowndes were James Burwell of Virginia, John W. Taylor of New York, Jonathan Moseley of Connecticut, Thomas B. Robertson of Louisiana, Samuel D. Ingham of Pennsylvania, and William Gaston of North Carolina. The committee was thus made up "with a strong majority of protectionists, but not with a majority of strong protectionists." [2]

Historians who have concerned themselves with Lowndes's

[1] On Feb. 23, 1815, the House had resolved that the secretary of the Treasury be directed to report to Congress at the next session a proposed tariff of duties for their consideration (*American State Papers: Finance*, III, 85. The secretary's report with the recommended schedule of rates follows, ibid., pp. 85–95).

[2] Edward Stanwood, *American Tariff Controversies of the Nineteenth Century* (2 vols., Boston and New York, 1903), I, 139.

views on tariff protection are not in complete agreement. Edward Stanwood in his study of American tariff controversies has stated that Lowndes "accepted fully and frankly the principle of protection."[3] More recently, Norris W. Preyer has suggested on the contrary that Lowndes harbored a hostility toward manufacturing but supported a protective tariff primarily out of considerations of national defense.[4] William W. Freehling reiterates Preyer's thesis as to the basic motive of Lowndes's qualified nationalism, adding that the duties of 1816, "while designed to be protective, were actually too low to protect."[5] Perhaps a closer look at Lowndes's handling of the Tariff of 1816 and his reaction to the effort to increase the rates in 1820 will help to clarify his views on the subject.

In formulating the revenue program in 1816, the Committee of Ways and Means generally followed the outline and schedule of rates suggested in the annual report of the secretary of the Treasury, Alexander Dallas. The report showed that under the permanent laws already in force, the Treasury Department anticipated a net annual revenue of $25,278,840; the changes recommended by the secretary were expected to yield an additional $90,660. Estimated annual civil, diplomatic, military, naval and miscellaneous expenses amounted to $9,628,669, to which would be added $6,150,000 representing the interest on the national debt (which stood at $120 million), bringing the ordinary annual expense of operating the government in 1816 to $15,778,669.[6]

Dallas's report also contained, along with a suggested schedule of import duties, an explanation of how the rates of duties in the suggested schedule had been determined: "The amount of duties should be such as will enable the manufacturer to meet the importer in the American market upon equal terms of profit and loss. There still, however, remains a diversity of opinion as to the amount which will be competent, and the aim of this report will be to strike the medium which appears to be best established from all the information which has been collected."[7] Clearly, adequate

[3] Ibid.

[4] Preyer, "Southern Support of the Tariff of 1816—A Reappraisal," *Journal of Southern History*, 25 (Aug. 1959): 306–7. See also Charles M. Wiltse, *John C. Calhoun, Nationalist, 1782–1828* (New York, 1944), pp. 104, 124.

[5] Freehling, *Prelude to Civil War, The Nullification Controversy in South Carolina, 1816–1836* (New York and Evanston, Ill., 1968), p. 95.

[6] U.S., Congress, *Annals of Congress*, 14th Cong., 1st sess., p. 518.

[7] Ibid., 16th Cong., 1st sess., p. 2127; *American State Papers: Finance*, III, 85–95.

protection of American manufactures meant to Secretary Dallas a schedule of rates high enough to negate the importer's advantage over his American competitor. Equally clear, and even more important, is the fact that Dallas did not intend the rates to be high enough to give the American manufacturer an advantage over the importer. Lowndes emphasized this concept in the debates; he always maintained that to give any clear advantage to the American manufacturer would place at a corresponding disadvantage those portions of the population engaged in commerce and agriculture, branches of American industry that he considered as important, if not more so, than manufactures.

Another fact of no small significance, and one which demonstrates the fundamental consistency of Lowndes's position respecting the tarriff, is that the rates suggested by Secretary Dallas and those advocated by Chairman Lowndes were based on solid information. Subjoined to the secretary's report in voluminous tabular detail—actually more than Lowndes would have required—was substantially "all the information in respect to the state of [American] manufactories in 1816." [8] Minute examination and careful analysis of such information was meat and drink to Lowndes. Midway through the session, committee member Thomas Robertson of Louisiana declared that the chairman had become "better acquainted with the fiscal concerns of the nation than any member of this House." [9] An acute observer of the Washington scene stated that Lowndes had "discovered a very general, profound and extensive knowledge of finance; a subject in itself dry and difficult, and to which very few citizens of this country have devoted much of their leisure. To Mr. Lowndes, however, it appears to be a branch of political science peculiarly pleasing, and to which he is much devoted both from inclination and habit." [10] These observations underscore the fact that Lowndes's judgment on the rates of impost that would offer adequate protection to domestic manufactures in 1816 rested on his mastery of an immense body of pertinent factual detail on the subject.

The Ways and Means report, "from the polished pen of Mr. Lowndes," was introduced by the chairman on Tuesday, January 9, 1816. Twelve resolutions that closed the report embraced two

[8] *Annals of Congress*, 16th Cong., 1st sess., p. 2127.

[9] Ibid., 14th Cong., 1st sess., p. 1261.

[10] George Watterson, *Letters from Washington* (Washington, D.C., 1818), p. 96. The author was Librarian of Congress (Samuel F. Bemis, *John Quincy Adams and the Foundations of American Foreign Policy* [New York, 1949], p. 253).

principal objectives: to improve the nation's financial condition while maintaining sufficient military might to guard against the possibility of foreign aggression and to provide for the rapid extinguishment of the national debt.[11] Because the duties on imports were expected, as usual, to furnish the considerable revenue required to accomplish these objectives, the tenth resolution, calling for an average increase of 42 percent in import duties after June 30, 1816, commanded the greatest attention. This resolution, taken up on February 8, 1816, read: "*Resolved*, That it is expedient to amend the rates of duties upon imported articles, after the 30th of June next, as that they shall be estimated to produce an amount equal to that which would be produced by an average addition of 42 percent to the permanent rates of duties."[12] Agreed to without a dissenting vote, the resolution was referred back to Lowndes's committee. It spent the next twelve days fashioning a schedule of rates in the form of a bill which the chairman introduced in the House on March 20.

The rates that Lowndes introduced and advocated throughout the debates were slightly lower than those suggested by Secretary Dallas; this does not necessarily mean that the chairman of Ways and Means harbored a hostility toward manufactures. A better case could be made for Lowndes's superior ability to interpret data. Not only the chairman but a majority of the committee considered the lower schedule sufficient to the purpose: to enable the American manufacturer to meet the importer on equal terms of profit and loss.

That the reported schedule was too low to satisfy more zealous protectionists was immediately apparent. No sooner had the bill been read through than Solomon Strong of Massachusetts opened debate by moving to increase the proposed duty of 25 percent ad valorem on both imported woolen and cotton manufactures to 33⅓ percent on cottons and 28 percent on woolens.[13] Chairman Lowndes thereupon took the opportunity to present to the House a full exposition of his views. Unfortunately, the entire speech was not recorded;[14] the reporter merely noted that Lowndes spoke against the motion, "taking a clear and comprehensive view on the subject of protecting duties generally," and explained why the committee had reported smaller duties on the articles named than were recommended by the secretary of the Treasury.

[11] Washington, D.C., *Daily National Intelligencer*, Jan. 13, 1816.
[12] *Annals of Congress*, 14th Cong., 1st sess., p. 939.
[13] Ibid., p. 1234.   [14] See Stanwood, I, 142.

When Strong withdrew his motion the next day, the Speaker of the House, Henry Clay, "moved to amend the bill by increasing the duty on imported cottons from twenty-five to thirty-three and a third percent. Mr. C. made this motion, he said, to try the sense of the House as to the extent to which it was willing to go in protecting domestic manufactures—assuming that there was no difference of opinion on the propriety of such protection, but only on the degree to which encouragement should be carried." [15] Clay disagreed with the basic premise of the Ways and Means report. To Clay the purpose of protective duties, aside from producing revenue, was to stimulate the growth of domestic manufactures. For this purpose, which he took pains to identify with the national interest, the duties recommended by Ways and Means were, he said, too low. To stimulate growth in this branch of domestic industry, Clay would have raised the rates high enough to give the American manufacturer a clear advantage over his foreign competitor. Lowndes preferred his own view of protection to that of the Speaker, and restated the committee's position. His reasons were not evident in the reporter's laconic remarks: "He entered into an ample and particular defense of the system reported on the subject by the committee, when the question on Mr. Clay's motion was decided in the negative—ayes 51, nays 43." [16]

Clay was undaunted. He still favored a "thorough and decided protection by ample duties" but was willing to settle for 30 percent on cotton goods. His resolution was supported by Samuel Ingham of Pennsylvania, member of Ways and Means and among its members the chief advocate of Secretary Dallas's higher schedule. Again Lowndes defended the committee report, but a majority of the House found 30 percent an acceptable duty on cottons, and Clay's motion carried, 68 to 61.[17]

Even so, the question was far from being resolved. Discussion on the rates continued into April before the matter was settled to the satisfaction of Chairman Lowndes and a majority of the House. On March 23, Daniel Webster, having consulted with the nation's leading manufacturers of textiles, moved to set the duty on cottons at 30 percent ad valorem for two years, 25 percent for two more years, and 20 percent thereafter. Chairman Lowndes assented to the motion. Although he was satisfied that 25 or even 20 percent would give sufficient protection, he supported the motion, "persuaded that it would eventually produce a state of things which he

---

[15] *Annals of Congress*, 14th Cong., 1st sess., p. 1237.
[16] Ibid.   [17] Ibid., p. 1247.

thought most desirable." [18] With Lowndes's support, Webster's motion passed, but on April 3, when the cottons question was combined with that of woolens, the duties on both were finally fixed at 25 percent for three years and 20 percent thereafter. Lowndes, of course, voted for the reduction.

The discussions on other articles did not produce interest so high or so general as had those on textiles. But this easing of tensions did not lessen the labor of the committee chairman. Scores of resolutions were introduced to alter the rates recommended by the committee on the multitude of items to be taxed, and on almost every one Chairman Lowndes found it necessary to rise and explain a point, to clarify a misconception, to reiterate the committee's position, to defend its recommendations, quietly but firmly resisting all efforts to alter the basic purposes of the bill.

Lowndes's opinion appears to have carried great weight with his colleagues, and usually only a few words from him determined the success or failure of a proposal. Henry Southard of New Jersey proposed to increase the duty on gunpowder from six to ten cents per pound; "After a few words from Mr. Lowndes in reply . . . the motion was negatived." William Milnor of Pennsylvania moved to reduce the rate on tin plates; "Mr. Lowndes offered a few arguments in support of the duty proposed by the bill, and in opposition to the amendment; after which the motion was negatived." Isahel Stearns of Massachusetts wanted the provision regulating the duty on woolens broadened; his suggestion was approved, "being accepted by Mr. Lowndes." Ingham moved that the duty of six cents per pound on gunpowder be raised to eight cents, "which was assented to by Mr. Lowndes, and agreed to by the House." Nathaniel Ruggles of Boston would have had copper sheets included in the list of copper articles protected by a duty of four cents per pound. "This motion was supported by the mover, Mr. Milnor, Mr. Stearns, and Mr. Webster, and opposed by Mr. Lowndes; and ultimately negatived, without a division." [19] Gradually it became clear that while the views of Chairman Lowndes regarding specific rates were flexible, he intended the Tariff of 1816 to offer the American manufacturer no more than an equal opportunity in the marketplace.

Reported by the Committee of the Whole, on April 4 the amended bill was on the point of final passage when John Randolph moved to strike out the section that fixed a minimum price on imported cotton goods. This provision, recommended by Secre-

[18] Ibid., p. 1270.   [19] Ibid., pp. 1268, 1270, 1275, 1283.

tary Dallas, provided that "all cotton cloths, whose value shall be less than 25 cents per square yard, shall be taken and deemed to have cost 25 cents per square yard, and shall be charged with duty accordingly." This "minimum principle" was designed to provide protection against cottons produced by the cheap labor of India and the power looms of England.[20] Randolph followed up his motion with an attack on a tariff that would levy "an immense tax on one portion of the community to put money into the pockets of another." Samuel Ingham of Pennsylvania, an ardent protectionist, "thought the House was becoming restive and confused" and fetched in Calhoun from a committee meeting to meet the Southern Cassandra's attack.[21] Calhoun proved entirely equal to the task; the minimum principle was saved, and the tariff bill passed the House on Monday, April 8, 1816, by a vote of 88 to 54.[22]

The Tariff Act of 1816 received final approval on April 27 and went into effect on July 1 of that year. Imports dropped from a postwar high of $147 million in 1816 to $99 million the following year, then climbed again to $122 million in 1818, the last year of the postwar boom. During the same thirty-month period, the excess of imports over exports fluctuated similarly, from $65 million in 1816 down to $12 million the following year, and up again to $28 million in 1818.[23] These figures show that even in 1818, by far the best year in terms of volume of imports under this tariff, importation was down $25 million from 1816, representing a reduction of 17 percent. Combine these figures with those of 1817 and the average reduction becomes 25 percent. Even when half the total for the banner year of 1816 is included, the average annual reduction of imports under this tariff before the Panic of 1819 is still 20 percent.

Notwithstanding these statistics, historians have persisted in asserting that the duties imposed by the Tariff of 1816 were too low to protect. This may be true. The claim was repeated often enough in the debates of 1816 and 1820 to make it the most familiar protectionist refrain. But the protectionist, when challenged by doubting Thomases who represented commercial and agricultural interests, had no convincing proof. The assertions of protectionist

---

[20] F. W. Taussig, *The Tariff History of the United States* (New York, 1923), pp. 76–77. The minimum principle had originated with Francis W. Lowell, whose Boston Manufacturing Company was to derive the greatest benefit from it (Stanwood, I, 140–41).

[21] Wiltse, p. 120.

[22] *Annals of Congress*, 14th Cong., 1st sess., p. 1352.

[23] U.S., Bureau of the Census, *Historical Statistics of the United States, Colonial Times to 1857* (Washington, D.C., 1960), p. 538.

and historian alike appear to have been based on the assumption that a protective tariff is one which gives the American manufacturer a clear advantage over the importer. Although it is true that during the 1820s this came to be the commonly accepted meaning of the term, it was not so in 1816. Such a doctrine would never have been admitted by the secretary of the Treasury or the chairman of Ways and Means, the two men most responsible for the 1816 rates. If their statements on the subject can be accepted at face value, and there is no evidence to suggest that they should not be, their clear intention was to give the manufacturer no more than an equal opportunity in the American market. Lowndes always felt that the rates were sufficient for the intended purpose, and no one has yet furnished conclusive proof that he was mistaken. In short, the Tariff of 1816 was adequately protective in the sense that the term was then understood by those who wrote the law.

As was to be expected, the Tariff of 1816 satisfied few if any of the more ardent protectionists. Agitation in favor of higher protection continued after the law went into effect, and it gathered momentum during the Panic of 1819. At the same time antiprotection sentiment grew among commercial and agricultural interests, who saw themselves deriving too few of the benefits and bearing too much of the burden of import duties. These circumstances set the stage for another and more bitter quarrel over the question of protective duties.

When the issue came before the House in 1820, Southern opposition to the proposed increase in rates was virtually unanimous. Historians have assumed that this opposition grew out of the disappointment of Southern expectations that the 1816 law would promote the growth of manufactures in the South.[24] More recent scholars, notably Preyer, have proved this assumption to have been groundless. Preyer has effectively demonstrated that "it was not a desire for manufacturing, but a combination of prosperity, patriotism and promises that had swayed Southerners" in 1816.[25] None of these conditions of 1816 obtained in 1820. Prosperity had ended with the Panic of 1819; the Anglo-American rapprochement had by 1820 removed patriotism as a significant reason for encouraging

[24] Freehling, pp. 94–95, states that "this standard interpretation is based on no more than the historian's faith in economic causation." A search of the William Lowndes Papers, Southern Historical Collection, University of North Carolina, Chapel Hill, and the Lowndes Papers, Library of Congress, Washington, D.C., has revealed nothing in William Lowndes's correspondence to support the standard interpretation.

[25] Pp. 321–22.

American manufactures; and the clamor for higher duties showed all too plainly that protectionists had no intention of keeping promises made four years earlier that protective duties were a temporary expedient to offset the effect of heavy British importations.[26] Yet, in spite of the changed circumstances, the manufacturing interests based their campaign for higher rates on the old ground of national interest, which had served so well in 1816.[27]

Other circumstances that led Southerners to oppose the tariff bill of 1820 included an important change in committee structure and responsibility. When the House organized on December 8, 1819, the initiative for revising tariff laws might have been supplied either by the Committee of Ways and Means or the Committee of Commerce and Manufactures, the latter chaired by Thomas Newton of Virginia, whose antitariff views were well-known. But the House, with a protectionist majority of roughly nine to seven, disregarded the objections of Newton and divided his committee in two, creating a new Committee of Manufactures and leaving Newton in charge of the Committee of Commerce. Speaker Clay promptly staffed the new committee with protariff men headed by protectionist Henry Baldwin of Pennsylvania.[28] Baldwin later explained that it was not then clear whether his committee or the Committee of Ways and Means, responsible for revenue measures, should initiate tariff legislation.[29]

At this point the secretary of the Treasury, William H. Crawford of Georgia, threatened to frustrate the designs of protectionists when he reported against an increase in rates, expressing concern that such action might reduce imports to such a degree that the federal revenue program would be endangered.[30] The Ways and Means Committee, in apparent agreement with Secretary Crawford, took no action toward revising the tariff schedule, depending on the existing law, supplemented by loans, to meet the fiscal needs of the government.[31] Thereupon Baldwin's committee, without clear authority or instructions to do so, seized the initiative and drew up a new tariff bill. Baldwin admitted that his committee alone had drawn up the new schedule, without the assistance or cooperation of the Treasury Department and, more importantly,

[26] Ibid.   [27] *Annals of Congress*, 16th Cong., 1st sess., pp. 1916–21.
[28] Ibid., pp. 705–7.
[29] Baldwin said on April 21, 1820, that "the Committee of Manufactures was a new one; its powers and duties were undefined by any rule; the various subjects referred to them related as well to the revenue and commerce of the country, as its manufactures" (ibid., p. 1917).
[30] Ibid.   [31] Ibid.

without making any effort to investigate the general condition of manufacturing in 1820 in order to provide a systematic, rational justification for the proposed increases. Moreover, in defending the bill, Chairman Baldwin revealed that his committee intended to effect a historic change in the revenue system from a primary reliance on impost duties—a system which Baldwin pronounced a failure—to a system depending principally on internal excise taxes. In short, the bill was designed to give such a clear advantage to domestic manufactures over foreign imports that the former not only would be given ample protection but could be expected to replace the latter as the principal source of federal revenue through excise taxes.[32] Opponents of the bill could thus base their opposition on any one of the above considerations, and all of them were alluded to in the course of debate.

The Virginia delegation led the opposition in defense of agriculturalists while several representatives of commercial interests in New England voiced the objections of their constituents. It was William Lowndes, however, who made the strongest attack on the proposed tariff and delivered the "weightiest" speech against it, although his position as chairman of Foreign Affairs was much less influential regarding tariff legislation than the post he had held in 1816.

Lowndes's principal objection to the bill was the committee's failure to make a systematic examination of the relative condition of manufactures in the American economy, as his committee had done in 1816, in order to establish the necessity of the proposed increase in protective duties. Without such an inquiry, the committee could offer no rational basis for the rate of increase on specific duties. Shortly after Baldwin introduced the bill on March 22, 1820, Lowndes offered this resolution to correct the deficiency:

Resolved, That the Committee on Manufactures be instructed to report to this House such evidence as it may be in their power to present, showing the several rates of wages given, and expense of all kinds incurred in the different branches of manufacture which, in their opinion, require additional encouragement, with the prices of their product, so as to exhibit the profit which, at the present prices of subsistence, materials, and labor, and the present value of land, buildings, and machinery, may be obtained in such manufacture, skillfully and economically conducted.[33]

Lowndes was confident that such an investigation would show that all branches of the American economy alike had suffered in the

[32] Ibid., pp. 1916–21.　　[33] Ibid., pp. 1848–49.

Panic of 1819 and that the fall in wages and prices of raw materials had more than offset the depressed prices of manufactured goods. Indeed, as Preyer has shown, manufactures had been injured less by the panic and depression than other portions of the economic community, such as commerce and agriculture.[34]

Antitariff men, led by the Virginia delegation, rallied behind Lowndes, producing the first serious test of protariff strength in the House. Opponents of the Lowndes resolution, led by Baldwin, asserted that the revision of the tariff had been proposed by the Committee of Manufactures "from considerations of national policy, and not from a minute investigation of details; that the information asked was not such as a committee of this House ought to be required to give," nor had such information ever been given before.[35] Lowndes disagreed and furnished facts to prove that the bill drawn in 1816 had been based on precisely such information as he now called for.[36] Nevertheless, his resolution was defeated, 72 to 90, with the Committee of Manufactures voting unanimously against it.[37] The result drew from Lowndes the observation that the House, in rejecting his resolution, "had refused all evidence as to the proper degree of encouragement, and left the defense of the bill to the same vague considerations which would support a duty of one hundred per cent as well as one of forty. They took they knew not how much from the people; they gave they knew not how much to the manufacturer."[38]

In his major speech against the bill, delivered on April 28, 1820, toward the close of debate as was his custom, Lowndes summed up the principal objections of the opponents of the bill. Fully one third of his speech was devoted to the arbitrary and haphazard way in which the proposed increases had been determined by the committee. In elaborating this point, Lowndes asked:

Had it ever been contended, not merely that manufactures should be encouraged, but that the bounty to be given should not be limited by any determined relation to the necessity of the manufacture, or the fair profits to the manufacturer? You say that it is important to encourage the manufacture of cotton. Be it so. We know that, however it be disguised, this can only be done at the expense of other classes of society. Is it not proper to inquire what expense is necessary; what would be adequate?[39]

---

[34] P. 320.
[35] *Annals of Congress*, 16th Cong., 1st sess., pp. 1861–62.
[36] Ibid., pp. 2126–27.   [37] Ibid., pp. 1861–62.   [38] Ibid., p. 2126.
[39] Ibid., p. 2125.

He went on to explain that when duties were laid on articles not produced by domestic manufacture, the additional price paid by the community went into the public treasury; but when duties were laid on imported articles of a type produced within the country, the price of all the articles, domestic as well as imported, would rise, but only part of the additional price paid by the community would go into the public treasury, and the other part would be received by the manufacturer who produced the domestic article.

If, for instance, one hundred million of pounds of sugar were consumed annually in the United States, and three-fourths of this amount were furnished by domestic industry, an additional duty of one cent the pound would cause the consumers of sugar throughout the country to pay one million of dollars more in the price of the article, than they would otherwise do—would impose upon the people a new tax of one million; but of this sum, less than $250,000 would be received by the Government, and $750,000 by the sugar planter.[40]

Lowndes stated that the principal difference between himself and those who supported the bill was explained by this hypothetical case. In his view, if Congress determined to encourage the production of an article such as sugar by an additional bounty, then it was duty bound to inquire carefully what sum would be necessary for this object.

To justify the tax, it was necessary to determine that the nation had such an interest in the establishment of the additional sugar plantations to which the bill was expected to give rise, that it was worth its while to contribute annually seven hundred and fifty thousand dollars to their support, and that a contribution of less than seven hundred and fifty thousand dollars would not cause their establishment. If the bounty in question were greater than the value of the object justified . . . we applied the money of the country injudiciously; but if a less bounty would produce the effect which we desired, we gave it away without object and without excuse. It was in this view that he had asked the Committee of Manufactures information to show what were the duties upon foreign importation which would give to our manufacturers a reasonable profit on their capital and labor. Everything beyond this was not a liberal encouragement of manufactures, but a profuse and capricious donation of the public money.[41]

Nobody could tell for certain whether the House would be guilty of such a breach of public faith in passing the bill, for the information that could answer the question had been withheld. It is important

[40] Ibid., pp. 2125–26.   [41] Ibid., p. 2126.

to note here that not once did Lowndes question the principle of protection, but only the degree.

To this principal objection to the bill, Lowndes added several other points to counter the arguments of its advocates. He denied that the existing system of revenue based primarily on import duties had proved a failure and effectively demonstrated that a system of excise taxes, even if practicable, would be no improvement. He refuted the argument that a protective tariff such as the one proposed would benefit the agricultural community, pointing out that the prices of its products, since production always exceeded the domestic demand, were determined by the state of the world market and hence beyond the remedy of protective duties. In fact, both commerce and agriculture, he maintained, as well as every part of the manufacturing community not in competition with foreign producers, stood to be injured by the bill. They would all share in its burden without participating in its profits.

Admit that it is in our interest to manufacture articles which we could procure at cheaper rates from abroad, it must be still more to our interest to manufacture such as prove themselves adapted to our circumstances by being able to bear foreign competition. Our capital and labor are limited, and in directing the largest amounts of these into branches which require most encouragement, we really divert them from those into which they would flow with most advantage. Thus every branch of industry which is entirely safe from foreign competition . . . must be injured by the encouragement of those which draw from them their resources of capital and labor.[42]

To Lowndes the most reasonable method of imposing duties on imports in order to encourage domestic manufactures was "to lay a very small and equal duty upon all manufactures, which would leave the relative inducement to engage in each unchanged."[43]

The protectionist majority, content with its own view of what constituted a reasonable tariff, effectively countered all efforts to block the bill's passage. It passed the House by a vote of 91 to 78 on April 29, but many of its opponents found satisfaction two days later when it was defeated in the Senate by a single vote.[44] The margin of victory was too slender, however, to allow much rejoicing in the antitariff camp.

The role of William Lowndes in this four-year period best illustrates the shift in sentiment among thoughtful Southerners from

[42] For the complete text of Lowndes's speech, see ibid., pp. 2115–35; for the quotation, see ibid., p. 2118.
[43] Ibid., pp. 2123–24.   [44] Ibid., pp. 672, 2155.

support of the protective Tariff of 1816 to opposition to the Baldwin tariff bill of 1820. The significance of the tariff struggle in 1820 was apparent to most, if not all, of those who participated in it. Lowndes saw it quite clearly. The matter that most troubled his perceptive mind was not that increases had been proposed or that the term "protective duties" was taking on a new and broader meaning than he wanted to admit, but that there was a clearly discernible trend toward setting up rates which could rest on no rational basis, that there was a lack of what might well be termed common sense in framing the tariff. "What he regretted most," Lowndes said, "in the course pursued by the Committee of Manufactures, was, that they suggested no standard by which the sufficiency of the encouragement which they proposed could be tested, and promised, therefore, no limitation to the burden which might be imposed on the country." [45] The words proved prophetic. Protectionists had caught the scent, and over the next twelve years they would pursue their prey to the brink of disunion.

[45] Ibid., p. 2128.

7   Executive Leadership in the Monroe Administration

Harry Ammon

S INCE the presidency of Franklin Delano Roosevelt, historians
and political scientists have been increasingly fascinated with
both the theory and the practice of presidential leadership.[1] Most
writers, accepting the necessity of vesting vast power in one person
to achieve the political ends of the modern state, have concluded
that the "best," the "most successful," or the "ablest" presidents
were those who formulated distinct policies and at the same time
vigorously implemented their measures by persuasion, by the exploitation of public opinion, by the patronage, or by some feat of
legerdemain. Implementation here primarily refers to securing congressional approval, for there are obviously other areas and other
problems toward which executive leadership must be directed. This
view has been so widely accepted that the only presidents usually
deemed worthy of admiration or praise are those customarily
labeled "strong." Executives not fitting this pattern are neglected
and often denigrated; they seem devoid of interest, and their administrations apparently offer little to illuminate present developments. That they may have operated on an entirely different
concept of the role of the executive in the federal structure has
seemed singularly unimportant.

Consequently, among pre-Civil War presidents only Washington, Jefferson, Jackson, and Polk have been accorded anything but
passing notice. Washington, other considerations apart, has merited attention as the first incumbent in the presidency. About Jefferson there has been some ambiguity of feeling. Although it is
admitted that he subscribed to a theory of leadership limiting the
role of the executive, at the same time historians have stressed that
he exerted greater direct influence over Congress than his predecessors. Jackson, of course, is particularly favored because he
seems the ideal prototype of the modern president, unhesitatingly
impressing his will on both Congress and the Supreme Court.

The study of executive leadership during the Jeffersonian Re-

---

[1] As for example, Richard E. Neustadt, *Presidential Power: The Politics
of Leadership* (New York, 1960).

publican era is hampered by certain inherent difficulties. In the first place there was little contemporary awareness in an articulate or self-conscious way that this aspect of the presidency should be distinguished from the overall functions of the office. Neither the presidents, the politicians, nor outside observers thought specifically in these terms. The absence of a contemporary vocabulary formulating the problems of leadership makes it necessary to analyze executive conduct in relation to congressional action as the only means of understanding the practices then in use. Unfortunately it is by no means easy to fathom the inner workings of these early administrations. No one thought it necessary to record techniques of leadership or to evaluate the effect of presidential influence on Congress. Although it is possible to scrutinize in considerable detail the operations of Congress, the activities of the presidents are not so easily traced. Consequently, the interrelationship between the executive and legislative branches remains elusive.

To these general observations there is one notable exception— the administration of James Monroe, for which the voluminous diary of John Quincy Adams offers the most detailed account of the day-to-day conduct of the executive department of any presidency before that of Lincoln.[2] The Monroe administration faced a variety of problems requiring the executive to formulate policy and exert leadership. The means used by Monroe provide a unique exposition of the usages and theory of presidential leadership in the Republican era. At the same time the particular techniques that Monroe employed were influenced by changing political circumstances and bore, as well, the stamp of his personal character.[3]

[2] John Quincy Adams, *Memoirs of John Quincy Adams, Comprising Portions of His Diary from 1795 to 1848*, ed. Charles Francis Adams (12 vols., Philadelphia, 1874–77).

[3] Monroe's ability as a leader has largely been underestimated. Historians of this era have not understood that he followed Jeffersonian practice with modifications. In comparison to subsequent presidents, such as Jackson, he seems to give the impression of inactivity. However, once his concept of executive leadership is examined, he emerges in quite a different light. The harshest judgment is that of Leonard White in *The Jeffersonians: A Study in Administrative History, 1801–1829* (New York, 1951), p. 28: "Monroe not only believed that the President should allow Congress to make up its own mind in domestic matters without influence from the Chief Executive; with an occasional exception he put his theory into practice. The greatest political issue of his day was the admission of Missouri and the status of slavery in the Louisiana Territory. During all the bitter debates, he remained silent and abstained from interference in the struggle. When the bill was finally laid on his desk he asked Cabinet advice on its consti-

When Monroe entered office in 1817, he inherited a loose conglomerate of precedents and a vague body of Republican doctrine about the nature of the presidential office and his function as a leader. Within this framework he mapped out his course after making adjustments required by the changed character of American politics after the War of 1812. The Republicans, having come to power in 1801 on a wave of protest against executive domination of the government, had taken a rather simplistic view of the position and role of the president within the federal structure, depicting him as but the agent for carrying out the will of the people enunciated in Congress. The legislature was accorded (in theory at least) a central position as the source of all legislation and the proper agency to guide the destiny of the nation. Only in the realm of foreign affairs was the president recognized as possessing independent authority, subject, however, to strict constitutional limitations. This was the theory, but as has often been noted, Jefferson exerted a more powerful influence over Congress than his Federalist predecessors. Apart from having his messages read by a clerk, it cannot be said that Jefferson remained in the remote sphere defined by Republican theory. On the contrary, he actively directed affairs through the agency of congressmen who functioned as recognized (if unofficial) spokesmen for the administration. In the deployment of his congressional forces, Jefferson had the inestimable advantage of a highly unified party, although not organized in the modern sense. In the first decade of the nineteenth century, the Republicans were not so much bound together by a common set of principles as by the fervor generated during the long contest against the Federalists; their strongest link was a vivid fear that if they did not preserve a solid front, their opponents would return to power. Consequently, Jefferson was able to carry out widely unpopular measures, such as the embargo, and, on occasion, by secret

---

tutionality and eventually gave it his signature. His course of action was perhaps politically wise, perhaps politically inevitable, but it abdicated leadership." More recently James Sterling Young, *The Washington Community, 1800–1828* (New York, 1966), p. 187, asserted that Monroe's record was "barren of any evidence of executive leadership." George Dangerfield expressed much the same view in his *Era of Good Feelings* (New York, 1952), pp. 97, 188, 326, but modified his conclusions slightly in his more recent *Awakening of American Nationalism* (New York, 1965), p. 22. One of the few writers to accord Monroe some positive merit as a leader is Stuart Gerry Brown, *The American Presidency: Leadership, Partisanship, Popularity* (New York, 1966), pp. 7–12, 70–74, 230. See also Harry Ammon, *James Monroe: The Quest for National Identity* (New York, 1971).

instructions secure the enactment of measures contrary to policy outlined in his public declarations. Jefferson also reinforced party loyalty by exerting his considerable personal charm at the numerous White House functions at which loyal Republicans were welcomed. In addition, he utilized the congressional contacts that his cabinet members enjoyed. His task of leadership was much simplified by the high turnover (over 50 percent) in House membership every two years, which prevented the evolution of rival leadership groups within Congress. To a great extent the legislature was dependent upon the executive for guidance on specific measures.[4]

Madison, who hewed to the line mapped out by Jefferson, met with less success. Internal divisions within the party and the resurgence of Federalism narrowed his margin of support in Congress. Moreover, he never enjoyed Jefferson's popularity with the rank and file of the party, many of whom could not convince themselves that the author of the *Federalist* papers was a fountainhead of pure Republican principles. In 1810, when his administration seemed on the verge of collapse, he reestablished firmer executive leadership by replacing Secretary of State Robert Smith, universally condemned as incompetent, with James Monroe. This appointment antagonized the "invisibles" in the Senate, but the administration was strengthened through Monroe's ability to establish a successful liaison with a rising group of Republican leaders, best known as War Hawks. This new rapport with Congress gave Madison's policies a much firmer outline in the six months preceding the declaration of war.[5]

The background provided by his experience in the Madison cabinet and his familiarity with Republican attitudes toward the presidency shaped Monroe's conduct while in office. He never doubted the responsibility of the president to provide leadership, but he was aware that he was expected to remain within the limits imposed upon him by the Constitution and by existing usages. He considered it a great disadvantage that the president, unlike the British cabinet, could not call upon official spokesmen in the legislature to explain policies and reply to critics but instead had to rely upon the services of congressmen who volunteered to defend the administration. To overcome this handicap, Monroe frequently used his annual messages to anticipate objections to administration

    [4] White, pp. 45–59; Young, pp. 90, 128–30, 163–78.
    [5] On Madison's leadership, see Roger H. Brown, *The Republic in Peril* (New York, 1964).

measures.[6] For this reason, he customarily included lengthy passages favorable to the Latin American insurgents. Adams, who never relished such phrases of sweeping approval to the cause of liberty in South America, nonetheless had to admit that the president's statements were highly effective in warding off Clay's efforts to force congressional action in favor of recognition, contrary to administration wishes. These public avowals of sympathy for the revolutionary cause made it impossible for the advocates of recognition to accuse the president of indifference to the cause of independence in Latin America.[7]

Monroe was quite aware that failure to supply executive leadership might jeopardize administration policy. In 1819, when Spain failed to ratify the treaty negotiated earlier in the year, Monroe was uncertain whether to advocate immediate occupation of Florida or to announce that he considered the treaty valid but was willing to defer occupation until Spain had time to reconsider her action. He unhesitatingly ruled out the suggestion that he make no recommendation to Congress, for this would lead to no action whatsoever, which in his opinion had happened all too frequently during the Madison administration. On such matters, he told Adams, Congress expected the executive to show the way.[8]

In his dealings with Congress, Monroe had to be very cautious, for the members, who accepted the theory of legislative supremacy, were hypersensitive about executive interference, particularly in domestic concerns. Any overt step taken by the president was likely to raise cries of executive meddling, to the detriment of presidential programs. Of this peculiar sensitivity, Monroe had a most unpleasant experience early in his first term. In his annual message of 1817, the president included a passage expressing the opinion that since the Constitution did not specifically grant Congress the power to authorize federal construction of internal improvements, it should be so amended. In this pronouncement, Monroe was honoring the Constitutional tenets of both Jefferson and Madison. On two occasions, but in less precise terms, Madison had also expressed doubts concerning the constitutionality of federal internal improvements. These publicly stated reservations, however, had not prevented congressional enactment early in 1817 of a bill allocating the bonus paid by the Bank of the United States for its charter (and future dividends from government-owned stock) for the pur-

---

[6] Adams, *Memoirs*, IV, 457 (Nov. 29, 1819).

[7] Ibid., V, 199–200 (Nov. 12, 1820).

[8] Ibid., IV, 450–53 (Nov. 27, 1819).

pose of internal improvements. Most congressmen were stunned when Madison vetoed this bill just before he left office. Either they had not attached such a narrow interpretation to his comments, or they had been persuaded that congressional action would be sufficient to convince the president that his views were erroneous. Moreover, since Jefferson and Madison had signed bills for the construction of the Cumberland Road, there seemed no valid reason why this measure should not be approved.

Although Monroe considered the construction of a nationally planned system of roads and canals essential for the full development of the resources of the country, loyalty to the views of his predecessors as well as private conviction led him to reiterate Madison's constitutional objections in his first annual message. He deemed it only just that these views should be stated to Congress at the beginning of his administration in order to expedite the process of amending the Constitution.[9] To his dismay, not only was his advice ignored, but he was harshly assailed for attempting to restrict the freedom of the legislature by telling it in advance what it could not do. The sharpest comments on his behavior came from Speaker Henry Clay, who informed the House:

The Constitutional order of legislation supposes that every bill originating in one House shall there be deliberately investigated, without influence from any other branch of the legislature, . . . and be remitted to the other House for a free and unbiassed consideration. Having passed both Houses, it is to be laid before the President—signed if approved, and if disapproved to be returned, with his objections to the originating House. In this manner, entire freedom of thought and action is secured, and the President finally sees the proposition in the most matured form which Congress can give to it. The practical effect, to say no more, of forestalling the legislative opinion, and telling us what we may or may not do, will be to deprive the President himself of the opportunity of considering a project so matured and us the benefit of his reasoning, applied specifically to such propositions; for the Constitution further enjoins it upon him to state his objections upon returning the bill.[10]

Monroe, who above all was scrupulous in his observance of the Constitution, was angered by these suggestions of improper con-

[9] For a detailed account of this complex issue in the Monroe administration, see Joseph H. Harrison, Jr., "The Internal Improvement Issue in the Politics of the Union, 1783–1825" (Ph.D. diss., University of Virginia, 1954).

[10] U.S., Congress, *Annals of Congress*, 15th Cong., 1st sess., Mar. 13, 1818, p. 1373.

duct.[11] For all his outward amiability, he was not one to give up easily where fundamental issues were involved. Convinced that it was entirely proper for the executive to voice opinions on such vital matters, he drafted a lengthy essay expounding his views on internal improvements. He originally planned to append it to his third annual message in 1819, taking advantage of the technicality that the new Congress then assembling would not be familiar with his views. In spite of the importance he attached to the question, he held it back, yielding to the arguments of his cabinet, who reminded him of the irritation his statement had produced in 1817; they could see no reason why his conclusions should now meet a friendlier reception. Moreover, they felt it quite unlikely that Congress would propose an amendment such as Monroe advocated. The opportune moment to present the essay did not come until 1822, when Congress enacted a bill providing for the collection of tolls to keep the Cumberland Road in repair. Monroe vetoed the measure without consulting his cabinet. He then transmitted his essay to explain his action.[12] The president's effort to guide Congress in the direction of an amendment authorizing internal improvements not only was one of the most notable failures in his exercise of legislative leadership but it also demonstrated the perils of a frontal approach to Congress on domestic issues.

In exercising leadership, Monroe was denied one principal advantage enjoyed by his Republican predecessors—party loyalty. So ardently did the Federalists embrace him after the War of 1812, and so great was his own conviction of the wisdom of inaugurating an era free from party conflict, that he could not rally the Republicans to the side of the administration by raising the specter of Federalist power.[13] From the moment that Monroe adopted as his

[11] Monroe to Madison, Dec. 22, 1817, April 28, 1818, in James Monroe, *The Writings of James Monroe*, ed. Stanislaus M. Hamilton (7 vols., New York, 1898–1903), VI, 46, 49; Adams, *Memoirs*, IV, 70 (March 28, 1818). In his efforts to reconcile the fact that his predecessors had signed bills extending the Cumberland Road, Monroe received little comfort from Madison, who confessed that these earlier bills had probably been signed "doubtingly or hastily" without sufficient reflection (Madison to Monroe, Dec. 27, 1817, in James Madison, *The Writings of James Madison*, ed. Gaillard Hunt [9 vols., New York, 1900–1910], VIII, 430–37).

[12] Adams, *Memoirs*, IV, 462–63 (Dec. 2, 1819); *A Compilation of the Messages and Papers of the Presidents*, ed. James Daniel Richardson (10 vols., Washington, D.C., 1908), II, 142–83.

[13] As early as March 12, 1817, Crawford observed in a letter to Albert Gallatin that Federalist approval of Monroe was a prime factor in loosening the old party ties (Gallatin Papers, New-York Historical Society, New York City).

guiding principle the maxim that he was not the "leader of a party, but the head of a nation," he repudiated, for all practical purposes, party solidarity as a means of carrying his programs into effect.[14] In establishing viable substitutes for party loyalty, Monroe did not move outside the path established by Jefferson and Madison. Thus he made no effort to exploit the patronage or to use his personal popularity by appealing to the people over recalcitrant legislators. Monroe, like his predecessors, made many appointments from congressional ranks, but these selections do not seem to have been coordinated to any significant degree with presidential policies. Monroe deplored the custom, but he considered it too well entrenched to abandon without unnecessarily offending the members of Congress, who had come to expect such advancement.[15]

During his tour of the nation begun in New England in 1817 and continued in the South and West in 1819, Monroe had within his grasp a unique opportunity to assert leadership by capitalizing on his undoubted personal popularity, but he completely rejected this possibility. His tour, like the less extensive one undertaken by President Washington, was intended to give all segments of the nation an opportunity to affirm their loyalty to the Union. Above all, he hoped to provide a suitable occasion for a reconciliation between the Federalists and the Republicans. Throughout his journey, Monroe carefully avoided references to current issues. He responded to the endless public addresses with vague phrases affirming the necessity of preserving republican institutions as the best guarantee of liberty and extolling the revolutionary heritage of the nation. Whenever attempts were made to draw him out on specific issues, he resorted to generalities. He saw himself not as a personal hero but as the embodiment of a national ideal. "He made himself," as Stuart Gerry Brown has commented, "personally known, thereby touching new generations with something of the glamor of the revolutionary age. They had seen and heard one of the Founding Fathers, not the less affecting because he was the last to hold the Presidency." [16] This was indeed the proper role for a leader whose carriage bore the motto *Principia non homines*.[17]

Unwilling to seek new methods of legislative management, Monroe adapted existing practices to his needs. Like his predecessors he relied heavily upon personal contact with congressmen, not so much seeking them out as making himself constantly available.

[14] Quote is from Jonathan Roberts to Nicholas Biddle, Jan. 30, 1817, Biddle Papers, Library of Congress, Washington, D.C. Monroe repeated this phrase to many others.

[15] Adams, *Memoirs*, IV, 72 (April 4, 1818).　　　[16] P. 12.

[17] Philadelphia *Aurora*, April 4, 1818.

Every day he received a stream of callers at the White House, greeting them informally in his office. At the constant succession of White House dinner parties and at the regular evening receptions, the president's warmth, courtesy, and simplicity of manner won him many friends. In dealing with Congress on certain highly technical matters, such as questions involving colonial trade, the executive enjoyed the considerable advantage of possessing detailed information. Without permanent staff members and with a constantly changing membership, congressional committees had no choice but to turn to the executive.[18] From time to time, individual members (most frequently committee chairmen) undertook to defend administration measures. Unfortunately such support could not be depended upon. In a body proud of its independent role, congressmen often went to great lengths to avoid the imputation of being executive spokesmen by opposing administration measures for no other reason than to prove their independence. Thus in the spring of 1818 Congressman John Forsyth of Georgia, chairman of the House Committee on Foreign Relations, after ardently upholding the president's program earlier in the session suddenly sponsored a resolution contrary to Monroe's wishes authorizing the occupation of Florida. At the president's request, William H. Crawford, the secretary of the Treasury, who was on intimate terms with Forsyth, went to see the congressman. Although unable to persuade his fellow Georgian to drop the resolution, Crawford brought back the agreeable news that it would not be endorsed by the committee.[19]

Adams's explanation of Forsyth's aberrant behavior was undoubtedly not far from the mark. On March 22, he recorded in his journal:

The Chairman of the Committee of Foreign Relations has always been considered as a member in the confidence of the Executive, and Mr. Forsyth acted thus at the last session. The President has hitherto con-

[18] See comments on this point in Adams, *Memoirs*, IV, 31, 212 (Dec. 26, 1817, Jan. 6, 1819). White, pp. 101–6, comments on the evolution of the committee system. One of the most notable examples of complete dependence on executive leadership was in connection with the West Indian trade. The House Committee on Commerce relied entirely on the executive for the framing of the various restrictive measures (known as Navigation Acts) intended to force Britain to open the West Indian trade to American merchants (Adams, *Memoirs*, IV, 495–504 [Jan. 3–13, 1820], V, 519 [May 7, 1822], and F. Lee Benns, *The American Struggle for the British West Indian Carrying Trade*, Indiana University Studies, X, no. 6 [Bloomington, 1923]).

[19] Adams, *Memoirs*, IV, 66–70 (March 18–28, 1818); Crawford to Monroe, March 22, 1818, Monroe Papers, Lib. Cong.

sidered him as perfectly confidential, and directed me to communicate freely to him the documents concerning foreign afairs. . . . Early in the course of the session of Congress I observed a paragraph circulating in the newspapers, intimating that the Chairman of the Committee of Foreign Relations was destined to a mission abroad, and Prussia was specially named as the Court to which he would be accredited. Mr. Clay, who has been marshalling his forces for a system of regular opposition to Mr. Monroe's administration in sneering hints and innuendoes, had been continually stinging Forsyth, as if he were a dependent tool of the Executive. Forsyth is a man of mild, amiable disposition and good talents, but neither by weight of character, force of genius, nor keenness of spirit at all able to cope with Clay. He has suffered himself to be goaded by Clay not only into disavowals of any subserviencey to the views of the Executive, and to declarations in the face of the House that he did not care a fig for the Administration or any member of it, but into the humor of proposing measures which the President utterly disapproves. From mere horror of being thought the tool of the Executive he has made himself the tool of Clay's opposition.[20]

Under Monroe the cabinet became the indispensable tool for exercising leadership. It is impossible to say whether Monroe constructed his cabinet with this eventuality in mind, but it is interesting to note that he wished to include two of the major political figures (and rivals for the succession) — William H. Crawford, to be continued as secretary of the Treasury, and Henry Clay, to serve as secretary of war. Crawford agreed, but Clay refused, for he was unwilling to serve in a lesser post than that held by his rival. Monroe would not offer the State Department to either, for he wished to disassociate that office from the presidential succession and to blunt the charge made by Northern leaders that the government was dominated by Southerners. To achieve this end he turned to John Quincy Adams, a New Englander and former Federalist, who had been long absent on a series of diplomatic missions.[21] No one, including the president, guessed that Adams would rapidly become a principal contender for the succession and acquire a formidable congressional following. Unable to find a Westerner whom he deemed qualified for the War Department, Monroe selected John C. Calhoun, who, as a member of the House, had sustained Madison's war measures. In spite of his youth, Calhoun enjoyed a substantial congressional following and was soon regarded as a major contender for the presidency. The two remaining members of the cabinet were of lesser importance. The secretary of the Navy, Benjamin Crowninshield, was a holdover

[20] Adams, *Memoirs*, IV, 65–66. Forsyth was made minister to Spain.
[21] Monroe to Jefferson, Feb. 23, 1817, Monroe, *Writings*, VI, 3.

from the Madison administration. When he departed in 1818, Monroe replaced him with Martin Van Buren's coworker in New York, Smith C. Thompson, a choice designed to improve the administration position in Congress. Attorney General William Wirt, while not commanding a specific following, was a much-admired and well-liked lawyer.[22]

The decline of party loyalty as a cohesive force in Congress made it necessary for the president to rely heavily upon his cabinet. Far more than any previous incumbent Monroe depended for the success of his measures upon the molding of a consensus within the cabinet. The innumerable cabinet sessions, so amply recorded by Adams, make this abundantly clear. The president was not driven to confer at such length by a desperate need for advice, for on most critical issues his mind was already made up, but to hammer out a common agreement and obtain a commitment to the decisions reached in the cabinet. Whether or not the secretaries actively mobilized their congressional backers, consensus was essential, for, as Monroe commented to Adams in 1819, once it was known that the cabinet was not united, then the enemies of the administration seized upon that fact and exploited it to undermine his program.[23] It is significant that Monroe avoided bringing before the cabinet issues on which he was certain that the differences of opinion were so fundamental that a consensus could not be reached. Thus he never discussed the constitutional aspects of internal improvements or the issue of the restriction of slavery in Missouri except in the most casual way. Debate on these controversial issues would have simply advertised the disharmony within the cabinet. Monroe's most notable failures in executing policies were precisely those efforts for which he did not have the united support of his department heads—obtaining an amendment authorizing federal internal improvements, preventing a large-scale reduction of defense expenditures after the Panic of 1819, and establishing a slave trade convention with Great Britain in 1824. He achieved his greatest successes on issues on which unanimity had been obtained—the endorsement of Jackson's conduct in Florida and the acceptance of the Treaty of 1819 with Spain in spite of Spanish delay in ratification.[24]

[22] Charles M. Wiltse, *John C. Calhoun: Nationalist, 1782–1828* (New York, 1944), pp. 138–41.

[23] Adams, *Memoirs*, IV, 450–53 (Nov. 27, 1819).

[24] Clay to Amos Kendall, Jan. 8, 1820, in Henry Clay, *The Papers of Henry Clay*, ed. James F. Hopkins and Mary W. M. Hargreaves (Lexington, Ky., 1959—), II, 752. Too much has been made of Clay's opposition.

Perhaps no episode so fully illustrates Monroe's methods as the controversy precipitated by Jackson's seizure of St. Marks and Pensacola during the invasion of Florida in 1818. The president first learned of Jackson's arbitrary action, not authorized by the orders issued to the general, when he was in Norfolk in June touring the fortifications of the Chesapeake area. Cutting his inspection short, Monroe hastened to the capital, but since official reports from Jackson had not yet been received, he left for his nearby estate in Loudoun County, Virginia. Adams was rather disapproving of the president's departure, which struck him as procrastination in the face of the "rapidly thickening" storm of public denunciation of Jackson's behavior. There was nothing to keep Monroe in Washington, however, for until the other members of the cabinet (summoned from their summer retreats) had arrived and until he received official accounts from Jackson, nothing could be done. By leaving the capital, Monroe simplified the problem of dealing with protests from the Spanish minister, enabling Adams to put him off until the president's return. As soon as Jackson's dispatches arrived, Monroe returned to the capital for a week of cabinet discussions.[25]

The cabinet was sharply divided on the issue, which not only involved grave constitutional questions but also touched directly upon the personal ambitions of the secretaries, for Jackson's rising fame made him a likely rival for the presidential succession. All the secretaries but Adams unhesitantly urged that the general be publicly reprimanded for exceeding his orders. Adams, on his part, recommended not only that the president approve Jackson's conduct but also that the United States retain the posts until Spain agreed to cede Florida. The secretary of state did not agree with the president's contention that the seizure of the posts was an act of war amounting to an invasion of the congressional power to declare war. Quite unintentionally, Adams gave rise to a misunderstanding about Monroe's initial position in this controversy. The secretary of state began his account of these meetings by observing that the president and all the other secretaries wished to condemn the general. That this statement does not correctly represent Mon-

---

He was, of course, highly articulate, but he never blocked a major administration measure. Clay did not use his power as Speaker to dominate congressional proceedings; his continued reelection during this era of intense intraparty conflict depended on his distribution of committee assignments to all factions (see Young, pp. 131–33).

[25] Washington, D.C., *National Intelligencer*, June 19, 1818; Adams, *Memoirs*, IV, 103–7 (June 26, 1818).

roe's views is apparent from Adams's subsequent narrative. In this particular instance, Adams's single-minded preoccupation with his own point of view led him to lump all those disagreeing with him in the same camp. In fact, Adams's entries in his diary make it quite clear that Monroe agreed with neither party in the cabinet, but that he sought a middle ground which would pacify Jackson's friends and appease his enemies, relieve the administration of the constitutional dilemma, and at the same time retain the advantage over Spain resulting from the general's activities in Florida. In his summary of the proceedings of the last cabinet session on July 20, Adams commented that the president continued to treat him with "candor and good humor . . . but without any variation from his original position." This cannot mean that Monroe still wished to repudiate Jackson, for the cabinet had agreed the day before to adopt the formula that Jackson had exceeded his orders, but that he had done so on the basis of information received during the invasion which made the seizure of the posts unavoidable to achieve the objectives of the campaign. In order to relieve the executive of the imputation of invading the war power of Congress, the posts were to be restored to Spain. On the same day (July 19) on which the cabinet agreed to this policy, Monroe wrote Jackson explaining the administration position, and Attorney General Wirt at the president's request drafted an editorial along similar lines for the Washington *National Intelligencer*. All Adams meant by his comment on the twentieth was that the president still did not agree with him that Jackson should be fully supported by the administration. From the outset Monroe preferred a course between the two extremes in the cabinet.[26]

Cabinet consensus did not automatically mean congressional approval, for the secretaries could not completely control their

[26] Adams, *Memoirs*, IV, 108–14 (July 15–20, 1818); Dangerfield, *Era of Good Feelings*, p. 138, accepts Adams's statement of face value, but Samuel Flagg Bemis, *John Quincy Adams and the Foundations of American Foreign Policy* (New York, 1949), p. 136, is more cautious. For an account of the issues involved in the dispute over Jackson, see Wiltse, pp. 76–81. Although Monroe did not spell out his policy in detail before the cabinet session, a letter he wrote to Madison on July 10, 1818 makes it quite clear that he had no intention of repudiating Jackson: "He [Jackson] imputes the whole Seminole war to the interference and excitement, by the Spanish authorities in the Floridas, of the Indians, together with foreign adventurers imposing themselves on these people for the agents of foreign powers. I have no doubt his opinion is correct, though he has not made his case as strong as I am satisfied he might have done" (Monroe, *Writings*, VI, 53–54).

supporters on an issue arousing such strong passions. Many congressmen felt that Jackson's thoughtless conduct, which could easily have plunged the nation into war with Spain, ought to be severely censured. Yet the administration stemmed the move (ably led by Clay) to censure Jackson by a solid majority—a victory which Crawford attributed to the fact that Monroe brought the full weight of his influence to bear on Jackson's behalf.[27] The administration position was strengthened by the knowledge that Adams had begun negotiations with the Spanish minister for the cession of Florida.

The intensification of the rivalry over the succession after December 1821, when Calhoun formally announced his candidacy, made it more difficult for Monroe to maintain consensus. In 1824 disunity within the cabinet was directly responsible for the frustration of administration efforts to conclude an agreement with Great Britain to suppress the international slave trade. This agreement was the result of the determined campaign by the British government to destroy the African slave trade by international action. Monroe, adhering to the traditional American view of neutral rights and sensitive to popular antagonism toward America's recent enemy, had at first rejected British overtures, for he was unwilling to grant British naval officers the right to search American ships merely on the suspicion of their being engaged in the slave trade. In the spring of 1823, however, Monroe, impressed by indications of a shift in American opinion, authorized Adams to instruct Richard Rush, the American minister in London, to negotiate an agreement in harmony with congressional resolutions recommending that the United States seek international agreements condemning the slave trade as piracy. This proposal had the great advantage of making it unnecessary to grant the right of search specifically, for pirates could not claim the protection of any national flag.[28] Monroe attached great importance to the slave trade convention, for he believed that a concession on an issue to which the British attached so much importance might open the way to a resolution of outstanding Anglo-American problems.[29]

Monroe discussed the proposal at length with the cabinet and

[27] Crawford to Albert Gallatin, July 24, 1819, Gallatin Papers; *Annals of Congress*, 15th Cong., 1st sess., pp. 515–1136.

[28] See P. J. Staudenraus, *African Colonization Movement, 1816–1865* (New York, 1961) and Hugh B. Soulsby, *The Right of Search and the Slave Trade in Anglo-American Relations, 1814–1862* (Baltimore, 1931).

[29] Bemis, pp. 471–552.

obtained the approval of all the secretaries. Crawford, who not only was a charter member of the American Colonization Society but had also actively lobbied on behalf of the congressional re-solves condemning the slave trade, was enthusiastic. Secretary Adams, on the other hand, did not approve this radical departure from the long-established American position on the right of search. Furthermore, he anticipated considerable public resent-ment when it came to the point of actually permitting British offi-cers to search American ships on the high seas.[30]

After Canning accepted the American convention with incon-sequential changes, Monroe expected prompt approval when he submitted the treaty to the Senate on April 30, 1824. Not only had the cabinet been united, but the House resolutions of 1823 con-demning the slave trade as piracy had been adopted unanimously. To his chagrin and embarrassment, it was at once apparent that such serious objections were being raised about permitting British officers to search American ships that the treaty was in jeopardy. The opposition was organized by John Holmes of Maine and Martin Van Buren, two staunch Crawford partisans, who sought to pillory Adams for sacrificing a basic national right. Instead of mounting a frontal attack, they concentrated on promoting an amendment limiting the right of search to African coastal waters, a modification not likely to be accepted by the British.[31] As soon as Monroe realized the strength and character of the opposition, he moved rapidly to exert his influence in behalf of ratification. Asking his old friend Senator John Taylor of Caroline to delay the vote, Monroe drafted a special message which he submitted on May 21. The president reminded the senators that the nation had a commitment to ratify a treaty which the United States had initiated and which the British government had accepted almost without change. Stressing the fact that no basic right had been conceded, Monroe condemned the proposed amendment as incom-patible with the objectives of the two powers. As a further prod to the Senate, Monroe attached copies of the House resolve of the previous session. All this was secondary to his main argument: "It cannot be disguised that the rejection of this convention cannot fail to have a very injurious influence on the good understanding between the two governments." [32] Impervious to the president's

---

[30] Adams, *Memoirs*, VI, 148–51 (June 19–20, 1823).

[31] Ibid., VI, 317, 338 (May 3, 18, 1824).

[32] Ibid., VI, 344 (May 21, 1824); *Messages of Presidents*, II, 243–47.

appeal, the Senate ratified the convention with the restrictive amendment.[33]

Before the final vote was taken, Monroe appealed to Crawford to intervene in behalf of the agreement that he had so ardently advocated the year before. At this time the secretary of the Treasury, who had suffered a shattering physical collapse in September 1823, was still prostrated—unable to sign his name, attend cabinet sessions, or discharge the duties of his office.[34] To Monroe's consternation, Crawford not only declined to intervene but maintained that he had never approved the draft convention when it had been before the cabinet. Although angered by the refusal of the secretary of the Treasury to restrain his followers, Monroe charitably attributed Crawford's assertion that he had never endorsed the convention to memory damage resulting from the secretary's illness. Adams, however, never doubted for a moment that Crawford was responsible for the sudden outcry over a measure inevitably identified with the secretary of state.[35] Adams may have been mistaken in this conclusion, but there is no doubt that Crawford's backers were indeed bitter toward Monroe, for they interpreted the president's neutrality in the electioneering as indicating a preference for Adams.[36] Monroe's gloomy forebodings that the Senate modification of the convention would prevent a general settlement with England proved correct. Canning refused to accept the amended text of an agreement negotiated in accordance with American wishes. Shortly after receiving the text of the convention, Canning suspended the negotiations under way with Rush on other issues, thus closing the door on a general rapprochement.[37]

The occasions on which the president worked directly with individual congressmen are difficult to isolate, for such arrangements depended on personal interviews and were usually outside the purview of the secretary of state. So discreetly were such relationships handled that the only instance in which it is possible to obtain a tantalizing but still incomplete glimpse of presidential influence exerted through an individual member of Congress oc-

[33] For Senate proceedings, see Niles' Weekly Register, June 12, 1824.

[34] On Crawford's illness, see Wiltse, 277–78.

[35] Adams, Memoirs, VI, 344–45, 356, 428 (May 21, 25, Nov. 10, 1824); Bemis, pp. 434–5.

[36] Washington Republican, Feb. 5, 1824. The British chargé, Addington, also commented on current hostility toward Monroe in his dispatch to Canning on August 2, 1824, Foreign Office Papers, 5/186, Public Records Office, London, photostat, Lib. Cong.

[37] Bemis, pp. 523–27.

curred in 1820 during the Missouri debates. This episode strikingly highlights the limitations imposed on presidential leadership by existing usages. From the outset of the crisis precipitated by the attempt to exclude slavery from Missouri, Monroe, though deeply concerned at the threat to the Union, was hemmed in by the fact that the Missouri question was a purely congressional affair, arising in the ordinary course of legislative business and involving a matter entirely within the jurisdiction of Congress. Open interference on his part would have been instantly resented. His position was made doubly difficult by the fact that as a Southerner and a slaveowner he would only raise the suspicions of both restrictionists and proslavery forces if he made any public declarations of policy.

Like most Americans, Monroe did not grasp the critical nature of the conflict over Missouri until after the beginning of the debates. His concern was immediate for he saw the threat to the Union unless the matter were resolved. It must be remembered that Monroe shared the opinion expressed by nearly all the leaders of the day that the attempt to exclude slavery masked a bid for power by the Northerners as well as an effort to restore the old party system, which he considered a source of so much evil in the past. From this point of view a solution maintaining the existing balance of power seemed eminently sound and statesmanlike. When the debates began Monroe felt handicapped because he had no confidential agent he could utilize who was not a member of the administration. His son-in-law, George Hay, who frequently served in this capacity, was unable to leave Richmond where he was attending the session of the state legislature.[38] Nonetheless, from a very early stage in the discussions, Monroe was informed of behind-the-scenes moves to compromise the issue. A month before Senator Jesse Thomas introduced his proposal to exclude slavery from the Louisiana Purchase north of 36° 30′, Monroe was aware of the measure and indicated his approval.[39] Monroe's prin-

[38] Hay to Monroe, Jan. 5, 1820, Monroe Papers, New York Public Library, New York City; Hay to his wife, Feb. 12, 1820, Monroe Papers, Lib. Cong.

[39] Monroe mentioned the possibility of a compromise to Adams on Jan. 8, 1820 (Adams, *Memoirs*, IV, 498–99). The secretary was frankly skeptical but admitted that there might be an "underplot" with which he was unfamiliar. Monroe wrote George Hay, Jan. 10, 1820 (Monroe Papers, N.Y. Pub. Lib.), explaining that the compromise would be on the basis of a division of the territories. It has been said that Monroe intended to veto the compromise until the last minute. This conclusion is based on a very rough draft of an undated veto message printed in U.S., Congress, *Con-*

cipal point of contact with the architects of the compromise was through Senator James Barbour of Virginia, who sponsored the first compromise attempt by linking the admission of Maine with that of Missouri. Barbour hoped that this move would induce the restrictionists to admit Missouri as a slave state, since the enabling act of Massachusetts authorizing the formation of a state from the District of Maine was only valid until March 1, 1820. On February 2 Barbour, who estimated that he had a majority of one in the Senate for his combined bill, conferred with Monroe about his strategy. The president, deeming this margin too slim, suggested that Barbour separate the two measures to permit the immediate admission of Maine. He felt that this act of generosity might arouse sufficient gratitude among the Northerners to permit action on Missouri without restriction.[40] The president also suggested that the Southern members of Congress meet to plan joint action. Barbour did not follow the president's advice—the two bills remained linked through their Senate career.

Monroe again cooperated closely with Barbour when they labored with limited success to persuade Virginia party leaders to accept the compromise. Monroe and Barbour did not win approval of the compromise, but they did prevent the state legislature from taking any drastic action. All but four members of the state delegation in Congress voted against the compromise proposal.[41]

Monroe's relations with his cabinet during the Missouri crisis provide an interesting commentary upon executive practices. Except for private remarks made to the secretaries individually, Monroe did not discuss the Missouri question with his cabinet until March 3, the day the compromise bill was passed. He had an excellent reason for this silence (it was not from indecisiveness, as some writers have suggested): he knew that his secretaries held irreconcilable views about the proposal to exclude slavery from Missouri. Adams fully approved restriction, while Wirt, Calhoun, and Crawford upheld the Southern point of view.

---

gressional Globe, 30th Cong., 1st sess., Appendix, p. 67 (I have been unable to locate the original.) A careful reading of this draft leaves no doubt that it was intended only to apply to a bill excluding slavery from Missouri, an action to which he was absolutely opposed. There is nothing in the draft to suggest that it was to be applied to a compromise involving the Louisiana Purchase.

[40] Monroe to Barbour, Feb. 3, 1820, *William and Mary College Quarterly*, 10 (1901): 9.

[41] For an account of this affair, see Glover Moore, *The Missouri Controversy, 1819–1821* (Lexington, Ky., 1953).

Premature discussion would not only produce unpleasant friction but also damage the prospects of compromise by publicizing the disharmony within the administration.

In taking up the compromise bill Monroe resorted to a procedure which he never employed on any other occasion: he asked the secretaries for opinions in writing on two questions. First, did Congress have the power to restrict slavery in the territories? Second, was the word "forever" in the compromise bill effective only during the territorial phase, or was it binding on new states formed in this region? All were united in conceding that Congress had the power to restrict slavery in the territories, but Adams disagreed with his colleagues in maintaining that it constituted a permanent ban on future states. After some sharp exchanges between Adams and Crawford, Calhoun, aware of the president's desire for unanimity, proposed that the second question be reworded. He suggested that they be asked whether the word "forever" was consistent with the United States Constitution. Since all answered affirmatively, they were left free to append individual interpretations. Monroe gave the completed opinions to Adams to place in the files of the State Department. The president's wish to have a permanent record was not achieved. In 1848, during the debates on the Oregon Territory when the slavery question was again raised, a search of the files of the department revealed that the cabinet opinions had vanished. Calhoun, a participant in the Oregon debates and the only survivor of the Monroe cabinet, could not recall the occasion at all.[42]

During the next session of Congress a second and equally acrimonious controversy developed over passages in the Missouri constitution offensive to the restrictionists, who moved to suspend admission until they were expunged. A major crisis seemed imminent when a compromise arrangement failed in the House by three votes. While Speaker Clay maneuvered to reverse the decision by presenting a revised compromise resolution, Monroe summoned Nicholas Biddle from Philadelphia. Biddle, a close friend and adviser of the president and one of the government-appointed directors of the Bank of the United States, brought sufficient pressure to bear on the Pennsylvania delegation to persuade three of its members to change their votes. His labors eased the way for

[42] Adams, *Memoirs*, V, 5–9 (Mar. 3, 1820); *Congressional Globe*, 30th Cong., 1st sess., Appendix, p. 57. The word "forever" did not appear in the original of the Thomas proposal introduced on Feb. 3; it was not added until Feb. 17 (*Annals of Congress*, 15th Cong., 1st sess., pp. 363, 367, 427).

the passage of the new compromise measure by a six-vote margin. When Monroe told Madison that Clay's revised bill would now be adopted, he said nothing of his own involvement apart from the cryptic comment: "Mr. Biddle is now here, and has rendered some service in this important occurence." [43]

On the basis of this slender evidence it would be improper to conclude that Monroe's intervention had a decisive effect on the adoption of either the first or second Missouri Compromise, although the fact that he and other members of the administration were known to favor them must have been useful to the promoters of the arrangement. Monroe's activities are important in that they demonstrate the cautious way in which the president was compelled to work when handling sensitive issues that were properly within the jurisdiction of Congress. Within the limits of current usages Monroe at least was willing to involve himself in the process of resolving the conflict.

On matters that directly affected his own perogatives, Monroe had no need to use secretive methods. In January 1822, when the Senate refused to confirm two minor military appointees for reasons Monroe considered an invasion of his right to make nominations, he declined to withdraw the names and condemned the Senate action in a sharply worded message. So convinced was he of the correctness of his constitutional position that he left the posts unfilled during the remainder of his term.[44] His determination to uphold Indian land rights established in the agreement between Georgia and the federal government in 1802, when that state ceded her lands, resulted in an angry conflict with the Georgia delegation in 1824. Again he defended his conduct in a vigorous special message.[45]

These two incidents, as well as the hostility to the slave trade convention in 1824, were a direct outgrowth of the disintegrating effect of presidential rivalries upon administration unity. Monroe himself did not grasp that leadership based on cabinet consensus could not survive without some stronger force than that provided by his personal persuasiveness or the respect he commanded as a revolutionary hero. At some point the ambitions of rival candidates would dictate that their interests made it necessary to attack ad-

[43] Moore, pp. 163–4; Monroe to Madison, Feb. 17, 1821, Madison Papers, Lib. Cong.

[44] *Annals of Congress*, 17th Cong., 1st sess., Senate, Executive Proceedings, Jan. 20–April 30, 1822, pp. 470–510; Adams, *Memoirs*, V, 486–88 (April 13, 1822); *Messages of the Presidents*, II, 129–36.

[45] See Wiltse, 193–97.

ministration policies associated with their rivals. Monroe was naturally distressed by the internecine rivalry, but he still reiterated his confidence in the viability of a government without parties. "Surely," he wrote Madison in 1822, "our government may get on and prosper without the existence of parties. I have always considered their existence the curse of the country, of which we had sufficient proof, more especially in the late war." Yet he could offer no suggestions as to how this desirable goal might be achieved except the vague hope that "virtue" and public opinion would counteract the destructive force of factional rivalry.[46] While assertions of confidence in the efficacy of such factors were a usual part of the Republican faith, they were insufficient to the task at hand. The leadership methods and attitudes shaped in Jefferson's administration perished with Monroe. Although Monroe was unaware of the development, at the very end of his second term Martin Van Buren was embarking on the self-imposed task of restoring (as he saw it) the old Jeffersonian Republican party that had been destroyed by Monroe's policy of party amalgamation. Van Buren's efforts were ultimately crowned with success in the Adams administration when he welded together the surviving Crawfordites, the Jacksonians, and the supporters of Calhoun.[47] Since John Quincy Adams, who would have preferred to continue the Republican tradition using Monroe's techniques, did not enjoy the support of Van Buren's coalition (which effectually dominated Congress), his attempts at leadership were abortive.[48] Van Buren was not, as he imagined, engaged in a work of restoration, for the party that resulted from his labors accepted a different concept of executive leadership and made use of techniques, notably the patronage, which the older Republicans had avoided on the federal level. In the long run, these new attitudes and practices exerted a more lasting impact on the presidency than those shaped by Jefferson.

[46] May 10, 1822, Monroe, *Writings*, VI, 289.

[47] For this important development, see Robert V. Remini, *Martin Van Buren and the Making of the Democratic Party* (New York, 1959).

[48] On Adams, see Samuel Flagg Bemis, *John Quincy Adams and the Union* (New York, 1956), chap. 5.

8 John C. Calhoun, Secretary of War, 1817-25: The Cast-Iron Man as an Administrator

Carlton B. Smith

J OHN C. CALHOUN is best known as a political philosopher, the spokesman of the states' rights South, and a sectionalist extraordinaire. Students of Calhoun mention his "nationalist" period. They hastily include him among the War Hawks of 1812, give a passing nod to his support of the protective tariff and internal improvements, and rush on to his role in the political wars of the Era of Good Feelings. The impression of Calhoun conveyed to the student of American history is that of an old, bushy-haired, "cast-iron man" with dark, penetrating eyes—"a moral and mental abstraction" [1] capable only of political intrigue, philosophical debate, and lofty pontification. Yet this South Carolinian for nearly eight years served as one of the nation's most effective secretaries of war. There were no abstractions in the War Department, only the hard facts of budgets, organization, and day-to-day operation of the largest and most complex branch of the executive. The office of secretary of war required a man familiar with practical realities, not a philosopher. It required a master of public administration.

Calhoun's biographers have scarcely scratched the surface of this important phase of his life. The "definitive" biography of the South Carolinian by Charles M. Wiltse devotes barely fifty pages of its three volumes to Calhoun's years as secretary of war. Other biographers are even less generous,[2] although they all concede

---

[1] Harriet Martineau labeled Calhoun "the cast-iron man, who looks as if he had never been born," and Virginia Howell Davis (Mrs. Jefferson Davis) dubbed him "a moral and mental abstraction." Both descriptions are conveniently found in Gamaliel Bradford, *As God Made Them: Portraits of Some Nineteenth Century Americans* (Boston and New York, 1921), p. 89.

[2] W. Edwin Hemphill lists the number of pages devoted to Calhoun as secretary of war by his biographers in John C. Calhoun, *The Papers of John C. Calhoun*, ed. Robert Lee Meriwether and W. Edwin Hemphill (Columbia, S.C., 1959–), II, xii–xvi.

that he was an able member of the Monroe cabinet. Margaret Coit compares him to Alexander Hamilton; [3] William Trent, not an admirer of Calhoun, grudgingly admits that he possessed "executive powers of the first rank"; [4] Arthur Styron maintains that he was "no doubt the greatest Secretary of War until Jefferson Davis occupied that office"; [5] Wiltse points out that after Calhoun had brought order to the department, it "long served as the model after which other departments were patterned," and, with von Holst, quotes *Niles' Weekly Register:* "the order and harmony, regularity and promptitude, punctuality and responsibility, introduced by Mr. Calhoun in every branch of the service, has never been rivalled, perhaps, cannot be excelled – and it must be recollected, that he brought this system out of chaos." [6] There is, then, a general consensus among students of Calhoun's career that while he was secretary of war his administrative ability "was soon exhibited in so marked a degree as to induce the belief that he was then in his most appropriate sphere." [7] But none of them has seen fit to discuss in detail the reasons for this favorable judgment of Calhoun as a public administrator. One is compelled to agree with Edwin Hemphill that "every revelation and interpretation of John C. Calhoun's accomplishments in his new role as an executive should be welcomed." [8]

Scholars have not agreed on a definition of public administration: for some it is "organization, personnel practices, and procedures"; for others it is "that part of the activity of a body or group of men which is concerned with the management of the affairs of that body or group." [9] These definitions are inadequate, better

[3] Coit, *John C. Calhoun: American Portrait* (Boston, 1950), p. 135.

[4] Trent, *Southern Statesmen of the Old Regime* (New York, 1897), p. 163.

[5] Styron, *The Cast-Iron Man: John C. Calhoun and American Democracy* (New York, 1935), p. 135. Styron was echoing William E. Dodd, who made the same judgment twenty-four years earlier in his *Statesmen of the Old South; or, From Radicalism to Conservative Revolt* (New York, 1911), p. 109.

[6] Wiltse, *John C. Calhoun: Nationalist, 1782–1828* (New York, 1944), p. 297; *Niles' Weekly Register*, 26 (March 27, 1824), quoted by Wiltse and by H. von Holst, *John C. Calhoun* (New York, 1899), p. 41.

[7] Jefferson Davis, "Life and Character of the Hon. John Caldwell Calhoun," *North American Review*, 145 (Sept., 1887), quoted in *John C. Calhoun: A Profile*, ed. John L. Thomas (New York, 1968), p. 16.

[8] Calhoun, *Papers*, II, xii.

[9] John A. Vieg, "The Growth of Public Administration," in *Elements of Public Administration*, ed. Fritz Morstein Marx (2d ed., Englewood Cliffs, N.J., 1946), p. 6; M. Ruthnaswamy, *Principles and Practices of Public Administration* (4th ed., Allahabad, India, 1962), p. 1.

suited to a definition of the management of a bureaucracy in the interest of self-preservation. Much more satisfactory explanations of what administration meant to Calhoun are those of Leonard White: "the direction, coordination and control of many persons to achieve some purpose or objective," and Woodrow Wilson: "Public administration is detailed and systematic execution of public law." [10] To Calhoun, administration was neither the organization nor the personnel practices but "the application of the laws and regulations." [11] An administrator applied the law, executed policy, and achieved the desired results.

Modern students of public administration have pictured the ideal executive as a man with single-mindedness and faith in the future, who can coordinate the activities of a large number of subordinates in order to accomplish his objectives. His job is not "being but doing." [12] One of the most pressing of his objectives is "the most efficient utilization of resources," with the "elimination of waste." [13]

The United States War Department in 1817 was an administrator's nightmare. It was "nearly foundering," "at best a mediocrity, at worse a disgrace." Following the resignation of John Armstrong in August 1814, the office of secretary was filled by five different men. During the year preceding Calhoun's assumption of the office, the day-to-day affairs of the department were conducted by the chief clerk.[14] Promising only industry and firmness, the tall, lean, thirty-five-year-old South Carolinian approached his new task with boundless self-confidence. It was this self-confidence, perhaps, which emboldened him "to embark upon a ship apparently already sunk." He came from a successful career in the House of Representatives where he had won a host of

[10] White, *Introduction to the Study of Public Administration* (4th ed., New York, 1955), p. 2; Woodrow Wilson, "The Nature of Administration," in *Basic Issues in Public Administration*, ed. Donald C. Rowat (New York, 1961), p. 36.

[11] Calhoun to Henry Clay, Dec. 11, 1818, Calhoun, *Papers*, III, p. 380.

[12] John A. Vieg, "The Chief Executive," in *Elements of Public Administration*, p. 163; Harlan Cleveland, "A Philosophy for the Public Executive," in *Perspectives on Public Management: Cases and Learning Designs*, ed. Robert T. Golembiewski (Itasca, Ill., 1968), p. 15; George A. Graham, "Essentials of Responsibility," in *Elements of Public Administration*, p. 513.

[13] White, p. 3.

[14] Francis Paul Prucha, *The Sword of the Republic: The United States Army on the Frontier, 1783–1846* (New York, 1969), p. 134; Calhoun, *Papers*, III, xiii, II, xxxii–xxxiii.

friends with his sparkling conversation, his charming manners, and unerring logic.[15] Surveying the varied responsibilities of his department, which included the army, pensions, bounty lands, militia claims, road construction, armament production, the military academy, and Indian affairs, young Calhoun observed to a friend: "The farther I look into its concerns, the more I am impressed with the magnitude of its duties."[16] He also was immediately impressed with "the awkwardness of the present organization," but working fourteen and fifteen hours a day, he soon felt that he was making progress toward determining "the precise state of the disease" that afflicted his new responsibility.[17]

Under Calhoun's dispassionate direction the department became the most efficient agency of the federal government. His Hamiltonian pessimism toward human nature and his cynical distrust of politicians and vested interests made him an administrator of cool precision.[18] He believed, as Ralph Gabriel has pointed out, that "no public official can be trusted unless he knows that he is being watched."[19] This is not to say that Calhoun was a pessimist in all respects. He had an overwhelming faith in the present and future greatness of the United States. But in administration he felt it was far wiser to assume that if something could go wrong, it would; and he organized the department so that errors would be minimized and responsibility for them fixed.

His professional relationship with people was firm and at times curt. Certain regulations and principles were to be adhered to; he saw no need in wasting time with lengthy explanations. When Dr. Benjamin Waterhouse of Boston presented a voucher for $27.00, Calhoun bluntly told him that the expense was "not justified by law or regulation." The amount was small, "but the principle is deemed important." There was no need for further explana-

[15] Coit, pp. 120–22, 131–32; Wiltse, pp. 144, 151; Bradford, pp. 93, 102–3; Gerald M. Capers, *John C. Calhoun—Opportunist: A Reappraisal* (Gainesville, Fla., 1960), p. 63; Styron, p. 97.

[16] Calhoun to Charles J. Ingersoll, Dec. 14, 1817, Calhoun, *Papers*, II, 16.

[17] Calhoun to General Winfield Scott, Sept. 5, 1819, Confidential and Unofficial Letters Sent, 1814–35, Record Group 107, National Archives, Washington, D.C., p. 108; Calhoun to Charles Tait, July 20, 1818, Calhoun, *Papers*, II, 408.

[18] Samuel P. Huntington, *The Soldier and the State: The Theory and Politics of Civil-Military Relations* (Cambridge, Mass., 1957), pp. 214–15; William W. Freehling, "Spoilsmen and Interests in the Thought and Career of John C. Calhoun," *Journal of American History*, 52 (June 1965): 26, 42.

[19] Gabriel, *The Course of American Democratic Thought* (2d ed., New York, 1956), p. 107.

tion.[20] Calhoun believed in fair and impersonal treatment of all, in the interest of the general welfare. The department, after all, had many divergent interests to serve.

When it came to the overall organization and supervision of subordinates, Calhoun had definite ideas. The central theme of his administration was "a more rigid enforcement of responsibility and economy." [21] Some twentieth-century students of government have listed the principles of public administration, including such items as duty, obedience, authority, coordination, and hierarchy. Others have denied that there are such principles, since for every rule, there are numerous exceptions. Significantly experts today seldom mention economy as one of these principles; instead they most frequently speak of authority, but without a corresponding stress on responsibility. When Lynton K. Caldwell compared the administrative principles of Hamilton and Jefferson, he found that the only one they shared was responsibility.[22]

The young South Carolinian set about his task by seeking to concentrate authority at the center and then drawing definite lines of responsibility in all parts of the organization; he demanded top proficiency from his subordinates. His task was not an easy one. Authority and responsibility in the many-headed hydra could not be prevented from overlapping. Neither the Constitution nor Congress had clarified the chain of command. Did authority pass from the president through a civilian-politician secretary and thence to both military and civilian subordinates, or were there two lines of authority emanating from the president? Was there a political-administrative line of command from the chief executive to the secretary, and in addition, a military chain of command from the commander-in-chief to the ranking army officer?

Calhoun intended a single chain of command in which all communication between the army and the president would pass through the secretary of war. Under the army organization of 1817, with its separation into a northern and southern division, the two commanding generals, having no common military superior, reported to the secretary. Neither Calhoun nor the general

[20] Calhoun to Dr. Benjamin Waterhouse, Sept. 29, 1818, Calhoun, *Papers*, III, 172.

[21] Calhoun to Henry Clay, Dec. 11, 1818, ibid., p. 380.

[22] Ruthnaswamy, pp. 10–19; White, pp. 41–42; Herbert A. Simon, "The Proverbs of Public Administration," in *Basic Issues in Public Administration*, p. 58; Caldwell, *The Administrative Theories of Hamilton and Jefferson: Their Contribution to Thought on Public Administration* (Chicago, 1944), pp. 24–30, 130–37.

officers of the army wanted a single commander, and this was reflected in the secretary's report of December 12, 1820; but as the result of an executive and congressional compromise, the office of commanding general of the army was created by the act of 1821. Since neither the executive nor Congress had anticipated the office, the duties and authority of the post were left undefined. Theoretically the creation of the office meant that one man would exercise military command over the entire army, but in fact the general regulations of 1821 gave the secretary of war authority over the staff bureaus and presumably the line, while the actual duties of General Jacob Brown, the newly appointed commanding general, were left to be informally defined by the secretary. Headquartered in the capital, he was overshadowed by the secretary and the president and did little more than advise, write reports, and implement executive decisions. The commanding general never really accepted his inferior status, and in time the office grew somewhat independent of the secretary and more directly responsible to the president. This duality of command reached its height in the army regulations of 1836. The secretary commanded the bureaus and the staff of the department; the commanding general exercised authority over the line of the army. Claims of authority often overlapped. This polycentric system was the one flaw in Calhoun's organization. Within it lay the seeds of civilian-military discord that was not to be calmed until twentieth-century reorganization.[23]

The problem of an indefinite chain of command was illustrated for Calhoun by two experiences with the army's most honored officer, Andrew Jackson. They taught the young secretary the need for definite lines of authority with corresponding responsibility.

During the administrative confusion that accompanied the War of 1812, orders to field commanders originated from both the president and the secretary of war with little regard for the procedural propriety of routing them through the division commanders. This practice continued sporadically after the war, and in 1816, Acting Secretary of War George Graham ordered Major Stephen Long from his survey of the upper Mississippi to New

---

[23] Leonard D. White, *The Jeffersonians: A Study in Administrative History, 1801–1829* (New York, 1956), pp. 240–41; Samuel P. Huntington, "Civilian Control and the Constitution," *American Political Science Review*, 50 (Sept. 1956): 695; Huntington, *The Soldier and the State*, pp. 208–9; William B. Skelton, "The Commanding General and the Problem of Command in the United States Army, 1821–1841," *Military Affairs*, 34 (Sept. 1970): 117–18.

York without notifying Andrew Jackson, the commander of the southern division. Jackson, who had sent Long up the river to survey the area in anticipation of Indian hostilities, was aghast to discover in January 1817 that Long was in New York and had published his survey in a newspaper there. The general shot off a blunt protest to Graham and received the cold reply that War Department orders took precedence over those of the division commander. The hero of New Orleans then put the matter before the president. When Monroe failed to render a satisfactory and prompt opinion, an enraged Jackson issued a division order from Nashville on April 22, 1817, prohibiting the men of his command from obeying any orders from Washington unless they came through his office.[24]

General Winfield Scott pronounced Jackson's order mutinous, and a war of words was soon under way; the War Department loftily tried to ignore the affair, at least until Monroe could find a secretary of war. It was left to Calhoun to resolve the problem. On December 29, 1817, just after taking office, he issued a conciliatory general order which held that "as a general rule all orders will be issued in the first instance, to the commanders of division." This supported Jackson's position that for the sake of discipline, the chain of command should run through the division commanders; but, Calhoun's order also retained the secretary of war's prerogative of issuing orders "directly to officers commanding departments, posts, or detachments, and to any officer attached to the division commander." [25] Calhoun accompanied a copy of the order to Jackson with a pacifying letter pointing out that its provisions "accord with your views." A calmed Jackson replied: "Responsibility now rests where it should, on the officer issuing the orders; and the principle acknowledged is calculated to insure that subordination so necessary to the harmonious movement of every part of the military machine." [26]

[24] Wiltse, pp. 150–51; James Parton, *Life of Andrew Jackson* (3 vols., Boston, 1870), II, 371–82.

[25] Calhoun, *Papers*, II, 42–43.

[26] Calhoun to Jackson, Dec. 29, 1817, ibid., pp. 43–44; Jackson to Calhoun, Jan. 20, 1818, *American State Papers: Military Affairs*, I, 697 (hereafter cited *ASP:MA*). The secretary of war had to remind Jackson several times that the lines of authority ran directly from staff officers, such as the commissary officers and surgeons, to their superiors in Washington and not through the division commander (Calhoun to Jackson, Dec. 22, 1818, Aug. 10, 1819, Confidential and Unofficial Letters Sent, RG 107, National Archives, pp. 98–101, 104–6).

Calhoun's second experience of the command system also involved the impetuous Jackson. There had been continuing trouble with the Seminole Indians on the Georgia-Florida border. In December 1817 Secretary Calhoun authorized General Edmund P. Gaines to pursue them into Spanish territory and attack them there. "Unless," he added, "they should shelter themselves under a Spanish post. In the last event, you will immediately notify this Department." [27] Jackson was ordered to assume personal command of operations on the border and received copies of the orders to Gaines. It is apparent from Calhoun's orders that he conceived the operation as having the limited objective of pacifying the Seminoles. When President Monroe urged him to instruct Jackson not to attack any Spanish posts, Calhoun did not feel it necessary to add to his orders; apparently he felt that his previous instructions were clear enough. Monroe informed Congress in March 1818 that Jackson would not enter Florida unless in pursuit and in any event had been ordered to respect Spanish authority. [28]

When the report from Jackson arrived recounting the capture of the Spanish fort at St. Mark and the execution of Arbuthnot and Ambrister, alleged British agents, Calhoun dashed off a letter to the general which attempted to explain the international implications of the action and made clear his opinion as secretary of war that Jackson had exceeded his orders and had acted entirely on his own responsibility. Pursuit of Indians into Florida was justified, but an attack on a Spanish fort was tantamount to a declaration of war. Calhoun requested an explanation which might appease the Spanish government, and he warned Jackson that if Spain inquired as to whether the secretary had ordered the operation, he would be compelled to reply, "I did not: it was the act of the general." [29]

From the tone of the letter, it seems that Calhoun was less disturbed by the results of Jackson's boldness than by the fact that he had exceeded his instructions. Twelve years later Vice-President Calhoun reminded President Jackson that his immediate concern had been the general's transcendence of orders and that he had

[27] Calhoun to Gaines, Dec. 16, 1817, *ASP:MA*, I, 689.

[28] Calhoun to Jackson, Dec. 26, 1817, Monroe to Calhoun, Jan. 30, 1818, Calhoun, *Papers*, II, 39–40, 104; Special Message to Congress, March 28, 1818, in *A Compilation of the Messages and Papers of the Presidents*, comp. James D. Richardson (20 vols., Washington, D.C., 1913), II, 601.

[29] Calhoun, *Papers*, II, lxxxvi–vii; Jackson to Calhoun, April 8, May 5, 1818, *ASP:MA*, I, 700–702; Calhoun to Jackson, July 19, 1818, Calhoun, *Papers*, II, 400–401.

"neither questioned your patriotism nor your motives." [30] Jackson, confident that he had acted under higher orders emanating from the president, felt free to violate the orders of the War Department; whether or not the instructions in the mysterious Rhea letter (if such a letter existed) actually originated with President Monroe, the implication was that the secretary of war could be bypassed in the chain of command.[31] This placed Jackson in the position of violating his own principles set down in the Long incident. It seemed that the division commander could not be bypassed, but a civilian secretary could; in effect Jackson's interpretation placed the military sector of the War Department above the civilian and tacitly posited a direct line of command and responsibility from the president to the military. Unfortunately this problem has never been fully resolved.

Calhoun weathered these crises of command with firmness and dispatch without making an enemy of the sensitive general. These incidents served to illustrate to the new secretary of war the necessity of clarifying the lines of control on all levels of the department. He turned the lessons learned to good use when he confronted the problem of developing a system of efficiency and economy in his department.

Calhoun immediately found himself under considerable pressure to economize, and it is his reaction to this demand that best illustrates his attachment to the principles of responsibility and economy. The War Department was by far the most complex agency of the executive branch and, therefore, the least efficient and the most wasteful. Calhoun noted that "little heretofore has been done to give exactness, economy, and dispatch to its monied transactions." [32] His task was to impose that required exactness and economy upon the department and, at the same time, restrain those who would indiscriminately reduce its budget to a point that would impair the efficient conduct of its duties.

The drive for retrenchment began immediately following the War of 1812. The national debt had increased by $80 million to a total of more than $110 million in 1815. Military expenditures had climbed precipitously during the war until they reach a peak of more than $16 million in 1816. The following year expenditures

[30] Calhoun to Jackson, May 27, 1830, quoted in Parton, II, 508–9.

[31] Wiltse, p. 160; Parton, II, 433–37; Richard R. Stenberg, "Jackson's 'Rhea Letter' Hoax," *Journal of Southern History*, 2 (Nov. 1936): 480–96. Harry Ammon has reexamined all the evidence in *James Monroe: The Quest for National Identity* (New York, 1971), pp. 414–17.

[32] Calhoun to Charles J. Ingersoll, Dec. 14, 1817, Calhoun, *Papers*, II, 16.

were cut to under $9 million, but the department faced a deficit of over $45 million in unsettled accounts.[33] In 1821, after the post-war depression had made economy essential, Congress enacted legislation that drastically reduced the size of the army.[34]

The young secretary of war and former respected member of the House of Representatives recognized the overwhelming demand for a reduction of expenditures but also realized the possible consequences of drastic cuts. He tried to restrain Congress as much as possible. In his report of December 1818, he urged Congress to consider the growth of the nation when it debated the size of the army. It was a fallacy, he argued, to compare the army of 1802, responsible for the garrisoning of twenty-seven posts, with that thought necessary in 1818, when there were seventy-three posts to be garrisoned. "Our present establishment," declared the secretary, "when we take into the comparison the prodigious increase of wealth, population, extent of territory, number and distance of military posts, cannot be pronounced extravagant." He cautioned against the reduction of supply expenditures and in fact urged the improvement of the daily ration. As for pay reduction, that was out of the question. The pay was already inadequate because as money depreciated, the pay had remained the same.[35]

Where could savings be obtained if not by reducing size, supplies, or pay? Calhoun's ready answer was that much could be saved by more efficient administration: "Here all savings are real gain, not only in a moneyed, but a moral and political point of view. An inefficient administration, without economy or responsibility, not only exhausts the public resources, but strongly tends to contaminate the moral and political principles of the officers who are charged with the disbursements of the army." [36]

The secretary of war set about organizing his department into bureaus, each with a head responsible for its efficiency. Responsibility was the key to Calhoun's concept of efficient administration. This reorganization was completed by December 1818, and the

---

[33] Annual Report of the Secretary of the Treasury, Dec. 8, 1815, Report of the Secretary of the Treasury, Feb. 7, 1820, Report of the Comptroller of the Treasury, Nov. 26, 1822, *American State Papers: Finance*, III, 8, 488–90, IV, 2 (hereafter cited *ASP:F*).

[34] "Act to Reduce and Fix the Military Peace Establishment," March 2, 1821, U.S., *Statutes at Large*, III, 615–17.

[35] Report to the House, Dec. 11, 1818, *ASP:MA*, I, 779, 780–81. The aggregate strength of the army at the time was 7,676 (Francis Paul Prucha, *A Guide to the Military Posts of the United States, 1789–1895* [Madison, Wis., 1964], p. 143).

[36] *ASP:MA*, I, 780.

general rule then in operation was that "every article of public property, even the smallest, ought, if possible, to be in charge of some person who should be responsible for it." [37] On the eve of the reduction of 1821, Calhoun, with a respectful nod to economy as "a very high political virtue," warned that it was not true economy to cut the military establishment to a point which would render it unfit to meet the dangers of war.[38] The road to true economy, he pointed out once again to the House Committee on Public Expenditures, was that which his department was following: "to hold the head of each subordinate department responsible for the disbursements of his department." [39]

The success of any program of fiscal responsibility depended to a great extent on the efficient functioning of supply. This area of activity most frequently furnished opportunities for graft and excessive expense because here the objectives of the department often clashed with the greed of private interests. An efficient, economical system of supply had never been devised. At the outbreak of the War of 1812, the system "lacked integration, responsibility, unity, and energy and was utterly inadequate." [40]

During the war it became evident that a reorganization of the supply system was imperative. The letting of contracts to private individuals to supply garrisons and armies in the field in a given area without the imposition of any stringent restraints or standards gave many persons an opportunity to profit at the expense of defeat. In reports to the House of Representatives in December 1814, General Scott, General Gaines, and Colonel John R. Fenwick agreed with Secretary of War Monroe that the contract system of supply was unworkable. The contractors were beyond the control of the military, and if their cost for foodstuffs went up, they substituted a less expensive item (usually whiskey) or defaulted; consequently, supply was often inadequate and erratic. General Gaines reported that no rations had been delivered for his troops for two weeks.[41]

Soon after the war, with problems of supply again plaguing the department, this time on the Florida frontier, Secretary Calhoun wrote sympathetically to General Jackson that "the inefficiency of provisioning our army by contract furnishes abundant

[37] Ibid.   [38] Report on Reduction, Dec. 12, 1820, ibid., II, 191.

[39] Feb. 11, 1822, ibid., p. 345. Responsibility was essential in view of the number of persons involved in disbursement: in 1822 War Department funds passed through 291 disbursing agents (Annual Report of the Secretary of War for 1823, ibid., p. 554).

[40] White, *Jeffersonians*, pp. 214, 224–26.   [41] *ASP:MA*, I, 600–601.

evidence of the incompetency of the contract system in war." [42] Calhoun himself had sponsored a resolution in the House in 1814 calling for a modification of the system, but to no avail.[43] The system was finally abolished in 1818, and a commissary system was substituted. A commissary general was authorized to contract for the purchase of all supplies, but, while under the old system the contractor was responsible for delivery to designated posts in a given district, now he was to deliver supplies in bulk to a depot where they would be inspected by a subsistence officer and turned over to the quartermaster corps for distribution. The new system was to go into gradual operation as the old contracts expired.[44]

Calhoun, in his annual report that December, strongly defended the new system and labeled the former reliance upon civilian companies to transport supplies absurd. He pointed out that because of the scattered locations of the army, efficient and adequate supply in the United States was inevitably more difficult and expensive than in Europe. The problem was in "enforcing a proper responsibility and economy" upon both the army and the contractor.[45]

The secretary was eminently successful in his program of economy. He could justly claim to have significantly reduced the cost of supplying the army.[46] In addition, a comparison of expenditures of the years 1821 and 1824 shows that while the other departments of the government increased their outlays by $1,552,-272, the War Department spent $613,222 less in the latter year.[47] Calhoun could also point out with pride in his last annual report that the outstanding accounts of the department had been reduced from more than $45 million dollars to less than $3.5 million.[48]

Calhoun had begun his administration by working fourteen to fifteen hours a day, but his concept of administrative efficiency

[42] Calhoun to Jackson, March 2, 1818, Calhoun, *Papers*, II, 169.

[43] Nov. 10, 1814, House of Representatives, U.S., Congress, *Annals of Congress*, 13th Cong., 3d sess., pp. 550–51.

[44] April 14, 1818, *Statutes at Large*, III, 426; Erna Risch, *Quartermaster Support of the Army: A History of the Corps, 1775–1939* (Washington, D.C., 1962), pp. 182, 202.

[45] Report to the House, Dec. 11, 1818, *ASP:MA*, I, 780–82.

[46] He estimated that the savings totaled more than $750,000 over the three-year period 1819–22 (Annual Report of the Secretary of War for 1822, ibid., II, 467).

[47] Annual Reports of the Secretary of the Treasury for 1822 and 1825, *ASP:F*, IV, 14–15, V, 164–66.

[48] Calhoun to the President, Dec. 3, 1824, Letters sent to the President, 1800–1863, RG 107, National Archives, II, 130.

did not require him to shoulder this heavy load indefinitely. Once procedures that insured proper responsibility had been established and the channel of authority and control was reasonably well-defined, the head of each bureau was "freed from detail, and has leisure to inspect and control the whole." [49] Thus, when he left office, the secretary of war had little to do but sign his name and make those decisions only he could make as they were brought to his attention by his efficient staff. [50]

This rather cursory look into several facets of Calhoun's administration of the War Department has attempted to demonstrate the need for a more thorough examination of the "cast-iron man" as an administrator. Calhoun's theme of responsibility and economy constitutes only a part of the intricate management of his subordinates and his relations with the public and politicians. In addition, Calhoun's relationship with Congress, his role in policy making as a member of Monroe's cabinet, and the relationship of his department to private business interests need to be investigated in more depth. As we survey the lack of research, we can agree with the words of the young man from South Carolina: "We have, indeed, much to do." [51]

[49] Calhoun to Henry Clay, Dec. 11, 1818, Calhoun, *Papers*, III, 381.
[50] Ibid., II, xlviii.
[51] Calhoun to Major General Jacob Brown, Dec. 17, 1817, ibid., p. 22.

Simon Bernard, the American System, and the Ghost of the French Alliance

Joseph H. Harrison, Jr.

OF THE United States after 1815, Henry Adams wrote,

The long, exciting, and splendid panorama of revolution and war, which for twenty-five years absorbed the world's attention and dwarfed all other interests, vanished more quickly in America than in Europe, and left fewer elements of disturbance. The transformation scene of a pantomime was hardly more sudden or complete than the change that came over the United States at the announcement of peace. In a single day, almost in a single instant, the public turned from interests and passions that had supplied its thought for a generation, and took up a class of ideas that had been unknown or but vaguely defined before.[1]

It is a fine passage and a sound generalization about nineteenth-century American history. Yet, like most sweeping summaries of change, it slights the case for continuity. It was not immediately apparent on the morrow of Waterloo that the age of revolutionary upheaval had ended; in Latin America, for example, it had hardly begun. Nor was it clear that peace in Europe, however calming to controversy over neutral rights, meant good relations between the United States and the United Kingdom.

Henry Clay, pleading in the winter of 1815–16 for retention of taxes he thought necessary for defense, reminded the House of Representatives "that the power of France, as a counterpoise to that of Great Britain, is annihilated" and warned "that this country must have many a hard and desperate tug with Great Britain, let the two Governments be administered how and by whom they may. That man must be blind to the indications of the future who cannot see that we are destined to have war after war." [2] John C. Calhoun looked for war with either Spain or England. The United States was "rapidly improving in the very particulars in which [the latter

---

[1] Adams, *History of the United States of America during the Administrations of Thomas Jefferson and James Madison* (9 vols., New York, 1889–91), IX, 80.

[2] Ibid., IX, 109; Clay, speech of Jan. 29, 1816, in House of Representatives, U.S., Congress, *Annals of Congress*, 14th Cong., 1st sess., pp. 776–92. See also Henry Clay, *The Papers of Henry Clay*, ed. James F. Hopkins and Mary W. M. Hargreaves (Lexington, Ky., 1959–), II, 140–59.

country] excels." Would "the greater Power permit the less to attain its destined greatness by natural growth, or will she take measures to disturb it?" The South Carolinian left no doubt as to which answer he considered realistic.[3]

Similar views were expressed, at nearly the same time, by the leading members of the Virginia dynasty and the Adams dynasty, by Rufus King, Alexander J. Dallas, and such prominent publicists as Mathew Carey and Hezekiah Niles.[4] A majority of the Fourteenth Congress, meeting in temporary quarters while rebuilding of the Capitol began among the ruins left by General Ross, concurred. It voted, at heavy political cost, for the retention of direct taxes. It approved an enlarged navy and a peacetime military establishment of ten thousand, rank and file, with two major generals (Jacob Brown and Andrew Jackson) and four brigadiers of the line. Also wanted were strong coastal fortifications and a national system of roads and canals for military and commercial— as well as political—reasons. Economic self-sufficiency as a national goal was a corollary of the same assumptions; hence the widespread acceptance of a new national bank and of a protective tariff. Clay especially, conscious of America's isolation as a republican power in the post-Napoleonic world, would presently look to Latin America for partners in an "American System" to counterbalance the Holy Alliance.[5]

Most of this program was supported, albeit with some qualifications, by President Madison and his heir-apparent, Secretary of State Monroe. The administration favored an army twice as large as Congress could be induced to vote—and three new military academies as well. Secretary of War William H. Crawford, late minister at the Tuileries and Bonapartist sympathizer, had reason to know that the collapse of the French Empire had left much military talent unemployed. On April 24, 1816, his friend James Barbour of Virginia—who was also the friend and neighbor of Madison and, as chairman of the Senate Committee on Military Affairs, a frequent spokesman for them both—introduced a resolu-

[3] Calhoun, speech of Jan. 31, 1816, in House of Representatives, *Annals of Congress*, 14th Cong., 1st sess., pp. 829–40; see also John C. Calhoun, *The Papers of John C. Calhoun*, ed. Robert Lee Meriwether and W. Edwin Hemphill (Columbia, S.C., 1959–), I, 316–31.

[4] Bradford Perkins, *Castlereagh and Adams: England and the United States, 1812–1823* (Berkeley and Los Angeles, 1964), pp. 156–72.

[5] Joseph Hobson Harrison, Jr., "The Internal Improvement Issue in the Politics of the Union 1783–1825" (Ph.D. diss., University of Virginia, 1954), pp. 326–32. For Clay's first use of the term "American System," see his speech of May 10, 1820, in House of Representatives, *Annals of Congress*, 16th Cong., 1st sess., pp. 2233–39; also Clay, *Papers*, II, 853–60.

tion which cleared Congress in three days and was approved by the president on the 29th. It provided "That the President of the United States be, and he hereby is, authorized to employ, in addition to the corps of engineers as now established, a skillful assistant whose compensation shall be such as the President . . . shall think proper, not exceeding the allowance to the chief officer of that corps." [6] On November 16 following, a commission as "assistant engineer with pay and emoluments of a brigadier general" was accordingly bestowed on Simon Bernard, a baron of the Empire and French general of brigade for whom the government of Louis XVIII had no present use.[7]

Born April 26, 1779, at Dole, former capital of the Franché-Comté, or Free County of Burgundy, this artisan's son had grown up in a locale appropriate for the rearing of engineers, military or civil. The Rhine-Rhône Canal (or Canal Napoléon as it was styled when both rivers were equally French) was under construction during most of his life; it passes through the town by the River Doubs. The principal event of Dôlois history was still the great siege of 1636 when the townsmen, loyal to their Spanish Hapsburg sovereign, had successfully resisted for three months a French army under the father of the great Condé. (Besançon had replaced it as the provincial capital when the French finally conquered the area a generation later.) [8]

Desperately poor but armed with a glowing recommendation from his schoolmaster-priest to the great Lagrange, Bernard had walked to Paris at sixteen to enroll in the Ecole central des travaux publics, shortly renamed Ecole polytechnique, from which he graduated second in the class of 1797. Beside Lagrange, its faculty then included Berthollet, Chaptal, Prony, and Bernard's eventual and particular patron, Gaspard Monge.[9] From their lecture rooms he went almost immediately to the Army of the Rhine

---

[6] *Annals of Congress*, 14th Cong., 1st sess., pp. 344, 351, 1439, 1452; U.S., *Statutes at Large*, III, 342.

[7] Francis Bernard Heitman, *Historical Register and Dictionary of the United States Army from Its Organization, September 29, 1789, to March 2, 1903* (2 vols., Washington, D.C., 1903), I, 214; also Bernard record in Record Group 94, National Archives, Washington, D.C.

[8] Armand Marquiset, *Statistique historique de l'arrondissement de Dole* (2 vols., Besançon, 1841–42), passim.

[9] André-Marcel Berthelot, "Ecole polytechnique," *La Grande Encyclopédie, inventaire raisonné des sciences, des lettres, des arts* . . . (Paris, 1886–1903). See also "Discours prononcé par M. le comte [Louis-Mathieu] Molé à l'occasion du décès du M. le baron Bernard, au Chambre des pairs, séance du 22 février 1840," in *Le lieutenant général Baron Bernard 1779–1839* (Besançon, 1894), pp. 35–36.

and seventeen years of service not untypical of what the French like to call *l'épopée*—years of wounds, long rides, and desperate fighting, with love interest provided by a Bavarian noblewoman, Maria Anna von Lerchenfeld, who became Madame Bernard.[10] Though distinguished in reconnaissance before Austerlitz, Bernard did best in Dalmatia, where he chased Montenegrin guerrillas and built roads for Marshal Marmont. (The great road from Ragusa to Zara and Trieste was doubtless one of the public works that caused no less a reactionary than the emperor Francis to express regret that the French had not stayed longer.)[11] In 1811 he was put in charge of the fortifications of Antwerp—the most important assignment of its kind then in Napoleon's power, we are told, since "in his struggle with England all his attention and all his hopes were concentrated on the Scheldt, and he had conceived the vastest plans" for that city.[12] Here Bernard won praise from the civil engineers who were his coworkers and formed a friendship with the alert young politician and man of letters, Matthieu Molé, who was already at the head of the Department of Public Works (Ponts et chaussées). Aide-de-camp to Napoleon in 1813 and an officer of the Legion of Honor, Bernard served heroically in Germany. He was promoted to *maréchal de camp* in the spring of 1814, after the Battle of Arcis-sur-Aube, and before the Empire fell he was a baron.

Napoleon liked him: "I shouldn't be surprised," he told Molé, if

[10] *Baron Bernard*, an anonymous compilation obviously prepared under family supervision, includes several commemorative speeches and extracts from surviving correspondence. See also Marquiset, I, 224–51; Gustave Gautherot, *Biographie du général Simon Bernard, né à Dôle* [sic, the accent is now obsolete] *le 28 avril 1779, mort à Paris le 5 novembre 1839, aide de camp de Napoléon Ier, major général* [sic] *de génie aux Etats-unis, ministre de la guerre sous la monarchie de juillet* (Besançon, 1901); Jean-Baptiste-Gaspard Roux de Rochelle, *Notice sur le général Bernard, lu à la société de géographie dans le séance de 3 janvier 1840* (Paris, 1840); Charles Durozoir, s.v. "Bernard, Simon, baron," *Biographie universelle* (Paris, 1842–65); E. Franceschini, s.v. "Bernard, Simon, baron," *Dictionnaire de biographie française* (Paris, 1933–); "Bernard, Simon, baron," *Dictionnaire biographique des généraux et amiraux français* (Paris, 1934); Thomas Marshall Spaulding, s.v. "Bernard, Simon," *Dictionary of American Biography*.

[11] "Discours par Molé," p. 40; Gautherot, pp. 8–9; Robert William Seton-Watson, *The Southern Slav Question and the Habsburg Monarchy* (London, 1911); Arnold Joseph Toynbee, *A Study of History* (12 vols., London, 1934–61), V, 367.

[12] "Discours par Molé," p. 41; Louis-Antoine Fauvelet de Bourrienne, *Memoirs of Napoleon Bonaparte*, ed. R. W. Phipps (4 vols., New York, 1891), III, 7–8.

this blond youngster "would have preferred Washington to me; what do I care? Do they think I only look for men without convictions? I don't ask anyone to think as I do; I ask everyone to help me make the French the first people of the world." Bernard was one of his best engineers, remarkable for his courage, "sense of duty, uprightness, truth. . . . I put these qualities ahead of everything; I want that known. Bernard is a plebeian and a self-made man. *L'enfant de ses œuvres,*" he smiled at the aristocratic Molé, "*c'est comme moi, et cela m'intéresse toujours.*" [13]

For the rest, the emperor thought him "an excellent bricklayer" who did not understand politics and should stick to his trade.[14] The events of 1815 tended to bear this judgment out. Bernard had fared well under the First Restoration, receiving the Order of St. Louis and the rank of *général de brigade* (equivalent to that which he already held); he nonetheless rallied to Napoleon during the Hundred Days, joined the Waterloo campaign, and even sought to accompany the emperor into exile. He was then much distressed when refused active duty in the royal service, banished to Dole, and ordered to remain there under police surveillance. Neither Gouvion St. Cyr nor his successor at the War Ministry, Marshal Clarke, duc de Feltre, inclined to forgiveness, though Bernard protested that the king would now find him "a faithful and zealous subject," ready to defend "the legitimate dynasty of the Bourbons, without which neither France nor the happiness of the French people could exist." He acknowledged sadly that "raison d'état" was doubtless against him at the moment.[15]

It was, and he had a growing family to maintain. Foreign employment beckoned. In August 1816 he advised Clarke that he could enter either the Dutch or the Bavarian army (he said nothing of the Russian despite later accounts of brilliant offers from the Czar) but feared that either might involve service against France. Fortunately, "the United States of America are just now fortifying their frontiers by sea and land." They had accepted his services as "foreign engineer." He knew what he owed his own country;

[13] "Discours par Molé," p. 42. I have left the conclusion of this passage in its idiomatic original.

[14] Durozoir. Another version of the story is in Paul, vicomte de Barras, *Memoirs of Barras, Member of the Directorate,* ed. George Duruy (4 vols., New York, 1855), IV, 364–65, where Napoleon, angered by a plea for constitutional government which the engineer has ventured, calls him the *son* of a bricklayer.

[15] Bernard to Clarke, May 3, 1816, dossier de Simon Bernard, Bibliothèque de service historique de l'armée, Château de Vincennes, Vincennes, Seine (hereafter cited as Bernard dossier).

he was not resigning but asking for leave. He assumed that "in serving the United States, I serve the natural interests of my fatherland." [16]

Hostility to England, though he did not mention it to the minister, may have had as much to do with this conviction as any partiality for America. He was imbued, said a later friend and eulogist, with feelings derived from the recent wars and could "believe himself still serving his own country while he organized, *against a rival nation*, a vast system of fortifications and defense. An illustrious Frenchman," after all, was associated with the achievement of American independence; another Frenchman might now help to consolidate that achievement.[17] The example could rarely have been far from Bernard's mind, for it was through the mediation of Lafayette and under his "paternal protection" that the creation of a place for the younger man in the service of the United States had been arranged.[18]

Secretary Crawford, who had known Bernard in France, was also involved, and Albert Gallatin, Crawford's successor at the Paris legation, equipped the engineer with "letters stating that he was the seventh in rank in [his] corps, and inferior to none in reputation and talents." [19] As the protégé of Lafayette, he could count on an American welcome; the "Hero of Two Worlds" assured his friend Jefferson that Bernard had "remained," despite his association with Napoleon, "a stranger to the intrigues, rewards, and principles of the [Imperial] Court." The former president himself, in a gracious note of welcome, congratulated the Union "on the acquisition of your talents, which, directing our preparations for war, are most likely to continue it a land of peace and safety." [20]

[16] Bernard to Clarke, Aug. 1, 1816, ibid.

[17] Félix Barthe, in *Baron Bernard*, pp. 13–14.

[18] Bernard to Soult, duc de Dalmatie, Feb. 5, 1831, Bernard dossier. See also "Discours par Molé," p. 44.

[19] James Monroe to Andrew Jackson, Nov. 16, 1816, *The Writings of James Monroe*, ed. Stanislaus Murray Hamilton (7 vols., New York, 1898–1903), V, 348–49. See also William Harding Carter, "Bvt. Major [*sic*] Gen. Simon Bernard," Journal of the Military Service Institution of the United States, 5 (May–June 1913): 306–14.

[20] Lafayette to Jefferson, Sept. 16, 1816, Jefferson to Bernard, March 3, 1817, Jefferson Papers, Library of Congress, Washington, D.C. For this and other material in both the Jefferson and Jackson Papers, I have used the photostats in the Bernard Collection, Fort Monroe (Va.) Casemate Museum and am indebted to its curator, Dr. Chester W. Bradley, indefatigable collector of Bernard material on both sides of the Atlantic.

Lafayette had been sure that Bernard's "companions will love him," [21] and doubtless his French companions—of whom several arrived with him at New York in the fall of 1816—did. The American engineers, graduates of an academy painfully inferior in size and repute to the Ecole polytechnique but fiercely proud of their recent exploits against the British, were otherwise disposed.[22] The administration had tried hard to forestall their complaints. Bernard was to serve on a Board of Fortifications with two senior officers of the corps; with them would be joined, at each locality, the ranking engineer and the ranking naval officer stationed there. In case of disagreement, the Frenchman could prevail only by convincing his colleagues. President-elect Monroe pronounced him "a modest, unassuming man, who . . . understands that he is never to have Command of the Corps, but will always rank second in it." [23]

None of this allayed the bitterness of his first two full-time colleagues on the Board of Fortifications. Their resentment blended military punctilio and American chauvinism. It may have owed something to Bernard's reluctance to explain his opinions in a language he had just commenced to learn, and it was doubtless enhanced by awareness that his credentials with the general public far outweighed their own. Brevet Brigadier General Joseph Gardner Swift, chief engineer since 1812, was not naturally diffident. He had been the first graduate of the military academy and had directed the fortification of New York—no bad equivalent to Antwerp—with energy and acclaim. But to have studied under Jonathan Williams was not quite the same as to have been a pupil of Lagrange and Monge, and to have served—however capably— with James Wilkinson at Chrysler's Farm was rather less glorious than to have been the last officer at Napoleon's side on the field of Waterloo.[24]

[21] Lafayette to Jefferson, Sept. 16, 1816, Jefferson Papers.

[22] For their achievements in the war, see Adams, IX, 235–36; and, more copiously, George Washington Cullum, *Campaigns of the War of 1812–15, against Great Britain, Sketched and Criticised, with Brief Biographies of the American Engineers* (New York, 1879), passim; also the biographical sketches cited below.

[23] Monroe to Jackson, Nov. 16, 1816, Jackson Papers, Lib. Cong.

[24] Cullum, pp. 151–96; also Cullum, *Biographical Register of the Officers and Graduates of the United States Military Academy at West Point, New York, from Its Establishment in 1802 to 1890* . . . (3d ed., 4 vols., Boston, 1891–1904), I, 51–56; Thomas Marshall Spaulding, s.v. "Swift, Joseph Gardner," *DAB*. For Bernard at Waterloo, see Barras, IV, 364–65; for his

Swift protested Bernard's appointment, tried to shunt him off to a professorship at West Point (where Captain Claude Crozet, another of the French party, would do much to raise the level of instruction), and went on protesting. Finally, toward the end of 1818, Swift resigned his commission to become surveyor of the Port of New York. In conversation and in writing, for the rest of a long life, he did not cease to belittle Bernard—"an excellent bureau officer, a cold-hearted man; not in any sense a man of genius." [25]

Still less "liberal," at least according to Swift, was Brevet Colonel William McRee, late chief engineer to General Brown on the Niagara frontier, third-ranking officer of the corps (not counting Bernard), and perhaps its most brilliant figure. His resignation followed hard on Swift's. But the civilian authorities stood firm. James Monroe could remember Washington's almost total reliance on French engineers with Du Portail at their head, and residents of the capital city could hardly have forgotten L'Enfant. [26] As for John C. Calhoun, who became secretary of war in December 1817 and made himself the driving force behind the fortification program, Swift complained that he helped "to infect members of Congress with an idea that General Bernard had a transcendent genius, and therefore . . . must be consulted upon all public works; as if he had been possessed of intuitive knowledge of a subject that could only be acquired by actual residence in our country a suitable period of time." [27]

Calhoun was fond of Swift, who later supported him for the presidency and whose authority over construction of fortifications —though not over their location and design—he wished to increase. But he apparently thought ballistic and hydraulic problems much the same on both sides of the Atlantic, and he stuck by his foreign expert. Moreover, Bernard, whose "popularity" his arch-enemy

---

ignorance of English in 1816, attested by his aide, Major Poussin, see *Baron Bernard*, pp. 24–25.

[25] *The Memoirs of Gen. Joseph Gardner Swift, LL.D., U.S.A., First Graduate of the United States Military Academy, West Point, Chief Engineer U.S.A. from 1812 to 1818*, [covering the period] *1800–1865* (privately printed, c. 1890), passim, esp. pp. 179–80.

[26] For McRee, see Cullum, *Campaigns*, pp. 202–33, and *Biographical Register*, I, 59–63; also Heitman, I, 682. The role of Du Portail and his associates is characterized by Douglas Southall Freeman et al., *George Washington, A Biography* (7 vols., New York, 1948–57), I, 571A. With Lafayette and Steuben, they were standing exceptions to the derogatory generalizations about foreign officers in the American service.

[27] Swift, p. 149.

conceded, clearly won support among the naval officers with whom he had to work and a degree of acceptance, at least, from most of the army engineers.[28]

So far as the record shows, Colonel Walker Keith Armistead, Swift's successor, coexisted peaceably with the Frenchman. So did Brevet Major General Alexander Macomb, who took over the engineers when the army was halved in 1821 and directed them until he succeeded Brown as commanding general seven years later; he himself, despite prewar service in the corps, seems to have been regarded by it as something of an outsider.[29] Macomb's two successors at its head, Charles Gratiot and Joseph Gilbert Totten, were Bernard's closest American collaborators.

The former, a St. Louis Creole who had been Harrison's chief engineer in the Northwest, became Bernard's closest friend among American professionals and the executant of his most ambitious design for a fort. With Totten, defender of Plattsburg and (in the long run) the most considerable American military engineer of his generation, Bernard's relations were less cordial, though it is not true that the two of them could only work together at a distance. From the time that Totten replaced McRee on the Board of Fortifications until Bernard revisited France in 1830, their cooperation was almost continual.[30]

It was, of course, absurd — and the sort of unfairness that Swift and his friends must have anticipated — for Bernard's devoted aide, Major Guillaume Tell Poussin, to claim that his chief had created the American frontier defense system singlehandedly. But in

---

[28] Calhoun's relationship with Swift is cogently discussed by editor W. Edwin Hemphill in Calhoun, *Papers*, II, lix–lx, lxxi–lxxii. See also Charles M. Wiltse, *John C. Calhoun: Nationalist 1782–1828* (New York, 1944), pp. 171, 205, 272, 274, 316. That both naval officers and local engineers often agreed with the Frenchman is clear from the frequency with which his judgment was preferred to those of Swift and McRee. For his intimacy with Commodore Jesse D. Elliott, see, especially, Bernard to Elliott, April 26, May 6, 1835, Jackson Papers. In the former, Commodores Charles Morris and Lewis Warrington are also mentioned as friends.

[29] For the corps' view of Macomb, a few years later, as an outsider, see Douglas Southall Freeman, *R. E. Lee, A Biography* (4 vols., New York, 1934–35), I, 124–27.

[30] For Gratiot, a neglected figure of some importance, see ibid., I, 131; he was Lee's first patron in the service. His collaboration with Bernard is extolled by Roux de Rochelle, himself French minister at Washington under Charles X (ibid., pp. 13–14). For Totten, see Cullum, *Campaigns*, pp. 65–88, and *Biographical Register*, I, 63–67; also William Addleman Ganoe, s.v. "Totten, Joseph Gilbert," *DAB*. For the tradition that he and Bernard had to work far apart, see Carter, pp. 312–13.

fourteen years he had "worked on practically every fortification from Maine to Texas," [31] prepared elaborate plans for the defense of the Gulf and Canadian frontiers, and "made dispositions equally scientific and effective to close the entrances of American rivers *to the English*." [32]

His plans were sharply criticized. Local particulars aside, he favored larger forts than those to which the Americans were accustomed—and even Swift admitted that here he was usually right. He also had a preference—its influence may have been baleful—for structures of a pentagonal design.[33] Few of his works were to be adequately tested in war; Fort Monroe, Virginia, his chef d'œuvre, "so nearly impregnable that no land attack on it was worth the planning," [34] played a great part in securing Union control of Hampton Roads and the lower Virginia peninsula; but it never had to stand siege. The fate of Fort Pulaski, Georgia, less distinctively Bernard's but influenced by him and also considered impregnable, suggests a failure to allow sufficiently for future improvements in artillery: its walls were easily breached in 1862 by the fire of rifled guns.[35]

But Bernard's American labors were not confined to military engineering. A national system of roads and canals, supplemented by river and harbor improvements, was considered—by Calhoun especially—an essential part of the national defense. In 1822 Bernard and Totten surveyed the Ohio and Mississippi rivers; in 1823 (with Commodore William Bainbridge) they studied the feasibility of a breakwater at the capes of Delaware Bay. In January 1824, with Canvass White of the Union Canal Company and Benjamin Wright, principal engineer of the Erie, they examined

[31] Poussin, in *Baron Bernard*, pp. 24–25.   [32] Marquiset, I, 228.

[33] Swift dismisses "General Bernard's pentagons" as having "since been found inappropriate" (p. 149). The reference is to a controversy between the Frenchman and Captain James Gadsden (with whom he also clashed over the fortification of Mobile Bay) regarding the proper defense of the Mississippi passes. The subject has been more fully discussed by Virgil B. Davis, "Simon Bernard and the United States Board of Engineers [for Fortification]," a paper presented to the Alabama Academy of Science at Auburn, April 1970. But see Bernard's Report on the Defense of the Gulf of Mexico Frontier, RG 77, National Archives.

[34] Douglas Southall Freeman, *Lee's Lieutenants: A Study in Command* (3 vols., New York, 1942–44), I, 695.

[35] Joseph Tyrone Derry, *Georgia* (Clement Anselm Evans, ed., *Confederate Military History* [12 vols., Atlanta, 1899], VI), pp. 88–91. Fort Hamilton, N.Y., Fort Washington, Md., and Fort Caswell, N.C., were also especially Bernard's.

alternate routes for the Chesapeake and Delaware Canal and settled, definitively, on the line of St. George's Meadows.[36] After the passage of the General Survey Act in April of that year, Bernard, Totten, and John Langdon Sullivan, former superintendent of the Middlesex Canal, were constituted the first Board of Engineers for Internal Improvement.

The six succeeding years, stretching from the Survey Act to the Maysville veto, marked the culmination of the American System in the field of public works. Bernard, with two boards to serve on instead of one, had to "reconnoitre all the coasts, descend the smallest rivers, traverse mountain ranges and marshes"[37] by turns. He acquired, and recorded in charts, maps and reports, a command of American topography which few native Americans can have equaled.

Yet in these very years the American System was being undermined. A states' rights resurgence, perceptible if impotent for several years and fueled by the growing unease about slavery, gathered strength from the reaction against the election of John Quincy Adams, his coalition with Henry Clay, and the uninhibited nationalism of his first annual message. Caught up in this reaction was Bernard's patron and former chief, Calhoun, now vice-president, whose plans and priorities—only a little diluted—continued to dominate the Department of War. The military rationale of the postwar nationalism had been weakened, too, by the improvement of relations with Great Britain; when the Monroe Doctrine was promulgated, so hardened an Anglophobe as Hezekiah Niles could envision England as fighting beside America against Bourbon France and the other "Holy Allies."[38]

Not all Americans were so ideological. Richard Rush, American minister in London, still believed that "France, . . . toujours France, belle France, is our best and true connexion abroad, and must be for years to come." An alliance with the Bourbons had proved advantageous in 1778. He thought "the French marine . . . the only one that will be able, in conjunction with ours, to make head against the English" and mused that "it would be strange if the first foreign power we have a war with, should be Mexico,

[36] Edward Burr, Memoranda relating to Brevet Brigadier General Simon Bernard, Assistant in the Corps of Engineers, U.S.A., 1816–1831, RG 77, National Archives; U.S., Congress, *Senate Documents*, 18th Cong., 1st sess., no. 1, pp. 27–36; ibid., no. 70, p. 6.

[37] Poussin, in *Baron Bernard*, pp. 24–25.

[38] *Niles' Weekly Register*, March 15, 1823.

with *England* as her ally." [39] But such premonitions were rare in the 1820s.

Bernard should have felt at home with an administration that included this Francophile, not to mention so ardent an admirer of Napoleon as Henry Clay. He was bound to sympathize with the new president's zeal for internal improvement. Yet in the sharpest controversy of his later American years he would find Adams and his secretary of war, the genial James Barbour, less staunch supporters than Monroe and Calhoun had been.

The first task assigned the Internal Improvement Board, and one which Bernard personally directed, was the survey of the Chesapeake and Ohio Canal route from Georgetown via Cumberland, Maryland, to Pittsburgh along with its projected extension to Lake Erie. His report was not submitted until October 1826; it included an elaborate comparison between ancient and modern public works with emphasis on the economy—the proportioning of means to ends—that modern respect for the value and dignity of labor entailed; "these conditions being fulfilled, such monuments justly become the objects of national pride; and combined with the civil and political institutions, the arts and sciences, literature, and naval and military achievements, form an union of glory around which the sympathies of the country are rallied, are strengthened, and are continued. Thus we perceive all the enlightened Governments of the present time to favor such undertakings."

The proposed canal, Bernard asserted, "has no equal in any country, either in relation to the works of every kind which its construction will require, or to the immense political, commercial, and military advantages which will result." It was "a work truly national; . . . beyond the means, always limited, of private enterprise," and much too important to be postponed. The growing West must have access to the Atlantic, and the Alleghenies, "a chain of mountains of secondary rank," should not "bar the progress of a nation as enterprising as ours, still less darken the prospects of this great federal empire." The canal would be a supreme technical achievement, and its cost, as Bernard made no effort to conceal, would far exceed that of any public work the country had yet seen.

Its width and depth, he and his colleagues proposed, should be the same as those of the Erie and Ohio canals; its length a mere

[39] Rush to Charles Jared Ingersoll, Feb. 14, 1821, Rush Papers, Princeton University Library, Princeton, N.J.

341 miles compared with the Erie's 362. But its lockage would total 3,158 feet, as against 688 for the Erie, 1,451 ¼ for the London-Liverpool navigation, and 1,458 for the yet uncompleted canal (so familiar to Bernard) between the Rhine and Rhône. It would require 398 locks and take 188 hours (nearly eight days and nights) to traverse. Use of railways or inclined planes at the highest points was not ruled out. But the engineers preferred a tunnel, 4 miles and 80 yards long, beneath the 856-foot ridge of the Alleghenies (the Standedge Tunnel through the Pennines, longest in Britain, was 3 miles and 15 yards). Their final estimate of expenses came to $22,375,427.69.[40]

Financially this was bad news. The Erie Canal had cost only $7 million. The Chesapeake and Ohio Canal Company, as incorporated by three states and by Congress on behalf of the federal district, was allowed a capital of only $6 million. Bernard was proposing to spend more than $8 million on the relatively easy eastern section (Georgetown to Cumberland) alone. One earlier estimate for the entire work had run below a million and a quarter. And the company must now sell its stock, as yet unissued, in a market badly shaken by the British Panic of 1825.[41]

President Adams, however, was enthusiastic and anxious for the federal government to lend its support with a generous subscription. In preparing his second annual message, he rejoiced that the engineers found the canal practicable, instead of lamenting that they had pronounced it costly. "Its utmost cost," he said (invoking a criterion remote from the peacetime taxpayer's mind) would be less that "of a single year of War." It would actually be a new source of revenue, helping to liquidate the public debt, and to have served in the Congress that undertook the project would "be a title to the veneration of after times." [42]

[40] "Report of the Board of Internal Improvement on the Chesapeake and Ohio Canal, comprising the plan and estimates of the same, October 23, 1826," U.S., Congress, *House Documents*, 19th Cong., 2d sess., no. 10. The signatories are Bernard, Poussin—then captain in the Corps of Topographical Engineers—and William Howard, civil engineer, the two latter signing as assistants to the Board. The comparisons are included in the report itself, pp. 37–40. For the priority given this project, see Macomb to Bernard, May 30, 1824, RG 77, National Archives.

[41] Walter Stanley Sanderlin, *The Great National Project: A History of the Chesapeake and Ohio Canal*, Johns Hopkins University Studies in History and Political Science, vol. 64 (Baltimore, 1946), pp. 52–56.

[42] Draft in Adams Family Papers, Massachusetts Historical Society, Boston; I have used the microfilms in the Lib. Cong. (hereafter cited as Adams Microfilms), roll 478.

To the president's pained surprise, Henry Clay demurred. He doubted, in cabinet, that the canal could be completed. He thought Bernard's estimate of the cost was too low. Even if finished the work would have "small utility. It would not divert the great mass of the trade of the Western country from New York and Philadelphia," whatever the hopes of the capital city. Except along its immediate route, "there was very little interest in it . . . , and none at all in the Western country generally."

Secretary Barbour supported Clay; Secretary Rush, the president. No one said anything about railroads, though George Stephenson's first demonstration on the Stockton and Darlington line had occurred the previous year. Adams decided to let the engineers' report stand alone, transmitting it to Congress without personal comment.[43] Clay and Barbour, for their part, kept their doubts to themselves in the convention that the canal's promoters held at Washington, December 6–9, 1826. The main purpose of that assemblage, it was later recalled, was "to neutralize and overthrow, in the judgment of the *public*, the estimate" of expenses from that "high and accredited source," the Board of Engineers— by arguments quite the opposite of the Kentuckian's.[44]

This campaign was led by two congressmen, Charles Fenton Mercer of Loudoun County, Virginia, and Andrew Stewart of Uniontown, Pennsylvania, who managed to dominate discussion of the subject for months to come. Both spoke for interested communities; each was an enthusiast for this project and for internal improvement generally. Mercer was also a crusader against slavery and for education, while Stewart's principal interest was the tariff.[45]

After Bernard had warned the promoters early in 1826 that his estimates would much exceed theirs, Stewart, who had just be-

[43] John Quincy Adams, *Memoirs of John Quincy Adams Comprising Portions of His Diary from 1795 to 1848*, ed. Charles Francis Adams (12 vols., Philadelphia, 1874–77), VII, 190–91, Nov. 30, 1826.

[44] *Report to the Stockholders on the Completion of the Chesapeake and Ohio Canal to Cumberland, with a Sketch of the Potomac Company, and General Outline of the History of the Chesapeake and Ohio Canal Company, from Its Origin to February 1851* . . . (Frederick, Md., 1851), pp. 32–34. For the membership of the convention, see Washington, D.C., *Daily National Intelligencer*, Dec. 7, 1826.

[45] Charles Henry Ambler, s.v. "Mercer, Charles Fenton," *DAB;* Solon Justus Buck, s.v. "Stewart, Andrew," ibid. There is a valuable sketch of Mercer in John Henry Hobart, *The Correspondence of John Henry Hobart* (Arthur Lowndes, ed., *Archives of the General Convention* [6 vols., New York, 1911–12]), III, 94–97.

come chairman of the House Committee on Roads and Canals, had tried already to cushion the expected shock. He had ascribed the engineers' figures (still unreleased) "not so much to the intrinsic difficulties, as to the magnificence and durable character of the plan proposed," given greater weight to earlier and less professional surveys, and insisted that "the *tariff* and *internal improvement* constitute one 'American system' of policy and must stand or fall together." [46]

In the subsequent canal convention Mercer was chairman of the central committee, Stewart of the committee on estimates. The former paid tribute to Bernard's "unassuming personal and moral worth" as well as his "indefatigable industry" but at the same time contrived to call attention both to the engineer's foreign birth and to the fact that his experience had been gained in "military fortification." The general and his colleagues, said Mercer (who had himself dreamed of studying at the Ecole polytechnique and of living on terms of intimacy with its great savants),[47] had "failed only where less ability was competent to the task . . . , under the impression, perhaps, that the work . . . would readily command the wealth of a nation"—in other words, that money was no object.

"Tariff Andy" was harsher. He admitted the honesty of the engineers but impugned their knowledge of construction costs, wages, and the like. For "want of accurate local information they . . . had been betrayed into great errors," and he predicted that the cost of the canal would "not exceed one fourth" of the board's calculations.

These reassurances "had the most instantaneous and vivifying effect." The convention voted its thanks and its confidence. The Mercer and Stewart reports were embodied in a memorial which was presently referred to the House Committee on Roads and Canals—of which, by happy coincidence, Mercer was now chairman and Stewart the ranking member. The committee's report of January 19, 1827, omitted criticism of the engineers but recommended a federal subscription of $2.5 million.[48]

---

[46] U.S., Congress, *House Reports*, 19th Cong., 1st sess., no. 72, especially pp. 1–24, May 22, 1826.

[47] Mercer to Hobart, June 13, 1803, Hobart, *Correspondence*, III, 225–26.

[48] *House Reports*, 19th Cong., 2d sess., Jan. 30, 1827, no. 90, appends the report of the central committee, pp. 70–88. For that of the committee of estimates see Washington *National Intelligencer*, Dec. 11, 1826. See also *Acts of the States of Virginia, Maryland, and Pennsylvania, and of the Congress of the United States, in Relation to the Chesapeake and Ohio*

Some semblance of objectivity was still needed, and thirty-two congressmen joined in petitioning the president to submit the board's estimates and those of the convention "to such practical civil engineers, as have long engaged in the actual construction of the various canals of the several states, with a view to reconcile the *apparent* disagreement." [49] Since the lower estimates were derived from such engineers, mostly surveyors with on-the-job training, the intent of the petition was obvious. John Quincy Adams, of all presidents, should have stood by his experts. But the Adamses were very much a part of the Washington community; the president esteemed Mercer, an independent but valuable supporter in the House; and piety to the memory of General Washington, long the foremost advocate of the Potomac route to the West, may have played its part.

In any case, Adams referred the matter to James Geddes and Nathan S. Roberts, two of the Erie Canal fraternity, and they did what was expected of them, making a survey of their own but taking the promoters' word for prices. They cut Bernard's estimate for the eastern section by approximately 45 percent.

The sequel, or part of it, is well known. By an act of May 24, 1828, an opposition-dominated Congress authorized a federal subscription of $1 million (10,000 shares at $100) in Chesapeake and Ohio stock. At the same time it empowered the three cities of the District of Columbia—Washington, Alexandria, and Georgetown—to subscribe, between them, another $1.5 million.[50] The president's wife observed that "all here are beside themselves with joy[,] none of us knowing exactly why but all anticipating mines of wealth from what will probably ruin many." [51]

To her husband his principles seemed vindicated. He could not "restrain" himself, he told his son Charles, "from crying the Io triumphe of internal improvement. It floats upon the future surface of the Chesapeake and Ohio Canal. All the waters of opposition too are broken by the Breakwater in the Delaware," for which Con-

---

Canal Company; with the Proceedings of the Convention which Led to the Formation of the Said Company . . . (Washington, 1828); and *Report to Stockholders, 1851.*

[49] Italics mine.

[50] The whole affair is concisely summarized in Daniel Hovey Calhoun, *The American Civil Engineer, Origins and Conflict* (Cambridge, Mass., 1960), pp. 113–15. See also Carter Goodrich, *Government Promotion of American Canals and Railroads* (New York, 1960), pp. 76–79.

[51] Louisa Catherine Adams to George Washington Adams, May 24, 1828, Adams Microfilms, roll 485.

gress had voted $250,000 on the previous day. The canal company soon completed organization, chose Mercer for president, and hired the adaptable Benjamin Wright as chief engineer. Adams retained his euphoria long enough, in that year of political disaster, to savor the one great public triumph of his presidency, the ground-breaking ceremony of July 4.[52]

Had he—and Bernard—been right about the canal's economic importance, the chief executive's optimism would have been admired and his political failures as little remembered as those of De Witt Clinton in New York. Barring railroads—the Baltimore and Ohio commenced on the same day as the canal and was built much more rapidly—a waterway from Washington to Pittsburgh might have repaid the cost; Bernard's plans might have ultimately prevailed, and his fame rivaled that of Riquet or Brindley, Telford or De Lesseps. As it was, the Chesapeake and Ohio's eastern section did not reach Cumberland until 1850. Its cost, though the excess over Bernard's calculations is largely attributable to rising prices, was more than $11 million. The western section was never even begun.[53]

The management of the company in 1851 made Bernard a posthumous amende honorable, lauding "the elaborate, well digested, and disinterested estimate of a corps of the ablest engineers in America, guided by [Bernard's] matured experience," that their predecessors had so rashly "cast aside and condemned." Sadly it was conceded that "a body of men, however upright and intelligent, are easily satisfied of what they greatly wish to believe." [54]

None of the other projects for which the general made surveys during those hectic six and a half years held out such possibilities of fame as a waterway across the Appalachians. The Delaware Breakwater was the first American attempt at a great artificial harbor, but its successful completion failed to avert the decline of the Port of Philadelphia.[55] The Muscle Shoals of the Tennessee were among the country's major obstacles to inland navigation, but the canal opened around them in the 1830s proved short-lived.[56] A

[52] J. Q. Adams to Charles Francis Adams, May 28, 1828, ibid.; Samuel Flagg Bemis, *John Quincy Adams and the Union* (New York, 1956), pp. 102–3.

[53] D. H. Calhoun, p. 155; Sanderlin, passim.

[54] *Report to Stockholders, 1851*, pp. 32–34.

[55] Another such work, at the mouths of the Mississippi, was discussed by the board in its report of Nov. 29, 1828 (*Senate Documents*, 20th Cong., 2d sess., no. 5).

[56] Susan Goode Douglass, "Canals and River Improvement in Alabama, 1819–1840" (M.A. thesis, Auburn University, 1970), pp. 80–81.

canal across Cape Cod, for which Bernard and Poussin prepared
elaborate plans, had been mooted by New Englanders at fifty-year
intervals since the days of Governor Bradford; it finally came to
fruition between 1909 and 1914.[57]

Most arduous of Bernard's labors was that on which he spent
much of the year 1827, "voyageant dans les forêts désertes des
Florides." [58] Here he surveyed three sides of a quadrilateral – the
north-south line of the St. Marys and St. Johns Rivers and two
east-west routes, one from the former stream to the St. Marks, the
other from the St. Johns to Tampa Bay. He came down with fever
before the task was finished, and since bands of hungry and dis-
gruntled Seminoles were roaming the area, his discomforts cannot
have been wholly physical. But despite the strategic importance
ascribed by Calhoun and others to a trans-Florida waterway, this
undertaking remained in limbo.[59]

Technically less interesting, politically more so, was the project
for a second great national road that absorbed more of Bernard's
time than any other scheme save the Chesapeake and Ohio Canal.
A first-rate highway from Washington to New Orleans had been
regarded as a national objective since the Louisiana Purchase.
Calhoun had given it a high priority in 1824, and three alternative
routes had been exhaustively surveyed. The westernmost – corresponding roughly to modern U.S. 11 – had received Bernard's
personal attention and was favored by the House Committee on
Roads and Canals, now chaired by Joseph Hemphill of Philadelphia. That body further proposed, in March 1830, to combine this
road with another which the Adams administration had projected
from the federal capital to Buffalo.

Politically, this was a bid for Northern support; militarily it
would provide at once for two of the outposts most threatened in
1814. As a sop to economizers, and to hold the initial estimates
down to $2.5 million, the committee proposed an "earthen turn-
pike" (or "mud road" as one critic jeered) with some admixture of
gravel where absolutely necessary. Such a wagon road of fifteen

[57] William Barclay Parsons, "Cape Cod Canal," *Annals of American
Academy of Political and Social Science*, 31 (Jan. 1908): 81–91; Frederick
Freeman, *The History of Cape Cod: The Annals of Barnstable County,
Including the District of Mashpee* (2 vols., Boston, 1858), I, 333, 493;
Henry Crocker Kittredge, *Cape Cod: Its People and Their History* (Boston
and New York, 1930), pp. 292–93.

[58] Bernard to Ferdinand Machera, Oct. 28, 1827, Bibliothèque municipale
de Dole, Jura.

[59] *Senate Documents*, 20th Cong., 2d sess., Feb. 19, 1829, no. 102.

hundred miles in the dawn of the railway age seemed obsolete to some, though Thomas Hart Benton would agitate nearly two decades later for a turnpike between the Missouri and the Columbia. But it was a combination of constitutional objections and the rivalries between the proponents of different routes through the South that caused the defeat of the Buffalo–New Orleans Road bill.

That defeat destroyed, at least for the moment, any claims to national importance for the Maysville and Lexington Turnpike Company, ostensibly a purely Kentucky undertaking but one which was proposing to construct part of an hypothetical third national road from Zanesville, Ohio, to Florence, Alabama. This would have linked the Cumberland Road, earliest national project of its kind, to the western route between Washington and New Orleans; but without the second road there was small occasion for the third, and President Jackson's veto of the Maysville bill could rest on the unassailable ground of distinction between national and local measures.[60]

But the message of May 30, 1830, and the simultaneous rejection of three other internal improvement bills unmistakably signaled abandonment of the program launched in 1824.[61] A large part of Bernard's occupation was going if not gone. Happily, two months later legitimism foundered in France, and the July Revolution opened the door for the lapsed Bonapartist of 1815.

Once again it was Lafayette, now a power in his own land for the last time, who intervened in Bernard's behalf, transmitting to him in September the compliments of Louis-Philippe on both his French and American services. The engineer lost little time in obtaining leave; he returned to France, was feted at Dole where he declaimed on "liberty . . . conquered by the people and for the people," and was encouraged at Paris where Marshal Soult was now minister of war.[62] Assured of employment at home, he came back to America to wind up his affairs, resigning on July 8, 1831, in a stately exchange of letters with President Jackson. To Gratiot, now chief engineer, he expressed "regret to separate from officers with whom I have been associated for nearly fifteen years and from

[60] Joseph Hobson Harrison, Jr., "Martin Van Buren and His Southern Supporters," *Journal of Southern History*, 22 (Nov. 1956): 450–51.

[61] Jackson vetoed a subscription to the Washington and Rockville Turnpike Company on the same day that he struck down the Maysville Bill. Simultaneously, he pocket-vetoed both a river and harbor bill and a further federal subscription to the indisputably national Louisville and Portland Canal Company. The impact is discussed in Goodrich, pp. 41–43.

[62] Bernard to Soult, Feb. 5, 1831, Bernard dossier; Gautherot, p. 18.

whom I have received so much attention and regard." His friend replied with warm acknowledgment of Bernard's "incessant services" and the "zeal and ability with which they were conducted." It was later noted that the "assistant engineer"—though employed on works that had cost, all told, more than one hundred million francs—returned to his native land "just as rich, just as poor" as when he left it.[63]

The July Monarchy brought him honors rather than reputation. He became, within a few years, aide de camp to the king, lieutenant general, grand officer of the Legion of Honor, and peer of France. He was twice minister of war—for three days in the fall of 1834 during the farcically brief Bassano ministry and from September 1836 to March 1839 under his old friend Count Molé. But he appears to have been an inept politician, an unpopular minister —an object of jealousy as an engineer ("grand terrassier"), perhaps of resentment as a longtime expatriate, of ridicule for planning the defense of Paris by means of detached forts. We are told that he made administrative reforms, and his record was probably better than anything he could say for it in the Chambre des pairs. When he died, September 5, 1839, he was governor of the Palais-Royal, and there was a fine funeral at the church of St. Roch with interment in the Montmartre cemetery. The eulogists dwelt exclusively on the Napoleonic and American phases of Bernard's career. Lewis Cass, President Van Buren's minister, was much in evidence.[64]

Cass had been high in the administration that had jettisoned the American System; his successor at the War Department, Joel Roberts Poinsett, who presently put the officers of the army into mourning for their old French comrade, had recently cashiered Charles Gratiot.[65] Yet Cass's presence at least testified to the peaceful resolution of the preposterous crisis that in 1834–35 had

[63] Bernard to Jackson, July 6, 1831, Jackson to Bernard, July 6, 1831, Jackson Papers; Bernard to Gratiot, July 11, 1831, Gratiot to Bernard, July 13, 1831, RG 94, National Archives; Poussin, in *Baron Bernard*, pp. 24–25.

[64] Gautherot, pp. 21–27; Franceschini; Durozoir; and the anonymous sketch "Bernard, Simon, baron," *Dictionnaire des parlementaires français, comprenant tous les Membres des Assemblées françaises et tous les Ministres français depuis le 1er mai 1789 jusqu'au 1er mai 1889* . . . (Paris, 1889–90). For the eulogies, see Baron Bernard, pp. 12–25.

[65] Freeman, *Lee*, I, 157–58, acquits Poinsett of personal hostility toward the chief engineer in the matter of that officer's accounts; he says nothing of Poinsett's own chief. There are strong hints of resentment at Gratiot's continued fervor for federal internal improvements in Van Buren to Andrew Jackson Donelson, Aug. 26, 1832, Van Buren Papers, Lib. of Cong.

threatened war between the United States and France—a war which could have made nonsense of half of Bernard's career.

The possibility of war was one on which Bernard's American enemies were probably pleased to dilate then, as their *epigones* certainly were in afteryears. George Washington Cullum, future general and personal disciple of Swift, would question whether it had been "good policy to take from the Bourbon army one permitted by his sovereign to enter our service, not from love to us, but rather that he might plan defenses against England, then deemed the common foe of both America and France; and was it statesmanship to introduce a Grecian horse within our Trojan walls, perhaps in time to be turned against us?" Had not Bernard, in fact, "carried abroad the secrets of our coast defense" and then risen high in the service of his own government? Who could doubt, in the event of "hostilities with France, what would have been [his] course of action"? [66] Another officer in the same tradition was certain that the engineer's dangerous knowledge was "placed at the disposal of his country and that France at any time in the following thirty years" might have used it to advantage in a war with the United States.[67]

That French forces would ever have attempted the systematic reduction of American coast defenses seems most unlikely. Bernard himself had always considered the Republic "attached to France by all the sympathies which could unite two great nations." [68] To his old friend Commodore Jesse D. Elliott, who put in at Le Havre on his way home from command in the Mediterranean, he warmly defended the good faith of the French executive in supporting the spoliation claims treaty of 1831. And, while avoiding direct criticism of "your worthy President," he insisted that "in a case like this the duty of men at the head of affairs consists in their doing every thing to temper those feelings which might arise out of too great national susceptibility." Repeatedly, Bernard appealed for "harmony . . . between two great nations, whom political principles and common interest must keep united." He insisted that "the two nations want each other: by remaining friends they will show the world that similarity of liberal principles is a tie which ought not to be broken." [69] But the affinity between the nations of

[66] Cullum, *Campaigns*, p. 61.

[67] Burr, Memoranda relating to Bernard, RG 77, National Archives.

[68] Bernard to Soult, Feb. 5, 1831, Bernard dossier.

[69] Bernard to Elliott, Apr. 26, 1835, Jackson Papers; see also Bernard to Elliott, Apr. 19 and May 6, 1835, ibid. The commodore, whose Jacksonism extended to the use of Old Hickory's visage as figurehead for his

Andrew Jackson and Louis-Philippe was becoming more and more dubious.

When an American president who invoked the shibboleths of Jefferson could say, "I know them French. They won't pay unless they are made to," when a British government could concern itself to avert a possible French blockade of American ports, or a French minister plan (as Guizot soon would) to thwart the growth of the United States in the interests of Latin culture and the balance of power, the ghost of the old alliance had been laid.[70] Neither John Quincy Adams, in his memorial tribute to Lafayette, nor Henry Clay, in the Senate report that rejected Jackson's belligerence toward France, made any reference to the traditional friendship between the two countries.[71]

In a world so changed, the memory of Bernard's work soon faded. His French friends might picture him roaming the New World wilderness like a Chateaubriand hero, equipping a nation with complete sets of public works, military and civil, but, after all, not that much had been done, and Bernard had by no means done all of it. Nor had he, despite high character and professional skill, impressed his personality upon his times—by contrast with his model, Lafayette, he appears colorless. Most of his charts and plans, with the bulk of his personal papers, presumably perished when the Paris Arsenal, commanded by his son Major Columbus Bernard, was burned by the Commune in 1871.[72] His elaborate reports are scattered through the American State Papers, the National Archives, and the documentary midden-heaps of the House and Senate.

---

flagship the *Constitution*, was an excellent pipeline. See Leonard F. Guttridge and Jay D. Smith, *The Commodores* (New York, 1969), p. 315.

[70] Henry Blumenthal, *A Reappraisal of Franco-American Relations 1830–1871* (Chapel Hill, N.C., 1959), pp. 35–43, 74–77; Sébastien Charléty, *La monarchie de juillet (1830–1848)* (Ernest Lavisse, ed., *Histoire de France contemporaine depuis la Révolution jusqu'à la paix de 1919* [9 vols., Paris, 1920–22], VI), pp. 112–17, 123.

[71] Bemis, pp. 309–12. For Clay's report from the Senate Committee on Foreign Relations, Jan. 6, 1835, see Washington *National Intelligencer*, Jan. 10. The same omission is conspicuous in the paper's own moderate editorials of Dec. 6, 1834, and subsequent dates.

[72] Gautherot, p. 27. Bernard's materials were doubtless available to Poussin, later a most unacceptable French minister to the United States, for his monographs *Chemins de fer américains . . .* (Paris, 1836), and *Travaux d'améliorations intérieures projetés ou exécutés par le Gouvernement général des Etats-Unis d'Amérique de 1824 à 1831* (2 vols., Paris, 1843). The surviving papers are in the possession of Mme la baronne Bernard d'Opeln Bronikowski, Paris.

There remains a portion of the Chesapeake and Ohio Canal, now a national monument. The Delaware Breakwater reposes, a little remote from the main channels of commerce, between Cape Henlopen and Cape May. A line of forts, some of them still occupied, one (Fort Monroe) an acknowledged masterpiece, still guards the Atlantic seaboard and the Gulf—some were alerted against enemy attack as late as 1898. One wonders if our missile silos will age as harmlessly in the twenty-first century.

10 James Barbour, a Progressive Farmer of Antebellum Virginia

Charles D. Lowery

J AMES BARBOUR, born June 10, 1775, in Orange County, Virginia, sprang from a society deeply rooted in the agrarian economy. A product of that society, he accepted as basic articles of faith the propositions that the yeoman farmer, the husbandman who tilled his own acres, was the chief factor in God's great experiment in human well-being and that agriculture, the primary source of all wealth, was superior to any other economic endeavor. Born to farming, he loved the rolling hills of the Virginia Piedmont that his grandfather, the earliest settler in Orange, had first cultivated in the early 1730s, and for fifty years he farmed the same familiar lands, not with the exploitative techniques employed by his grandfather and father, but in the careful, scientific manner of the experimental agriculturalist. Coming of age at a time when the agrarian economy of his state and region was threatened with collapse, he devoted himself to the task of helping to ameliorate the cumulative effects of almost two centuries of ruinous farming and to the preservation of the agrarian society of which he was so inseparably a part.

Like many gentlemen farmers of his day, Barbour was active in state and national politics. His public career spanned the period from 1798 to 1829, during which time he served for ten years in the Virginia legislature, three terms as governor of the state, two terms as United States senator, and as secretary of war under John Quincy Adams and United States minister to England. During those years he established himself as a powerful figure in the Republican party, especially at the state level where he was closely associated with the ruling Richmond Junto. With the disintegration of the party in the 1830s, he emerged as a prominent Whig, helping to organize the state party and serving in 1840 as president of the Harrisburg convention that nominated William Henry Harrison for president. Though overshadowed on the national scene by such contemporaries as Clay, Webster, and Calhoun, he played an active and important role in the political history of the country during the Jeffersonian and Jacksonian periods.[1] But during his long public career, his attachment to the land that sustained him, his fondness of things agrarian, did not diminish. Throughout, he maintained a lively interest in farming and during his lifetime contributed significantly to the Virginia agricultural reform movement, a movement which led to a revitalization of the state's economy in the generation before the Civil War.

Although a great deal has been written about the reform efforts of such men as Edmund Ruffin, John Taylor, and Thomas Jefferson, the equally important endeavors of men such as Barbour have been overlooked. Actually, Barbour played a major role in the Virginia agricultural revival, both as a private citizen and public official. As a private citizen he set a personal example of progressive farming worthy of emulation very early in the century, when the prevailing tendency was to follow the old course of abuse and exploitation; as a public official he sought not only to call attention to specific agricultural maladies but also to point out remedies. His interest in scientific farming brought him into close association with a number of farmers in the Piedmont section who through research, experimentation, and exchange of ideas contributed substantially to the advancement of scientific agriculture. In short, he was in the vanguard of that small group of gentlemen farmers whose vision and experimentation were eventually to restore soil fertility and bring a return of prosperity to much of the depressed region of the state.

Barbour was a highly successful planter in a period when success did not come easily. His plantation was a model of good management and progressive farming. One of the wealthiest planters of his region, he owned in 1830, at the time of his retirement from politics, over 20,000 acres of land, some of which was in scattered parcels in areas as distant as Florida and Mississippi. His main plantation, Barboursville, contained some 5,000 acres in the vicinity of the Southwest Mountains in Orange and Albemarle counties. A smaller plantation located to the north on the Rapidan River consisted of 2,000 acres of rich bottom land. To work the plantations he maintained a large labor force which in 1830 comprised eighty-one adult slaves. Including land, slaves, livestock, buildings, and other improvements, Barbour possessed at this time property worth at least $300,000, the greatest part of which had been acquired through his own labors rather than through in-

[1] Charles D. Lowery, "James Barbour: A Planter and Politician of Ante-Bellum Virginia" (Ph.D. diss., University of Virginia, 1966).

heritance. This of itself is convincing evidence of his success as a planter.[2]

Barboursville was located in an area of rolling hills bounded on the east by the small Southwest Mountains and on the west by the hazy Blue Ridge, which like a giant backbone separates the Piedmont from the Shenandoah Valley. With its commanding view, well-kept fields, and handsome buildings, the plantation was impressive. Dominating the estate was an imposing neoclassical home designed by Jefferson, a splendid structure of warm red brick and contrasting white Doric columns. On both fronts, which faced north and south, were large pediment porticoes adorned with massive columns.[3] On the south side of the house was a formal garden laid out in squares over three acres of ground and surrounded by brick serpentine walls. Walks lined with grass and flanked by double rows of boxwood crisscrossed the garden, and a small flower-bordered stream spanned by three rustic bridges meandered lazily through. A short distance from the main house stood a number of smaller structures—an ice house, a carriage house, a long row of stables, and the slave quarters.[4] As a whole, the plantation had the appearance of a small, neat, well-ordered community.

Barbour's success as a planter was due in no small part to the early interest he took in published works on scientific agriculture. When at the turn of the century an increasingly profitable legal practice provided him with the financial resources to acquire land and establish a plantation, he began to add agricultural treatises to his library—Arthur Binn's *A Treatise on Practical Agriculture*, several works by the noted English farmer Arthur Young, and copies of transactions from various agricultural societies.[5] Always anxious to acquire studies that would increase his store of scientific knowledge, he read widely and profited from the information gleaned, showing none of the traditional reluctance of farmers to adopt new techniques or to benefit from the experiences of others.

[2] Deeds, Tax Receipts, and Miscellaneous Records, Barbour Papers, University of Virginia Library, Charlottesville; James Barbour Account Book, ibid.; Orange and Albemarle County Land and Personal Property Books, Virginia State Library, Richmond.

[3] I. J. Frary, *Thomas Jefferson: Architect and Builder* (Richmond, 1950), pp. 97–98; Fiske Kimball, *Thomas Jefferson, Architect* (Boston, 1916), pp. 73–74; *Homes and Gardens in Old Virginia*, ed. Frances A. Christian and Susanne W. Massie (Richmond, 1932), p. 337.

[4] *Homes and Gardens*, pp. 337–39; Frary, p. 97; Barbour Account Book, Barbour Papers.

[5] List of Books, 1805, Barbour Papers.

Learning from Humphrey Davy's *Agricultural Chemistry* that soil acidity was responsible for the small benefit derived from vegetable manures, he sought a remedy in liberal applications of lime.[6] John Taylor's *Arator* confirmed his belief in the efficacy of deep plowing and crop rotation.[7] He showed a keen interest in his friend Edmund Ruffin's experiments with marl and obtained an early edition of *An Essay on Calcareous Manures*.[8] He subscribed to a number of pioneer farm journals and frequently contributed articles to Ruffin's *Farmers' Register* and John S. Skinner's *American Farmer*.[9] In short, he believed that solutions to some of the agricultural problems of his day could be found on the printed page.

Virginia agricultural practices in 1800, when Barbour began to emerge as a planter of some importance, had improved very little since colonial days. Generally the old system of the seventeenth and eighteenth centuries still persisted, and the same exhaustive methods of planting were widely practiced. The Tidewater area, where grain crops now dominated, had yielded its position as the tobacco-growing center to the more recently settled Piedmont, but an increase in the price of tobacco resulted almost invariably in a rapid return throughout the Tidewater to the old staple. The persistence of tobacco culture saw also the continuation of all its attendant evils. New land was cleared and planted for three or four years in tobacco, followed by five or six years in corn, and then abandoned to sorrel, sage, and pine.[10]

Statements made by travelers in Virginia during the late eighteenth and early nineteenth centuries give ample evidence of the continuation of exhaustive cultivation, of wasted lands and abandoned fields, of the air of poverty and despair that had settled on much of the state. To some, it was as if an "angel of desolation had cursed the land." Landowners generally were "in low circumstances, the inferior rank of them wretched in the extreme," while agriculture had reached its "lowest grade of degradation." [11] The

[6] Miscellaneous File, 1820, ibid.

[7] James Barbour, "On the Improvement of Agriculture, and the Importance of Legislative Aid to That Object: Description of the South West Mountain Lands," *Farmers' Register*, 2 (April 1835): 705.

[8] Miscellaneous File, 1836, Barbour Papers.

[9] *Farmers' Register*, 2–9 (1834–41): passim; *American Farmer*, 1–12 (1819–31): passim.

[10] W. A. Low, "The Farmer in Post-Revolutionary Virginia, 1783–1789," *Agricultural History*, 25 (July 1951): 123–24.

[11] William Strickland, *Observations on the Agriculture of the United States of America* (London, 1801), p. 49.

duc de la Rochefoucauld-Liancourt observed that in sixty miles of travel around the city of Richmond he found not a single well-cultivated field. Depleted by long tobacco cultivation, the land was poor and barren; soil untreated by manures created a condition "inferior to almost all the other states of America." [12] Large areas of the state, both in the Tidewater and Piedmont, were described as scenes of ruin and desolation that "baffle description—farm after farm . . . worn out, washed and gullied, so that scarcely an acre could be found in a place fit for cultivation." [13] Although there were many "gullied fields interspersed with broom straw and stunted pines," there were "no meadows, no luxuriant fields of clover, no rich crops of grain, no large and fat cattle, and indeed nothing that indicates good husbandry." [14]

By 1800 the day had clearly passed when the Virginia farmer could readily buy new land cheaper than he could improve the old. Indeed, the old system had been so exploitative that good land was virtually nonexistent. A planter had the choice of either improving the old lands or moving to the newer regions of the West and lower South where virgin soil was abundant. Although Orange County, more recently populated than the Tidewater, suffered less extensively from abusive agricultural practices than the older areas, it too had been subjected to many of the same ruinous practices. Much of the land that Barbour acquired in Orange and Albemarle consisted of farms that had been exhausted by their owners before they migrated to new regions.

One of the major factors contributing to soil exhaustion was the mode of plowing. Plows generally used in Virginia at the turn of the century were inadequate instruments that, by turning a super-ficial furrow, loosened the topsoil but left an unbroken hard stratum beneath, thus creating a shallow surface which was quickly washed away by the heavy summer rains. Although deep plowing was known, it was seldom practiced.[15] Beginning about 1800 Barbour experimented extensively with new types of plows and new methods of plowing. He acquired and used new, improved iron models capable of penetrating the subsoil and by 1804 was using large plows requiring from three- to five-horse teams that cut the earth to a depth of eight to ten inches. He experimented also with winged plows, iron moldboards, "duckbill" colters, and

[12] Cited in Avery Craven, *Soil Exhaustion as a Factor in the Agricultural History of Virginia and Maryland, 1606–1860*, University of Illinois Studies in the Social Sciences, vol. 13, no. 1 (Urbana, 1925), p. 3.

[13] *Farmers' Register*, 1 (Aug. 1833): 150.

[14] Craven, p. 85.   [15] Ibid., pp. 89–90.

improved hillside plows, and those which proved most effective he put into general use.[16]

In addition to his experimentation with deep plowing, Barbour devised new ways to fight soil erosion. He abandoned the ruinous system of cross plowing, which was employed widely on corn lands, and planted instead by drill. Although he used plows of special design, such as Randolph's hillside plow, and used the horizontal method of cultivation on the rolling hills, this in itself was not sufficient to prevent washing of the steeper slopes. The unusually heavy summer rains to which the Piedmont was subject continued to cause great damage, and in August 1813 the "disastrous effect" of ten inches of rain falling in a twelve-hour period prompted Barbour to seek additional preventive measures. After considerable study and analysis, he devised an effective system of hillside-ditching which involved the digging of ditches at suitable intervals on the steeper hillsides to carry off the storm water and drain the horizontal furrows. This system stopped erosion even on the steepest slopes. "The land within or below these ditches," he informed members of the Albemarle Agricultural Society, "becomes almost as valuable as the valleys, and when cured of their galls is worth $100 the acre." [17]

A major task which confronted Barbour and his neighbors was that of restoring and maintaining soil fertility. To accomplish this, Barbour experimented widely with various systems of fertilization and crop rotation. Manure production and liberal applications of various forms of fertilizer were basic components of his agricultural system. In the first decade of the century he began experimenting with animal manure, plaster, and cover crops. Animal manure, though highly beneficial, was always in short supply. When practicable, his livestock was penned and the offal mulched with straw and cornstalks, but the quantity produced, though carefully conserved, was never sufficient for general use.[18] In the second decade of the century he conducted small-scale experiments with marl, but he found an equally effective and less expensive substitute in the form of lime, which he employed successfully for a while. He finally settled on gypsum or plaster, a mineral which, when applied liberally to his wheat fields and used in conjunction

[16] Bills, Receipts, and Business Papers, 1800–1830, Barbour Papers; Barbour, "On the Improvement of Agriculture," pp. 705–6.

[17] Barbour, "On the Improvement of Agriculture," pp. 705–6.

[18] Barbour Ledger, Account Book, Business Papers, and Miscellaneous File, Barbour Papers.

with clover cover crops, increased yields by as much as 100 percent. He employed this same system successfully with other grain crops such as corn, rye, and oats.[19]

Deep plowing and fertilization produced the best results when used in conjunction with a judicious system of crop rotation, and Barbour incorporated all three practices into his agricultural system. Sufficiently familiar with the works of Arthur Young to know that crops differ in their demands on soil nutrients, he sought to develop a system of rotation which would give maximum yields without exhausting the soil and at the same time would provide continuity of employment for the labor force and work stock. Although he never devised a system which could be applied uniformly to all his land, he did employ a number of systems which produced good results. These ranged from the simple but effective three-field system to a more elaborate seven-field system. The former, which he employed on certain of his upland wheat fields, consisted simply of two years of wheat followed by a year of ungrazed clover. The difficulty with this system was that it entailed heavy use of plaster and could be applied only to the better lands. On less fertile upland ground he followed a more involved six-field system of corn, wheat, clover, clover, wheat, and clover. Occasionally tobacco was included in a more complex seven-field system, but generally it was grown on the bottom lands of his river plantation where the richer soil permitted a less elaborate system of rotation in which tobacco was followed by wheat and two years of clover.[20]

Barbour did not abandon tobacco as did some of his neighbors, but neither did he make it the cornerstone of his plantation economy; rather he integrated it into an intelligent system of general farming which included wheat and other grains.[21] Indeed, by 1800 wheat had become for him a more important money crop than tobacco. In wheat as in tobacco production, he was careful to employ scientific techniques. In contrast to those farmers who simply scattered seed on unprepared ground, he tilled the soil carefully, planted with drills, and fertilized heavily. Through judicious use of

[19] Barbour Ledger, ibid.; Barbour, "On the Improvement of Agriculture," pp. 704–5; Barbour to John S. Skinner, May 5, 1820, *American Farmer*, 2 (May 1820): 55.

[20] Barbour, "On the Improvement of Agriculture," pp. 704–5; Barbour Ledger and Sims Brockman to Barbour, Dec. 22, 1828, Barbour Papers.

[21] Bills, Receipts, and Business Papers, Barbour Papers; Lewis C. Gray, *History of Agriculture in the Southern United States to 1860* (2 vols., New York, 1941), II, 752–69.

cover crops and plaster, he consistently harvested yields much greater than the Piedmont average of seven bushels per acre.[22]

Along with many other progressive farmers, Barbour constantly sought ways to combat more effectively the diseases and insects, such as the smut and Hessian fly, which menaced wheat crops. From his friend John S. Skinner, editor of the *American Farmer*, and neighboring farmers he obtained many varieties of wheat seed with which he conducted carefully controlled experiments in the period 1813–19, hoping to discover a seed resistant to both the fly and the smut.[23] Early experiments were disappointing. It appeared that every variety of seed was subject to the ruinous fly, which seemed a "calamity without remedy." When Barbour sought a solution by delaying planting from August to October, he found that winter frosts killed much of the crop, but in 1815 he began to meet with encouraging results. In the fall of that year he planted on an experimental basis twenty pounds of Columbian or Lawler wheat, which produced a crop totally free of the insect. Subsequent tests showed that Lawler wheat resisted the fly when other varieties were almost totally destroyed. Emboldened by these findings, he planted most of his wheat acreage with the Lawler seed in 1817. The results were gratifying; the crop was large and unblighted.[24]

In 1819 Barbour reported to the Albemarle Agricultural Society the results of his experiments with Lawler wheat and warmly extolled its fly-resistant qualities. It was far more resistant than the more popular purple straw and bearded wheats, and the quality and size of its yields were comparable and perhaps superior to the other varieties. The danger with it lay in late planting. If planting were delayed beyond the proper season by as much as a single week, the crop became subject to heavy damage from smut and rust.[25]

Next to the Hessian fly, the greatest enemy of Virginia wheat was smut. Although Barbour had not been previously troubled by that blight, he noticed it for the first time in his early wheat in the spring of 1816, and by the following year it had become a major problem. To combat the disease he soaked his seed wheat in a saline solution immediately before planting. Imperfect or diseased

[22] Barbour to William M. Barton, Dec. 15, 1824, *American Farmer*, 7 (May 1825): 60; Barbour, "The Cultivation of Wheat," ibid., 1 (Dec. 1819): 301–2.

[23] Barbour to Skinner, May 5, 1820, ibid., 7 (May 1825): 60; Barbour, "Cultivation of Wheat," pp. 301–2.

[24] Barbour, "Cultivation of Wheat," pp. 301–2.   [25] Ibid., p. 302.

seeds floated to the surface and were removed. He then mixed with each bushel of seeds a gallon of slaked or hydrated lime and a bushel of plaster, and the whole was thoroughly mixed and immediately planted. Of all the many elaborate tests that he conducted to find a smut-resistant seed, this procedure, he informed neighboring farmers at a meeting of the Albemarle Agricultural Society, had proved the most successful. Seeds prepared in this manner produced crops almost totally free of smut, while control seeds, omitted from the process, produced heavily blighted crops.[26]

Although wheat and tobacco were his chief money crops, Barbour produced other items that, taken as a whole, constituted an important source of income. Corn was grown in large quantities, not only for feeding his slaves and livestock but also for sale on the local market. He maintained a large herd of merino sheep whose wool brought good prices. He raised fine thoroughbred horses that were sold throughout the South, sometimes bringing as much as $1,500 each; one of his better stallions earned $5,000 in stud fees in a single year.[27] He distilled whiskey and brandy for sale locally.[28] Through this sort of diversification he was able to hedge against losses in wheat and tobacco production and at the same time to achieve maximum utilization of his labor force.

Although scientific agricultural techniques were a *sine qua non* for nineteenth-century Virginia farmers, nothing was more essential to successful large-scale farming than a reliable, stable labor force. This Barbour found in slavery. A large slaveholder who, during most of his adult life, owned between 100 and 150 bondsmen, he succeeded through careful management and efficient utilization of labor in making the "peculiar institution" profitable.[29] His plantation records do not bear out the assertion that slavery was unprofitable, nor is there anything in his experience to suggest that the institution, by its very nature, precluded soil reclamation, crop diversification, or agricultural innovation. Moreover, the agricultural adjustments that he made were not contingent upon cap-

[26] Ibid.

[27] Barbour Account Book, 1830, and J. S. Moore to James Barbour, Jr., Nov. 15, 1842, William Bagley to Barbour, July 21, 1830, Gabriel Moore to Barbour, July 7, 1832, William Terrill to Barbour, Dec. 26, 1833, Barbour Papers; Clement Eaton, *Henry Clay and the Art of American Politics* (Boston and Toronto, 1957), p. 73.

[28] Bills, Receipts, and Business Papers, 1800–1842, passim, Barbour Papers.

[29] Orange County Personal Property Books, 1800–1842, Va. State Lib.; Barbour Ledger, Barbour Papers.

ital derived from the sale of surplus slaves to the lower South. Through profits obtained from routine farming operations he was able to invest in fertilizers and improved equipment, experiment with new methods, and diversify his crops without reducing his labor force.[30]

Speculation on whether or not slave labor was as profitable as free labor can only be termed an exercise in futility, since adequate materials for comparison do not exist. Too many variables in the form of climatic conditions, nature of crops, and cost accounting systems exist to make any really significant comparisons between the free labor farms of the North and West and the slave plantations of the South.[31] Certainly the thesis that slaveowners made money in spite of slavery rather than because of it does not apply in Barbour's case, nor, one suspects, does it apply to many of his neighboring planters. Except in unusual years, such as those following the Panic of 1819, Barbour rather consistently earned profits that, by whatever method of cost accounting used, represented a good rate of return on his capital investment.[32] And this does not take into account such concealed sources of profit as personal services rendered by domestics, natural increase of slaves, and appreciation of land values resulting from improvements wrought by slave labor.

Barbour encountered no insuperable obstacles in training his labor force to perform the different tasks required by scientific and diversified farming. Admittedly, it might have been easier to train and supervise hands in the routine chores of staple production alone, and the temptation, especially when tobacco prices were good, to resort to the one-crop system must have been great; but experience and business acumen suggested that diversification held the greatest promise of success. The success that Barbour had indicates that slave labor proved far more adaptable than many scholars have believed.[33] Good management was essential for success in any complex agricultural operation such as Barbour's, and its absence, rather than any inherent limitation of slave labor,

[30] Barbour Ledger, Account Book, and Business Papers, 1800–1842, Barbour Papers.

[31] See Thomas P. Govan, "Was Plantation Slavery Profitable?", *Journal of Southern History*, 8 (Nov. 1942): 513–14.

[32] Barbour Account Book and Business Papers, 1800–1842, Barbour Papers.

[33] See especially Eugene D. Genovese, *The Political Economy of Slavery: Studies in the Economy and Society of the Slave South* (New York, 1967), pp. 124–44.

seems to have been the decisive factor in the failure of other Southern plantations.

The efficiency of slave labor depended to a large extent upon the health and morale of slaves, a fact of which Barbour was well aware. Within obvious limits, he did all he could to keep his chattels happy. A firm master who tempered judgment with wisdom and benevolence, he believed that humanity, no less than the simple dictates of self-interest, demanded good treatment. He held a deep affection for his "people" and showed a genuine concern for their well-being. His close attention to their physical needs and his sympathetic treatment were designed to win their affection, for he felt that a personal attachment between slave and master was mutually beneficial.[34]

Proper treatment of bondsmen, Barbour informed members of the Albemarle Agricultural Society, involved, among other things, close attention to their basic needs. They should be well fed, properly clothed, closely attended in sickness, and adequately housed. Revealing what may have been a better understanding of nutritional requirements than was possessed by those planters who fed their slaves only corn meal and salt pork, he urged fellow planters to include milk, garden vegetables, and daily allotments of lean meat in the slave diet. Each hand, he continued, should be allowed at least three suits of clothing per year—a durable warm suit for winter and two linen suits for summer. In sickness or in the infirmities of old age, the slaves had an incontestable claim to the immediate and humane attention of the master. When medical attention was needed, the master should "give of his stores" and affection with "no sparing hand." The raising of children should be entrusted to an elderly nurse who, uniting kindness with firmness, would assume primary responsibility for their immediate well-being. The careful attention that Barbour gave to proper diet, sanitary living quarters, and treatment of the sick paid handsome dividends—for more than twenty-five years he lost not a single adult through illness, a remarkable record. Not only was his slave family healthy; it also doubled in size in less than twenty-five years.[35] With his policy of humane treatment Barbour combined a program of incentives and rewards. Special privileges, holidays, and other bonuses were awarded the deserving. The cost of such a

[34] Barbour, *Address of James Barbour, Esquire, President of the Agricultural Society of Albemarle, at Their Meeting of the 8th of November, 1825* (Charlottesville, Va., 1825), p. 9.

[35] Ibid., p. 10.

policy was trifling, and the effect was "manifestly beneficial." It "inspired gratitude toward the master" and became a "stimulus to good conduct." [36]

Like so many of his contemporaries, Barbour in principle disliked the institution of slavery but could see no feasible way of abolishing it. It was, he believed, a necessary evil. Echoing Aristotle and anticipating the arguments of such proslavery spokesmen as John C. Calhoun and George Fitzhugh, he said that a laboring class, "whether bond or free, white or black," must exist in every community, for it constituted "the indispensable foundation of the social fabric." Given the present circumstances, any attempt to alter the social fabric would, he feared, prove disastrous. "Any effort forcibly to disturb their relation with a view to the change of their condition, which can be attempted only by those who do not foresee, or seeing are reckless of the consequences, cannot fail to make worse the condition of the slave. For our own daily experience teaches us that the condition of the slaves, when well treated, is infinitely preferable to that of free people of color . . . , who, ignorant, insolent, and demoralized . . . and with no ostensible means of acquiring their subsistence . . . , are reduced to prostitution, theft . . . and begging." [37] Thus Barbour, like so many other Southern planters, viewed slavery as something more than a purely economic institution. But it is doubtful that he would have allowed mere sentimental attachment to a social institution to prevent him from disposing of his slaves had they been an economic burden.

One of the most vexatious problems of running a large plantation in Barbour's day was that of finding capable managers. The overseer system so widely employed was almost universally condemned. In an address to the Virginia Agricultural Convention in 1836, Barbour expressed the sentiment of most intelligent farmers when he pointed out the evils of the system.

Were I to select the most disastrous of all causes which have contributed to our misfortunes, I would say at once, it was the lack of capacity of proprietors to manage their estates. Instead of personally superintending them . . . , they have deputed their management to hireling superintendents, not infrequently as ignorant as themselves —and to complete their ruin, have paid these hirelings with a share of the crop. These, as was natural, looked only to the present year— the future being left to take care of itself. The lands capable of producing, were annually cultivated till exhausted; improvements of every kind neglected, and in effect, the whole country by this simple

[36] Ibid.   [37] Ibid., p. 11.

process was as though it had been under an annual rack-rent—with no restrictions on the tenants, and with no supervision by the proprietors.[38]

Barbour did not share the conviction held by a majority of planters that overseers as a class were vicious and unreliable. Undue prejudice, he believed, was indulged against them, and this in turn contributed to the evils of the system by robbing the overseer of self-respect and creating unnecessary suspicion between proprietor and manager. These attitudes combined with penurious salaries to create in the overseer a continual restlessness and disposition to annual change.[39]

To combat the evils of the managerial system, Barbour believed that the overseer should be treated with greater respect and understanding and that the proprietor should make every effort to inculcate in him a sense of responsibility and self-respect. Nor should the proprietor expect too much of the overseer too soon. "Indeed it is impossible that he can succeed so well the first year—he has to learn the wishes of his employer, and the disposition of the hands under him—the capacity of the latter for labor—the different kinds of soil he has to cultivate, and a long list of details which cannot be acquired in a year." [40] For the evils of the system, he believed that the proprietor was as culpable as the overseer.

Barbour himself sought to achieve managerial stability by giving his overseers a stake in their work in the form of liberal wages, substantial bonuses, and indulgences of various sorts. "Instead of grudging them their wages," he said, "I rejoice that while they are securing my independence, they are acquiring one for themselves." As a result of this approach, Barbour encountered far less difficulty than most of his neighbors in obtaining and keeping able managers. His principal manager stayed with him for more than twenty years, performing his task with "honesty, industry and zeal." [41]

The steadily declining condition of agriculture in Virginia in the early 1800s, dramatized by the rising tide of emigration to the lower South that threatened to depopulate the older areas, gave a sense of urgency to the activities of agricultural reformers like Barbour who, seeking to preserve the agrarian order, joined together in cooperative ventures designed to explain and improve

---

[38] "Address to the Agricultural Convention of Virginia," *Farmers' Register*, 3 (March 1836): 685.

[39] Barbour, *Address to the Agricultural Society of Albemarle*, pp. 11–12.
[40] Ibid.   [41] Ibid.

the economy of their section. One of the most popular ventures was the agricultural society. Although many such groups were organized in Virginia during this period, none was more successful than that centering in Albemarle and embracing the neighboring counties of Orange, Amherst, and Fluvanna. Organized in May 1817, the Albemarle Agricultural Society—"perhaps as brilliant for the number assembled as had ever gathered in the name of agriculture"—did much in the 1820s and 1830s to improve farming practices. Barbour, along with Jefferson, Madison, John H. Cocke, Joseph C. Cabell, and Thomas Mann Randolph, was a leader of the group.[42]

At the organizational meeting of the society a committee of five was appointed to draw up rules and objectives. Serving on the committee were John Patterson, Jefferson, Cocke, Cabell, and Barbour. During the summer the five men worked at their assignment, and in October they presented to the organization a list of ten "Objects for the Attention and Enquiry of the Society." First, and principally, was the cultivation of the primary staples of wheat, tobacco, and hemp for market. Next came the subsidiary articles for the support of the farm: corn, barley, oats, and other grains; peas and beans; turnips, potatoes, and "other useful roots"; and grapes and other fruit. Third were the care and services of useful animals for saddle or draught and the destruction of noxious insects, reptiles, fowls, and quadrupeds. The report encouraged the discovery and promotion of improved agricultural techniques through experimentation with crop rotation, the adoption of new implements of husbandry, and the use of manures, plaster, green dressings, and fallow. Members were urged to keep close records of their experiments and were invited to report the results to the society.

After approving these objectives, the society organized with Madison as president, Thomas Mann Randolph and John H. Cocke as vice presidents, Peter Minor as secretary, and Isaac Cole as treasurer. The steering committee included Randolph, Cabell, Cocke, and Barbour. A sort of agricultural catechism to be used by the members in reporting their farming practices, including questions about crop rotation, yield per acre, methods of fertilization, and labor-saving machines, was then adopted. Plans were made for

[42] Rodney H. True, "Early Days of the Albemarle Agricultural Society," *American Historical Association, Annual Report for the Year 1918* (2 vols., Washington, D.C., 1921), I, 243–45; Charles W. Turner, "Virginia Agricultural Reform, 1815–1860," *Agricultural History*, 26 (July 1952): 81–83.

the establishment of a nursery from which members might secure plants and trees; a committee was appointed to examine the possibility of importing blooded horses to improve Virginia racing stock; and other measures were proposed to improve agriculture.[43]

For the next several decades the society was an active agent in promoting reform. It held agricultural fairs where premiums were given to outstanding exhibitions, conducted plowing contests to determine the most effective types of plows, gave bonuses to its members for significant agricultural innovations, established a manufactory for farm implements, and supported internal improvements designed to improve markets of the section. Barbour was a leading spirit in the organization. He served on most of the important committees during the early years of its existence and attended the meetings with as much regularity as his duties in Washington permitted. He presented several important papers on various agricultural experiments that he had conducted, delivered speeches on other topics of interest, and exchanged ideas with members of the society. In recognition of his contributions to scientific farming, the society in 1825 elected him to succeed Madison as president.[44]

Throughout the 1820s and 1830s Barbour maintained a lively interest in agricultural reform. With prominent farmers from other sections and countries, including the famous English agriculturalist Sir John Coke of Norfolk, he discussed agrarian problems and urged neighboring farmers to adopt new, improved methods.[45] But farmers as a group were slow to abandon traditional practices. Old evils persisted, and for Barbour and other progressive farmers this was a matter of growing concern. Out of this concern grew the Virginia Agricultural Convention of 1836.

The convention, called for the specific purpose of discussing agricultural problems and proposing solutions, met in Richmond in January 1836. Progressive farmers from all parts of the state attended. Barbour, who had been instrumental in convening the assembly, was chosen president.[46] In the major address to the con-

<hr>

[43] True, "Early Days of the Albemarle Agricultural Society," pp. 244–51.

[44] Rodney H. True, ed., "Minute Book of the Albemarle (Virginia) Agricultural Society," American Historical Association, *Annual Report for the Year 1918*, I, 263–349.

[45] Robert A. Brock, *Virginia and Virginians* (2 vols., Richmond, 1888), I, 119.

[46] Barbour to Edmund Ruffin, July 23, 1835, *Farmer's Register*, 3 (Sept. 1835): 274–75; Barbour, "Address to Agricultural Convention of Virginia," p. 685.

vention he pointed to the magnitude of the agricultural problems confronting Virginia and proposed several remedies.

I call your attention to a spectacle without an example in any other part of the globe. Vast regions, once the abode of a numerous population, of plenty, and of social happiness, have been recommitted to the forest—and their original inhabitants, the wild beasts, reestablished in their primitive dominion. That a result of this kind has occurred where a barbarous conqueror, Attila-like, has swept the face of the country with the besom of desolation, or where dread misrule has caused the population to recede before the rod of the oppressor is true—but in no instance where the hoof of the conqueror has not defiled the land, and where peace and freedom have held undisturbed sway as in our case, has such a thing occurred. Other large portions of the commonwealth . . . still present the most discouraging prospects—wasted fields, houses threatening their inhabitants with their fall—and depopulated districts—while our people by the tens of thousands, are leaving us. . . . When and how these great mischiefs are to be stayed in their career, are questions that address themselves with an irresistible pathos to every lover of his mother land.

Many factors had contributed to the plight of Virginia's "tillers of the soil." The greatest of these, Barbour believed, was the failure of proprietors to manage their own estates. They turned management over to "hireling superintendents" who, with no restrictions or supervision, butchered the land and laid waste the once fertile fields. The overseer system, as practiced by most Virginians, was a primary cause for agricultural decline. Another contributing factor was emigration. Virginia, Barbour noted, had been for more than half a century "the great hive from which have gone numerous swarms of emigrants to the south and west." Two groups remained behind: "the well-to-do who are too comfortable to move, and the indigent who are too poor to move. . . . The head and tail of society are thus left; the vital part attends the emigrants."

The reluctance of farmers to adopt improved agricultural techniques worsened the situation. Despite the development of improved practices and methods, old customs persisted. Exhausting crops were planted until the soil was capable of producing nothing but sorrel, persimmon, and weeds. Little or no effort was made to ameliorate the land by fertilization or rotation.

In enumerating the causes of agricultural paralysis and decline, Barbour contended that the state of Virginia society could not be overlooked. For many years it had been passing through a "violent revolution." Ancient and wealthy families, once a numerous class, had disappeared. Young men raised in the "luxurious indulgence" of the wealthy families all too often lacked enterprise and motivation. Sticking "like suckers to the parent stock, . . . they have exhausted it, and all have gone down together."

Barbour was confident that Virginians possessed the means to correct these evils. Although there existed no remedy to the waste of centuries, a judicious program of reform perseveringly pursued would, in time, bring a return of prosperity to the agricultural community. He then proposed to the convention two measures that he believed would help bring about improvement. A state agricultural board, composed of outstanding agriculturalists and representing the agrarian interest of the state, should be created to promote and coordinate reform and to act as a pressure group to secure from the legislature laws aiding agriculture. Secondly, an agricultural professorship and an experimental farm should be established at the University of Virginia. The professor should be a man of broad experience and training, capable of applying scientific knowledge from many fields to the exclusive domain of agriculture. The experimental farm would serve as the proving ground for new farming methods and techniques. Experiments with different soil types, fertilizers, and improved varieties of seeds and plants might be conducted to great advantage on such a farm and the results made known throughout the state. By fostering reform and seeking to determine the best farming practices, the agricultural professor and the experimental farm would perform a great service to farmers of the state.[47]

The Agricultural Convention adopted Barbour's recommendations, incorporating them into a petition addressed to the General Assembly. But the legislature, as in the past, took no action, and the efforts of Barbour and other reformers came to nothing. The House of Delegates did debate a bill in 1839 which would have established a board of agriculture, but the measure failed.[48]

Although Barbour was not the first Virginian to propose an agricultural professorship, he was apparently the first to stress emphatically the value of an experimental farm. Of both ideas he was the foremost and ablest champion. As early as 1825, when he became president of the Albemarle Agricultural Society, he had strongly urged that both be created; and despite the failure of numerous petitions to move the legislature to action, he had continued to advocate the move, adding proposals for the establish-

[47] Barbour, "Address to Agricultural Convention of Virginia," pp. 685–89.
[48] Turner, "Virginia Agricultural Reform," p. 85.

ment of an agrarian press for the state.[49] In 1830–31, when he had
been briefly a member of the legislature, he had submitted a bill
embodying his schemes, only to see it rejected.

It was in vain I urged that in a society boasting of its exclusive
agricultural character, the legislature had never dispensed the slightest
aid to its encouragement; that while the tillers of the earth had paid
ninety-nine hundredths of the cost of the University, their particular
interests had been entirely overlooked. . . . To my mortification . . .
the proposals . . . which have long been favorite objects with me
. . . fell still-born. They appeared as scandal to the Jews, and folly
to the Greeks. There was a headlong member . . . who condescended
merely to denounce them as smelling too strong of the tariff.[50]

Although the legislature declined to act upon Barbour's proposal
for an agricultural professorship and experimental farm, it did
finally respond favorably to the pressure that he and others exerted
for a state board of agriculture. Created by the General Assembly
in 1841, the Virginia Board of Agriculture was composed of eight
prominent agriculturalists representing the Tidewater, Piedmont,
Valley, and Trans-Allegheny regions of the state, who were to
meet annually to suggest measures of agricultural improvement.[51]

In December 1841, when the board held its first and only meeting, Barbour was elected president and Edmund Ruffin corresponding secretary.[52] In a report to the General Assembly, Barbour gave
a brief summary of the board's goals, the foremost of which was
"to remove the blighting evil of injudicious agriculture." To promote improvement, it would attempt to draw together and as-
similate the vast store of agricultural knowledge and, after careful
study, incorporate it into an agricultural code to serve as a guide
and encyclopedia for farmers. By embodying the best knowledge
that science and experience could offer, the code would serve, he
hoped, as a "tool of inestimable value" to both the experienced and

[49] The Albemarle Agricultural Society in 1822 appropriated $1,000 for
the purpose of establishing an agricultural professorship at the University
of Virginia. It is not known whether John H. Cocke, who suggested the
appropriation, or some other person initiated the move, but Barbour was
an early supporter of the idea. True, "Early Days of the Albemarle
Agricultural Society," pp. 253–54.

[50] Barbour, "On the Improvement of Agriculture," p. 704; H. G. Good,
"Early Attempts to Teach Agriculture in Old Virginia," *Virginia Magazine
of History and Biography*, 48 (1940): 345–46.

[51] Rodney H. True, "The Virginia Board of Agriculture, 1841–1843,"
Agricultural History, 14 (July 1940): 97–98.

[52] Ibid., p. 94.

inexperienced farmer. To promote further reform, advisory committees composed of outstanding husbandmen would be created in each county. Farmers of the county might address inquiries to this committee, and each individual member would serve as a sort of county agent, encouraging reform and advising farmers of his respective district. Finally, the board hoped to give new direction to the course of Virginia agriculture and society.

Agriculture should be the first object of civilized man; its condition is a fair test of the state of society; when it is defective all conditions suffer—when it prospers all partake of its prosperity. Every patriot should esteem it among his first duties to do all in his power for its advancement: the apathy too prevalent everywhere should cease—a new impulse should be imparted by the zealous friends of agriculture —and the public mind, diverted from an engrossing devotion to party politics, should be made to perceive that this great interest has claims on its attention. For while the bickering, the rise and fall of heated partisans, and their baneful influence on society shall be forgotten, or be remembered only to be deplored, the achievements of agriculture, by the aid of science and experience, will endure forever, and in their progress will dispense blessings in all coming time to human kind. The board indulges the hope that its labors will not be altogether unavailing in producing this new direction of sympathies and feelings, so propitious to the success of agriculture.[53]

Apparently the legislature was unimpressed by this statement; it abolished the board in 1843.

Although Barbour did not live to see this action taken, the board's demise would have been for him a great personal disappointment. Believing as he did that the noblest of God's creatures was the tiller of the earth, and fearful that Virginia's agricultural decline presaged ruin of the agrarian society, he was particularly anxious to see the legislature extend every encouragement to farmers of the state.

Legislative enactment of those measures which he and fellow reformers urged undoubtedly would have abetted agricultural progress, yet the real obstacle to reform was not the legislature but rather the farming masses, who seemed utterly resistant to change. Farmers as a group were notoriously slow to abandon practices, however ruinous, that carried the weight of custom. Few would admit, or seemingly could recognize, that the exploitative methods of their fathers and grandfathers could not be continued without disastrous results. Rather than change their habits, they chose instead to emigrate to the virgin lands of the Southwest where they

[53] Barbour, "Report of the Board of Agriculture to the General Assembly of Virginia," *Farmer's Register*, 9 (Dec. 1841): 688–89.

could profitably continue the soil-mining form of agriculture traditionally practiced. A large percentage of those who remained behind were subsistence farmers unable to raise the capital necessary to move. It was they, also, who were generally the most resistant to change. In the final analysis, the availability of cheap land elsewhere may well have been the greatest single obstacle to agricultural reform in Virginia.

If one views Barbour's record and experience as an example of what might have been accomplished within the limits of a slave society, it must be concluded that the potential for developing a sound agricultural economy based on slave labor was great. It is a mistake to assume that such labor was adaptable only to staple crop production, that the wasteful methods of exploitative farming are attributable exclusively to it, or that the institution of slavery, impervious to reform, was on the road to ultimate extinction by the 1830s. It is true that agricultural reform in Virginia was largely unsuccessful until the supply of fresh land in the South and West was exhausted and until economic depression, resulting from declining staple prices and rising production costs on worn-out soil, forced upon planters a choice between reform or ruin. But when that time came, it was slaveholders like Barbour, Edmund Ruffin, and John H. Cocke who generally took the lead. They sounded the call for reform, promoted agricultural societies and fairs, experimented with crop rotation and fertilizers, devised new farming methods, employed and sometimes designed improved implements, and in general demonstrated that slaves could be used successfully in a system of scientific, diversified farming. In demonstrating the superiority of this type of agriculture over the old system of monoculture, Barbour and a few other enlightened farmers prepared the way for a new era of productive agriculture in Virginia.

11   "Situation Ethics" and Antislavery Attitudes in the Virginia Churches

Patricia Hickin

From the antebellum years to the present time, critics have condemned the Southern clergy for their failure to wage a vigorous crusade against slavery. Instead of battling valiantly against black bondage, Southern churchmen fought against Northern abolitionism, they denounced the efforts of radicals who wanted the churches to condemn slavery as sin, they refused to expel slaveholding communicants from their churches, and they gave up the battle for emancipation in their own states. And when some of them went so far as to point out what they considered to be the merits of slavery, they shocked their antislavery contemporaries and won for the Southern churches a proslavery reputation.

Historians have especially deplored what they have seen as the churches' shift from antislavery views in the late eighteenth century to proslavery attitudes in the antebellum years.[1] It is impossible to determine today precisely to what extent the Virginia clergy abandoned earlier antislavery notions and became apologists for slavery. The evidence, however, indicates that until the 1850s there was no sharp turning point in attitudes toward slavery. Even in the immediate pre-Civil War years many clergymen continued to disapprove of slavery "in the abstract." But few in any period were willing to agitate for its removal. Rare indeed was the minister who would suggest any means but African colonization to bring an end to slavery, and of those clergymen who supported colonization only a few engaged in a significant amount of public agitation for even that moderate measure.

How could Southern churchmen have made peace with an institution that exploited black men so brazenly? Why did they not protest vehemently against chattel slavery? One obvious reason was the pressure of laymen who thought slavery was "too delicate" a

---

[1] See especially Dwight Dumond, *Antislavery: The Crusade for Freedom in America* (Ann Arbor, Mich., 1961), pp. 344–48; Robert McColley, *Slavery and Jeffersonian Virginia* (Urbana, Ill., 1964), pp. 148–54.

topic for discussion; another was the competition among the various denominations for new members and the consequent desire to avoid taking a stand on hotly controversial subjects. But perhaps the most important reason was the typical clergyman's own ambivalent attitudes toward the peculiar institution. Though he might question the morality of slavery, he was well aware of the problems of emancipation. When he attempted to calculate the consequences of complying with abolitionist demands for immediate emancipation, he was likely to be appalled at the outcome he envisioned. Knowing full well that Southerners—whatever the hue of their skin —were not so filled with the Christian spirit that they could overcome the dangers and temptations of racism, a clergyman could easily conclude that disaster would follow in the wake of emancipation.

In other words, Virginia clergymen found it difficult to escape the "situational" problem created by slavery. Most found it impossible to join their Northern abolitionist brethren who urged Southerners to emancipate their slaves without considering the consequences of the act—to trust in God, do what was right, and leave the results to the Almighty. The conflict between the increasingly absolutist morality of Northern agitators who insisted that slavery was sin and the relativist morality of Southern opponents of slavery eventually made cooperation between the two groups inconceivable.[2] No matter how deeply a Virginia clergyman deplored slavery or favored emancipation, he rarely argued against the peculiar institution without incorporating in his argument some aspect of what today would be called "situation ethics."

In two books published in the 1960s, Professor Joseph Fletcher, one of the most widely known expositors of situation ethics, attempted to spell out the meaning and the demands of the situationist approach to moral decisions. Basically, situationists argue that no action is intrinsically good or bad. To make a moral judgment one must take into consideration the circumstances that determine the act. The only intrinsic bad, says Fletcher, is malice; the only intrinsic good is love. To determine whether any act is good, one must ask the all-important question: what is the loving thing to do? But this question immediately necessitates a second question: what

---

[2] John L. Thomas, "Antislavery and Utopia," in *The Antislavery Vanguard: New Essays on the Abolitionists*, ed. Martin Duberman (Princeton, N.J., 1965), pp. 240–69; and David Brion Davis, "The Emergence of Immediatism in British and American Antislavery Thought," *Mississippi Valley Historical Review*, 49 (Sept. 1962): 209–30, emphasize the perfectionist thrust of radical abolitionism.

is love? Fletcher argues that love and justice are synonymous. They are not words denoting different ways of ordering life, for *"justice is love distributed, nothing else."* The loving act and the just act are always one and the same; one determines the loving or just act in any situation by asking, what action—under the circumstances—is needed to bring the greatest love to the greatest number of people? Such a question is necessary because this world is imperfect. Barring the advent of the millennium, there is no hope of making a utopia of this earth. In an imperfect world the best that any man can do in a given situation may sometimes seem evil. At such a time he must determine his action by deciding which of the alternatives open to him will bring the least evil to the fewest people and the greatest welfare to the most people. Although man must be armed with certain principles—for situationists are not antinomians—he must also know when to apply those principles and when to depart from them. To the situationist the means employed can be judged only by the results it produces: *"only the end justifies the means; nothing else."* [3]

When Virginia clergymen talked about slavery their approach was basically situationist. Armed with the principle that slavery in the abstract was wrong, they believed that the South was in a situation in which it would be dangerous to apply that principle. When abolitionists argued that slaveholding was an intrinsic sin, Southerners refused to agree: whether slavery could be condemned as sin would depend on the circumstances. When abolitionists urged immediate emancipation, most Virginia clergymen replied that emancipation under the circumstances would not be a loving act. If the Negroes were emancipated in the United States, predicted the prominent Presbyterian William Mayo Atkinson of Virginia in 1834, the white race would not be the greatest sufferer. Virginians knew it was impossible to bring on the millennium, and they were not "so ignorant of human nature as to seek human happiness by turning loose a nation of semibarbarians to starve upon the earth or perish by the sword." Masters were unwilling to emancipate their slaves because they were convinced that "they will confer no boon upon the slave by setting him free—and this they infer from a comparison of the condition of the mass of our slaves with the mass of our free negroes." [4]

[3] Fletcher, *Situation Ethics: The New Morality* (Philadelphia, 1966), pp. 30–37, 63, 65, 87, 99, 102, 120–23, 127–33; Fletcher, *Moral Responsibility: Situation Ethics at Work* (Philadelphia, 1967), pp. 14, 17–19, 21–23, 33, 42–52, 56.

[4] Atkinson to Josiah F. Polk, Jan. 27, 1834, American Colonization Society Records, vol. 56, Library of Congress, Washington, D.C.

Slavery, said Virginians repeatedly, is an evil, but abolition would be a worse evil. The only way to free the Negro in fact as well as in law was to send him back to Africa where he could not be oppressed by white men. The greatest welfare for the greatest number could be achieved only by emancipation with colonization, not by emancipation alone. "What an awful state of society," speculated Presbyterian clergyman William Henry Foote in 1833, "would Garrison's plan of emancipation bring about!" The free Negroes "are here a miserable race." [5] Colonization, declared one Virginian after another, is the "only practicable way." [6]

Situationist arguments seem to have become increasingly important to Virginia clergymen as the nineteenth century progressed, but at no time—even in the supposedly antislavery period of the revolutionary era—were Virginians so utopian and perfectionist in their thinking as to believe that circumstances could be ignored. Of the principal denominations (Episcopal, Methodist, Presbyterian, and Baptist) in postrevolutionary Virginia, only the Episcopalians failed to take an official stand against slavery. The other churches made some moderately strong statements, but the strength of their late-eighteenth-century declarations has frequently been exaggerated by selective quotation on the part of historians. Dwight Dumond, for example, has quoted the statement of Virginia Baptists in 1790 in which they declared that "slavery is a violent deprivation of the rights of nature and inconsistent with a republican government and therefore [we] recommend it to our brethren to make use of every legal means to extirpate this horrid evil from the land." But he has not called attention to the next clause: the Baptists continued by praying that the Virginia legislature would "proclaim the great Jubilee, consistent with the principles of good policy." Dumond also failed to point out that although Virginia law at the time permitted voluntary manumission, the church did not make slaveholding a matter of discipline. [7]

Of the four major denominations in Virginia, the Methodists had the longest history of opposition to slavery and were the only large body theoretically committed to the doctrine of Christian perfection; yet even in their earliest days, when they were relatively

---

[5] Foote to Ralph R. Gurley, Sept. 19, 1833, ibid., vol. 53.

[6] Patricia Hickin, "Antislavery in Virginia, 1831–1861" (Ph.D. diss., University of Virginia, 1968), pp. 247–308 passim.

[7] Dumond, p. 346 (where the year is given incorrectly as 1789); Robert B. Semple, *History of the Rise and Progress of the Baptists in Virginia* (Richmond, 1810), p. 79. See Garnett Ryland, *The Baptists of Virginia, 1699–1926* (Richmond, 1955), pp. 150–55, for the action and inaction of Virginia Baptists in the postrevolutionary period.

few in number, they were unable to overcome a situationist approach to slavery. When the end of the Revolution brought the separation of the Methodists from the Anglican communion and the arrival in the states of the fervently antislavery Methodist Anglican priest and doctor of civil law, Thomas Coke, some American Methodists were willing to follow his advice to take a strong stand against slavery. In the organizational meeting of the Methodist church in 1784, Coke persuaded the conference of preachers, none of whom was from Virginia, to include in the discipline a statement directing Methodists on pain of expulsion to free their slaves.[8] The rule specifically provided that Virginians, who constituted almost half of American Methodists, were to have two years to comply. Although the state legislature in 1782 had passed a law permitting masters to manumit their slaves and allowing the freed blacks to remain in the commonwealth, Virginia Methodists denounced Coke's rule so vigorously that it was suspended six months later. In its place was substituted the relatively innocuous–and more situationist–statement: "We do hold in the deepest abhorrence, the practice of slavery; and shall not cease to seek its destruction by all wise and prudent means." [9]

The Virginia Conference did agree, at the urging of Dr. Coke, to petition the state legislature in 1785 for either immediate or gradual emancipation of slaves. Each preacher received a copy of the memorial to circulate, some prominent men were known to favor the petitions, and there were some optimistic–but vain–hopes that it might succeed. Within the next few years a handful of Methodists joined the largely Quaker abolition societies in Richmond and Alexandria, and some Methodists manumitted their slaves, but most Virginia Methodists were listless opponents of slavery. The General Conference of the church in 1796 firmly urged specific steps to eradicate "this enormous evil" from the Methodist church, but by 1798 Bishop Francis Asbury concluded that slavery would

---

[8] Donald G. Mathews, *Slavery and Methodism: A Chapter in American Morality, 1780–1845* (Princeton, N.J., 1965), pp. 9–10. The rule was omitted from later editions of the 1784 discipline. See *A Form of Discipline for the Ministers, Preachers, and Members of the Methodist Episcopal Church in America. Considered and Approved at a Conference Held at Baltimore . . . On Monday the 27th of December, 1784* (4th ed., Elizabethtown, N.J., 1788).

[9] *The Statutes at Large: Being a Collection of All the Laws of Virginia*, ed. William Waller Hening (13 vols., Richmond, 1823), XI, 39–40; *Minutes of the Annual Conferences of the Methodist Episcopal Church*, I, 24 (1785), quoted in Mathews, p. 12. See also Dumond, pp. 343–44.

exist in Virginia "perhaps for ages; there is not a sufficient sense of religion nor of liberty to destroy it." [10]

By 1816 the position of the church was almost totally situationist in its approach. The General Conference declared that it was "as much as ever convinced of the great evil of slavery," but because state laws concerning manumission varied, it would allow each annual conference to form its own regulations concerning slaveholding among both the laity and the clergy.[11] The new rule meant that for Southern Methodists slaveholding was more or less officially condoned. In 1806 the Virginia legislature had repealed the voluntary manumission act of 1782; slaves freed after the new act was passed had to leave the state within one year after emancipation or run the risk of reenslavement.[12] For some years the church did not substantially change its position on slaveholding,[13] and Virginia Methodists found its policy no barrier to membership.

Like Virginia Methodists, Virginia Presbyterians insisted on a situationist approach to slavery. The first action on slavery taken by the Virginia Synod of the Presbyterian church apparently came in 1800 when the synod declared it to be the "indispensable duty of all who hold slaves" to "educate the young among them for . . . freedom," and "to liberate them as soon as they shall appear to be duly qualified for that high privilege." But the synod had little sympathy for the doctrine that slavery was sin per se: to refuse to hold communion with "any who may differ from us in sentiment & practice in this instance would . . . [at the present time] be a very unwarrantable procedure." All would readily admit that the enslavement of so many Africans had been wrong in the first place, but because of varying circumstances Christians might differ as to the best measures to adopt to bring about universal liberty.[14]

[10] Lucius C. Matlack, *The History of American Slavery and Methodism from 1780 to 1849* (New York, 1849), pp. 18, 19; *Journals of the General Conference of the Methodist Episcopal Church*, I, 22–23 (1796) (hereafter cited as *M.E. Journal*); Francis Asbury, *The Journal and Letters of Francis Asbury*, vol. II: *The Journal, 1794–1816*, ed. Elmer T. Clark (3 vols., Nashville, 1958), p. 151; Mathews, pp. 14, 17, 23.

[11] *M.E. Journal*, I, 93 (1808), 169–70 (1816); *The Doctrines and Discipline of the Methodist Episcopal Church* (New York, 1817), pp. 211–12.

[12] *The Statutes at Large of Virginia, From October Session 1792, to December Session 1806, Inclusive . . . Being a Continuation of Hening*, ed. Samuel Shepherd (3 vols., Richmond, 1835–36), III, 252.

[13] Mathews, pp. 302–3.

[14] Ms Minutes, Synod of Virginia, II, 54–58 (1800), quoted in Ernest Trice Thompson, *Presbyterians in the South*, vol. I: *1607–1861* (Richmond, 1963), pp. 326–27. In 1795 the General Assembly had deplored slavery

Almost twenty years later, in 1818, the Virginia delegates to the Presbyterian General Assembly joined in the unanimous approval of a relatively strong statement on slavery. It declared the "voluntary enslaving" of the Negroes a "gross violation of the most precious and sacred rights of human nature; as utterly inconsistent with the law of God, which requires us to love our neighbors as ourselves." Christians were dutybound to work for the abolition of slavery. Nevertheless, the assembly expressed its sympathies for those who abhorred slavery but lived in slaveholding communities "where the number of slaves, their ignorance, and their vicious habits generally, render an immediate and universal emancipation inconsistent with the safety and happiness of the master and slave." The assembly recommended that all Presbyterians support the newly organized American Colonization Society; that they encourage the religious instruction of slaves; that they attempt to prevent cruelty to slaves, particularly the separation of slave families; and that they suspend from church any communicant who sold a slave "in communion and good standing with our Church" against his will. But slaveholding itself was not to be a matter of discipline.[15]

The major American denominations were thus clearly more interested in maintaining peace and harmony among their members than in waging a campaign against slavery. By 1820 a major factor in enabling churches in Virginia to take a position on slavery without offending an undue number of citizens was the rise of the African colonization movement and the organization of a society to promote the deportation of Negroes. From its beginning the precise goal of the American Colonization Society, as it was commonly called, was as unclear as its official title: The American Society for Colonizing the Free People of Color of the United States. Some supporters contended that its purpose was to emancipate and colonize every American Negro; others argued that it existed only to send away those blacks who had already been freed; still others stated that it expected to provide a home for voluntarily manumitted slaves but had no goal of universal emancipation.[16] Al-

but advised Presbyterians to live "in charity and peace" with those with whom they disagreed (*Minutes of the General Assembly of the Presbyterian Church in the United States of America,* 1795, p. 103, quoted, ibid., p. 325).

[15] *Minutes of the General Assembly of the Presbyterian Church in the United States of America* (Philadelphia, 1818), pp. 688, 691–94.

[16] The best and most recent history of the American Colonization Society is P. J. Staudenraus, *The African Colonization Movement, 1816–1865* (New York, 1961); but see also Philip Slaughter, *The Virginian History of African Colonization* (Richmond, 1855).

though the colonization society seems always to have had an antislavery image in Virginia (despite its noncommittal statements and frequent protests that it had no intention of undermining "property rights"), a member accused of being an "abolitionist" could always argue that he only wanted to get rid of the troublesome free Negro population, or that he simply hoped to help spread the gospel to the "dark continent" of Africa. Under such circumstances it is not surprising that all the major denominations in Virginia gave the American Colonization Society their official approval [17] and that none is known to have taken any other significant stand on slavery in the 1820s.

Despite the inactivity of the churches, the 1820s saw a growing discontent with slavery in the Old Dominion. Agricultural depression in the South, together with the rise of industry and the economic growth of the free states, led numerous Virginians to question the expediency and the morality of slavery. Adding to their qualms was the rising fear that the Southern market for Virginia's excess slave population would soon close. States in the deep South were expected to forbid the importation of more Negroes; many Virginians feared their beloved commonwealth would be overrun by blacks.[18] In August 1831 the alarming news of the Nat Turner insurrection spread throughout the state. For the first time in Virginia history, slavery became a subject open to discussion; for a few months the most popular topic of thought and conversation in the state was the question of the feasibility of emancipation and colonization. In January 1832 the House of Delegates—its galleries packed with visitors and newspapermen—discussed the possibilities of gradually abolishing slavery and deporting the freedmen. But two weeks of spirited speechmaking brought Virginia no closer to abolition; the house refused to take any action in support of emancipation.[19]

[17] Slaughter, pp. 107–8.

[18] See, for example, *Alexandria Gazette*, April 30–July 21, 1827; *Richmond Whig*, Jan. 30, Feb. 17, July 6, Oct. 5, 1824, Feb. 22, Aug. 2, 1825, Feb. 24, July 4, 1826, Nov. 22, 1828, Jan. 2, July 14, July 24, Sept. 12, Sept. 18, 1829.

[19] The most significant antislavery discussions in the Richmond press are to be found in the *Whig* on Sept. 29, Oct. 17, Nov. 17, Dec. 2, 6, 16, 23, 1831, Jan. 2, 13, 19, Feb. 7, 1832; and in the *Enquirer* on Oct. 25, Nov. 4, Nov. 18, Dec. 10, Dec. 24, 1831, Jan. 5, Jan. 7, Feb. 16, March 3, March 10, 1832. A number of the most important speeches are in Philip A. Bolling et al., *Speeches in the House of Delegates of Virginia on the Policy of the State in Relation to Her Colored Population* (Richmond, 1832). See also Joseph Clark Robert, *The Road from Monticello: A Study of the Virginia Slavery Debate of 1832* (Durham, N.C., 1941).

In the aftermath of the insurrection and the slavery debates, a few Virginia clergymen seized the opportunity to advance their emancipationist views. One of the most colorful was the Reverend John Hersey (1786–1862), an itinerant Methodist minister. Traveling in central Virginia, "Father Hersey" had won an enviable reputation as a fervent exhorter and a true man of God. A fanatical believer in Christian holiness, he was so pious that a Quaker friend remarked that Hersey's soul would go up to heaven "like a rocket" when he died.[20]

Soon after the Virginia legislature ended its debates on the peculiar institution, Hersey wrote his *Appeal to Christians on the Subject of Slavery.*[21] In it he incorporated many of the arguments of modern situationists. The "grand requisition of the Gospel," wrote Hersey, was to love the Lord God with all one's heart and soul and mind and one's neighbor as one's self. Applying the imperative to love to the slavery question, he argued that no Christian would say that anyone who was "blessed with the light of the Gospel" but did not fulfill the command to love could be received into heaven. Since slaves were among the children of God, it was virtually impossible to love their Father supremely and yet hold them in bondage. Christians should remember that black men were their brothers: "Would it be esteemed honorable, or merciful, or affectionate in any human being," asked Hersey, "to hold his own brother in bondage for life, and make a slave of him?" Christians were compelled by the Gospel to love all their neighbors, "the *Africans*, the *slaves*, the *beggars*," as themselves. Could they ever hope to do so while holding slaves in bondage? [22]

Hersey clearly believed the answer was no. Yet he also thought that circumstances should determine the time and means of emancipation. Despite his theories of Christian perfection, Hersey was

[20] F. E. Marine, *Sketch of Reverend John Hersey, Minister of the Gospel of the M. E. Church* (Baltimore, 1879), pp. 6, 9, 92.

[21] No copies of the first edition are extant, but several libraries have copies of the second edition, published in Baltimore in 1833. A copy of the third edition, John Hersey, *An Appeal to Christians on the Subject of Slavery* (3d ed., Baltimore, n.d.), which contains a new introduction, is in the Swarthmore College Library, Swarthmore, Pa. Page numbers in the following citations refer to the third edition.

[22] *Appeal*, pp. 55–66. Compare Fletcher's statement that "Christian situation ethics has only one norm or principle or law. . . . That is 'love'— the *agapē* of the summary commandment to love God and the neighbor." "Situation ethics," Fletcher points out, "does not ask *what* is good but how to do good for *whom;* not what *is* love but how to *do* the most loving thing possible in the situation" (*Situation Ethics*, pp. 30, 52).

too much a situationist to believe that slavery could be ended without colonization. Custom, prejudice, and pride, he wrote, had led almost every American, regardless of the section of the country in which he lived, to consider "black skin as a badge of disgrace or inferiority." Freeing Negroes and keeping them in the United States "would not better their condition, or cause them to be more respected, happy, or independent"; in America the black man would always be "degraded, insulted, and oppressed." Fortunately, Liberia was flourishing, and although it would not be "desirable or prudent" to remove all American slaves to the African colony in one, two, or even ten years, it would be possible to do so within the next three or four decades by colonizing one hundred thousand slaves per year. To emancipate and colonize that number, estimated the naive Hersey, would cost three million dollars annually. The needed money could easily be raised, he urged, if the two million Christians in the United States would each contribute a mere dollar and a half per year—just three cents per person per week.[23] African colonization would bring the greatest welfare for the greatest number of Americans, black and white.

Many Virginians apparently approved of Hersey's arguments. His *Appeal* sold well, and in 1833 a second edition was published. According to an introduction to a later edition, Hersey "preached and circulated the work publicly, for some time, in the southern states." The book was well received until the rise of the "ultra-abolitionists" in the North. In 1835, when they began to inundate the slaveholding states with publications that Southerners considered inflammatory, excitement against antislavery agitation from whatever source ran rampant. That fall, a Richmond committee of vigilance seized and burned a number of copies of Hersey's book.[24]

Historians of the antislavery movement have paid surprisingly little attention to the American Anti-Slavery Society's pamphlet campaign in 1835–36.[25] But in Virginia it appears to have aroused more bitterness against abolitionists than did any other single occurrence in the antislavery movement before John Brown's raid on

[23] *Appeal*, pp. 86–88. Hersey's estimate of expenses was based only on the $30 passage which the American Colonization Society charged for each emigrant.

[24] Ibid., pp. v–xi. Also see *Richmond Whig*, Sept. 7, 1835; Hersey to Brother Drake, Oct. 6, 1835, printed in *Richmond Whig*, Oct. 23, 1835.

[25] For brief comments on the campaign, see Louis Filler, *The Crusade against Slavery, 1830–1860* (New York, 1960), p. 97; Clement Eaton, *The Freedom-of-Thought Struggle in the Old South* (rev. ed., New York, 1940, 1964), pp. 197–98; John Hope Franklin, *The Militant South, 1800–1861* (n.p., 1956), pp. 87–88.

Harper's Ferry in 1859. Because it took place just as a major presidential contest was getting under way, it became a partisan issue. Hoping to stigmatize Democratic aspirant Martin Van Buren as an abolitionist, Virginia Whigs took the lead in arousing excitement against the pamphlets and in encouraging local groups of citizens to press the legislature to protest against the flow of materials from the North.[26]

The excitement that swept Virginia and the rest of the South on the heels of the pamphlet campaign convinced many church-affiliated Virginians that slavery was—at least temporarily—too delicate a topic for discussion. A typical course was that of the Richmond *Religious Herald*, an important Baptist weekly newspaper which frequently carried antislavery news. A few weeks before the pamphlets began to reach the South, Editor William Sands wrote that "slavery beheld in any light is an evil of tremendous magnitude" and that thousands of Southerners so acknowledged it. Although he complained that Northern abolitionists often made unfair attacks on slavery, he urged Southerners to "betake ourselves to God in earnest prayer for direction, and agitate among *ourselves* the best means of ridding our land of an evil which many thousands *most deeply interested* deplore." [27] A few weeks later, as the pamphlets began arriving, Sands warned that the "harsh invective and unmeasured abuse which are poured unsparingly on the holders of slaves, will certainly arouse their anger, but can never convince them of the propriety of the course recommended to their attention." No good could come from such abolitionist agitation, and its tendency to weaken the bonds of union and "produce jealousy and discord" were to be deeply regretted. Southerners could not permit any "foreign interference." Abolitionists might "irritate and goad" the South by "their intemperate zeal, and harsh vituperations," but they would never win it to their cause by such means.[28]

In the late summer of 1835 a prominent Baptist clergyman, Andrew Broadus, pastor of a church in Caroline County, wrote the *Herald* that he had recently received some of the pamphlets and had returned them with the comment that he favored emancipation but that the North should share in the problems it would involve. Like most Virginians, he was particularly indignant when radical abolitionists refused to consider the consequences of emancipation

---

[26] See *Richmond Whig*, July 24–Nov. 3, 1835, and cf. *Richmond Enquirer* for the same period of time.

[27] July 3, 1835.   [28] July 31, 1835.

and advised slaveholders to set free their bondsmen without fear and to leave the consequences up to God. Why, he asked, did abolitionists offer such advice when they refused to come South because they were afraid of the consequences to themselves? [29] After the pamphlet campaign, the *Herald* published only one antislavery item, an excerpt from a Boston newspaper which maintained that immediate emancipation in Antigua seemed to be working well.[30]

Although Virginians and other Southerners reacted bitterly to radical abolitionist agitation, some of them found the antislavery writings of less extreme Northerners highly convincing. A favorite work among antislavery Virginians was William Ellery Channing's *Slavery*, first published in 1835.[31] Channing believed slavery was inherently evil "and evil continually," but he had lived briefly in Virginia as a young tutor and consequently understood and respected the situational dilemma in which Southerners found themselves. Among the Virginians impressed by Channing's arguments was the Reverend Charles W. Andrews, an Episcopal clergyman who was the nephew of Bishop of Virginia William Meade and who served as an efficient agent of the colonization society in Virginia for two years in the mid-1830s. In 1836 he wrote in a private letter that Channing's book was "a powerful and searching argument." [32]

Channing opened his essay by maintaining that the most important question to be determined in any consideration of slavery was the moral question; he was writing in an attempt to help the public reach a valid conclusion concerning the morality of the "peculiar institution." Slavery raised the matter of character, for Christianity inculcated and made manifest "Universal Love." Christianity taught its believers to "respect human nature in all its forms, in the poorest, most ignorant, most fallen." [33]

Channing was willing to recognize the difficulties created by varying situations. He would not attempt to "pass judgment on the character of the slaveholder," because "the same acts in different circumstances admit and even require very different construction."

[29] *Religious Herald*, Sept. 11, 1835.   [30] Feb. 19, 1836.

[31] Channing, *Slavery* (3d ed., rev., Boston, 1836). Channing made very minor changes in the second and third editions of his book.

[32] Charles W. Andrews to Ralph R. Gurley, Feb. 11, 1836, Amer. Colonization Soc. Recs., vol. 63; Hickin, pp. 86, 284, 290–96. For additional evidence of Virginians' receptivity to Channing's arguments, see Samuel M. Janney to J. Miller McKim, Dec. 1, 1843, Cornell Slavery Collection, Olin Library, Cornell University, Ithaca, N.Y.

[33] *Slavery*, pp. 2–9.

Nevertheless, he wrote, there was no right of property in man. The "claim of property in a human being is altogether false, groundless. No such right in man can exist. A human being cannot be justly owned. To hold and treat him as property is to inflict a great wrong, to incur the guilt of oppression." There was no higher crime than to steal a man and reduce him to slavery. It was equally wrong to hold him in slavery. Men could not be property because they were rational, moral, immortal beings created in the image of God. They were made to be ends, not means; people, not things. Man "was made for his own virtue and happiness." Such an end was not "reconcilable with his being held and used as a chattel." [34]

Channing knew that some people would not agree that all men should have rights: they would argue that the "General Good" necessitated certain restraints. But when people spoke of the "Public Good," they meant the safety, power, affluence, and arts of a state; whereas Channing argued that the "Moral Good" was the "Supreme Good." The "General Good" should mean not only the security and prosperity of a state but also its inward and moral worth. The welfare of the individual should not be sacrificed to the power of the state. [35]

It was essential that the means used to remove slavery be determined by the slaveholders who knew their slaves and who must live peacefully with them after emancipation. Masters must admit that they could not rightfully hold other men as property. The fetters should be struck off gradually; slaves should have guardians, not masters. If the freedmen would not work from natural motives, the laws of vagrancy should be applied to them. However, emancipated slaves could be motivated to support themselves and their families by being given land, bounties, and rewards and by having their homes made inviolate. Emancipation would have its evils, but these would be less pronounced than the evils of slavery. [36] Insofar as the immediate emancipators were concerned, their principles and sympathy for their fellow creatures were honorable, but the tone of some of their publications had been "fierce, bitter, and abusive." They had erred in advocating immediate emancipation, for such rapid action would be inconsistent with the well-being of the slave or the state. [37]

What qualities made Channing's work acceptable to a number

[34] Ibid., pp. 14, 21, 25, 27, 31, 36–37.   [35] Ibid., pp. 41–47.

[36] Ibid., pp. 128–38, 142. Channing also explicitly declared that colonization would be acceptable to the North if undertaken as a means of general emancipation.

[37] Ibid., pp. 149–53, 169–73.

of Virginians? In the first place, he directed his attack against the institution rather than against slaveholders. He indulged in no name-calling, he expressed no bitterness or animosity, and he made no indiscriminate generalizations. He recognized that some slave-holders were seriously troubled by the institution, and he under-stood that some men held slaves not simply as means to their own welfare but because they were concerned about the welfare of the slaves and wanted to see that they received the best treatment pos-sible. In other words, he did not force all Southerners or all slaveholders into the category of sinner, and he realized that cir-cumstances—not an exceptional amount of innate depravity—led Southerners honestly to view slavery in a different light from Northerners. In addition he offered some practical suggestions for emancipation, he did not advocate immediate and unconditional abolition, and he argued that Southerners should be in control of the emancipation process. Thus he did not add to the fear of social chaos the additional threat that Southern whites would lose the control of their own destiny to outsiders. By tact, basic good will, and his respect for the situation that Southerners faced, Channing was able to advance a strong moral indictment of slavery which won the approval of a number of Virginians.

At the very time that Channing's book was finding acceptance in Virginia, tension was increasing between Northern and South-ern members of the Baptist, Methodist, and Presbyterian churches as Virginia clergymen battled every Northern attempt to make slaveholding per se a matter of church discipline. The generaliza-tion is frequently made that the schisms of the 1830s and 1840s reflected not only the growth of abolitionism in the North but also an increasing commitment to slavery in the South. Certainly, Southern sensitivity to abolitionist agitation had risen with the heightened demands of Northern abolitionists. But the essence of the disagreements concerning slavery can be interpreted in every case as a conflict between Northern attempts to impose absolute rules concerning slaveholding and Southern insistence that the situation—the circumstances—must be taken into consideration. The growth of abolitionism in the North did not necessarily mean a change in Southern attitudes to slavery; Southern churchmen had always insisted that the situation must be the determining factor in any action concerning slavery.[38]

[38] It has also been suggested that the Baptist and Methodist churches, faced in the late eighteenth century with the option of promoting anti-slavery principles and remaining small or relaxing them and attracting many new adherents, chose the latter course (W. W. Sweet, *Virginia*

The first major denomination to divide over the peculiar institution—and other issues—was the Presbyterian. The split came in 1837 between "New School" and "Old School" members, between New School revivalists who believed in almost instantaneous repentance and conversion and Old School men who continued to believe in the doctrine of election and thought conversion took months and even years of spiritual preparation. New School men were more likely to be immediate emancipationists who wanted to bring Southern slaveholders to a rapid realization of their sins, while Old School men were certain that both immediate conversion and immediate emancipation were impossible dreams. Although the schism between New School revivalists and Old School Calvinists reflected sectional patterns less closely than did the Baptist and Methodist ruptures of the mid-1840s, Northerners dominated the New School assemblies and the South controlled those of the Old School.[39]

The antagonism of Virginia Presbyterians—most of whom were in sympathy with Old School beliefs—to abolitionist insistence that slaveholding was sin did not mean that they no longer regarded the peculiar institution as an evil. Antislavery opinion not only remained pronounced in the Presbyterian stronghold of the Valley of Virginia after the schism, it may even have increased in the 1840s.[40] Among those who campaigned most ardently in that decade for emancipation with colonization were several of the most prominent Old School clergymen and laymen.[41] The relatively small number of Virginia Presbyterians who adhered to the New School were probably even more opposed to slavery than were Virginia's conservative Calvinists.[42]

Methodism: A History [Richmond, 1955], pp. 198–99; Virginius Dabney, *Liberalism in the South* [Chapel Hill, N.C., 1932], pp. 65–66; and Mathews, pp. 22–29, 60, 191, et passim).

[39] Elwyn Smith, "The Role of the South in the Presbyterian Schism of 1837–38," *Church History*, 29 (March 1960): 44–63.

[40] William Gleason Bean, "The Ruffner Pamphlet of 1847: Some Antislavery Aspects of Virginia Sectionalism," *Virginia Magazine of History and Biography*, 61 (July 1958): 260–82; [Henry Ruffner] to Samuel M. Janney, Dec. 31, 1847, Samuel McPherson Janney Papers, Friends Historical Library, Swarthmore College; J. W. Paine to William McLain, June 16, 1849, Amer. Colonization Soc. Recs., vol. 114, pt. 2.

[41] Among these were the Reverend Henry Ruffner (see below, pp. 207–8), his son William Henry Ruffner, and the Reverend Rufus W. Bailey (Bean, pp. 260–82; Hickin, pp. 310–29, 414–20).

[42] Thompson, I, 541–42; *Minutes of the* [New School] *General Assembly of the Presbyterian Church in the United States of America*, 1853, pp. 333–39.

Antagonism over slavery may not have been the principal factor in precipitating the Presbyterian split of 1837, but it was assuredly the dominant issue in the more ominous and clearly sectional Methodist and Baptist schisms of the 1840s. The Baptist church, highly congregational in its organization, divided after Northern Baptists opposed the licensing of a slaveholder as a missionary.[43] The more highly centralized Methodists had to deal with two similar disputes in one year: the ordination of James O. Andrew, a reluctant slaveholder of Georgia, as bishop; and the appeal of Francis A. Harding, whom the Baltimore Conference—in keeping with its tradition of not allowing its ministers to hold slaves—had refused to ordain as a minister because his wife owned slaves.[44]

The formation of the Southern churches did not mean that the members had all become converts to the idea that plantation slavery was a positive good. It was still common for them to regard the institution as an evil that could not be abolished without creating a problem of even greater proportions. Southern Baptists and Methodists alike insisted that it was Northern abolitionist members who were changing the rules. Southern Baptists claimed that they wanted only to adhere to the old platform of their Trienniel Conventions;[45] and the Baptist *Religious Herald*, which supported the separation, declared that Southern men generally lamented slavery and considered it an evil but believed that unconditional emancipation would be a worse evil.[46] Southern Methodists proved to their own satisfaction that they were acting within the Methodist tradition by including in their discipline exactly the same statement on the evils of slavery that had been part of the discipline of the entire church for the past twenty years.[47]

In the mid-1840s the Baptist and Methodist schisms caused Virginians to give the slavery problem more attention than they had done in recent years. Many observers and participants regarded the

---

[43] Robert G. Torbet, *A History of the Baptists* (Philadelphia, 1950), pp. 299–313.

[44] A brief, recent, and scholarly account of the Methodist schism is Mathews, pp. 246–82.

[45] *Religious Herald*, May 2, 9, 16, 23, 1844, May 15, 22, 29, 1845.

[46] Ibid., May 23, 1845.

[47] John N. Norwood, *The Schism in the Methodist Episcopal Church, 1844* (Alfred, N.Y., 1923), pp. 100–101; Sweet, pp. 240–42; *Journals of the General Conference of the Methodist Episcopal Church, South, 1846*, pp. 74–75. Ten years passed before Methodists from the lower South were able to modify, over border-state opposition, antislavery statements in the Southern Methodist discipline (Washington *National Era*, June 29, 1854).

divisions of the two largest denominations in the nation as the vanguard of the disruption of the Union. At the same time the question of Texas annexation intensified Northern opposition to slavery
and increased the dangers of schisms in other denominations as
well. Among the Virginia clergy of the small church bodies who
attempted to take a moderate stand on the issue in order to prevent
a division of their churches was Alexander Campbell (1788–1866),
one of the founders of the Disciples of Christ. In his discussion of
the morality of slavery Campbell offered a new situationist approach. Unlike Virginians who believed slavery was wrong in the
abstract but situationally justified, Campbell contended that slavery in the abstract was not immoral but that the institution was
inexpedient in nineteenth-century America.

A native of northern Ireland, Campbell had followed his father
to the United States in 1809 and had settled in Brooke County in
the northern Virginia Panhandle between Pennsylvania and Ohio.
He seems always to have been somewhat opposed to slavery, but
despite his antislavery convictions, Campbell undertook no campaign for emancipation until after the Nat Turner rebellion, when
he added his voice to the growing demands for abolition.[48] In a
January 1832 editorial in his religious journal, the *Millennial Harbinger*, published in Bethany, Virginia, he declared that Virginia
must take steps to free its Negroes. Slave labor, he argued, was
more expensive and less productive than any other kind and had
laid waste the lands of eastern Virginia. Unless an end was put
"to this all-prostrating evil," Virginia would become a wilderness
with a few scattered inhabitants. Campbell, like most other antislavery Virginians of his day, advocated a plan of *post nati* emancipation and colonization. He urged that the ten millions of dollars
that had theretofore been appropriated each year to pay off the national debt be used in the future to colonize both free and enslaved
Negroes beyond the boundaries of the United States.[49]

More than a decade later, in 1845, after the rupture of the Baptist and Methodist churches, Campbell set forth even more explicit
views on the morality but inexpedience of slavery. In a series of

[48] *Memoirs of Alexander Campbell*, ed. Robert Richardson (2 vols. in 1,
Cincinnati, 1866), I, 501, II, 367–69; Harold L. Lunger, "Alexander
Campbell's Political Activity and Views," in *The Sage of Bethany: A
Pioneer in Broadcloth*, ed. Perry E. Gresham (St. Louis, 1960), pp. 149–
50; *Christian Baptist*, Aug. 3, 1823; *Millennial Harbinger*, June 1845, p.
259.

[49] *Millennial Harbinger*, Jan. 1832, pp. 14–20; *Memoirs of Campbell*,
II, 367–69.

essays in the *Harbinger*, he examined the question of the morality of slavery, concentrating on what the Bible had to say about the institution. Campbell and the Disciples had long held that the only absolute guide to morality was a literal interpretation of the word of the Bible; other principles were to be a matter of opinion and were not to constitute an article of faith. In discussing the moral aspects of the master-slave relationship, Campbell argued that the "simple relation of master and slave" was not "necessarily and essentially immoral and unchristian." Slavery was in fact an institution recognized in the Bible. Under certain circumstances and certain regulations, slavery was "altogether lawful and right." [50]

Nevertheless, Campbell declared, the municipal law that spelled out the nature of the master-slave relation might be "altogether immoral." The New Testament did not sanction "the *legalized treatment* of either masters or slaves according to the American or any other code"; he would "not say that the New Testament authorizes a master to treat his servants as he treats his mules or his oxen," merely taking good care of their physical needs. Slaves had minds and "souls as well as bodies." They had a right to a stable family life and to moral and religious training. No master could withhold such rights from his bondsmen "without the forfeiture of Christian character and Christian privilege, no matter under what code of laws such injustice be perpetrated." [51]

Moreover, the institution of slavery was not in harmony with the "spirit of the age" or with "the peculiar genius of our American population and political institutions." That a time would come when free labor would "appear incomparably more honorable, more profitable, and more favorable to domestic and state prosperity and happiness" Campbell thought almost certain. Two more censuses like those of 1830 and 1840—which showed the free states advancing in commerce, education, and general prosperity much more rapidly than the slave states—would not "leave a pin in all the South on which to hang a doubt." At no "very far distant day" Virginia could be expected to abandon slave labor for free.

Campbell had always abjured the two most prominent tenets of the abolitionists, "that the *relation of master and slave is morally wrong*" and "that *immediate emancipation is the imperious duty of every master.*" But he had long opposed American slavery on what

[50] *Millennial Harbinger*, April 1845, p. 145, June 1845, p. 257; H. Jackson Darst, *Ante-Bellum Virginia Disciples: An Account of the Emergence and Early Development of the Disciples of Christ in Virginia* (Richmond, 1959), p. 1.

[51] *Millennial Harbinger*, May 1845, pp. 194–96, 233–37.

were actually situational grounds: because of its abuses and its demoralizing influence and because it impoverished the states and communities in which it continued to exist. The best means of ending slavery was to terminate it gradually by state constitutional action. Apparently Campbell in the mid-1840s was no longer making colonization a *sine qua non* for emancipation; he suggested that Virginia might, for example, pass a law providing that every slave born after 1800 would be free at the age of twenty-one.

Campbell had thus begun to grope toward an ethical system very similar to the "new morality." The "philosophy of expediency," he wrote, "though not well developed," was "susceptible of a very clear development." Actions that were not obligatory or positively required might "by the influence of circumstances, become praiseworthy, meritorious, and sometimes necessary with reference to very great and moral results." In other words, Campbell believed that there were certain acts without intrinsic moral value which became good or bad because of the situation. Thus Campbell saw no intrinsic sin in slavery: "in certain cases and conditions" it was "morally right." But *"in this age and in this country"* it was *"not expedient."* [52]

Arguments that slavery was inexpedient were heard with increasing frequency in Virginia in the 1840s.[53] In the throes of a severe agricultural depression and sensitive to the fact that the state had lost its earlier position of leadership in the Union, many citizens attributed Virginia's decline and poverty to the presence of slavery. Other churchmen besides Campbell seized on the widespread discontent to agitate against the institution, sometimes condemning slavery only on grounds of expediency and political economy, sometimes touching on the morality of the institution. Private letters indicate that many Virginians who refused to discuss the morality of slavery in public nevertheless felt it to be a moral wrong; they argued on grounds of practicality because abolitionist agitation had made them overly sensitive to moral

[52] Ibid., June 1845, p. 263.

[53] See, for example, Samuel M. Janney to Sydney Howard Gay, July 4, 1846, Gay Papers, Columbia University Library, New York City; Janney to Richard Janney, Aug. 20, 1845 (draft), [Henry Ruffner] to Janney, Dec. 31, 1847, Janney Papers; Robert R. Howison, *A History of Virginia, from Its Discovery and Settlement by Europeans to the Present Time* (2 vols., Philadelphia, 1846–48), II, 519; Richmond *Southerner*, n.d., quoted in Washington *National Era*, May 25, 1848; Washington *National Era*, Jan. 7, June 7, Nov. 18, Nov. 25, 1847, Sept. 6, 1849, et passim.

arguments.[54] Such Southern antislavery writers knew that the self-esteem of their fellow citizens—so long condemned as sinners—would tolerate few implications of wickedness.

Because these men—unlike Campbell—seemed to have little concern for the welfare of the blacks and because they were not attempting to deal with the question of the morality of slavery, their arguments do not quite lie within the realm of situation ethics. Such an antislavery advocate was the Reverend Henry Ruffner, the Presbyterian pastor who was president of Washington College in Lexington from 1836 to 1848. Though Ruffner had moral scruples concerning slavery,[55] in his 1847 *Address to the People of West Virginia*,[56] he did not deal with the moral implications of slavery but argued against the institution solely on grounds of white welfare. Ruffner declared that the prosperity of western Virginia, and perhaps of the eastern portion of the state as well, would be promoted by gradual emancipation accompanied by removal of the Negroes. In those states where free labor was used exclusively, the population growth was more rapid; agriculture, manufactures, and commerce were flourishing; and the level of education and intelligence was much more advanced than in the slave states. Ruffner did not propose that slavery be abolished in eastern Virginia, where the slave population was eight times as large as in western Virginia, but he thought it imperative that the western portion of the state act immediately.

Although Ruffner's stand on slavery caused controversy from the very beginning,[57] early reaction to it seems to have been largely favorable. Not only were many western Virginians hospitable to Ruffner's plan for emancipation, but to Ruffner's "joyful surprise" many eastern Virginians, particularly in the part of the state near Washington, also reacted favorably.[58] A number of newspapers, many of them in western and northeastern Virginia, also applauded the renewal of discussion concerning slavery; and the

[54] See [Henry Ruffner] to Samuel M. Janney, Dec. 31, 1847, Janney Papers; Rufus W. Bailey to William McLain, Nov. 13, 1848, Amer. Colonization Soc. Recs., vol. 112.

[55] [Ruffner] to Samuel M. Janney, Dec. 31, 1847, Janney Papers.

[56] [Ruffner], *Address to the People of West Virginia* (Lexington, Va., 1847).

[57] See John W. Brockenbrough to William Henry Ruffner, July 21, 1858, Papers of Henry Ruffner and William Henry Ruffner, Historical Foundation of the Presbyterian and Reformed Churches, Montreat, N.C.

[58] [Ruffner] to Samuel M. Janney, Dec. 31, 1847, Janney Papers.

Lexington Gazette carried the *Address* in serial form.[59] Ruffner was so encouraged by the favorable reaction to his *Address* that he made plans to rewrite and reissue his pamphlet, omitting those parts which were applicable only to western Virginia and to circulate it more extensively east of the mountains. Stimulated by the initial response, a number of Lexington's "most discreet and influential citizens" also began to consider the establishment of an antislavery newspaper.[60]

Neither the revised pamphlet nor newspaper seems to have appeared. A decade later Ruffner declared that the antislavery party had not won the support they had expected. A number of editors and politicians had objected to the "movement as ill-timed, while northern abolitionism was raging." [61] The approaching end of the Mexican War, the question of slavery in the Mexican Cession, and the upcoming presidential election all played a part in convincing political men that a movement would then be ill timed. On the other hand, in 1849, eighteen months after the appearance of the pamphlet, Dr. J. W. Paine, the owner of a Lexington book store that sold Ruffner's *Address*, wrote the American Colonization Society that "this part of the state is already ripe for a scheme of gradual emancipation." [62]

Several outstanding clergymen in the Episcopal church, which included in its membership some of the largest slaveholders in Virginia, argued that slavery was moral and expedient under the circumstances, but were concerned about the issue nonetheless. The church never took an official stand on slavery, but it repeatedly gave its blessing to the colonization movement, and a number of Virginia Episcopalians were among the colonization society's most ardent supporters.[63] Like so many other Virginia churchmen, they

[59] *Lexington Gazette*, Oct. 28–Nov. 25, 1847. The Washington *National Era*, Nov. 18–Dec. 30, 1847, carried a number of excerpts from Virginia newspapers approving Ruffner's pamphlet. See also Howison, II, 510–20, for indication of widespread approval in Virginia of Ruffner's position.

[60] Ruffner to William McLain, Sept. 7, 1847, Amer. Colonization Soc. Recs., vol. 107; [Ruffner] to Samuel M. Janney, Dec. 31, 1847, Janney Papers.

[61] Ruffner to Kanawha *Republican*, July 15, 1858, quoted in Bean, p. 275.

[62] Paine to William McLain, June 6, 1849, Amer. Colonization Soc. Recs., vol. 114, pt. 2.

[63] For example, see L. Minor Blackford, *Mine Eyes Have Seen the Glory: The Story of a Virginia Lady, Mary Berkeley Minor Blackford, 1802–1896, Who Taught Her Sons to Hate Slavery and Love the Union* (Cambridge, Mass., 1954); Martin Boyd Coyner, "John Hartwell Cocke of

viewed the deportation movement as the only practicable means of freeing the Old Dominion from the evils of slavery. Among the most effective and enthusiastic colonizationists in the early years of the movement was the Reverend William Meade, later bishop of Virginia.[64] In the last decade before the outbreak of the Civil War, another Episcopal clergyman, the Reverend Philip Slaughter, was the agent of the Colonization Society of Virginia.[65] Slaughter was at heart a scholar rather than an administrator; he was more effective as a historian of the colonization movement than at raising funds or promoting the manumission of slaves. In addition to publishing a state society newspaper,[66] Slaughter in 1855 published his *Virginian History of African Colonization*. By the mid-1850s eastern Virginians had become much less tolerant of antislavery sentiment than they had been in the mid-1840s, and the book reflects Slaughter's ambivalent attitude toward the merits of slavery.[67] Nevertheless, his arguments in favor of the deportation movement as a means of ameliorating—if not eliminating—slavery mark him clearly as a situationist.

Slaughter complained that abolitionists were a "one-idea party, demented about an abstraction." Every principle, maintained the clergyman, must undergo modifications in its application. Even abolitionists admitted this: they could be heard to say that there were times when a citizen's "imperative duty" was to kill despite the biblical injunction to the contrary. Yet these same men had seized hold of the abstraction that all men were created free and equal and had run it "like a ploughshare through society." To overthrow their fallacious arguments, men need not view all abstractions with contempt. The abstractions of truth, justice, and of God himself had their proper place in the world. Slaughter quoted an unnamed fellow Virginian with approval: society could not be im-

---

Bremo: Agriculture and Slavery in the Ante-Bellum South" (Ph.D. diss., University of Virginia, 1961).

[64] Standenraus, pp. 27–28, 31, 48, 50–54, 70–74, 169, 176–78, 184, 207; Slaughter, p. 9; John Johns, *A Memoir of the Life of the Right Rev. William Meade* (Baltimore, 1867), pp. 117–25; Minutes of the Virginia Branch, American Colonization Society (Nov. 4, 1823–Feb. 5, 1859), p. 1, Virginia Historical Society, Richmond.

[65] Slaughter, p. 98.

[66] Ibid., p. 101. The Richmond *Virginia Colonizationist* (1852–?) was a monthly publication.

[67] Slaughter's antislavery leanings show more clearly in two of his letters to the parent colonization society in Washington than in his book; see Slaughter to William McLain, April 17, 1856, Slaughter to Ralph Gurley, July 3, 1858, Amer. Colonization Soc. Recs., vols. 143, 152.

proved at a single bound, but only by degrees. Whenever "external improvements" ran ahead of "internal changes" they did no good, as the history of South American republics and the French Revolution demonstrated. When Christ came into the world, he did not set out to change the "external features and peculiarities" of the kingdoms of the world, except as they might "*gradually* and *silently*" be changed by the "permeating and all-pervading influence" of the kingdom of Christ.

Among such external features were war, polity, and slavery. In regard to all these there was an ideal situation, or "perfection," which would probably be realized in the millennium and ought to be approximated in the meantime. This state of absolute right called for the elimination of some of these relations and the modification of others. To achieve it was the objective of the kingdom of Christ. But how was Christianity "to realize in the *actual*, this beautiful and infinitely desirable ideal?" Christianity could not assault the defects and abuses directly, for that would bring it into collision with the government and result in the extermination of the church of Christ. It must consider the expedient in determining its approach: "In fixing her eye on the *right*, she [Christianity] maintains a high aim, and makes provision for progress: in regulating the pursuit of that object by the expedient, she has a wise reference to the nature of man and the condition of the world, as fallen; and takes care that the progress shall not be checked. *Right* gives an onward motion to the car; expediency keeps it from running off the track. Each is indispensable in its place; neither can be omitted."

Normal developments, said Slaughter, were gradual. The application of these principles to slavery was obvious. If it were an evil, it could not be cured in a single generation "without inflicting greater evils." Virginians should remember that Jefferson had urged that the first object in planning for the future of the unfortunate Negroes must be to establish a colony in Africa to introduce to the natives the arts of civilization. Slaughter was uncertain of the destiny of American Negroes, but he noted that the latest census showed that they were moving steadily toward the tropics. "With the Anglo-Saxon for their guide" they might spread out over Central America. That many would go to Africa Slaughter had no doubt. In the meantime Virginians could take comfort in the conviction that "their bondage here has been a blessing to them and is fraught with blessings to their fatherland." Out of evil so much good would flow as to "justify the ways of God to the master and the slave. The destiny of the black population of the United States is toward Africa. . . . His servants had better be about their master's work." [68]

Most Virginia clergymen were so overwhelmed by the situational problems of emancipation and their own desires not to offend their congregations that they avoided the slavery question altogether or, like Slaughter, played down their antislavery inclinations. But there seem always to have been a few clergymen, even in eastern Virginia, whose beliefs and expressions were more radical. In 1839 the Reverend J. M. Dickey, pastor of a Presbyterian church in Clarke County, sent some money from his Pisgah Congregation to the American Colonization Society and accompanied it with a note complaining about the controversy between colonizationists and abolitionists. Slavery, he wrote, was a sin which every Christian man should immediately abandon. It was a national sin bringing the curse of God. There was ample room for proponents of both colonization and abolition, and he thought the disagreements between them were unfortunate. [69] In Richmond in the 1850s an anonymous Presbyterian pastor repeatedly spoke out against slavery. Reportedly a strong abolitionist who opposed colonization, he prayed repeatedly for the poor oppressed slaves and often preached about slavery in his sermons. [70]

As might be expected, only the smaller pietistic sects in Virginia managed to maintain relatively firm antislavery principles. Only those religious societies with a literal interpretation of the Bible and a more nearly absolutist concept of morality were able to stay reasonably clear of slaveholding. Believing, for example, that war was always wrong and not situationally justifiable, they were ardent pacifists. Just as they believed that the preservation of one's society could not justify warfare, so they tended to believe that the welfare of society could not justify slavery.

Of the four principal pietistic sects in Virginia, the Society of Friends was the most important in the antislavery movement in Virginia. In 1784, two years after the state legislature passed a law permitting voluntary manumission, the Virginia Yearly Meeting required its members to free their slaves and to refrain from

[68] Slaughter, pp. ix–xvi.
[69] Dickey to Ralph R. Gurley, Sept. 20, 1839, Amer. Colonization Soc. Recs., vol. 75.
[70] Luther Griffing to William McLain, Oct. 25, 1854, ibid., vol. 136. Griffing was especially indignant because the clergyman had dared to pray for Anthony Burns, the fugitive slave from Virginia whose rendition to servitude from Boston created such excitement in New England abolitionist circles in 1854.

the practice of slave hiring. Within the next ten years, Virginia Quakers largely cleared themselves of slaveholding, although the victory was not easily achieved.[71] In 1788 Quaker discipline provided that Friends should not only be free of supporting slavery but should also "bear a faithful testimony" against the institution. A number of Virginia Friends became active in emancipation societies for a few years in the 1790s, but declining antislavery zeal in the state after 1800 caused the societies to become virtually defunct.[72] For many Quakers the problems of emancipation without colonization seemed too difficult to overcome. One Richmond Quaker, for example, declared in 1805 that although he hoped the state would not abandon its policy of permitting voluntary manumission, he "most sincerely" wished "that provision may be made for colonizing them [the Negroes] to themselves" for he believed "that it will require a great length of time and change of circumstances to make them and us happy together."[73] Not until the 1820s did Quakers again become especially active in antislavery endeavors. Once again emancipation societies supported by Friends, many of them advocating colonization, began to spring up in Virginia. Little is known of these antislavery organizations, but few if any continued to exist after the excitement caused by the Nat Turner rebellion.[74]

More than a decade lapsed before Virginia Quakers again undertook any significant antislavery agitation. By that time one of the most active antislavery crusaders in the South was Samuel McPherson Janney, a Quaker schoolmaster of Loudoun County and a member of the Baltimore Yearly Meeting of (Hicksite) Friends. Janney was not actually a situationist; there is no doubt

[71] *A Brief Statement of the Rise and Progress of the Testimony of the Religious Society of Friends, against Slavery and the Slave Trade* (Philadelphia, 1843), pp. 54–55, 56; William C. Dunlap, *Quaker Education in Baltimore and Virginia Yearly Meetings* (Philadelphia, 1836), pp. 478–79; Samuel M. Janney, *History of the Religious Society of Friends from Its Rise of the Year 1828* (4 vols., Philadelphia, 1859–67), III, 435.

[72] Weeks, *Southern Quakers*, pp. 213, 214–16; Weeks, "Antislavery Sentiment in the South," *Publications of the Southern Historical Association*, 2 (April 1898): 96–97; American Convention Minutes, 1796–1805, Historical Society of Pennsylvania, Philadelphia.

[73] Micajah Davis to James Milnor, Jan. 29 [sic], 1805, quoted in Acting Committee Minutes, Jan. 28, 1805, American Convention Minutes.

[74] Acting Committee Minutes, July 7, 1817, Aug. 2, 1819, Feb. 5, Nov. 7, 1828, Jan. 7, Dec. 17, 1829, March 18, 1830, ibid.; [Thomas Earle], *The Life, Travels, and Opinions of Benjamin Lundy* (Philadelphia, 1847), pp. 199, 210–11, 218, 226; Samuel M. Janney to Dillwyn Parrish, April 6, 1875, Janney Papers; Janney, *Memoirs*, pp. 11, 28–33; Filler, pp. 18–19.

that he considered slaveholding an immoral and corrupt institution that should be ended immediately. But because his agitation was directed at Virginians and he was aware of the problems of emancipation, he refrained from publicly attacking slavery as sin and instead argued against the institution on situational grounds. Certain by the mid-1840s that emancipationist sentiment was increasing in Virginia, Janney felt the time was ripe for antislavery endeavors. In 1844 he decided to write a series of essays "showing the disastrous effects of slaveholding in my native state, and the superiority of free labor in promoting prosperity and individual happiness." [75]

Janney argued that the principal reason for the poverty of Virginia was "the employment of laborers having no interest in the products of the soil, and without skill or knowledge to develope the resources" of the land. Unlike most other antislavery Virginians, he believed that the freedmen should be permitted to remain in the state. If the Negroes were emancipated, "protected by humane laws, and encouraged by the education of their children," they could become industrious workers. If Virginia's black laborers were given more incentive to produce, the commonwealth could advance more rapidly in education, agriculture, commerce, manufacturing, and transportation.[76] In tracts and in several newspapers, Janney's essays received extensive circulation in the Old Dominion. Many approved of his arguments, although few Virginians were willing to tolerate his ideas of emancipation without colonization.[77] Thus Janney, despite his privately held view that slavery was sinful, attempted to convert his fellow citizens to emancipation—even without colonization—by arguing that such a move would provide the greatest prosperity and welfare for the greatest number of all residents of the state regardless of color.

The three major remaining pietistic sects in Virginia—the Mennonites, Dunkards, and United Brethren—were largely composed of people of German ancestry, and were as opposed to

[75] Janney, *Memoirs*, p. 33; Janney, "A Review," *National Anti-Slavery Standard*, Sept. 7, 1843; Patricia Hickin, "Gentle Agitator: Samuel M. Janney and the Antislavery Movement in Virginia, 1842–1851," *Journal of Southern History*, 37 (May 1971): 159–90. The quotation is from Janney to Isaac T. Hopper, Dec. 15, 1844, in Janney, *Memoirs*, pp. 87–89.

[76] *Alexandria Gazette*, Dec. 11, 1844. Janney acknowledged his authorship of this unsigned letter to the paper in Janney to Isaac T. Hopper, Dec. 15, 1844, Janney, *Memoirs*, p. 88.

[77] Hickin, "Antislavery in Virginia," pp. 491–98; Hickin, "Gentle Agitator," pp. 169–74, 176–77. See also Janney to John H. Pleasants and R. H. Gallaher, Aug. 26, 1845 (draft), Janney Papers.

slavery as was the Society of Friends, but they did not have the Quaker tradition and concept of public responsibility. Unlike the Quakers, they tried to withdraw from the world; primarily interested in keeping their own skirts clear of sin, they did little to advance antislavery ideas outside their own societies. Slaveholding had never greatly tempted these industrious farmers and artisans who moved into the fertile Shenandoah Valley in the eighteenth century. Firmly convinced that worldly goods were a snare of the devil, they felt little desire to accumulate great wealth; believing that work was a way to win the Lord's blessing, they were not eager to emulate the social life of their more Cavalier neighbors across the mountains. Yet even they found it impossible to avoid some involvement with slave labor. Nevertheless they seem in general to have become more nearly absolutist in their opposition to slavery with the passing decades. Growing pressure from their Northern brethren and their own deep attachment to their faiths were undoubtedly major factors influencing them to reverse in their own sects the proslavery trend that dominated the larger Virginia denominations in the antebellum decades.[78]

In their attempts to refute the absolutist, perfectionist demands of radical abolitionists, most Virginia churchmen had been unable to advance an alternative situationist argument that could undermine the institution of human bondage. The problem with the situationist approach in any era—and in its antebellum Virginia application—is the problem of finite man. The clergymen could not make an objective and dispassionate assessment of the consequences of emancipation; instead, they assumed what they wanted to believe or what they were afraid not to believe: that dire results would accompany abolition without colonization. They predicted that the blacks would be turned loose on society without a guardian, that they would not work and would become a burden to society, that racial warfare would become inevitable, and that the black race would be exterminated. The greatest welfare for the greatest number of blacks and whites in America could be achieved only by emancipation with colonization.

Yet there was a situationist argument available to those who had the imagination to foresee a different outcome to the abolition of slavery. Samuel Janney advanced it most forcefully in the 1840s and found a fair number of Virginians who were willing to listen to his arguments. The consequences he foresaw were black and white men living together peacefully, the blacks becoming more

[78] Hickin, "Antislavery in Virginia," pp. 431–41.

productive because they would be free to improve their minds and because they would have incentives of money and opportunity for advancement. Greater individual productivity would mean greater prosperity for the state as a whole. In the same decade Alexander Campbell offered some of the same arguments and foresaw some of the same consequences.

How did the intellectual training, self-interest, experiences, and temperaments of Janney and Campbell differ from those of the clergymen who feared black freedom without deportation? How many Virginians were willing to accept emancipation without colonization? Contemporaries and historians have argued for more than a century as to whether civil war was necessary to bring an end to American slavery. Perhaps the answer lies in this very problem: would enough Southerners ever have come to believe as did Janney and Campbell? If so, when and by what means would the change of opinion have come about?

12   The Education of
a Virginia Planter's Son

Raymond C. Dingledine, Jr.

EDUCATION for the professions in the United States traditionally has included a variety of experiences. Enrollment at an
institution of higher learning with its formal classes also has
meant involvement in a community separate from the adult society
surrounding it; a community subjected to the boisterous and, at
times, riotous behavior of its youthful members, with an independence and pride of their own. The years of preparation have
involved parental advice, whether solicited or not, and earnest discussions with one's elders. The fledgling has been prone to avail
himself of opportunities for travel and personal observation, subjecting men and institutions of "the establishment" to critical
appraisal. The scion of Virginia's nineteenth-century plantation society was in a particular position to undergo such a multiplicity
of experiences as he prepared himself for the profession of law.

Nineteen-year-old William C. Rives, Jr., left his Albemarle
County home to enroll at the University of Virginia in the fall of
1844. He was the product of a planter aristocracy that was very
conscious of its roots in Jeffersonian Republicanism. His family's
plantation, Castle Hill, of prerevolutionary origin, had been inherited by Will's mother from the estate of her grandfather, Dr.
Thomas Walker, planter, land speculator, explorer, and personal
physician to Thomas Jefferson. It was located about twenty miles
north of Charlottesville, on the roads from Richmond and Orange
Court House. In 1765 Dr. Walker had erected a frame house; to
it the Riveses had attached a two-story brick structure in the
1820s and added wings later. The entrance drive to the house,
situated on a knoll, passed between rows of cedars until it reached
a circular drive framed by tall boxwood. Tulip and poplar trees
ringed the spacious lawn with a vista opening through the boxwood to give a view of the Piedmont to the east. Walker's frame
house in the rear had a beautiful view of the Southwest Mountains, Albemarle's foothills of the Blue Ridge.

Will Rives's father, William C. Rives, had been prominent in
state and national affairs for nearly three decades. Four terms in
the House of Delegates of the General Assembly of Virginia had
been followed by three in the federal House of Representatives.

There Rives had become associated with the rising Jacksonian element and had helped the general carry Virginia in 1828. His political labors had been rewarded by appointment as minister to France, where he had negotiated the important spoliation claims treaty of 1831. Elected to the Senate as a Jacksonian Democrat, he had supported the administration during the nullification controversy, had been "instructed" out of office with the emergence of the Whig party, and then had been returned by the Democrats. Disappointed as a candidate for the vice-presidential nomination in 1835, he had split with Van Buren over the subtreasury plan and had become a leader of the small Conservative Democrat faction. This had led Rives out of his party into "third party" status as a Conservative and then into the Whig party. In 1844 he was nearing completion of what would be his final term in the Senate. The remaining quarter-century of his life would be spent as a private citizen, except for a second mission to France under the Taylor-Fillmore administration and service in the Peace Convention in 1861 and the Provisional and Second Confederate Congresses.

The enrollment of his son and namesake at the University of Virginia must have been a source of satisfaction to the senator. He himself had studied under the personal direction of the institution's founding father, Thomas Jefferson. As a young state legislator he had worked actively and effectively for the bill establishing the university at Charlottesville. Ten years later he had been appointed to its board of visitors, a position which he still occupied and which enabled him to take an active interest in the institution's affairs.

The University of Virginia, with its provision for the student to elect a course of study by enrolling in one of eight schools, offered perhaps the finest education available in the South at the time. Henry St. George Tucker, a distinguished judge and legal author who had been instrumental in the establishment of the university's famed Honor System in 1842, held the professorship of law. Young Rives's academic career at Charlottesville turned out to be unexpectedly brief, however. Toward the close of his first session, he was expelled by the faculty "for evading the process of the Civil Authority" by refusing to appear in court and testify in connection with the student rioting that disrupted the university and caused suspension of classes in the spring of 1845.[1]

---

[1] William B. Rogers to William C. Rives [n.d.], transmitting resolutions of a faculty meeting of May 3, 1845, William Cabell Rives Papers, Library of Congress, Washington, D.C. Professor Rogers was secretary of the faculty.

Disorderly conduct, which ran the gamut from disruptive noise-making with split-quills and tin horns, shooting off firecrackers, firing pistols and guns, building fires on the Lawn, drunkenness, and gambling to breaking windows, physical assaults on members of the faculty, and destructive rioting, had plagued the university since its opening in 1825 and had resulted in the fatal shooting of a professor in 1840.[2] The riot of April 1845, precipitated by a surreptitiously organized band of students, featured breaking the blinds and windows of faculty pavilions on the Lawn, horseback-riding back and forth through the arcades, pistol shooting, and forced entry into the Rotunda. Disturbances on five out of seven nights of one week forced suspension of classes. Appeals to the student body to bring a halt to the disorder were in vain. Convinced that a decision at last had to be made whether the "laws of the land" or the rioters would prevail, the faculty requested assistance from the local justices of the peace and sheriff. Two hundred militia were brought to the grounds, and the county court convened.[3]

Before Christmas, Will had joined a band of "pseudo-musicians" that apparently had sallied forth on the Lawn on several occasions, but his group soon dissolved, and he had played no part in the April rioting.[4] Like most of his colleagues, however, he bitterly resented the faculty's resort to the civil authority. A student meeting denounced the violence but resolved that members would refuse to testify on the grounds that the proctor had exceeded his authority in sending out notices directing some students to come before the justices. Large numbers left the university. Those remaining, encouraged by local citizens led by Will's uncle, Alexander Rives of the Charlottesville bar, assembled in an effort to prevent the arrival of militia by resolving to restore order themselves. In Will's opinion, it was a particular "insult" to the students by the faculty that the troops still appeared, and many of the boys signed a pledge to withdraw from the university. Fearing that he would be summoned to testify, young Rives determined to follow the "most honorable course" and resign.[5]

[2] Philip Alexander Bruce, *History of the University of Virginia 1819–1919: The Lengthened Shadow of One Man* (5 vols., New York, 1920–22), II, 266–311.

[3] Faculty Minutes, VI, April 21, 1845, University of Virginia Library, Charlottesville. See also ibid., April 29, 1845; Bruce, III, 112–17.

[4] Rives, Jr., to Rives, April 23, 1845, Rives Papers.

[5] Rives, Jr., to Rives, April 23, 1845, ibid. See also Rives, Jr., to Rives, April 21, 1845, ibid.; Faculty Minutes, VI, April 29, 1845; Bruce, III, 115–17.

The son's position was staunchly upheld by his father. Illness had prevented him, as a member of the executive committee of the board of visitors, from responding to a faculty request during the disorders to come to Charlottesville. He was present for a meeting of the full board, however, and agreed that the court should determine how long to keep armed guards at the university.[6] Influenced by Will's reports, supplemented by the attitude of his brother, Alexander, who was critical of the faculty for getting overly excited and of the proctor for reveling in the exercise of authority,[7] Rives criticized errors made in dealing with the rioting. Deeply concerned, he sought the advice of President Thomas R. Dew of the College of William and Mary about how to deal with student discipline—the organization and government of colleges being one of the "most puzzling problems of the age." Dew's counsel was never to convict a student unless he admitted guilt and to avoid punishing "the mass," which just united the student body against the faculty.[8]

Controlling the conduct of students was indeed one of the "puzzling problems of the age." The college campus of pre-Civil War America was all too often the scene not merely of pranks and dissipation but of destructive rowdiness and rebellion against authority. The natural exuberance of youth, the need of release from the rigors of academic endeavor, and the conflict between "gown" and "town" were as old as universities themselves. Such additional factors as the influence of the vigor of a young nation of changing mores, the prevalence of violence in American society, and the resentment of youth toward the rules and regulations that marked college discipline of the time have been suggested in attempts at explanation.[9]

The experiences of the University of Virginia during its turbulent first quarter-century seem to reflect the particular difficulties of subjecting the proud and independent sons of the planter gentry to restrictions on their personal conduct. Jefferson's efforts to provide for extensive student administration of a system of self-

[6] Minutes of Board of Visitors, vol. 3, April 23 and 24, 1845, UVa Lib.

[7] He also was indignant over the accusation by some of the professors that he was serving as counsel for the students (Alexander Rives to Rives, April 21, 1845, Rives Papers). The faculty resented his unsolicited intervention (Faculty Minutes, VI, April 29, 1845).

[8] Dew to Rives, May 26, 1845, Rives Papers. Rives was attempting, unsuccessfully, to persuade Dew to accept the professorship of moral philosophy at the University of Virginia.

[9] John S. Brubacher and Willis Rudy, *Higher Education in Transition, An American History: 1636–1956* (New York, 1958), pp. 50–55.

government had failed, and the responsibility of the faculty for enforcing rules of discipline was conducive to an atmosphere of suspicion and hostility between students and professors. Prohibitions against gambling and drinking were impossible to enforce. Until their repeal in the early 1840s, the requirement of a dawn arising and the prescription of a uniform for off-campus wear were perennial causes of irritation. The refusal of the faculty, for a number of years, to grant a Christmas recess was regarded as unreasonable. These and various other regulations and decisions thus were added to such chronic irritants as dissatisfaction over food and housing.[10] Events of over a century later have revealed clearly that the instinct of students to question seemingly arbitrary rules and policies, to resent limitations on personal freedom, to band together in defense of their own, to refuse to cooperate with administrators against their fellows, and to resist appeals to off-campus police authority are not traditions buried with the past.

As has many a young man whose initial college experience was disrupted, Will Rives resumed his academic career elsewhere. In the fall of 1845 he headed north, with his mother and father, to enroll as a law student at Harvard. His mother admonished him to read his Bible each morning and evening and "hang on to the old faith." Citing Lord Chesterfield, his father advised noting all receipts and expenditures in a pocket book, a practice that would be of the "highest importance" throughout life.[11]

Harvard Law School, with its emphasis on the study of law as both science and philosophy, brought young Rives under the influence of two able professors. Supreme Court Justice Joseph Story "with his perpetual high spirits and brilliant, flashing mind, impressed, amused, and stimulated the students"; Simon Greenleaf, a Maine lawyer and one of New England's foremost legal scholars, "deliberate and thorough, taught them how to work, and aroused an ambition for learning." [12] Among the off-campus experiences afforded by Cambridge was an opportunity to stand for two hours in Boston's Faneuil Hall listening to Whig speakers, including the incomparable Daniel Webster, who was introduced as "Defender of the Constitution":

He was dressed with the most scrupulous elegance—buff vest with brass buttons—blue coat with brass buttons—white cravat—& exquisite

[10] Bruce, II, 66–68, 131, 207–16, 246–66, 276–84.
[11] Mrs. Rives to Rives, Jr., Sept. 3, 1845; Rives to Rives, Jr., Sept. 12, 1845, Rives Papers.
[12] Samuel Eliot Morison, *Three Centuries of Harvard, 1636–1936* (Cambridge, Mass., 1936), p. 240.

boots. He walked forward slowly & majestically—& "in his rising seemed a pillar of state."—After the reiterated cheering subsided—"his look drew audience & attention still as night or summer's noontide air." "There can be at least no mistake where we *are*" were his first words. . . . His appearance was very striking—& the upturning of his eyes as he said "for these matters they will have to answer at another & a *higher* tribunal" was truly awful.[13]

From his father, an orator of much note in Virginia, the young student received hints on developing his own public speaking ability. He was advised of the advantages of writing out a speech in advance so as to give "more correct & elegant expression" to his thoughts but was admonished on the necessity of extemporaneous speaking. Understanding a subject, concentration on it, and the orderly arrangement of thoughts were the essentials for extemporaneous delivery.[14]

The ten-month session at Harvard completed, Will headed back to Virginia on the long, tiresome trip typical of travel in antebellum America. He left Boston at 5:00 P.M. on July 1 by train for Norwich, Connecticut. An overnight steamboat trip in an uncomfortable stateroom allowed little sleep, and fog caused a late arrival in New York and missed connections with the morning train to Philadelphia. Leaving that city at 10:00 P.M., the weary traveler rode the train all night, reaching Baltimore at 5:30 in the morning and Washington in time to catch the 9:00 A.M. boat for Richmond. He reached Virginia's capital city around 6:00 that evening. After spending the night with friends, he left Richmond by train at 8:00 A.M., arrived at Gordonsville at 1:00 P.M., and after three hours of travel over the "abominable" road to Charlottesville, reached the gate to Castle Hill.[15]

The next two months afforded opportunity for reading, in which Will sought to pursue a "course of study" suggested some time earlier by his father, for contemplation and self-evaluation, and for discussions with father and older brother. After measuring his height of just under six feet one afternoon, the young man accepted the theory that a person was taller in the morning because the night's rest had removed pressure on the "vertebrate column" so that it was longer and one stood more erect. He noted the opinion of brother Francis that he lacked self-assurance with young ladies:

[13] Journal of W. C. Rives, Jr., Nov. 7, 1845, Rives Papers. Webster discussed such current issues as Oregon, Texas, Native Americanism, and the exercise of the suffrage.

[14] Rives to Rives, Jr., Feb. 25, 1846, ibid.

[15] Journal of Rives, Jr., July 1, 2, 4, 5, 6, 1846, ibid.

"I do not sufficiently feel the superiority of my sex. Instead of endeavoring to control I suffer myself to be controlled." [16]

Much discussion centered around Will's future plans. Francis was just getting established in law in New York City and would carry with him his father's admonition: "Take care under all circumstances, to exhibit in your conduct an example of irreproachable virtue and honor, and fortune can have no power over your happiness, whose seat is in the conscious mind." [17] His father was not in favor of beginning the practice of law in the city. He argued that college-educated men were apt to have an "absurd fastidiousness" and "deem it beneath them to associate with the great body of the people." The great men of the state, and of the nation, had been shaped by the experience of "familiar intercourse with the people," obtained by attending county court and participating in public meetings concerning county affairs. Many a young, educated lawyer failed in country practice because of poor business habits, dissipation, and loafing. Virginia was in the "infancy" of its development, and those who remained there would benefit. Moreover, one could engage in "healthful exercise" in the country and have opportunity for "moral & intellectual improvement"; "while a young man can improve himself in professional knowledge, & in readiness and fluency of speech, he acquires, by associating with people who all feel that they have rights & are resolved to maintain them, a certain frankness [,] manliness & independence of character, which he could not attain amidst the servility & corruption of a large city." [18] Francis, on the other hand, maintained that Virginia's progress was too slow to be of much value in a single lifetime. He pointed out greater chances for success in the city, the prospect of an annual income of $8,000 to $10,000 rather than $1,500, and more opportunity to marry an "appropriate" person rather than "someone inferior." [19]

Young Will felt his father's arguments to be slightly the stronger. He was also attentive to additional parental advice on how to develop the art of public speaking. Rives urged practice

[16] Ibid., July 8, 12, 27, 1846.

[17] Rives to Francis R. Rives, Aug. 23, 1846, quoted in ibid.

[18] Will recorded these as being essentially his father's words (ibid., July 10, 1846).

[19] Ibid. Francis cited $1,500 as the maximum annual income of his uncle Alexander, whom Rives considered one of Virginia's "most eminent criminal lawyers." In reflecting on his plans, Will estimated $1,000 as the maximum income to be expected if successful and not over $300 if "mediocre" (ibid., July 27, 1846).

in both "written composition" and "extemporaneous speaking," in which thoughts but not precise wording were prepared. He warned against overreliance on memorization as producing a lack of "readiness & boldness." He also opposed taking notes to reply to an adversary in debate, for reliance on them instead of on "mental faculties" would decrease forcefulness. The great barrier to developing as a speaker, he felt, was a tendency to think more of the language than of the subject. "Lack of words" was caused ordinarily by "lack of ideas." Finally, the veteran orator stressed the need of animation if one would be a successful speaker.[20]

In September 1846 Will returned to Cambridge to complete his studies. Then, in the spring, he came home to begin the practice of law. He took his oath as an attorney in Albemarle County and qualified before the county court and the Superior Court of Law and Chancery. Over nine months elapsed before the young lawyer had his first case, but there were social and civic activities. A dance, with the "belles" of the community present, lasted until midnight or after.[21] Attendance was required at three militia musters, two company and one regimental, a year.[22] There were opportunities to observe the political climate in Virginia and the nation in a presidential election year.

While attending the Albemarle county court early in February 1848, Will was impressed with the "extraordinary influence" the perennial Whig candidate, Henry Clay, exerted over his supporters. "He wields a greater personal influence than any man in the United States," the young man noted. It seemed to him, though, "rather a melancholy spectacle to see so eminent a statesman after such repeated defeats at the advanced age of 71 still fixing his affections upon the prospects of political elevation." He was amused by George W. Randolph's anecdote of an Irishman who returned to the United States after an absence of over two decades and asked if the current presidential candidate was the son of the Clay who had sought office thirty years earlier.[23]

A short time later, young Rives visited Washington, called on Clay, and could evaluate personally the venerable statesman:

Mr. Clay still preserves his divine voice, but I was disappointed in his looks. The public say that he looks exceedingly well. I thought that he looked old—his form shrunk—his clothes hanging loosely about him & his face furrowed & hair very thin[.] He said John Randolph of R.,

[20] Ibid., Aug. 30, 1846.   [21] Ibid., April 8, 1847.
[22] Ibid., April 10, 1847.
[23] Diary of W. C. Rives, Jr., Jan. 30–Feb. 10, 1848, Rives Papers. A single entry covers these dates.

he thought had paid him one of the greatest compliments he had ever received. "If you want to know Mr. Clay's opinions," said R., "you have but to look in his face." Mr. Clay's association with the church has had a happy effect upon his character—mollifying its asperities. He said that people crowded around him as if he had broken out of a menagerie, "as if," said he, with one of the peculiarly beautiful modulations of his sublime voice "I were anything more than *mortal* man." [24]

On the evening of that same Saturday, Will visited another elder statesman, former president John Quincy Adams, who, he observed:

though physically very infirm has much mental energy. he rises early —reads much—newspapers & pamphlets chiefly—& insists on receiving the public every Saturday evening. . . . [He] exemplifies what can be accomplished by energy of purpose & indominitable will. His voice is gone, he can scarce stand upon his feet, yet, I am told he rises early, studies diligently, attempts occasionally to address the house of representatives & rises to receive his friends. His physical machine appears to me almost wholly worn out.[25]

On Monday, while sitting in the Senate gallery, Rives heard an announcement that Adams was dying and that the House "had broken up in great confusion." Two days later the statesman was dead. "The emotions produced by the death . . . are highly creditable to the people. I had thought that partisan feeling had now arrived to such an height in this country that the due need of praise would not even on his decease be accorded to such a man as Mr. Adams. But all parties & all classes of society seemed to be impressed with the belief & with the feeling that a great man has fallen." The funeral was a "great pageant," attended by "throngs," both civilian and military.[26]

Before returning home, the young Virginian had an opportunity for a visit with "Mrs. Ex-Presidentess Madison who preserves her good looks astonishingly & receives with her usual affability and grace," and to see Mrs. Crittenden of Kentucky, "fair, fat and forty." [27] Earlier he had attended a White House reception and found President and Mrs. Polk "very gracious," although they confined their conversation with him to the weather.[28] He had also had a chance to hear anecdotes about John Randolph of Roanoke from former Congressman John S. Barbour. One dealt with an occasion when a relative had grabbed Randolph by the collar and "laid him across his knee & whipped him with twigs from a stable broom." Barbour had been with the brilliant eccentric during his

[24] Ibid., Feb. 19, 1848.   [25] Ibid.   [26] Ibid., Feb. 21, 24, 26, 1848.
[27] Ibid., Feb. 28, 1848.   [28] Ibid., Feb. 18, 1848.

last days, when he was "intoxicated almost the whole time" from "Virginia mint juleps." Even on his deathbed Randolph had reprimanded his doctor for incorrectly pronouncing the word "omnipotent." [29]

These experiences in the capital stimulated conversations between son and father at Castle Hill about the nation's statesmen. After one evening of such discussion, the son opined that Webster was "by far the greatest man, so far as *intellectual* power goes, in America." Calhoun was "remarkable" for his reasoning ability. His strength lay in his "Rati[o]cination" and "dry dialectics." Webster was notable not only "for his powers of ratiocination, but for his eloquence, his imagination, his force, his wit, his sarcasm, in a word for his sublime genius. Mr. Webster writes & speaks better English than any of our statesmen. Mr. Clay commits oftentimes the greatest inaccuracies. What can be more beautiful & impressive than Mr. Webster's oration on the anniversary of the landing of the pilgrims!" [30]

His initial year of practice afforded numerous occasions for Rives, now planning the development of his own plantation on his father's gift of the 771-acre Cobham estate adjoining Castle Hill, to observe and reflect upon life and problems in antebellum Virginia. A trip through the Piedmont to Goochland and Powhatan counties and a visit to Rock Castle plantation revealed that good lowland along the James River was selling for around $100 an acre but was producing a coarse-textured, heavy, rich tobacco which was not as desirable for chewing tobacco as the crop on the lighter soil of a county such as Fluvanna.[31] The young lawyer was left with the impression that Virginia's agriculture lacked system. Fences were "tumbling down, gates broken, bridges rotted down, horses used up, universal negligence & irregularity." He disagreed with those who felt no change could be made under slavery but felt that special effort was necessary for improvement. "He however who, with the disadvantages of our system, would succeed as an agriculturist must be regular, vigilant, energetic, & intelligent. We cultivate too much land & do not use manure—the foundation of all agricultural improvement. One should endeavour to get *beforehand* with the affairs of his plantation. We are almost invariably *behindhand* in all agricultural operations." [32] At Cobham, Will hoped to plant tobacco and, as far as possible, to use

[29] Ibid., Feb. 20, 1848.   [30] Ibid., April 9, 1848.
[31] Ibid., Nov. 11, 1847.
[32] Ibid., Nov. 15–Dec. 6, 1847. A single entry covers these dates.

"poor whites" and free Negroes who could be paid in the "produce of the plantation." [33]

Mingling among his fellow citizens while traveling or attending court days in Albemarle or nearby counties impressed the erudite young Harvard-trained lawyer with the ability and inclination of even a "motley group" of men to discuss a variety of subjects; "the genius of our institutions causes people to take an interest in all public affairs & to talk about & inquire into everything. The constant interchange of views & information between the people has produced intelligence which in turn begets the spirit of inquiry." This, he decided, was responsible for John R. Godley's observation, after his travels in the United States, that he had never met a *"stupid* American" and for the "superior intelligence" of lower and middle class Americans as compared with those classes in England. As Rives saw it, "the wealthy in America sometimes disdain mingling with their poorer but not humbler fellow citizens. The consequence is that, though in some cases more refined, they are often less intelligent & far less energetic. This remark applies to those who inherit wealth & not to those who achieve their own fortunes who in this country are usually men of popular talents and manners." [34]

Will became aware of the need to develop an easy and familiar manner with people, without becoming coarse, copying their "vulgarisms," or resorting to demagoguery. "All ceremony should be waived. Stately and formal courtesy should be dispensed with, & unaffected urbanity alone should be cultivated." He was impressed with John S. Barbour's observation that his "most reliable and attached friends were those in the humbler walks of life which he had treated with kindness. They respect a gentleman the more for not being *in every particular* one of themselves, while they are pleased and gratified by marks of his good will and attention." [35]

The monthly sessions of the county court brought together people from all parts of the county to transact business, renew acquaintances, and dispense and receive the latest news.

About 11 o'clock the hum of human voices near the court house becomes quite audible and it continues to increase until 2 and 3, and *four* o'clock in the afternoon when perhaps it reaches its *acme*. Many become intoxicated, and are seen reeling to and fro, and are at their wit's end. A fight too occasionally takes place to vary the monotony of the scene and there is always at such times an instantaneous rush on the part of the bystanders to surround the combatants and *to see*

[33] Ibid., Jan. 30–Feb. 10, 1848. A single entry covers these dates.
[34] Ibid., Feb. 13, 1848.   [35] Ibid., April 3, 1848.

the *fun!* It is but fair to remark that intoxication in Virginia is of far less frequent occurrence now than formerly, and a fight is, it must be said, a rare spectacle.[36]

Young Rives felt that Louisa Court House was the scene of more drinking than anywhere else in the state; there were usually some half dozen "drunken revellers who keep up their orgies throughout the night." [37] On one occasion, Melton's Inn at Louisa was the scene of dancing to the tunes of a fiddler. Elisha Melton, who had begun as a carpenter and had acquired a reported 20,000 acres, 100 or more slaves, and much of the property around the court house, held a candle to illuminate the dancing. An old man, nearly too drunk to stand, "insisted on giving dancing demonstrations"; other guests spent their time playing whist.[38]

The situation at nearby Fluvanna Court House, in the home county of Virginia's temperance crusader, John Hartwell Cocke, was in sharp contrast. At Palmyra, its county seat, there was no drunkenness and "no liquor sold, & the walls of the court House are decorated with Dr. Sewall's plates of the stomach—exhibiting the appearance of the internal coat of the stomach of the perfectly temperate man, the moderate wine bibber, the debauchee etc. etc. Whether this reform (for it is a most decided *reform*) is attributable to the exertions of the great advocate of temperance—Gen. Cocke—I am unable to say." [39]

Business transactions included not only buying and selling such livestock as horses and mules but also traffic in slaves. The clamor of the slave auctioneer, who on one occasion, Will noted, "recommended a negro woman because she had a fine suit of hair," [40] was particularly disturbing:

Those vile traffickers in human flesh—negro traders—invariably resort to the Court House on court days with a view to make purchases or to sell and it should be a matter of profound grief and mortification to every right minded Virginian to reflect how much they are encouraged. The very high price for slaves in the extreme Southern markets keeps up the demand for slaves & gives them a nominal value which so long as they remain within the limits of this state they are very far from possessing. Experience demonstrates that in a *grain growing* country *slave* labour cannot be employed to advantage. Whether the [*sic*] can be different in those southern states where cotton, rice, sugar etc. are the staples I am unable to say. It is a sad thought to reflect that Virginia *is* and *has been* a *slave breeding state*—rearing slaves not for her own uses and necessities but for transportation to other states.[41]

[36] Ibid., Feb. 4, 1848.   [37] Ibid.   [38] Ibid., March 13, 1848.
[39] Ibid., Feb. 4, 1848.   [40] Ibid., March 13, 1848.
[41] Ibid., Feb. 4, 1848.

Such a critical attitude toward the slave trade reflected the inheritance of this son of a planter-slaveholder. At various times his parents had indicated their adherence to the Jeffersonian tradition of moral concern about the institution of slavery and expectation of and desire for its eventual elimination. The elder Rives had been an active member of the American Colonization Society, serving as a vice-president of the Albemarle chapter. While he was living abroad, the pleasing contrast between most American institutions and European ones had emphasized to his mind "the melancholy anomaly of domestic slavery in our free institutions," [42] and he had wondered if it would not be wise to lay aside constitutional scruples and seek aid from the national government toward the colonization of Negroes. News of Nat Turner's rebellion had elicited his strong support for emancipation of the *post nati* and colonization. After efforts in that direction in the Virginia legislature had failed, Rives had continued to endorse colonization as holding out the future prospect of getting rid of "this consuming cancer of our permanent prosperity" while respecting property rights,[43] and he had written: "The extinction of slavery is one of those great revolutions, to which there is an inevitable tendency in the spirit of the age, so found in social ameliorations of every sort; & the wise & the good ought to look constantly to it with the sole desire of rendering the transition as safe & easy as possible." [44]

Just as such sentiments had not resulted in effective action, however, so the son's critical observations did not indicate a willingness to support actively the cause of antislavery. Nor did his experiences at Virginia's county courts presage a career as planter-lawyer in his native state. In the spring of 1849 he married Grace Sears, daughter of the prominent Boston merchant. After taking his bride abroad, when his father returned to France, Will settled permanently in Boston for the practice of law. His education, both formal and informal, had prepared him well, and the development and management of his Cobham plantation, where he built a home and spent his summers, insured a continuing connection with Virginia.

[42] Copy, Rives to Thomas Walker Gilmer, Oct. 29, 1831, Rives Papers.
[43] Rives to Robert Rives, May 19, 1832, ibid.
[44] Rives to Henry Rives, March 30, 1832, ibid.

13 The Many-Faceted Career of Judge William Hallam Tuck

Alden Bigelow

QUITE often, it seems, either analytical abstractions or nostalgic myths prevent us from really seeing personalities in history. Their frustrations and achievements, their domestic lives and workaday worlds are seldom revealed. Yet in addition to its grander themes history should include a broad range of representative lives. There is no better perspective on the social history of our past than that revealed by the study of such a man as Judge Tuck of Maryland. The purpose here is not to give a comprehensive sketch of Judge Tuck's personal life or even of his professional career. The sources that I am using do not lend themselves to that; they are the judge's papers, which are now in the private possession of Mrs. William Hallam Tuck of Upper Marlborough, Maryland, whose husband was the judge's grandson. For this study I have used extracts from the collection to describe the many-faceted career of the antebellum judge and indirectly the society in which he lived.

William Hallam Tuck was born in Annapolis, Maryland, on November 20, 1808.[1] His family had held a prominent position in Maryland for several generations, and he was related by birth to the Brookes, Chews, Bowies, and Spriggs, all well-known families of the Chesapeake Bay area. His father, Philemon Hallam Tuck, a lawyer, had greatly increased the family fortune through real estate ventures; this made it possible for William Hallam to attend the best schools and to take a high place in the society of the day.[2] He graduated from St. John's College in 1827 with the degree of Master of Arts. On June 23, 1843, he married Margaret Sprigg Bowie Chew, from Prince George's County. From the time of his marriage Tuck maintained a residence in both Upper Marlborough, Prince George's County, and Annapolis, Maryland.

Aided by his fine background William Hallam Tuck was able to distinguish himself as a lawyer, businessman, and citizen. He

---

[1] Clayton Colmon Hall, ed., *Baltimore: Its History and Its People* (3 vols., New York, 1912), III, 771.

[2] Ibid., p. 772.

served a number of terms as a member of the Maryland House of Delegates and was Speaker of the House during one term. His success in the business world led him to the presidency of the First National Bank of Annapolis. He was a director of the Baltimore and Ohio Railroad and represented the State of Maryland's stock in the railroad. He was a member of the Board of Governors and Visitors of St. John's College, and for half a century he was a member of the vestry of St. Anne's Church, Annapolis. He was appointed judge of the Circuit Court of Anne Arundel and Calvert counties, and at the time of his death in 1884 was president of the Board of County Commissioners of both counties.[3]

By 1845 Tuck had already established himself as something of a family patriarch. The many letters to him from his sister, Elizabeth E. Hamlin, and other relatives show that they looked up to him for family leadership, advice, and, not infrequently, money. For example, when his sister wanted money for a house, she wrote from Pittsburgh:

My motive for giving you the preference as a correspondent will be apparent from the proposal I have to offer for your consideration, which is done on my part without hesitation knowing your willingness to serve me should it be in your power to do so, altho Mr. Hamlin does not altogether approve of my application to you as your money may be otherwise invested. My plan if it would suit you is this for you to purchase a cheap house and lot for me to refund in annual payments principal and interest to you. . . . A few days ago . . . a man that we are acquainted with sold a good house and lot for $400 cash. In a few years our rent would amount to that sum and then we have nothing but the liberty of giving the house up when we can suit ourselves better.[4]

The judge's reply to this appeal can be deduced from another letter his sister wrote him about six months later:

How I would that we could see and converse awhile with you. I shall profit by your advice and procede with caution. If the deed is drawn in my name, I want you to hold a mortgage on the property until you are paid.[5]

The following month she wrote again:

As it was not in my power to procure a house and lot of the size and price that would suit my circumstances I concluded to take the

[3] Ibid.

[4] Elizabeth E. Hamlin to Tuck, March 28, 1844, William Hallam Tuck Papers in the possession of Mrs. William Hallam Tuck, Upper Marlborough, Maryland. All subsequent citations are from the Tuck Papers.

[5] Sept. 4, 1844.

lot that already has been described to you. . . . There is a man who lives in that place that has engaged to build me a good house for four hundred dollars, to pay him two hundred dollars to cover the whole expense, yard fixtures and all that appertains to a good dwelling included if you will let me have the two hundred dollars requisite to make the first payment.[6]

Finally, Elizabeth seemed satisfied with the help her brother had given her, telling him, "Your check . . . will relieve me from the embarrassment I was in. . . . I am glad to know that your wife has safely passed the time of nature's sorrow and I have no difficulty in thinking you very happy in your domestic relation, loving and being loved." [7] Tuck seems to have patiently endured his sister's reliance upon him and his money.

Judge Tuck's bills indicate that he and his family lived quite well. Many of the items needed for his household were sent from Baltimore by steamer. For example, a May 1844 notice from James Cox and Co., Baltimore, said, "By tomorrow's boat you will receive your renovated mattresses and six Venetian blinds." The amount of this bill was $66.22, and Cox added, "For which amount your check shall have a hearty welcome." [8] But apparently the judge was sometimes slow in making payments. Almost two years later, in March 1846, Cox wrote, "If entirely agreeable to you I should like very much by return mail to receive your check. . . . If remarks about being in want of money were not too stale, I would here repeat some of them, but the fact is people in business are always in want of funds." [9] His gentle tone, with no comments about interest payments on the unpaid balance, presumably indicate that he knew his customer was financially able to pay the bill. Finally in April, Cox politely wrote, "Below you will find a bill of your Venetian blinds. Your usual prompt attention to such little matters will in the present case much oblige." [10] When Cox was able to give his "hearty welcome" to the payment of this bill is not recorded.

Goods coming to Upper Marlborough or Annapolis from Baltimore were frequently delayed. Typically, Cochrain Brothers wrote, "You will be disappointed at not receiving the wardrobe by the steam boat today. The reason was the wagoner not coming at the time appointed . . . he just got down to the wharf when the steamboat was hauling out, and consequently had to bring it back . . . sorry for the disappointment." [11] Roads were so bad as to be often unusable. The water route from Baltimore to Upper Marl-

---

[6] Oct. 30, 1844.   [7] Jan. 23, 1845.   [8] May 29, 1844.
[9] March 10, 1846.   [10] April 21, 1846.   [11] May 18, 1848.

borough led down the Chesapeake Bay to the Patuxent River and thence up that river almost to Upper Marlborough. Of course Annapolis was an even easier run down the Bay to the mouth of the Severn River.

Judge Tuck's papers indicate the prices paid for various services and household goods in the 1830s and 1840s. The best calico curtain material was ten cents a yard, and the best linen was eight cents a yard.[12] The judge paid five dollars a pair for trousers [13] and five dollars for riding boots.[14] Mrs. Tuck paid forty-four cents a yard for velvet ribbon and six cents a dozen for buttons.[15] Corn whiskey was fifty cents a gallon.[16] When traveling to Washington as he did fairly frequently, the livery stable charged him "two horses fed and servant one meal 75¢." [17] Day wages are exemplified in a receipt from George Kendricks, who got six dollars for being a chain carrier on a surveying party for six days in August 1844. The milk bill for the Tuck family was ninety-seven cents for the month of May 1837. The sheriff charged one dollar and fifteen cents for summoning three witnesses in the same year, and in 1834 the judge paid twenty dollars a quarter for the rent of his office in Annapolis. One of the most interesting bills was the account submitted by John Davidson for the funeral of Henry D. Hatton, for whose estate Judge Tuck acted as executor in 1843:

Hinged-top walnut coffin	$16.00
Walnut case for ditto	7.00
Lining coffin with flannel and stuffing it with hair	6.00
Shroud	1.00
1 Saddle horse	1.00
Cash for ferriage	2.50
	$38.50 Total

With his duties as lawyer, judge, farmer, and businessman it is not strange that William Hallam Tuck had more to attend to than he could easily manage. His correspondents frequently urged him to take a case and then pestered him if he worked slowly. The widow Hilliary tried to bribe him with oysters if he would come to her home to discuss business. She wrote, "Having written to

[12] James Cox to Tuck, June 27, 1845.
[13] Lane and Tucker to Tuck, June 23, 1846.
[14] Ackland and Armiger to Tuck, Aug. 8, 1849.
[15] R. G. Etchison to Tuck, Oct. 6, 1856.
[16] J. B. Wilson to Tuck, Sept. 1, 1851.
[17] Carpenter's stable to Tuck, Oct. 21, 1849.

you some time since and receiving no answer I take the opportunity of informing you that I wish you as soon as convenient to come up as I want to see you on some very particular business." She added, "Please do not disappoint me." Apparently Tuck did not disappoint her in that instance, judging from a rather nagging letter he received the following year: "It has been some time since I heard from you. . . . I have been looking for you for two weeks. . . . Don't forget I have oysters for you." [18]

Judge Tuck's letters frequently mention family illness, and the letters to him show the special concern of his friends about his wife's health, which was not at all robust if one gathers correctly from frequent allusions to her "indisposition." [19] Perhaps bad weather and illness in the family forced Tuck to stay at home occasionally and postpone professional work. The country lawyer of a century ago appears to have missed a good deal more time at the office than his counterpart today.

As a lawyer much of William Hallam Tuck's work was in connection with acting as the trustee of an estate or as the executor or administrator of a will. Mrs. Catharine Townshend, widow of Samuel Townshend, depended upon him to handle her husband's estate and provide funds for herself and her six children. As Townshend's trustee, Tuck sold some land out of the estate so that the widow would have enough money to plant a crop for the coming year. Apparently the sale did not realize enough money, for she wrote: "I have been trying my best to do without calling upon you untill you had finally arranged the business, but it being just the time of pitching our crop and our Montgomery lands producing nothing of any account without the assistance of guano or some other help I find it impossible to do anything at this time without the assistance of a little money. . . . I have no other resource to look to but you." [20] Obviously the judge needed to be knowledgeable about real estate and farming practices as well as the law.

Frequently two or more relatives of a deceased client pulled at Judge Tuck in opposite directions to favor their claims to an estate. William Hilliary wrote from Baltimore:

My brother in March [1843] . . . appeared to be in a good deal of trouble and told me . . . that he had no way of paying me except by selling his blacks and [this] he did not want to do. He however worked upon the feelings of my wife and myself until he finally succeeded in getting me to give him a receipt for the claim, he promising that

[18] Eleanor B. Hilliary to Tuck, April 7, 1860, Nov. 23, 1861.
[19] See, for example, Tuck to Captain Tilden, Dec. 15, 1859.
[20] April 29, 1850.

he would double pay me and my family some future day. If he has
made no will and has made no reservation for me I shall certainly try
and get it if I can. He has left considerable property exclusive of his
daughter who is rich. I might as well have it as others as it is justly
due me.[21]

Eleanor Hilliary, the "rich daughter," was in no way disposed to
allow her uncle's claim. She scolded Tuck for even corresponding
with William Hilliary, complaining, "You wrote to my Uncle and
I was astonished . . . you have failed to comply with your promise. My health will not permit me to attend to anything that will
give me trouble. I looked upon you as a friend when I employed
you." [22] Tuck had great difficulty in working out a mutually satisfactory settlement of this estate.[23] It would have taken a Solomon
to please both parties.

Lawyer Tuck was the administrator of the estate of Robert
Bowie, his neighbor and relative, who died in 1846.[24] Like so many
Southern planters Bowie had little cash on hand and few securities,
and so to pay his debts the executor had to arrange for a sale of
land. This sort of business took much of Judge Tuck's time since
it involved finding a buyer. The length of time it took to find and
communicate with heirs and others who might have claims also
delayed the settling of estates. A typical bill, received by Tuck
over a year after Bowie's death, said curtly, "understanding you
to be an administrator on the estate of Robert Bowie . . . I take
liberty in enclosing an account against the said estate. I shall be
obliged if you will give it your immediate attention." [25] The amount
of this account is not indicated, but no doubt if it was large the
judge would have had to sell all or part of a crop, several Negroes,
or some land in order to make payment. Naturally, Tuck wanted
the best price for his old friend's produce; so he negotiated with
the Baltimore brokers, John Sullivan and Sons.[26] But just as
surely this procedure only further delayed and complicated his
duties as executor.

A majority of Judge Tuck's neighbors made their living by
raising tobacco. The fluctuations in tobacco prices were hard to
forecast, and as a result many farmers got into debt when the market dropped. Creditors placed many delinquent accounts in Tuck's
hands for collection, either by "gentle persuasion" or by due proc-

[21] Sept. 13, 1859.   [22] Dec. 10, 1859.
[23] Eleanor B. Hilliary to Tuck, Oct. 24, 1864.
[24] Copy of the will of Robert Bowie, Sept. 18, 1818.
[25] R. Taylor to Tuck, June 26, 1848.
[26] John Sullivan and Sons to Tuck, March 2, 1848.

ess of law. One such creditor, the company of Hopfeld and Schroeter of Baltimore, wrote the judge:

Enclosed we hand you a note against A. B. Berry . . . for $76.33 which we wish you to collect immediately. Should there be no prospect of getting the money very soon from him we would thank you to have it safely secured in such a way as will enable you to realize the money without waiting too long. We have sent this claim to you at the instance of Mr. John Duval . . . who recommended you as one who would give it your immediate attention. We would remark that many claims are lost for want of proper attention and hope that although this amount is small, yet it is of importance to us.[27]

Despite the argument that "many claims were lost for want of proper attention," it is apparent that Judge Tuck wanted to give debtors every opportunity to make good. Even though his clients often lacked his patience, forcing a planter into bankruptcy or a forced sale of his land was repugnant to Tuck's nature. One disgusted creditor said, "We placed in your hands for collection a claim against Samuel Phillips . . . nearly three and a half years since. We must confess we are a good deal surprised at the delay . . . as Mr. Phillips was considered entirely solvent. We are extremely anxious to bring our business to a close." [28]

The other side of the coin can be seen from the letters to Tuck from the debtors. William Hardesty lamented: "No doubt but the time has come when you might with the utmost propriety have looked for the fulfillment of my promise [to pay]. . . . The great falling in the price of tobacco . . . has ruined me. I hope you will receive this as a sufficient apology. . . . I hope that I shall be able in a month or two at the least to come up in a measure [with the money] or at furtherest no doubt in the spring.[29] Unfortunately, the coming spring did not see an end to Hardesty's indebtedness. Three and a half years later, he wrote: "I have been doing the best I could under the circumstances that I have been placed. Suffer me once more to say here is but fifty dollars that I can pay you at this time as I have judgments to meet which I cannot put off. . . . I have to ask . . . once more your indulgence until next spring.[30]

Some creditors were willing to settle for less than the full amount due them rather than take the matter to court.[31] Other

---

[27] Henry Hopfeld and Philip Schroeter to Tuck, Aug. 26, 1842.
[28] Flint, Cooke and Co. to Tuck, Jan. 16, 1847.
[29] Nov. 26, 1846.   [30] May 11, 1850.
[31] George Sylvester to Tuck, Feb. 27, 1859.

creditors were more abrupt.[32] But whatever the settlement procedure, Tuck kept for himself a percentage of the amount collected.
To judge from the tone of one letter to him, this amount was not
always clearly understood by the client. One wrote, "We see you
have charged for commission 10 percent. We have hitherto paid
5 percent for collecting and do not now expect to pay any more."[33]

In the Upper Marlborough of Judge Tuck's day most of the
larger planters used slave labor in their cultivation of tobacco. The
entire operation—starting the new plants in seedbeds in March,
transplanting to carefully prepared fields, cultivation and hilling,
cutting, stripping, drying, and getting the weed to market—required a well-trained gang of Negroes. Consequently there was a
brisk market in slaves. They were bought and sold, listed in wills,
used as collateral for loans, rented by the day, week, month, and
year, and sometimes freed. Much of Judge Tuck's legal practice
dealt with one or more of these economic aspects of slavery.

For example, as the executor of the deceased Bowie's estate,
Tuck tried to collect $400 that J. H. Somervelt owed the estate
for a certain slave he had bought. But Somervelt complained:

Mr. Bowie sold me a Negro Man as a strong sound and able bodied
Man. . . . I paid $400 and gave my note at six months. Now the
Negro is not such as he represented him to be. He is a perfect fool,
incapable of doing any farm work properly. If I were to send him
plowing corn or hoeing tobacco he would be just as likely to plow
up the corn or weed up the tobacco as anything else. Now I can prove
by my two overseers . . . that he is incapable of doing any work
properly. I once sold him to Mr. Sam Hands and had to take him
back.[34]

For this reason, Somervelt was not inclined to honor the debt to
Bowie. The decision as to whether or not to bring suit was up to
Tuck. Since there is no further correspondence available, it may
be assumed that he felt that Somervelt had indeed a "money-back
guarantee," and so the debt was uncollectable. One wonders if this
slave was subtly rebelling against his new master or, indeed, the
whole slave regime.

While some Maryland planters sold their slaves "down the
river" during hard times, others rented them out to more prosperous neighbors or used them to secure loans to keep their plantations going. Since Judge Tuck was prosperous, he occasionally
received such propositions as: "If you could loan the money for

[32] John Oren to Tuck, Oct. 16, 1847.
[33] Dinsmore and Kyle to Tuck, Feb. 8, 1848.   [34] Feb. 24, 1846.

six months I would mortgage a young servant man to you. I am very sensitive about selling servants for debt, but in the event of the money not being paid at maturity . . . I have entire confidence in you as a humane master." [35] Slaves were sometimes allowed to sell themselves. It would appear that almost like the Fuller Brush man they could go from door to door or plantation to plantation seeking a new master. One permit reads, "The bearer of this, (Milly), has permission from Mr. and Mrs. Osprigg to get a master for herself and family." [36] Contracts varied, of course, but the arrangement expressed by R. L. Hill seems usual: "I have been hiring a man from Benjamin Young for the present year. His time will be out on the eleventh of January and I would like to get him for another year. I have been paying $60 a year, feeding and clothing and would be willing to give the same again." [37]

Another indication of the status of slaves as property is revealed in a petition Judge Tuck presented to the Prince George's County Court for Samuel Hamilton:

> The petition of Samuel Hamilton humbly represents that at October ten, 1843 of said court his Negro man Daniel was convicted on an indictment for murder and sentenced to be hanged, and has since been executed in pursuance of said sentence.
>
> Your petitioner states that the Court at that time assessed and valued the said Negro at $350 and he humbly suggests that said valuation is less than his value . . . and that the Court did assess and value said Negro at $350 without any notice to himself or his counsel. . . . Your petitioner states that he is aggrieved by said assessment and if the Court will reopen the said question we will be prepared to show that the Negro was worth at least $500 and to show . . . that he is now paying one dollar per day for the services of a man to perform the same work.[38]

To support this petition, Tuck had had five of Samuel Hamilton's neighbors sign an affidavit swearing:

> We the undersigned neighbors of Samuel Hamilton having been well acquainted with Negro Daniel, late the property of said Hamilton, hereby certify that we knew him to be a good farm hand, capable of using carpenter's tools in doing most of the rough jobs of carpenter's work needing to be done on a farm and occasionally he was entrusted to keeping things about it in good order.
>
> And we further certify that we thought said Negro worth at least

---

[35] B. M. Beale to Tuck, June 11, 1856.

[36] This is the document in its entirety, dated Northampton, Sept. 27, 1854.

[37] Dec. 30, 1847.

[38] This portion of the petition is undated and unsigned.

$500 to his master, and that we really believe his services can not be now, nor since his death, replaced for the sum of $500.[39]

If "Negro Daniel" was as skilled as his neighbors said, then perhaps $500 was a minimum price for him.

The intricacies of the South's peculiar institution are only one aspect of the antebellum society that Judge Tuck's correspondence reveals. Through such miniature studies the historian can dispel the murky generalities and oversimplification that hide much of the past's reality. Tuck's experiences illustrate some of the responsibilities of a lawyer in antebellum Maryland and highlight a few of the existing local conditions of the day. It becomes clear that the prosperous lawyer-planter-patriarch of the Old South shared at least some of the so-called Yankee traits, such as dedication to hard work and business acumen. The multiplicity of Judge Tuck's efforts exemplify a characteristic of antebellum Southern life that has too often been overlooked.

[39] This undated affidavit is signed by John Turner, John Morsell, and Thomas P. Turner.

14 Edmund Fontaine and the Virginia Central Railroad

Elizabeth Dabney Coleman

TO MANY STUDENTS of American history the successful railroad entrepreneurs of the nineteenth century were men like Cornelius Vanderbilt and Jay Gould—mostly Northern and sometimes ruthless. An exception to this stereotype was Edmund Fontaine, a very Southern and staunchly upright railroad magnate. For twenty-two years he guided the Virginia Central Railroad, parent of the Chesapeake and Ohio Railway, through a spectacular period of growth, recurrent enemy raids during the Civil War, and its reorganization after the war. With imagination, honesty, energy, and administrative ability he drew together the elements of legislative support, private capital, labor, and engineering talent to help create one of the country's major transportation systems.

Born January 20, 1801, in Hanover County, Virginia, Edmund Fontaine was of Huguenot descent. He was a great-grandson of the Reverend Peter Fontaine, rector of Westover Parish, the first of the family to settle in Virginia. His father, Colonel William Fontaine, was a Revolutionary army officer who wrote an eyewitness account of the British surrender at Yorktown. His mother, Ann Morris, was a daughter of William Morris of Taylor's Creek, Hanover County, Virginia.[1]

Remembering him as a child, John Blair Dabney, Edmund Fontaine's first cousin and friend, noted his "quickness of apprehension, and aptitude in acquiring knowledge. His capacity was certainly good, and his progress such as to warrant the most favourable auguries." [2] William Fontaine died in 1810, and Edmund, one of nine children, soon began to make his way in the business

---

[1] John Livingston, "Edmund Fontaine," *Portraits of Eminent Americans Now Living, with Biographical and Historical Memoirs of Their Lives and Actions* (4 vols., New York, 1854), IV, 164; Ann Maury, *Memoirs of a Huguenot Family* (New York, 1853), pp. 444–47; *Genealogical Chart of the Fontaine and Maury Families*, lithograph by Sarony & Co. (New York, n.d.).

[2] John Blair Dabney, "Sketches and Reminiscences of the Dabney and Morris Families," 1850, p. 213, MS, University of Virginia Library, Charlottesville.

world. At about the age of seventeen he began to work in a mercantile establishment in Fredericksburg, Virginia, and learned business methods by practical experience. He acquired the habits of thrift, industry, and perseverance and began to accumulate property. He is said to have cultivated his exhausted farm land in Hanover County so well as to give "a vigorous impulse to agricultural improvement" in that section of the state.[3]

When he was twenty-four years old, Fontaine married his second cousin, Maria Louisa Shackelford. Portraits of the couple were painted later by Louis Mathieu Didier Guillaume.[4] Maria Louisa was shown with blue eyes and brown hair parted in the middle with a black lace mantilla fastened at the back and falling to her shoulders; her dress was black with delicate white lace collar and brooch. Edmund, blue-eyed and blond, was pictured wearing a black coat, white shirt and collar, and soft black satin tie. He was described as "about the middle stature. . . . His manners are affable, frank, and cordial. Personal firmness, quick sagacity, and uncommon energy of purpose are plainly marked in his countenance and bearing."[5]

The young couple lived in Hanover County at Beaver Dam, a home among fine old trees, which they shared with Fontaine's mother. According to her daughter-in-law, the elder Mrs. Fontaine was "most industrious" and "a beneficial example." Four sons and seven daughters were born to the Fontaines.[6] The parents showed great interest in the education of their children, who for the most part were taught at home. In 1837 they employed a graduate of Hampden-Sydney College to teach Latin, Greek, and all the branches of "a liberal English education." In 1844 a tutor who had credentials in English, French, geography, arithmetic, history, natural and moral philosophy, and chemistry was engaged specifically to teach the girls. A small "Classical School," limited to eight

[3] Ibid., pp. 213–14.

[4] *Richmond Portraits in an Exhibition of Makers of Richmond 1737–1860* (Richmond, 1949), p. 67. The portraits are in the possession of Charles E. Moran, Jr., of Charlottesville, Va., a great-grandson. Both Fontaine and his bride were great-grandchildren of William Dabney of Aldringham, Hanover County, Va. (William H. Dabney, *Sketch of the Dabneys of Virginia* [Chicago, 1888], pp. 101–6). They were both cousins of Major General J. E. B. Stuart, commander of the Cavalry Corps of the Confederate States of America, through this descent.

[5] Livingston, IV, 169.

[6] Maria Louisa Shackelford (Mrs. Edmund) Fontaine, "To My Grandchildren," MS in possession of author.

students, was conducted by a William and Mary graduate at Beaver Dam in 1850.[7]

The Fontaines were members of Trinity Church in the upper end of St. Martin's parish. In 1830 he was a church warden and member of the building committee. He was often a lay delegate to the conventions of the Protestant Episcopal Church in the Diocese of Virginia. He served on committees on finance, on the admission of new parishes, to memorialize the governor for a day of public thanksgiving, and on the religious instruction of "the colored people." After establishing a residence in Richmond at 606 North Sixth Street, he served as a vestryman of St. James's Church from 1854 until 1860.[8] It was said that he was a sincere Christian and that "his life and conversation have never disgraced his profession." [9]

At the age of thirty-three Fontaine was elected to the senate of Virginia, representing the counties of Hanover, Louisa, Fluvanna, and Goochland. He served two terms from 1834 to 1842. About the same time he was a justice of the peace in Hanover County.[10] He opposed the National Bank, the building of internal improvements by the federal government, the protective tariff, and Martin Van Buren's subtreasury plan.[11] A Democrat with conservative leanings, he sometimes drew the ire of the party regulars.[12] Of this period in his life it was said later: "he was more than a politician; he had genuine public spirit, and was the active friend and able advocate of internal improvements." [13] But Fontaine firmly believed that only local governments should support such improvements.

His most significant work in the senate was in securing the

[7] *Richmond Enquirer*, Nov. 21, 1837; *Richmond Whig*, Sept. 13, 1844; *Richmond Whig and Public Advertiser*, Nov. 15, 1850.

[8] Rosewell Page, *Hanover County, Its History and Legends* (n.p., 1926), pp. 52–53; *Journals of the Convention of the Protestant Episcopal Church, Diocese of Virginia, 1840* (Richmond, 1840), p. 7; ibid., *1852* (Washington, D.C., 1852), p. 25; ibid., *1865* (Richmond, 1866), p. 37; *Richmond Portraits*, p. 67; Murray McGuire and John B. Mordecai, *St. James's Church, 1835–1957* (Richmond, 1958), p. 57.

[9] J. B. Dabney, p. 214.

[10] William Ronald Cocke III, *Hanover County Chancery Wills and Notes* (Columbia, Va., 1940), p. 178.

[11] Joseph M. Sheppard, *Address to the Voters of the Senatorial District Composed of the Counties of Fluvanna, Goochland, Louisa and Hanover* (Richmond, 1838), leaflet in UVa Lib.

[12] Livingston, p. 165.

[13] *Richmond Whig and Advertiser*, Oct. 29, 1869.

passage through the upper house of the bill chartering the Louisa Railroad in 1836. He was also one of the persons in Hanover County chosen to receive subscriptions to its stock from individuals.[14] The Louisa Railroad was organized as a joint-stock company, and its capital was limited to $300,000. After three-fifths of the stock had been subscribed by individuals, the state supplied the remaining two-fifths of the capital. The president and a five-man directory supervised the business and appointed the operating personnel. Stockholders met annually to hear reports on the business, vote on major issues, and elect the president and three directors. The internal improvement companies in Virginia in which the state owned an interest reported regularly to the Board of Public Works. This group appointed the state's representatives on the various company boards, while the stockholders elected theirs. Fontaine was chosen to be one of the two directors of the Louisa Railroad to represent the state's interest.

Under the first president of the company, Frederick Harris of Louisa County, construction began in 1836. The route from Hanover Junction on the Richmond, Fredericksburg, and Potomac Railroad westward was surveyed by Moncure Robinson. Originally the railroad was to extend to Harrisonburg in the Valley of Virginia by way of Powell's Gap, a plan defeated later by legislators from Albemarle and Augusta counties, who won a more southerly and central crossing at Rockfish Gap.[15] A survey of the Rockfish Gap route had been made by State Engineer Claudius Crozet in 1839, and he had selected a site for a tunnel there through the Blue Ridge Mountains. Crozet had been trained as one of Napoleon's engineers in France; in Virginia he served as state engineer from 1823 until 1843 (with the exception of five years spent in Louisiana).

Crozet, Moncure Robinson, and Fontaine championed the cause of railroads in Virginia against the supporters of the James River and Kanawha Canal, to which the legislature gave priority.[16] At the time of the change in direction of the Louisa Railroad, Fontaine first proposed extending it to the Ohio River. The idea of connecting the two waterways had been presented first by George Wash-

[14] *Journal of the Senate of the Commonwealth of Virginia, 1836* (Richmond, 1836), passim.

[15] Charles W. Turner, *Chessie's Road* (Richmond, 1956), pp. 21–26, 30.

[16] Col. William Couper, *Claudius Crozet, Soldier-Scholar-Educator-Engineer (1789–1864)*, Southern Sketches, 1st ser., no. 8 (Charlottesville, Va., 1936), pp. 78, 80; R. W. Brown, *Moncure Robinson (1802–1891), Genius of America's Early Railways* (New York, 1949), p. 27.

ington,[17] and the James River and Kanawha Canal Company had hoped to accomplish the feat. That a railroad instead should do so was considered "chimerical." The "energy, zeal, and intelligence" with which Fontaine supported his proposal, however, the "boldness and vigor with which he pressed his arguments," and "his known business habits and qualifications" won for him the support of the stockholders and the public as "the safest and wisest guardian to whom its rising fortunes could be confided." [18] In 1845 he was elected president of the Louisa Railroad, which reached as far west as Gordonsville and had legislative approval to build to Charlottesville.

At the first meeting of the stockholders after Fontaine's election the future of the railroad was the chief business. At that time the RF&P operated its engines and cars over the Louisa's tracks, for the latter had no rolling stock of its own. In return the stockholders were paid regular dividends. Some of them were satisfied with this arrangement and did not wish to assume the risks of independence and expansion. Their persuasive new president, however, overcame their complacency, and he also convinced the legislature that the Louisa should build eastward into Richmond.

Within two years the Louisa bought its own engines and cars and began to handle its own transportation. But it was still under contract to the RF&P, which had a thirty-year monopoly to carry freight between Richmond and Fredericksburg. With independence as its aim, the company decided to build tracks into Richmond at the termination of the contract. The RF&P obtained an injunction to prevent the construction of these tracks, which would of necessity cross their own. To this injunction the Louisa replied with a request for a speedy judicial decision. President Fontaine threw up the first spade of earth on the eastern extension at Hanover Junction and later repeated it by order of the company's legal advisers. The injunction was denied by a lower court, a decision upheld by the Supreme Court of the United States in 1851. During the litigation between the two companies the eastern extension was begun early in 1849, William A. Kuper serving as chief engineer.

Financing this part of the line was another difficult problem. The legislature had approved an increase of $200,000 in the company's capital stock but had granted no funds beyond matching the insufficient $38,000 raised by individual subscriptions. Among

---

[17] *The Diaries of George Washington*, ed. John C. Fitzpatrick (4 vols., Boston and New York, 1925), II, 318–28.

[18] Livingston, IV, 168.

the board of directors there existed at that time a perfect agreement regarding the future of the road. They joined with the president to endorse the company's bonds for $24,400 to build into Richmond, and Fontaine donated one year's income from his crops to the cause. Company receipts were applied to its construction, and stockholders, who consented to having their dividends applied to the project, received company scrip payable in 1866 instead. Not until 1850 did the legislature endorse the company's bonds of $100,000 to complete the work. The bonds paid 6 percent, matured in thirty years, and were secured by a mortgage on the property. This method of financing the building of the road was later used several times.

The decision and faith of the officials even before the support from the state was granted laid the foundation, Fontaine thought, for the continuous railroad to the Ohio and the great results that followed. The company's ambition to become a major artery of commerce through the heart of the Old Dominion was recognized when the legislature on February 2, 1850, authorized its new name, The Virginia Central Railroad.

During the year the thrusts to the east and to the west continued. Trains rolled into Charlottesville on June 27, 1850, having just crossed the novel and newsworthy iron bridges over the Rivanna River and Moore's Creek. An increase of $300,000 in capital stock had been granted to build the twenty-one miles from Gordonsville to Charlottesville. About this time T. Colden Ruggles became chief engineer of the Virginia Central and served for three years. Then there was great rejoicing in Richmond on December 19, 1850, when trains arrived in time for the Christmas holidays. These twenty-seven miles from Hanover Junction to Richmond had cost about $332,000. In 1851 the state decided to increase its share of holdings to three-fifths and to appoint three directors, leaving the stockholders to elect two.[19]

As the road pushed farther west, public meetings continued to be held in advance in the communities along the proposed route

[19] Elizabeth Dabney Coleman, "The Story of the Virginia Central Railroad, 1850–1860" (Ph.D. diss., University of Virginia, 1957), pp. xiv–xvii, 1–29. For specific facts about the railroad see also the *Annual Reports of the Virginia Central Railroad Company*, hereafter cited as *AR*, or the *Reports of the Internal Improvement Companies to the Board of Public Works*, sometimes annual and sometimes biennial, hereafter cited as *BPW*. *Acts of the General Assembly of Virginia* are the source for legislation affecting the railroad.

for the purpose of raising subscriptions. In the finest oratory of President Fontaine the railroad was to become:

the Virginia link in that great chain which is to bind together our American Union in the strong bonds of mutual commerce and association, unite by a direct line the shores of the two oceans, open illimitable fields of oriental trade to our enterprise, and in time, by our steam connections with the Sandwich and South Pacific islands and the Chinese Empire, encircle the earth itself with a bright unbroken girdle, diffusing in its track the intelligence, the wealth, the refinement, and civilization of the age and country in which we live.[20]

Early in 1852 Fontaine of the Virginia Central and Charles F. M. Garnett, chief engineer of the Virginia and Tennessee Railroad, debated in the press the respective merits of the 4-foot 8½-inch standard gauge of the Virginia Central and the 5-foot broad gauge of the Virginia and Tennessee. Both lines were aiming for the Ohio River by the New River route. The Virginia and Tennessee had secured a subscription of $100,000 from the city of Richmond, and Fontaine wished to secure a similar one for his railroad. Garnett said he had good reason to fear so experienced a controversialist as Colonel Fontaine, whose armor was always bright and whose lance was always in rest. Colonel Fontaine replied that he only used his armor in defense of his railroad and never in attack.[21] The standard gauge was adopted for the Covington and Ohio Railroad, separately organized as an extension of the Virginia Central, and the city of Richmond voted subscriptions to the Virginia Central the next year.

The Virginia Central was completed to the base of the Blue Ridge at Mechum's River in 1852, an increase of $250,000 in capitalization having been approved by the legislature for this section west of Charlottesville. Crossing the mountain barrier was undertaken by the state itself, for construction there was too expensive for the Virginia Central to assume. The Blue Ridge Railroad was chartered separately and was built under the supervision of Claudius Crozet as chief engineer. For its use the Virginia Central paid tolls under an agreement with the state. The seventeen miles of the Blue Ridge Railroad cost about $100,000 per mile, totaling almost $1,700,000. Of the four tunnels required, the Blue Ridge, about a mile long through solid rock, excited the public imagination as no other did. Begun at both ends in 1850, a scene of wild

[20] Livingston, IV, 168.
[21] Coleman, pp. 176–79; *Richmond Whig and Public Advertiser*, Jan. 20, 23, 24, 26, 30, Feb. 3, 6, 13, 1852.

rejoicing erupted in December 1856 when the augers from each end met in the center within a half inch of each other.[22]

Meanwhile work on the slightly more than thirteen miles from Waynesboro to Staunton had begun. Materials for construction were hauled by wagon portage over the mountain. In the summer of 1853 the company officials decided to place a locomotive on the tracks west of Waynesboro and to that end arranged for teams of from eighteen to thirty-six mules to draw the engine, named "Frederick Harris," over the mountain—a remarkable sight on a hot July day.[23] Eager to bring the products of the Valley to Richmond before the completion of the tunnel, the officials also decided to adopt the plan of Charles Ellet, Jr., then chief engineer of the Virginia Central, for a temporary track across the mountain top. Completed in 1854, its grades were as steep as 600 feet to a mile and its special engines operated at a speed of only seven miles an hour. For four years it carried passengers and freight with only one accident.[24] The track was depicted by artist Edward Beyer in the lithograph *Rockfish Gap and the Mountain House* in his *Album of Virginia*, published in Richmond in 1858. That same year the Blue Ridge Tunnel was completed after eight years of construction, and the mountain-top track was dismantled.

The road between Waynesboro and Staunton had not been expected to exceed the allotted increase in capitalization of $300,000, but it did, perhaps because of the added expenses of portage over the mountain. Subscriptions of $55,000 by individuals in Augusta County and $20,000 raised by a countywide railroad tax, although matched by state funds, had not met the allotted capitalization. Again the president raised some of the needed money on his own credit, and again his action was justified, for within a short time after the track reached Staunton on March 20, 1854, the revenue of the road increased 60 percent.[25]

The approximately seventy miles from Staunton to Covington was the next segment to be built. Although the state had financed and constructed the line across the Blue Ridge, it did not wish to assume the task of constructing through and tunneling the more formidable Alleghenies. The Virginia Central was granted the

[22] Couper, pp. 36–66, 73–91; Coleman, chaps. 3 and 4; James Poyntz Nelson, *Four Tunnels in the Blue Ridge Region of Virginia on the Chesapeake and Ohio Railway* (Richmond, 1917).

[23] *Richmond Daily Enquirer*, July 26, 1853; *Staunton Spectator*, July 27, 1853.

[24] Ellet, *The Mountain Top Track* (Philadelphia, 1856).

[25] *Richmond Daily Dispatch*, Jan. 17, 1854; Coleman, chap. 6.

right to build, and increases in capitalization were made between 1850 and 1856 amounting to $2,000,000. As usual, individual and community subscriptions were received and matched by the state. Greenbrier and Monroe counties subscribed $50,000 each in their corporate capacities to bring the road in their direction. The city of Richmond subscribed $200,000 in 1853 and $100,000 in 1854 as it began to enjoy commercial benefits from the Valley connection. Earnings amounting to $600,000 were applied to this section. And finally in 1854 the Virginia Central issued $1,000,000 worth of bonds, with the company property as security, to help finance this portion. By 1857 the road was completed to the Jackson River, which remained the terminus until 1867. Up to this point the section had cost over $3,000,000, but by the year 1860 the net receipts of the company amounted to over $600,000.

On the eve of the war 195 miles of track were completed. Grading and masonry were finished from the Jackson River to Covington, the iron for laying the tracks had been purchased, and the state in 1860 had loaned $600,000 to complete these last ten miles. The company owned 28 locomotives, weighing from sixteen to twenty-eight tons, and 247 cars; its track was laid throughout with solid U or T rail, weighing fifty or more pounds per yard. Some 456 persons were in its employ. Its revenue came from carrying mails and express; from passengers, especially the lucrative springs traffic in the summers; and freight, including manufactures, merchandise, wheat, flour, tobacco, pig iron, and lumber.[26]

The railroad acquired a new role when the war broke out. Virginia railroads assembled in convention agreed to carry troops at two cents per mile and munitions, provisions, and material at half the rates in effect on May 1, 1861. Government business was to take precedence over all other business. Payment would be in bonds or treasury notes of the Confederate States of America at par whenever the secretary of the Treasury considered it necessary.[27]

The location of the Virginia Central in the state that became the chief battleground of the war and its function as a major feeder to the Confederate capital destined it to be a strategic target of the Union army. During the course of the war the Virginia Central helped to move troops to and from the Allegheny region, the Valley of Virginia, Richmond, and by rail connections to and from northern Virginia. On the return trips it brought back wounded men in ambulance cars and prisoners of war on their

[26] Coleman, chaps. 8, 9, 10.   [27] *BPW*, 1861, p. 91.

way to prison camps. The war quickly touched the Fontaine family personally. Edmund Fontaine, Jr., was killed in the First Battle of Manassas and was buried in the family cemetery at Beaver Dam.[28] For a time his sisters and matrons in the neighborhood operated a Convalescent Hospital near the Beaver Dam railway station, located about one mile from the Fontaine home.[29]

The erection by the Confederate government of a military warehouse near the Beaver Dam depot in 1861 made the area a prime target for enemy cavalry raids. In July 1862 raiders destroyed the warehouse and its contents. The operation of trains between Richmond and Gordonsville had to be suspended until a protective force north of the line could assure safe operation. Some forbearance on the part of the enemy during 1862 was attributed by Fontaine to their confidence that they would gain possession of Richmond and the railroad within a short time.[30] Shops and office were moved hastily to the Charlottesville area in the summer of 1862 and then were returned to Richmond as the threat passed. A much-needed connection between the Virginia Central and the RF&P within the city of Richmond was also completed that year.[31]

As the war progressed, shortages became more acute. Since most white men between eighteen and forty-five were serving in the army, the company purchased thirty-five Negroes to help fill its labor force; some of these ran away or were captured by the Yankees. Several Confederate railroads including the Virginia Central tried to secure railroad supplies through an agent in England. These supplies had to run the blockade, and a fourth of them were lost. Wood for ties, sawmills to cut them, and wagons and horses or mules to haul them had to be commandeered. Salaries had to be readjusted with the inflated Confederate currency. The president kept his pay down while giving a much larger salary to Henry D. Whitcomb, the Chief Engineer and General Superintendent.[32]

[28] Churchill Gibson Chamberlayne, *Ham Chamberlayne, Virginian* (Richmond, 1932), p. 22. Connections were with the Orange and Alexandria (now the Southern Railway), with which it shared its tracks from Charlottesville to Gordonsville, and with the RF&P at Hanover Junction.

[29] *Richmond Daily Dispatch*, Aug. 19, 1861.

[30] *AR*, 1862, pp. 11–12, 26; R. N. Scott et al., eds., *Records of the War of the Rebellion* (Washington, D.C., 1880–1901), ser. I, vol. XII, pt. III, p. 490 (hereafter cited as *WOR*). General Rufus King reported this raid.

[31] *AR*, 1862, p. 32; *Richmond Daily Dispatch*, May 28, June 10, July 26, 1862.

[32] *AR*, 1863, pp. 9–10, 17; *AR*, 1864, pp. 16, 26–27; entries of March 23, Sept. 31, Aug. 11, 1863, Dec. 10, 1866, Minutes of the Virginia Central Rail-

A skirmish at Beaver Dam depot in 1863 was succeeded by far more damaging raids during the next two years. Early in March 1864 Union soldiers shot at Fontaine several times near his home, but he escaped uninjured to the woods.[33] On the evening of May 9 undefended depot buildings at Beaver Dam and several unloaded trains that were accumulating stores for Lee (including nearly all his medical supplies) were destroyed. The smoke from burning flour and bacon, an estimated 1,500,000 rations, filled the air, and the heat became so intense that the wheels of the railroad cars melted out of shape.[34]

On May 10 J. E. B. Stuart stopped long enough at Fontaine's home to reassure himself of the safety of Mrs. Stuart and their children, who were staying there. When Stuart was mortally wounded the next day at Yellow Tavern, Dr. John Fontaine, surgeon and son of Edmund Fontaine, attended his cousin.[35] At one point during the war, a party of raiders ransacked the Fontaine home and threatened to burn it; one soldier brandished a pistol as he searched for brandy. "They carried away everything in the way of food, leaving us to starve," wrote Mrs. Fontaine. "After they left, we got some corn, and boiled some hominy, which was our living for several days." [36] Then, in October 1864 word came that a second son, John, serving as Medical Director of the Cavalry Corps of the Army of Northern Virginia, had been killed while

---

road Company, 1850–1869, Chesapeake and Ohio Railway Archives, Cleveland, Ohio (microfilm in Virginia State Library, Richmond; hereafter cited as VCR Minutes); Edmund Fontaine, Office of the Virginia Central Railroad Company, Richmond, to Thomas H. DeWitt, Secretary of the Board of Public Works, Dec. 19, 1866, Virginia Central Railroad Manuscripts, Va. State Lib.

[33] *Richmond Whig*, March 3, 1864; *Daily Richmond Enquirer*, March 7, 1864.

[34] *AR*, 1864, pp. 12, 28; Philip H. Sheridan, *Personal Memoirs* (2 vols., New York, 1884), I, 374; *WOR*, ser. I, vol. XII, pt. II, p. 177; vol. XXXIII, pp. 186, 189, 191, vol. XXXVI, pt. I, pp. 776–77, 790, 817, vol. XLVI, pt. I, p. 508. Generals Hugh J. Kilpatrick, H. E. Davies, Jr., and George Custer, the latter with Sheridan, led raids on Beaver Dam depot (Carter S. Anderson, "Train Running for the Confederacy," typescript copy of a series of articles in *Locomotive Engineering*, 1892–98, in Virginia Central Railroad Manuscripts, UVa Lib.

[35] Henry Brainerd McClellan, *The Life and Campaigns of Major-General J. E. B. Stuart* (Richmond, 1885), pp. 69, 410, 415.

[36] M. L. S. (Mrs. Edmund) Fontaine, "To my Grandchildren." The raid on the home is not dated except that it happened during the war. The house that Edmund Fontaine built burned in the Reconstruction period but daughter Lucy rescued the Guillaume portraits.

going to the assistance of a wounded general on the battlefield near Petersburg.[37]

A cavalry sweep from the west during the closing months of the war destroyed bridges and track for forty-six miles from Staunton to Keswick, burned all the station houses except those in Charlottesville, and damaged the track in the area. East of Trevilians all the station houses were destroyed except the Frederick's Hall depot and the Louisa passenger house. Track was torn up, crossties burned, and rails heated and twisted so that they could not be used until rerolled. The bridges over the Little River and the South Anna were burned, the latter for the fifth time during the war. The rolling stock was greatly damaged.[38]

After the defeat of the Confederacy and the occupation of Richmond by the Federal army, all operations of the railroad ceased pending Virginia's reorganization as Military District Number One. Fontaine's health by this time was so impaired by the pressures under which he had worked that he felt that he could not go on with any public business. He told his friend Henry Whitcomb that he planned to resign. Whitcomb communicated with the board, who objected to accepting the resignation. Fontaine was told that stockholders, bondholders, and citizens had remonstrated against his withdrawal. Confronted with appeals from many quarters, he resolved that if it cost him his life he would continue in the presidency for one more year.[39]

Next Fontaine and Whitcomb went to military headquarters to ask for permission to reopen the road. This was granted by General Edward O. C. Ord on April 19, 1865. According to Whitcomb, "the U.S. authorities in giving assent expressed themselves surprised at the request, and said politely but confidently that we, i.e. Col. Fontaine and his directors, would find it necessary to turn the road over to northern people who had means. However we were allowed to try – and we did." [40]

At that time about twenty miles of the road were operable for revenue, and there was a total of only $100 in gold left in the treasury. Not a bridge was standing between the South Anna

---

[37] Wyndham Blanton, *Medicine in Virginia in the Nineteenth Century* (Richmond, 1933), pp. 54, 276, 279, 315, 401; Henry B. McClellan, Headquarters Cavalry Corps [Petersburg], to Elizabeth Price [Mrs. John] Fontaine, 1864, Virginia Historical Society, Richmond; *WOR*, ser. I, vol. XLII, pt. I, p. 948, pt. II, p. 1171, pt. III, p. 1133.

[38] *AR*, 1865, p. 41; Sheridan, II, 112–23.   [39] *AR*, 1865, p. 7.

[40] Whitcomb to Richard Morris Fontaine, Jan. 31, 1905, Whitcomb letters in possession of Charles E. Moran, Jr., Charlottesville, Va.: *AR*, 1865, p. 41.

River and Staunton. Fifteen out of twenty freight houses between Richmond and the North Mountain had been destroyed, as well as passenger houses, water stations, and other less important buildings. The number of freight cars was reduced to 117.[41]

The company set to work. Manpower was then plentiful as soldiers laid down their arms and sought employment in civilian life. The first loan to be secured was $10,000 from Adams Express; the second was $5,000 from the president of the Baltimore and Ohio Railroad. Through the influence of General Ulysses S. Grant, whose men had wreaked havoc along the line, a thousand tons of railroad iron were procured at sixty dollars per ton on six-months' time—afterward extended to twelve months. At a public sale in Alexandria, Whitcomb purchased locomotives and cars on partial credit. Merchants along the line also extended credit for flour and bacon as some of the men accepted rations for part of their pay.[42] Finally, the legislature arranged for a loan of $300,000 to help rebuild the line. Bridges were restored by erecting pine-pole trestles or trusses, some of which remained in use for five or more years. There was never an accident on one of them, according to Whitcomb, who was with the company long thereafter. The frame for such a bridge, kept in hiding in case of emergency near the Cowpasture River for two years during the war, was brought out and used for a replacement.[43]

By July 23, 1865, the railroad was in operation to the Jackson River, and for the last half of the year the revenues began to average $45,000 per month, exceeding the expectations of the officers. Indebtedness of over $1,600,000 hung like a pall over the company, and the bondholders had to wait from mid-1864 until mid-1867 for their dividends, when some of the debt was funded to pay them. In that year revenue began to exceed ordinary operating expenses.[44]

When General Williams C. Wickham, a Confederate general who had been a Unionist before secession, was elected president of the company at the fall meeting of the stockholders in 1865, Fontaine told those present: "I feel, Mr. Chairman, something like a father who is parting with a son whom he had watched with parental anxiety until he was about to enter the world to buffet

---

[41] *AR*, 1865, p. 20; *AR*, 1867, pp. 39–40.

[42] Whitcomb to R. M. Fontaine, Feb. 23, 1905; VCR Minutes, May 17, 1865.

[43] Whitcomb to R. M. Fontaine, Feb. 23, 1905.

[44] *AR*, 1865, pp. 40–42; *BPW*, 1867, p. 95.

with the storms of life." And later, "Whatever credit has been awarded me, should be in part attributed to the support of the Board and the valuable services of the officers in all departments." To his successor he said of the office, "it is no bed of roses. . . . The duties of a President of a railroad at any time are laborious and harassing; but in the present financial embarrassment of the country, he will have a load to carry which I do not envy him, and from which I can truly say that I feel a sense of relief." Promising his support in trying to promote the interests of the company, Fontaine explained, "nearly half of all I own is invested in it, and if he can take better care of it than I could, I shall have occasion to thank him." [45]

Yet after a year's rest from executive duties, Fontaine was again a candidate for the presidency and was elected in the fall of 1866. He seemed to be fired with renewed zeal and energy to complete the road to the Ohio. In April 1867 the directors sent him and Whitcomb to New York City to purchase iron for the ten miles from Jackson River to Covington, and by September that section was completed. The iron purchased for the purpose on the eve of the war had been used for replacements during the conflict.[46]

Before the war the Covington and Ohio Railroad had been organized separately under the supervision of the Virginia Board of Public Works to connect with the Virginia Central and form its last link to the Ohio River. The state had appropriated some $4,800,000 to it by 1861, but in 1862 most of the territory in which the line was to lie became part of West Virginia.[47] Soon after the war the legislatures of Virginia and West Virginia cooperated and passed enabling acts to continue the public improvement so valuable to both. By 1867 the right to build the line was granted to the Virginia Central Railroad. The signing of the contract between the four commissioners of Virginia, the four commissioners of West Virginia, and President Fontaine of the Virginia Central took place at White Sulphur Springs, West Virginia, in August 1868. The name of the company was changed to Chesapeake and Ohio Railroad, and its capitalization was set at $30,000,000. A seal was adopted with the words "Chesapeake and Ohio Railroad Company" encircling the date September 1, 1868.[48]

Among the guests at the White Sulphur Springs at the time of

[45] *AR*, 1865, pp. 6–8.

[46] Whitcomb to R. M. Fontaine, Jan. 26, 1905; VCR Minutes, April 17, 1867; *BPW*, 1867, p. 89.

[47] *BPW*, 1861, p. 93.

[48] VCR Minutes, Aug. 25–Sept. 1, Sept. 30, 1868.

the ceremony was General Robert E. Lee, who had told Fontaine earlier that as a citizen of Virginia and well-wisher to the country he was "exceedingly anxious that the Central Railroad should be extended to the Ohio with all practicable expedition." [49] A Union general who was attempting to determine the sentiment of Southerners regarding many of the issues of reunion was also a guest at White Sulphur Springs. Lee gathered thirty-one Southerners in whom he had confidence, Fontaine being one of them, to sign a letter he drafted expressing their views. To Fontaine the war had been an aggressive one waged by the northern portion of the Old Union. [50] Now that it was over, however, he was ready to join Lee in expressing a desire for peace and restoration to the Union. The letter asked for a restoration of their rights under the Constitution and the right to self-government. Granted this, Lee said, the signers would obey the Constitution and laws of the United States, treat Negroes with kindness and humanity, and fulfill every duty incumbent on peaceful citizens, loyal to the Constitution of their country. They deprecated disorder and excitement as the most serious obstacle to their prosperity. [51]

The future success of the Chesapeake and Ohio Railroad depended upon financial arrangements of great scope. The president and directors decided to raise $10,000,000 through the sale of 7 percent bonds maturing in thirty years. It was to be the only mortgage on the company property; $2,000,000 of the amount was to be used to lift the indebtedness of the Virginia Central. Two firms agreed to handle the sale of the bonds: McGinnis Brothers and Smith of New York City, who would sell in the United States and Europe, and R. A. Lancaster of Richmond, who would sell only in the United States. At the same time a contract was signed with a Southern firm, Tredegar of Richmond, Virginia, to furnish railroad iron, iron bridges, and locomotives to the Chesapeake and Ohio. [52]

To encourage the sale of bonds in the newly formed company, the president and directors issued a pamphlet reviewing its history, describing the country through which it passed, and setting forth its easy grades, the favorable climate, and the shortness of route between the western states and the Atlantic. The two proposed

[49] Lee to Colonel Edmund Fontaine, July 9, 1867, Robert E. Lee Letterbook, 1866 Nov. 29–1870 Sept. 12, Va. Hist. Soc.

[50] *BPW*, 1861, p. 89.

[51] Lee to General W. S. Rosecrans, Minister &c. Mexico, White Sulphur Springs, W. Va., Aug. 26, 1868, R. E. Lee Letterbook.

[52] VCR Minutes, Aug. 25–Sept. 1, 17, 30, 1868.

prongs in West Virginia were pointed out: one at the mouth of the Kanawha River to connect with the railroads in Ohio, the other at the mouth of the Big Sandy River to connect with the railroads of Kentucky. The line was on nearly the same parallel with the Chesapeake Bay and Norfolk, the mouth of the Ohio River, and San Francisco. "It is not only national as regards the great agricultural, commercial and manufacturing interests of the country," the pamphlet stated, "but it is also important in a military point of view." Dividends amounting to over $1,300,000 had been paid by the company to date.[53]

Since the company thought that investors would be more interested in its bonds if it were "wholly free" from state control and in the hands of private interests, it decided to purchase the state's interest in both the Virginia Central and the Blue Ridge railroads.[54] This purchase had been provided for in the legislative acts organizing the Chesapeake and Ohio Railroad, and a time limit of two years after the passage of the act on March 1, 1867, had been set to accomplish it. A survey and estimates for a connection with the Richmond and York River Railroad was also ordered in October 1868 with a view to using it as the link between Richmond and the Chesapeake Bay.[55]

Before the stockholders' meeting late in November 1868 political forces were at work behind the scenes that would prevent the execution of some of these plans. On the third day of the meeting, General Wickham, a Unionist before secession, was elected to the presidency of the company along with an entirely new board of directors. Visibly trembling at times during the meeting, Fontaine, a conservative Democrat, retired from the chair without speaking. His minority strength lay with the individual stockholders present, who voted twenty-two to one in his favor. But the vote of the state shares and of most of the localities was for Wickham.[56]

For more than three decades Fontaine had devoted himself to his beloved railroad, and now, just as it seemed to be reaching its greatest era, he was cast aside. Fontaine died on June 26, 1869, at the age of 68. His contribution to southern railroading was elo-

[53] Edmund Fontaine, *History of the Chesapeake and Ohio Railroad, with a Map Showing Its Connections with the Pacific Railroad. Resources of the Country, Legislation of Virginia and West Virginia* (Richmond, 1868). The direct route from Richmond to Charlottesville (authorized by the legislature in 1856) would shorten the distance to the Ohio by 30 miles. Work on this "airline" had been postponed pending the westward thrust.
[54] VCR Minutes, Sept. 16, 1868.   [55] Ibid., Oct. 22, 1868.
[56] *Richmond Daily Enquirer and Examiner*, Nov. 27, 28, 30, 1868.

quently memorialized three days later in the *Richmond Whig and Advertiser:*

In announcing the death of Colonel Edmund Fontaine, we feel, as those who read it will feel, such a sense of bereavement as the death of few men could create. He was eminently an honest, upright, high-minded gentleman. . . . Years ago, he was elected President of the Virginia Central Railroad Company, and his able and efficient administration of the affairs of that company have indissolubly connected his name with its history and progress. . . . Under his auspices, and chiefly through his untiring efforts, a large scope was given to that company, expressed in its change of name from the Virginia Central to the Chesapeake and Ohio Railroad.

It was the ambition of his latter years to complete this grand trunk line and link his name with it forever. To that end he toiled and strove with an ardor and devotion that excited universal applause. A political change in the Directory, about twelve months ago, terminated forever his career as president of that company. . . . He was a finished gentleman, an enlightened and devoted patriot, and a bright example in all the relations of life.[57]

Leaders and laborers alike contributed to the building of the Chesapeake and Ohio Railway, but none more than Edmund Fontaine, who gave generously of his time, talents, and fortune to lay the foundations of the present system.

[57] June 29, 1869.

15   Nicholas P. Trist:
A Discredited Diplomat Vindicated

Robert A. Brent

THE name of Nicholas Philip Trist is not a household familiar, and even to serious students of history he is barely remembered as the diplomat who made possible the Treaty of Guadalupe Hidalgo in 1848. To a few others he may be known as the husband of one of Thomas Jefferson's granddaughters, as private secretary to Jefferson in his final years, as a White House confidant of Andrew Jackson. Trist was in fact associated with most of the great public figures of the first half of the nineteenth century, but as a public figure himself he flamed out after spectacular feats during the Mexican War and died in obscurity.

In November 1847, while in Mexico with Winfield Scott's invading army and charged by President James K. Polk with negotiating a treaty with the already beaten Mexicans under terms laid down by Polk and his cabinet, Trist decided to disobey an order recalling him to Washington. This decision was to affect him the rest of his life. Convinced that his government was making a grave error in breaking off the negotiations then beginning to bear fruit, and with the complete agreement of General Scott, Trist arrogated to himself a position that affected not only the United States but the future of the Republic of Mexico. When Polk had dispatched Trist to Mexico in the spring of 1847, he had hoped that gaining clear title to Texas, Upper California, and the New Mexico territory would silence both his war critics and those extreme advocates of Manifest Destiny. However, as both casualties and expenses mounted, and with his own leanings in the direction of expansion, the president began to feel that nothing less than the annexation of all of Mexico offered a practical way out of an unpopular war. Hence the letter of recall to his ambassador in Mexico, and Trist's subsequent decision to stay and negotiate a treaty based on his original instructions.

This direct insubordination and the eventual signing of the Treaty of Guadalupe Hidalgo in February 1848 constituted an action perhaps unprecedented in diplomatic annals. That the treaty was negotiated in accordance with Trist's original instructions, that it was reluctantly accepted by an infuriated president, was ratified by a still more reluctant Senate, and became the supreme law of the land, did not alter the fact that Trist had acted in direct violation of a presidential order, thus laying himself open to the wrath of the administration. When he finally returned to Washington in the spring of 1848, Trist became disheartened by what he termed duplicity on the part of the president. Trist remained firm in his belief that what he had done was in the best interests of his country, but realizing that he could expect nothing in praise and acceptance from Polk, he determined to leave public service for good. Polk made Trist pay for his disobedience; the president never received his former ambassador after Trist's return.

Consequently Trist found not only the government distasteful but also the city of Washington itself, and early in July 1848 he and his wife Virginia moved to Westchester, Pennsylvania.[1] Here, save for brief periods in New York and Philadelphia, the Trists remained for over twenty years. Once again, as he had many times before he entered government service, Trist contemplated practicing law, but he was dissuaded by friends who argued that his long absence from the legal profession would prove too great a handicap. Although he had been in financial straits many times in the past, never was Trist more in need than the first few years after his return from Mexico. He wrote in 1849 that he was at that moment "at the last grasp for immediate cash." [2] He still believed that the government owed him a considerable amount of money for the years 1847–48, but he was determined not to ask for it. If the money was not volunteered, he would not press his claims. Washington friends offered advice and help. Trist was informed that a position as a translator in the State Department under the Whig administration of President Zachary Taylor was his for the asking,[3] but he refused to consider the post. Winfield Scott, back in Washington once again as commanding general of the army, wrote, "What can I do? I take a lively interest in you and all who belong to you." [4] Robert Dale Owen urged Trist to go to England to live with some of Owen's relatives—any change of atmosphere was preferable to the brooding he was doing.[5] How Trist supported

---

[1] Trist to ———, July 7, 1848, Trist papers, University of North Carolina Library, Chapel Hill.

[2] Trist to Beverly Randolph, May 2, 1849, Trist Papers, Library of Congress, Washington, D.C.

[3] Beverly Randolph to Trist, Feb. 1, 1849, ibid.

[4] Scott to Trist, June 20, 1849, ibid.

[5] Owen to Trist, March 20, 1849, ibid.

himself from 1848–50 is a mystery. Browse Trist sent small checks from Louisiana as his brother's share of the profits from their cotton and sugar plantations there,[6] but these remittances hardly seem enough to have supported a family.

If Trist was poor financially, there is evidence that he was not lacking in contemporary prestige. He was solicited by a prominent firm of photographers with the plea, "we are very anxious to have in our gallery likenesses of all the great men of our nation."[7] Several writers asked him to read their manuscripts and to make any additions or corrections that were necessary. One author, recounting the Mexican War, suggested that Trist attack the Polk administration and tell the "true side of the story," but Trist declined.[8] Henry Randall, starting his work on Thomas Jefferson, posed several questions for the Trists to answer.[9] It is highly probable that many of Randall's detailed descriptions of Jefferson's family life came from these talks with Nicholas and Virginia Trist. A few years later Thomas Hart Benton begged Trist to come to Washington to help him with his book, *Thirty Years' View*. Benton had reached the period of the Mexican War and wanted Trist's advice and guidance. The Democratic senator also assured Trist that if he would present his monetary claims to the Senate, he, Benton, would do everything in his power to see that the claims were allowed.[10] Trist, a man of tenacious pride, refused. James Parton, biographer of Jackson, was another who sought and obtained Trist's aid.[11] Perhaps in rendering these services to eminent writers of the period, Trist did more for his country than he would have done through public service.

During the summer of 1851 the Trists moved to New York City, where he became clerk in the law firm of Fowler and Wells, in the Wall Street district.[12] This post was not permanent, and after a few years and much changing of residence in the city, the Trists moved back to Philadelphia. There Virginia ran a school for young ladies, teaching them the social graces and music,[13] while Trist

---

[6] H. B. Trist to N. P. Trist, Feb. 2, 1850, Trist Papers, UNC Lib. Browse explained that this money ($275) was Nicholas's share from the profits of the year 1849.

[7] England & Gunn to Trist, June 16, 1848, Trist Papers, Lib. Cong.

[8] Brantz Mayer to Trist, Aug. 19, 1848, Trist Papers, UNC Lib.

[9] Randall to Trist, March 10, 1851, ibid.

[10] Benton to Trist, Jan. 18, 1856, Trist Papers, Lib. Cong.

[11] Trist to Parton, May 31, 1860, ibid.

[12] Edward Spalding to Trist, Aug. 9, 1851, Trist Papers, UNC Lib.

[13] In the Trist Papers, Lib. Cong., are notes dated 1855 by Nicholas and Virginia Trist for the school.

took a position as railway clerk for the Wilmington and Baltimore Railroad Company. He remained with this company until 1870, rising in time to the job of paymaster, with a monthly salary of $112.50,[14] bitter medicine indeed.

With the approach of the Civil War, Trist's interest in politics reawakened. Thoroughly imbued with Jackson's principles regarding the sanctity of the Federal Union, he deplored talk of Southern secession. In an article in the New York *World* he quoted Madison's and Jackson's views on secession in the 1830s, stating that if they were alive, they would have disapproved just as much as they had thirty years earlier.[15] Trist confided to Winfield Scott that although he was a Southerner by birth, he was a Yankee by adoption and that his sympathies were all with the North in its struggle to preserve the Union.[16]

Despite his Southern heritage, Trist had long since abandoned the dogmatic states' rights policies of John C. Calhoun. Indeed, during the Jackson administration while working as a confidential secretary to Old Hickory, Trist had written many articles for newspapers damning the nullification movement of the 1830s. He had applauded Jackson's strong stand then and approved of Lincoln's strong actions after his inauguration in 1861. If nullification was abhorrent to Trist in 1832, secession in 1860 and 1861 was even more so—especially in light of the immense personal sacrifice he had made in what he imagined to be the best interests of the Union in 1847 when he refused Polk's recall order. Trist showed great interest in the military conduct of the Civil War, thoroughly approving of Lincoln's choice of commanders. He was especially enthusiastic about Generals McClellan and Pope, believing that they would surely defeat Lee and Jackson.[17]

Virginia was just as ardent in her views; she wrote, "you know my dear that I love the Union; and if we had . . . ceased to love it, I believe our prosperity would have lasted." [18] This is the only time Virginia lamented on paper her husband's actions in Mexico. She undoubtedly felt that had Nicholas loved his country less, he would not have remained in Mexico, and that their prosperity in government service would have been assured. In this whole period

[14] Virginia Trist to ——, July 8, 1864, Trist Papers, UNC Lib.

[15] Nov. 1, 1860.

[16] Trist to Scott, Jan. 12, 1861, Trist Papers, Lib. Cong.

[17] Trist to Edward Bates, Aug. 26, 1861, Robert Todd Lincoln Papers, Lib. Cong.; see also Trist to Cornelia Randolph, June 27, 1862, Trist Papers, UNC Lib.

[18] Virginia Trist to ——, Aug. 24, 1862, Trist Papers, UNC Lib.

after Trist's return from Mexico in 1848, there is abundant evidence that Nicholas and Virginia, in their late years, and despite (or more likely, because of) almost abject poverty at times, were closer than they had been at any time in their marriage.

Although it is difficult to trace the comings and goings of the three Trist children, some information is available on all of them. Pattie (Martha Jefferson) Trist, the eldest of the children, lived at home with her parents most of the time until she married in 1862. She had become engaged the previous year to a lawyer named John Burke and, after her marriage in July 1862, went to live with him in Alexandria, Virginia.[19] Hore Browse Trist, Jr., entered the University of Virginia in 1850, and after two years entered Washington University, from which he was graduated with a degree in medicine in 1855.[20] For a time after graduation he was a surgeon in the United States Navy, but in 1864 he married Miss Evelyn Waring of Washington and settled down to private practice in Baltimore.[21] Thomas Jefferson Trist was born a deaf mute and spent a great part of his life at the Philadelphia Institute for the Deaf and Dumb. After Trist returned from Mexico, he wrote to General Scott, asking for aid in placing his handicapped son in some government position.[22] Scott was evidently unable to help, for the youngest Trist remained a drain on the finances of his parents until their deaths.

Throughout these later years in Nicholas Trist's life, his many friends urged him to return to government service and often without his permission or knowledge recommended him for vacancies that occurred from time to time. Scott wrote to Trist in 1861, "I do not expect to recommend more than one friend, for any civil employment whatever under the next administration—I mean the friend who has been so shamefully neglected from September 1847." [23] True to his word, Scott urged Salmon P. Chase, Lincoln's secretary of the Treasury, to appoint Trist collector of taxes in Philadelphia. Scott said that Trist was wronged by Polk and treated with indifference by Taylor, Filmore, Pierce, and Buchanan, and that the government was greatly indebted to Trist,

[19] Virginia Trist to Pattie Burke, July 10, 1862, ibid.

[20] H. B. Trist, Jr., to N. P. Trist, Oct. 3, 1850, ibid.; Schole DeVere, *Students of the University of Virginia* (Baltimore, 1878), p. 43.

[21] This information has been gathered piecemeal from references in various letters in the Trist Papers at both the Library of Congress and Chapel Hill.

[22] Trist to Scott, May 19, 1849, Trist Papers, UNC Lib.

[23] Scott to Trist, Jan. 11, 1861, Trist Papers, Lib. Cong.

who had borne his banishment from government service grace-fully.[24] This plea fell on deaf ears, and Trist continued in his railway job. It is doubtful that Trist would have accepted had the position been tendered; his pride was indestructible.

Ever since 1848 Trist had been too proud to press Congress for the money due him for his Mexican mission. He had hoped that a grateful government would pay him without the necessity of filing a claim. As time passed, however, it became increasingly evident that this was not likely to happen and that if he wanted what was rightfully due him he must press his claims to the utmost. His friends urged him to do this. J. M. Forbes wrote in 1869:

Who but you would have ignored party claims and prejudices and sacrificed himself as you did to carry out a high toned national policy against the wishes of his own government. . . . Had you done what Polk and his crew of unscrupulous politicians expected and wanted, we would have annexed the mongrel population of Mexico, cut up into a dozen states, and we might now have been a Pro-Slavery Republic— converted into a military Propagandism, whose object would have been to extend slavery by force of arms all over this continent and its Islands, and perhaps all over South America too.[25]

Despite a pressing need for money, it was not for another year that Nicholas and Virginia Trist would allow the claim to be in-troduced into Congress. Trist had earlier reported to the Senate that he received as compensation for the mission:

Salary at $4,500 per year	$ 2,651.65
Outfit	4,500.00
Return allowance	1,125.00
Total	$ 8,276.65

Trist maintained that he should have received:

Salary at $9,000 per year	$ 8,827.40
Outfit	9,000.00
Return allowance	2,250.00
Salary as secretary of legation	1,961.65
Total	$22,039.05
Plus expenses	797.50
Grand total	$22,836.55

Subtracting $8,276.65 from the grand total, Trist felt that the government still owed him the sum of $14,559.90.[26]

[24] Scott to Salmon P. Chase, July 15, 1862, ibid.

[25] Forbes to Trist, July 10, 1869, ibid.

[26] Trist to S. M. Felton, June 18, 1868, ibid.

In July 1870 Charles Sumner, of the Senate Committee on Foreign Affairs, made a brief but moving speech summarizing Trist's career, the courage of his stand in 1847, and the shameful failure to adequately remunerate his services.[27] With a favorable report from the House Committee on Foreign Relations, a bill was introduced in the Senate by Sumner to pay Trist the money he claimed.[28] It was not until the next session that a vote was taken, but the tally was favorable, and on April 20, 1871, Trist was awarded the sum of $14,559.90, exactly as claimed.[29] Actually there never had been much question of the monetary bill passing. Over a period of many years, Senator Sumner had urged Trist to allow him to introduce measures to effect repayment. The sympathetic attitude on the part of the chairman of the Senate Committee on Foreign Affairs and of other members of the committee foreshadowed passage of the bill. Many other governmental officials were of the opinion that Trist had been wronged by Polk in 1848 and showed willingness to make restitution. With a favorable response from President Grant, passage was assured.

This money came at a time when it was sorely needed; the income of the Trist family had shrunk almost to nothing, and there were numerous debts to pay. Trist had been forced to give up even the small amount of money derived from his job as a railway paymaster in 1869 when the duties became too strenuous for his old age. The blessings derived from the government did not stop with the payment of money owed. The Grant administration, which took office in March 1869, proved to be a boon to the Trists in many ways. At the urging of Simon Cameron, senator from Pennsylvania, and others, Trist was named in the summer of 1870 to fill the vacant position of postmaster at Alexandria, Virginia.[30] Alexandria, then listed as a second-class city, had a postmastership which carried with it the handsome emolument of $2,900 per annum.[31] Aside from his earnings while in Mexico, this was more money than Nicholas Trist had made in one year since he left a diplomatic post as consul in Havana in 1841.

The change in his financial fortunes appears to have lightened Trist's burden in many ways, and during the next few years

---

[27] U.S., Congress, *Senate Reports*, 41st Cong., 2d sess., no. 261, pp. 1–2.

[28] U.S., Congress, Senate, *Journal*, 41st Cong., 2d sess., p. 1063.

[29] G. G. Van Dusen, *The Jacksonian Era* (New York, 1950), p. 245. "Never was a reward for services to a man's country more unjustly withheld or more richly deserved" (ibid.).

[30] Simon Cameron to ——, June 3, 1870, Trist Papers, Lib. Cong.

[31] *United States Official Postal Guide* (Boston, 1875), p. 364.

Virginia wrote that Nicholas seemed to be younger in spirit than he had been since he returned from Mexico. In one letter to her daughter, she said that at a recent party her husband stayed on the floor for nearly every dance and waltzed until dawn because "the spirit moved him." [32] Living in Alexandria gave the Trists a chance to be near Pattie and her husband, John Burke. Browse, Jr., who was a practicing physician in Baltimore, was another frequent visitor, and in many respects these last few years of Nicholas Trist's life were among his most pleasant. Freed at last from financial worries by a beneficent administration and surrounded by friends and relatives, Trist spent his few remaining years in comfort and happiness. [33]

Late in 1873 Trist was felled by a stroke and from that time never left his bed. On February 11, 1874, he died, surrounded by his family and close friends. The *Alexandria Gazette* noted his death, lauding him for his actions in the past: "Mr. Trist was a man of talent and note in this country." [34] The *Washington Chronicle*, [35] *Richmond Daily Dispatch*, [36] and *Jeffersonian Republican* [37] of Charlottesville, praised him highly for his public services.

The death of Nicholas P. Trist in 1874 closed a career which, though it never reached the heights many had expected, was certainly influential in shaping the destiny of the United States. Coming to a climax in the decade of the 1840s with the spirit of Manifest Destiny at its apex, Trist's career might well have taken another turn had he obeyed Polk's recall order. One can only wonder what the future of the United States might have been had the administration pursued a goal of absorbing all of Mexico. Would this have benefited the nation? What of the Mexican population? Would they have been better off living under the stable government of the Stars and Stripes? How much less stable would this nation have been had such a disparate population been absorbed? And lastly, one must wonder what Trist's future would have been. Would he have lived up to his earlier promise in government circles and moved on to higher positions of trust and responsibility? These questions can, of course, never be answered, but the weight of public opinion at the time and informed opinion since 1848 would seem to agree that Trist's action was in the best long-range

[32] Virginia Trist to Pattie Burke, Oct. 8, 1871, Trist Papers, Lib. Cong.

[33] Information for these last years is meager, and letters were few. What correspondence there is reflects the serenity and peace of mind at last enjoyed by the Trists.

[34] Feb. 12, 1874.   [35] Feb. 12, 1874.   [36] Feb. 12, 1874.

[37] Feb. 18, 1874.

interests of the United States and that had President Polk been permitted to carry out his scheme of absorption, the United States would have been saddled with an even greater guilt complex as a result of its actions toward its southern neighbor than it has today. Trist's decision was one of courage and, from a position of narrow self-interest, near-insanity. But the diplomat chose to place principle above self and thus sacrificed a promising career for the greater good of his nation.

Contributors

The dissertation title and the year the doctorate was granted by the University of Virginia are given for each contributor.

Harry Ammon (Ph.D., 1948: "The Republican Party in Virginia, 1789 to 1824"). Professor, Southern Illinois University. Dr. Ammon, who was a Visiting Professor at the University of Virginia in 1968–69 and has been a Fulbright Lecturer in Austria, is well known for his widely used dissertation and his important articles in the *William and Mary Quarterly* (coauthored with Adrienne Koch, 1948; 1963), *Journal of Southern History* (1953), *Virginia Magazine of History and Biography* (1953, 1963, 1966), and *Journal of American History* (1966). He has also written biographical sketches for the *Dictionary of Notable American Women, Encyclopedia Britannica,* and *Encyclopedia of World Biography.* In 1971 he published a definitive biography, *James Monroe: The Quest for National Identity,* and in 1973 a significant monograph, *The Genet Mission.*

Alden Bigelow (Ph.D., 1957: "Hugh Blair Grigsby: Historian and Antiquarian"). Associate Professor, Virginia Commonwealth University. Professor Bigelow, in addition to his teaching duties, has been the moderator of several educational television programs of historical interest.

John B. Boles (Ph.D., 1969: "The Religious Mind of the Old South: The Era of the Great Revival, 1787–1805"). Associate Professor, Towson State College. Dr. Boles has published articles in the *Southern Humanities Review* (1970), *Georgia Historical Quarterly* (1970), *Virginia Baptist Register* (1973), and *Journal of Popular Culture* (1972). He has also edited for microfilm publication the *Papers of William Wirt* (1971), and the *Papers of John Pendleton Kennedy* (1972). In 1972 he published a monograph, *The Great Revival, 1787–1805: The Origins of the Southern Evangelical Mind.* A Thomas Jefferson Fellow (1966–68) and Woodrow Wilson Dissertation Fellow

(1968–69) at the University of Virginia, he is now Book Review Editor of the *Maryland Historical Magazine*.

Robert A. Brent (Ph.D., 1950: "Nicholas Philip Trist: Biography of a Disobedient Diplomat"). Professor, University of Southern Mississippi. Professor Brent is the author of almost twenty articles which have appeared in such journals as *Revista de Historia de America, Southwestern Historical Quarterly, Southern Quarterly, Journal of Mississippi History, American Studies in the Philippines*, and *Proceedings of the Gulf Coast History and Humanities Conference*. He was a Fulbright Lecturer at the University of the Philippines in 1965–66. Dr. Brent is the author of three books: *Mr. Jefferson of Virginia: A Renaissance Gentleman in America* (1966), *The Episcopal Church in Mississippi, 1763–1966* (with Nash K. Burger, 1973), and *Nicholas Philip Trist: Disobedient Diplomat* (forthcoming).

Elizabeth Dabney Coleman (Ph.D., 1957: "The Story of the Virginia Central Railroad, 1850–1860"). Greatly interested in Virginia history, Dr. Coleman for years was a member of the staff of *Virginia Cavalcade*, which published some thirty-eight of her articles on various aspects of the Old Dominion's history. She also did basic research for the restoration of Christ Church, Lancaster County, Virginia. Dr. Coleman occasionally taught at the University of Virginia, both in the School of General Studies and in the Corcoran Department of History. Dr. Coleman was a great-granddaughter of Edmund Fontaine. She died in January 1972 as this volume was in preparation. Miss Ruth Evelyn Byrd has assisted the editor in checking and proofreading Dr. Coleman's article.

Raymond C. Dingledine, Jr. (Ph.D., 1947: "The Political Career of William Cabell Rives"). Professor and Head of the Department of History, Madison College. Professor Dingledine coauthored *Virginia's History* in 1956 and *Our Home: Virginia and the World* in 1962. These widely used textbooks were combined in 1965 as *Virginia's History and Geography*. In addition he has written a history of *Madison College: The First Fifty Years, 1908–1958* (1959), articles on Virginia for several encyclopedias, and "The Civil War and the Shenandoah Valley" in *Historic Preservation* (1968).

Edwin M. Gaines (Ph.D., 1960: "Outrageous Encounter: The Chesapeake-Leopard Affair of 1807"). Associate Professor, University of Arizona. Holder of a Fulbright Fellowship to England in 1955–56, Professor Gaines has published articles in the *Virginia Magazine of History and Biography* (1956) and *Essays in History* (1955). He has had a distinguished administrative career at Converse College, the University of Wyoming, and the University of Arizona. He was Visiting Professor at the University of East Anglia, Norwich, England, during the Fall Term, 1972, and returned to full-time teaching at the University of Arizona in January 1973.

Pendleton Gaines (Ph.D., 1950: "The Virginia Constitutional Convention of 1850–51: A Study in Sectionalism"). Dean of the Division of Continuing Education and Summer Session, University of Arizona. Like his brother, Pendleton Gaines has pursued a distinguished administrative career at several colleges and universities. He has been a dean at Birmingham-Southern College and Southern Methodist University; he was Director of Development at the University of Houston and President of Wofford College. In 1959 Dean Gaines assumed his present post at the University of Arizona. He has written and reviewed widely in the fields of education, academic administration, and history.

Joseph H. Harrison, Jr. (Ph.D., 1954: "The Internal Improvement Issue in the Politics of the Union, 1783–1825"). Professor, Auburn University. An associate editor of *The Papers of Thomas Jefferson* in 1957–58, Dr. Harrison's publications include "Martin Van Buren and His Southern Supporters," *Journal of Southern History* (1956); "Harry Williams, Critic of Freeman: A Demurrer," *Virginia Magazine of History and Biography* (1956), and in the same journal, "Oligarchs and Democrats: The Richmond Junto" (1970).

J. Edwin Hendricks (Ph.D., 1961: "Charles Thomson and the American Enlightenment"). Associate Professor, Wake Forest University. Among Dr. Hendricks's many publications are articles in the *Pennsylvania Magazine of History and Biography* (1965), *North Carolina Historical Review* (1968), and *Virginia Cavalcade* (1968). Another article, "Some Early American Impressions of India," was printed in *Images of India*, ed. B. G. Gokhale (Bombay, 1971). With C. C. Pearson he published *Liquor and Anti-Liquor in Virginia, 1619–1919* (1967). In addition he has read papers at several historical conferences. Recently Professor Hendricks became Director of the Historic

Preservation and Museum Training Program at Wake Forest University.

Patricia Hickin (Ph.D., 1968: "Antislavery in Virginia, 1831–1861"). Editor, Publications Branch, Archives Division, Virginia State Library. Before taking her present position, Mrs. Hickin taught at the State University of New York College at Cortland and Ithaca College. She held a National Endowment for the Humanities research grant in 1970–71, has published articles in the *Virginia Magazine of History and Biography* (1965) and *Journal of Southern History* (1971), and now is general editor of historical works published by the Virginia State Library.

Charles D. Lowery (Ph.D., 1966: "James Barbour, A Politician and Planter of Ante-Bellum Virginia"). Assistant Professor of History, and Associate Dean, College of Arts and Sciences, Mississippi State University. Professor Lowery taught at Ball State University before moving to Mississippi. The *Journal of Mississippi History* published his article, "The Great Migration to the Mississippi Territory, 1798–1819," and he has recently completed his biography of James Barbour. While at the University of Virginia he was a Thomas Jefferson Fellow in History.

John S. Pancake (Ph.D., 1949: "The General from Baltimore: A Biography of Samuel Smith"). Professor, University of Alabama, and Visiting Professor, Stillman College. Professor Pancake has taught at Alabama since receiving his doctorate. In that time he has published articles in the *William and Mary Quarterly* (1951), *Journal of Southern History* (1955), *Maryland Historical Magazine* (1952), and *History Today* (1973). The University of Alabama Press has just published his *Samuel Smith and the Politics of Business, 1752–1839* (1972), and a comparative study of Jefferson and Hamilton is forthcoming.

Norman K. Risjord (Ph.D., 1960: "The Old Republicans: Southern Conservatives in Congress, 1806–1824"). Professor, University of Wisconsin, Madison. Dr. Risjord has published articles in the *William and Mary Quarterly* (1961), *Journal of Southern History* (1967), and *Journal of American History* (co-author, forthcoming). His first book, *The Old Republicans: Southern Conservatism in the Age of Jefferson* (1965), has become a standard work. Two more recent books are *The Early American Party System* (1969), an edited volume of interpretative essays, and *Forging the American Republic, 1760–1815* (1973). Previously a Fulbright Teaching Fellow at Uppsala, Sweden, Dr. Risjord currently (1973–74) holds the British Petroleum Fellowship in American Studies at Dundee, Scotland.

George Green Shackelford (Ph.D., 1955: "William Short, Jefferson's Adopted Son, 1758–1849"). Professor, Virginia Polytechnic Institute and State University. Although Dr. Shackelford has published widely in such journals as the *Proceedings of the American Philosophical Society* (1956), *Virginia Magazine of History and Biography* (1965), and *Maryland Historical Magazine* (1969), has edited the *Collected Papers of the Monticello Association* (1965), and has another book forthcoming, *Edwardian Carriages in the Winmill Collection,* he is perhaps better known for his leadership in the field of historic preservation. He has set up three permanent museum exhibits: Historic House Museums at Smithfield Plantation House, Blacksburg, Virginia, and Morven Park, Leesburg, Virginia, and the Carriage Museum at Morven Park.

Carlton B. Smith (Ph.D., 1967: "The United States War Department, 1815–1842"). Associate Professor, Madison College. Author of "The American Search for a 'Harmless' Army," *Essays in History* (1964) and "John B. Floyd and the Secession Crisis," *Madison Studies* (1973), Dr. Smith formerly taught at Fairmont State College in West Virginia. He delivered a paper at the 1971 annual meeting of the Southern Historical Association.

Carl J. Vipperman (Ph.D., 1966: "William Lowndes: South Carolina Nationalist, 1782–1822"). Assistant Professor, University of Georgia. Dr. Vipperman's biographical study, *The Rise of Rawlins Lowndes,* is forthcoming from the University of South Carolina Press for the South Carolina Tricentennial Commission. He has also published articles in *Essays in History* (1964) and the *South Carolina Historical Magazine* (1969). At the University of Virginia he was a Thomas Jefferson Fellow in History, 1962–64. Before coming to Georgia, Dr. Vipperman taught at the College of Charleston.

Index